Screen Damage

Screen Damage

The Dangers of Digital Media for Children

Michel Desmurget

Translated by Andrew Brown

polity

Originally published in French as *La fabrique du crétin digital* © Editions du Seuil, 2019, © Editions du Seuil, 2020 for the abridged and updated version

This English edition © Polity Press, 2023

This book is supported by the Institut français (Royaume-Uni) as part of the Burgess programme.

INSTITUT
FRANÇAIS
ROYAUME-UNI

Polity Press
65 Bridge Street
Cambridge CB2 1UR, UK

Polity Press
111 River Street
Hoboken, NJ 07030, USA

ISBN-13: 978-1-5095-4639-8
ISBN-13: 978-1-5095-4640-4 (paperback)

A catalogue record for this book is available from the British Library.

Library of Congress Control Number: 2022935229

Typeset in 10.5 on 12 pt Sabon
by Fakenham Prepress Solutions, Fakenham, Norfolk NR21 8NL
Printed and bound in Great Britain by TJ Books Ltd, Padstow, Cornwall

The publisher has used its best endeavours to ensure that the URLs for external websites referred to in this book are correct and active at the time of going to press. However, the publisher has no responsibility for the websites and can make no guarantee that a site will remain live or that the content is or will remain appropriate.

Every effort has been made to trace all copyright holders, but if any have been overlooked the publisher will be pleased to include any necessary credits in any subsequent reprint or edition.

For further information on Polity, visit our website:
politybooks.com

CONTENTS

We must not reassure ourselves by thinking that the barbarians are still far away; for, while there are some peoples who allow the light to be snatched from their hands, there are others who stamp it out with their own feet.

Alexis de Tocqueville, *De la Démocratie en Amérique*

— INTRODUCTION —

WHO SHOULD WE BELIEVE?

The truth is there. The only things we invent are lies.

Georges Braque[1]

The consumption of digital media in every form (smartphones, tablets, television, game consoles, etc.) by the younger generations, for recreational purposes, is astronomical. During their first two years, children in Western countries spend, on average, nearly 50 minutes on screen time every day. Between 2 and 8 years, the figure rises to 2 hours 45 minutes. Between 8 and 12 years, it reaches 4 hours 45 minutes. Between 13 and 18 years, it exceeds 7 hours 15 minutes. Expressed as an annual total, that means more than 1,000 hours for a kindergarten pupil (1.4 months), 1,700 hours for a primary school pupil (2.4 months) and 2,650 hours for a secondary school pupil (3.7 months). Formulated as a percentage of waking time, these values represent, respectively, 20%, 32% and 45%. Added up over the first 18 years of life, this is the equivalent of almost 30 school years or, if you prefer, 15 years of full-time paid employment.

Far from being alarmed, many media experts seem to welcome the situation. Psychiatrists, academics, paediatricians, sociologists, consultants, journalists and so on make endless indulgent statements to reassure parents and the public. Times have changed, they say, and the world now belongs to the aptly named 'digital natives'. The very brains of the members of this post-digital generation have been modified – for the better, obviously. Their brains turn out, we are told, to be faster, more responsive, more suited to parallel processing, more competent at synthesizing immense flows of information, and better adapted to collaborative work. These developments represent an extraordinary opportunity for schools. They provide,

1

it is claimed, a unique opportunity to overhaul education, stimulate pupils' motivation, fuel their creativity, overcome academic failure and tear down the walls of social inequalities.

Unfortunately, this enthusiasm is far from unanimous. Many specialists denounce the deeply negative influence of current digital usage on development. All the dimensions of our humanity are affected, they point out, from the somatic (e.g. obesity, cardiovascular maturation) to the cognitive (e.g. language, concentration) and the emotional (e.g. aggressiveness, anxiety). All these assaults cannot ultimately leave academic success unscathed. Regarding that, moreover, it appears that the digital practices of the classroom for instructional purposes are not particularly beneficial either, as most of the available impact studies seem to indicate, including the famous international PISA evaluations. The director of this programme recently explained, about the process of digitizing education, that 'if anything, it makes things worse'.[2]

In line with these fears, several individuals and institutional players have opted to play safe. In England, for example, several head teachers have threatened to send the police and social services into homes that let their children play violent video games.[3] In Taiwan, a country whose schoolchildren are among the most successful in the world,[4] there is a law that lays down heavy fines for parents who, on the one hand, expose children under 24 months to any digital application whatsoever and, on the other, do not sufficiently limit the time that 2- to 18-year-olds spend on such activities (the stated objective is not to exceed 30 consecutive minutes).[5] In China, the authorities have taken drastic measures to regulate video game use among minors, on the grounds that this negatively impacts on their education.[6] Indeed, children and adolescents there are no longer allowed to play during the time slot normally reserved for sleep (10 p.m.–8 a.m.) or to exceed 90 minutes of daily exposure during the week (180 minutes at weekends and during school holidays). In the United States, a number of senior executives in the digital industries, including Steve Jobs, the legendary former boss of Apple, seem very keen to protect their offspring from the various 'digital tools' they market.[7] It would even seem, says the *New York Times*, that 'a dark consensus about screens and kids begins to emerge in Silicon Valley'.[8] This consensus is apparently strong enough to go beyond the domestic context; these geeks feel impelled to enrol their children in expensive private schools where there are no screens.[9,10] As Chris Anderson, former editor of *Wired* and now chief executive of a robotics company, explains: 'my [five] kids [6 to 17] accuse me and my wife of being fascists and

2

overly concerned about tech, and they say that none of their friends have the same rules. That's because we have seen the dangers of technology firsthand. I've seen it in myself, I don't want to see that happen to my kids.'[7] In his view, 'on the scale between candy and crack cocaine, it's closer to crack cocaine'.[8] As the French journalist Guillaume Erner, who holds a doctorate in sociology, puts it: 'The moral of the story is: you can put your children in front of screens, but those who make the screens will continue to put their children in front of books.'[11]

Who should we believe? At the heart of this tangle of contradictions, who is bluffing, and who is wrong? Where is the truth? Do our children, nourished by screens, comprise 'the smartest generation ever', as Don Tapscott, a consultant specializing in the impact of new technologies, assures us,[12] or are they rather 'the dumbest generation', as Mark Bauerlein, professor of English at Emory University, puts it?[13] More generally, is the current 'digital revolution' an opportunity for our offspring or a grim mechanism for creating imbeciles? The point of this book is to answer that question. For the sake of clarity, the analysis is organized into three main parts. The first assesses the reality of the original basic concept, one still very much alive, of the 'digital native'. The second analyses the twofold qualitative and quantitative nature of the digital activities of our children and adolescents. The third examines the impact of these activities. Different fields are then considered: academic success, development and health. Before continuing, however, three points must be clarified.

First, although it attempts to conform to the most rigorous academic standards, this book does not meet the formal criteria of scientific writing. This is mainly because it hopes to be accessible to everyone, parents, health professionals, teachers, students, etc. But also because it is fuelled by real anger. I am stunned by the partial, biased and unfair nature of the way many mainstream media treat screens. As we will see throughout the book, there is a huge gap between the unsettling reality of available evidence and the frequently reassuring (or indeed enthusiastic) content of journalistic discourses. This disparity, however, is not in the least surprising. It simply reflects the economic power of the digital recreation industries. Each year, these generate billions in profits. However, if recent history has taught us anything, it is that our industrial friends do not easily give up the profits they amass, even if this is detrimental to consumer health. At the heart of this war waged by mercantilism against the common good is a powerful armada of complacent scientists, overzealous lobbyists and professional merchants of doubt.[14] Tobacco, medicine, food, global warming, asbestos, acid rain, etc. – the list is full of instructive precedents.[14-25] It would be surprising if the digital recreational sector had escaped this assault. So I stand fully behind the sometimes mordant form of the present work, even though I understand that the emotions expressed in it might jar with the usual way one imagines a cold and objective science, a science which, by nature, is supposed to be incompatible with any form of emotional expression. I don't believe in this disembodiment. In writing this book, I was especially keen not to produce a boring essay, impersonal and stiff. Beyond the data which constitute the indisputable heart of this document, I wanted to share with the reader both my concerns and my indignation.

Second, my aim is not to tell anyone what to do, believe or think. Nor do I seek to stigmatize screen users or pass any critical judgement on the educational practices of any particular parent. I simply wish to inform readers by offering them as exhaustive, precise and sincere a synthesis as possible of the existing scientific knowledge. Of course, I understand the usual argument that we have to stop guilt-tripping people, worrying and alarming them by creating unnecessary 'moral panics' around screens. I also understand the army of self-righteous people who explain to us that these panics are the products of our fears and that they come with every form of societal or technological advance. The frightened little group of reactionary obscurantists – they tell us – have already tried to put the wind up us, for example, in connection with the pinball machine, the microwave, rock'n'roll, printing and writing (denounced in his time by Socrates for its possible impact on memory).

Unfortunately, however alluring they may be, these considerations are flawed. The thing is, if I may say so, that there are no studies establishing the harmfulness of pinball, microwave or rock'n'roll. At the same time, there *is* a solid body of work highlighting the positive influence on people's development of books and being able to read and write.[26,27] Therefore, what rules out a hypothesis is not its initial formulation but its ultimate evaluation. Some people were afraid of rock'n'roll. This fear was groundless; end of story. Others worried about writing. An extensive scientific literature has invalidated this fear; hurrah for that! The same goes for screens. Never mind the hysterical fears of the past. Only current scientific information should count: what does it say, where does it come from, is it reliable, how consistent is it, what are its limits, etc.? It is by answering these questions that everyone will be able to make an informed decision, not by muddying the waters and resorting to the well-worn evasions of alarmism, guilt or moral panic.

Third and finally, there is no question here of rejecting 'the' digital world as a whole and demanding, without further ado, the return of the wired telegraph, Pascal's calculating machine or tube radios. This text really is in no way technophobic! In many areas – linked, for example, to health, telecommunications, air transport, agricultural production and industrial activity – the extremely fruitful contribution of digital technology cannot be disputed. Who would complain about seeing automata operating in fields, mines or factories and performing all kinds of brutal, repetitive and destructive tasks which until then had to be carried out by men and women at the cost of their health? Who can deny the enormous impact that computing, simulation, data storage and data sharing tools have had on scientific and medical research? Who can question the value of software for word processing, management, and mechanical and industrial design? Who would dare to say that the existence of appropriate educational and documentary resources, freely accessible to all, is not a benefit? Nobody, of course. However, these indisputable benefits should not mask the existence of far more damaging advances, particularly in the field of recreational consumption – especially because, as we will have the opportunity to see in detail, this consumption alone counts for almost all of the digital activities of the younger generations. In other words, when the arsenal of screens on offer today (tablets, computers, consoles, smartphones, etc.) is made available to children and adolescents, they do not put them to clearly positive uses, but exploit them in an orgy of recreational usage which, as research irrevocably shows, is harmful. Certainly, if children and adolescents focused their practices on the most positive things that digital media can offer, this book would not need to have been written.

— PART ONE —

DIGITAL NATIVES
Building a myth

A [good] liar begins by making the lie seem like a truth, and ends up making the truth seem like a lie.

Alphonse Esquiros[1]

The ability of certain journalists, politicians and media experts to spread, quite uncritically, the most extravagant fables put about by the digital industry is quite breathtaking. We could just shrug these fables off with a smile. But that would be to ignore the power of repetition. Indeed, by dint of being reproduced, these fables end up becoming, in the collective mind, real facts. We then leave the field of substantiated debate and approach the space of urban legend – of a story 'that is held to be true, sounds plausible enough to be believed, is based primarily on hearsay, and is widely circulated as true'.[2] So if you repeat often enough that the younger generations have different brains and learning styles because of their phenomenal digital literacy, people eventually believe it; and when they believe it, their whole view of children, of learning and of the educational system is affected. Deconstructing the legends that pollute thought is therefore the first essential step towards an objective and fruitful reflection on the real impact of digital technology.

'A different generation'

In the wonderful digital world, there are many different fictions. Yet, in the final analysis, almost all of them rest on the same basic illusion: screens have fundamentally transformed the intellectual functioning and relationship to the world of young people, now called 'digital natives'.[3-7] For the missionary army of the digital catechism,

> three salient features characterize this [younger] generation: zapping, impatience and the collective. They expect immediate feedback: everything has to go fast, if not very fast! They like to work in a team and have an intuitive, even instinctive, cross-sectional digital culture. They have understood the strength of the group, of mutual aid and of collaborative work [...] Many shy away from demonstrative, deductive reasoning, 'step by step' argumentation, in favour of trial and error encouraged by hypertext links.[8]

Digital technologies are now 'so intertwined with their lives that they are no longer separable from them [...] Having grown up with the Internet and then social networks, they tackle problems by relying on experimentation, exchanges with those around them, and cross-functional cooperation on given projects.'[9] Let's face it, these kids 'are no longer "little versions of us," as they may have been in the past. [...] They are native speakers of technology, fluent in the digital language of computers, video games, and the Internet.'[10] 'They're fast, they can multitask and they can zap easily.'[11]

These developments are so profound that they render all old-world pedagogical approaches definitively obsolete.[8,12-14] It is no longer possible to deny the reality: 'our students have changed radically. Today's students are no longer the people our educational system was designed to teach. [...] [They] think and process information fundamentally differently from their predecessors.'[7]

> In fact, they are so different from us that we can no longer use either our 20th century knowledge or our training as a guide to what is best for them educationally. [...] Today's students have mastered a large variety of [digital] tools that we will never master with the same level of skill. From computers to calculators to MP3 players to camera phones, these tools are like extensions of their brains.[10]

Lacking the appropriate training, therefore, current teachers are no longer up to speed, they 'speak an outdated language (that of the pre-digital age)'.[7] Certainly, 'it is time to move on to another type of pedagogy that will consider the changes in our society',[15] because 'yesterday's education will not permit us to train the talents of tomorrow'.[16] And in this context, the best thing would be to give our prodigious digital geniuses the keys to the system as a whole. Freed from the archaisms of the old world, 'they will be the single most important source of guidance on how to make their schools relevant and effective places to learn'.[17]

We could fill dozens of pages with pleadings and proclamations of this kind. But that would hardly be of any interest. Indeed, beyond its local variations, this torrent of verbal diarrhoea is still centred on three major propositions: (i) the omnipresence of screens has created a new generation of human beings, totally different from the previous ones; (ii) members of this generation are experts in handling and understanding digital tools; (iii) to maintain any effectiveness (and credibility), the education system must adapt to this revolution.

No convincing evidence

For fifteen years now, the validity of these claims has been methodically assessed by the scientific community. Here again – unsurprisingly – the results obtained directly contradict the blissful euphoria of fashionable fictions.[2,18-27] As a whole, 'the digital native literature demonstrates a clear mismatch between the confidence with which claims are made and the evidence for such claims'.[26] In other words, 'to date, there is no convincing evidence to support these claims'.[23] All these 'generational stereotypes'[23] are clearly 'an urban legend'[2] and the least one can say is that 'the optimistic portrayal of younger generations' digital competences is poorly founded'.[28] The conclusion? All the available elements converge to show that 'digital natives are a myth in their own right',[19] 'a myth which serves the naïve'.[29]

In practice, the major objection raised by the scientific community to the concept of digital natives is disconcertingly simple: the new generation supposedly referred to by these terms does not exist. Undeniably, one can always find, by looking carefully, a few individuals whose consumption habits vaguely correspond to the stock stereotype of the over-competent geek glued to his screens; but these reassuring paragons are more the exception than the rule.[30,31] As a whole, the so-called 'Internet generation' is much more akin to 'a collection of minorities'[32] than a cohesive group. Within this generation, the extent, nature and expertise of digital practices vary considerably with age, gender, type of studies pursued, cultural background and/or socio-economic status.[33-40] Consider, for example, the time spent on recreational uses (figure 1, top). Contrary to the myth of a homogeneous over-connected population, the data report a great diversity of situations.[41] Thus, among pre-teens (8–12 years), daily exposure varies more or less consistently from 'nothing' (8% of children) to 'insane' (more than 8 hours, 15%). Among adolescents (13–18 years old) these disparities remain notable, even if they decrease a little to the benefit of significant users (62% of adolescents spend more than 4 hours per day on their screens for recreation). To a large extent, this heterogeneity aligns with the socio-economic characteristics of the household. Disadvantaged subjects thus display a very significantly longer average exposure (about 1 hour 45 minutes per day) than their privileged counterparts.[41]

Unsurprisingly, the tangled picture becomes even more complex when we include domestic uses related to the field of education (figure 1, bottom). Indeed, in this area too, the degree of inter-individual variability is considerable.[41] Take the pre-teens. These are distributed roughly evenly between daily (27%), weekly (31%), exceptional (monthly or less often, 20%) and non-existent (never, 21%) users. The disparity remains among adolescents, even if it then tends to diminish due to the high proportion of daily users (59%; these represented just 29% in 2015,[35] which reflects, as we shall be seeing in greater detail, the strong current movement towards digitalization in teaching). Once again, the family socio-economic gradient represents an important explanatory variable.[41] Thus, among 13- to 18-year-olds, privileged pupils are significantly more likely than their disadvantaged counterparts to use a computer every day for their homework (64% as against 51%, with an average duration of 55 minutes as against 34). However, disadvantaged adolescents tend to use their smartphones more (21 minutes compared to 12).[41] In short, presenting all these kids as a uniform generation, with homogeneous needs, behaviours, skills and learning styles, simply does not make sense.

A surprising technical ineptitude

Another essential objection regularly raised by the scientific community to the concept of digital natives concerns the supposed technological superiority of the younger generations. Immersed in the digital world, they are said to have acquired a degree of mastery forever inaccessible to the fossils of the pre-digital ages. This is a nice story – which unfortunately also poses several major problems. First, it is, until we have proof to the contrary, these same brave pre-digital fossils who 'were [and often remain!] the creators of

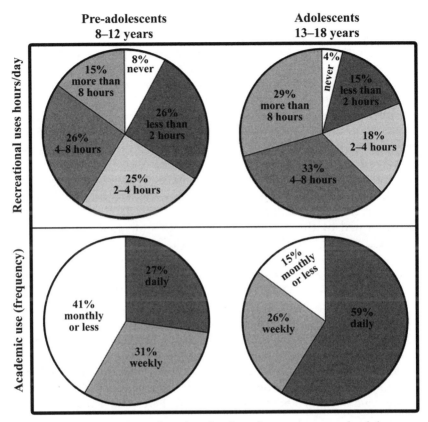

Figure 1. Time spent on digital technology by pre-teens and adolescents. Top: variability in time spent with screens for recreation. Bottom: variability in the use of screens for homework (in this case, the low daily usage time – pre-teens 22 minutes; teenagers 60 minutes – does not allow, as for screens for recreation, depiction in terms of slices of time). Some totals do not add to 100% due to rounding up.[41]

these devices and environments'.[42] Also, contrary to popular belief, the overwhelming majority of our budding geeks display, beyond the most utterly elementary recreational uses, a level of mastery of digital tools that is wobbly, to put it mildly.[28,36,43-6] The problem is so pronounced that a recent report by the European Commission placed the 'student's low digital competence' at the top of the list of factors that could hinder the digitization of the education system.[47] It must be said that, to a very large extent, these young people struggle to gain the most rudimentary computer skills: setting the security of their terminals; using standard office programs (word processing, spreadsheets, etc.); making video files; writing a simple program (whatever the language); configuring backup software; setting up a remote connection; adding memory to a computer; launching or disabling the execution of certain programs when the operating system starts up, etc.

And it gets worse. Indeed, beyond these glaring technical ineptitudes, the younger generations also experience appalling difficulties in processing, sorting, ordering, evaluating and synthesizing the gigantic masses of data stored in the bowels of the Web.[48-53] According to the authors of a study devoted to this issue, believing that members of the Google generation are experts in the art of digital information retrieval 'is a dangerous myth'.[48] This depressing finding is corroborated by the conclusions of a large-scale study published by researchers at Stanford University. For them,

> overall, young people's ability to reason about the information on the Internet can be summed up in one word: *bleak*. Our 'digital natives' may be able to flit between Facebook and Twitter while simultaneously uploading a selfie to Instagram and texting a friend. But when it comes to evaluating information that flows through social media channels, they are easily duped. [...] In every case and at every level, we were taken aback by students' lack of preparation. [...] Many assume that because young people are fluent in social media they are equally savvy about what they find there. Our work shows the opposite.[43]

Ultimately, this incompetence is expressed with 'a stunning and dismaying consistency'. For the authors of the study, the problem goes so deep that it constitutes nothing less than a 'threat to democracy'.

Certainly, these results are not surprising insofar as, in terms of digital capabilities, 'digital natives' use technology in a set of ways both 'limited'[34] and 'unspectacular'.[27] As we will see in detail in the next part, the practices of the younger generations revolve primarily around recreational activities that are, to put it mildly, basic and not very educational: TV programmes, films, series, social networks, video games, shopping sites, promos, musical and other videos of various kinds, etc.[35,41,54-6] On average, pre-teens spend 2% of their screen time on content creation ('such as writing, or making digital art or music').[41] Only 3% say they write computer programs frequently. These percentages rise to 3% and 2% respectively for adolescents. As the authors of a large-scale study of usage write: 'Despite the new affordances and promises of digital devices, young people devote very little time to creating their own content. Screen media use continues to be dominated by watching TV and videos, playing games, and using social media; use of digital devices for reading, writing, video chatting, or creating content remains minimal.'[41] This conclusion also seems to hold for supposedly ubiquitous academic uses. On average, these represent a quite minor fraction of total screen time: less than 8% among pre-teens and 14% among adolescents (13–18 years). In other words, as figure 2 illustrates, when using their screens, 8- to 12-year-olds spend 13 times more time on entertainment than on study (284 minutes as against 22 minutes). For 13- to 18-year-olds, it is 7.5 times (442 minutes as against 60 minutes).[41]

In this context, believing that digital natives are experts of the megabyte is the same as mistaking my pedal cart for an interstellar rocket; it's the same as believing that the simple act of mastering a computer application enables the user to understand anything about the physical elements and software involved. Perhaps this was (somewhat) the case 'before', in the heyday of early DOS and UNIX, when even installing a simple printer meant embarking on a Homeric journey. It's interesting, in any case, to relate this idea to the results of an academic study reporting that personal recreational use of a computer was positively correlated with students' mathematical performances in the 1990s, and more so in the 2000s (the age of millennials).[57] This is understandable if we remember that the use and function of home computers have changed drastically in two decades. For today's children and teenagers, as we have just said, these tools, which can be consumed endlessly without any effort or special skills, are mainly used for entertainment. Today,

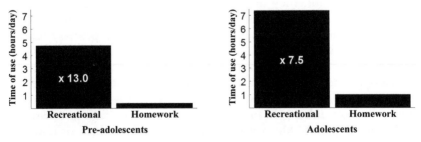

Figure 2. Time spent on digital uses at home for entertainment (recreational) and schoolwork (homework) by pre-teens (8–12 years) and adolescents (13–18 years). For details, see the text.[41]

everything is pretty much 'plug and play'. Never has the distance between ease of use and complexity of implementation been so great. It's now about as necessary for the average user to understand how their smartphone, TV or computer works as it is useful for Sunday gourmets to master the intricacies of the culinary art in order to eat at the Ritz; and (above all!) it's crazy to think that the mere fact of eating regularly in a large restaurant will allow just anyone to become an expert cook. In the culinary field, as in the computer field, there is the person who uses and the person who designs – and the former clearly does not need to grasp all the secrets of the latter.

For those who doubt this, a short detour through the population of 'digital immigrants'[a,7] might prove rewarding. Indeed, several studies report that adults are generally just as competent[23,34,38] and diligent[58-60] in digital matters as their young descendants. Even seniors manage, without great difficulty, when they deem it useful, to gain access to this new universe.[61] Take, for example, my friends Michèle and René. These two retirees have both clocked up over 70 years; they were born long before the spread of television and the birth of the Internet. They were 30 before they got their first landline phone. This hasn't stopped them, today, owning a giant flat screen, two tablets, two smartphones and a desktop computer; they can order their plane tickets on the Internet; use Facebook, Skype, YouTube and a video-on-demand service; and play video games with their grandchildren. More connected than her partner, Michèle is forever feeding the Twitter account of her walking club with selfies and punchlines.

Frankly, how can you believe for a single second that such practices are likely to turn anyone into a computer maestro or some coding genius? Any idiot can pick up these tools in a matter of minutes. After all, they have been thought out and designed with that in mind. So, as a senior executive in Google's communications department who chose to put his children in a primary school without screens explained to the *New York Times* recently, using these kinds of apps is 'supereasy. It's like learning to use toothpaste. At Google and all these places, we make technology as brain-dead easy to use as possible. There's no reason why kids can't figure it out when they get older.'[62] In other words, as the American Academy of Pediatrics explains, 'do not feel pressured to introduce technology

---

[a] This expression is used to describe 'older' users, born before the digital age – they are deemed to be less competent than digital natives.

early; interfaces are so intuitive that children will figure them out quickly once they start using them at home or in school'.[63] On the other hand, if the cardinal dispositions of childhood (and adolescence) have not been sufficiently mobilized, it is generally too late subsequently to learn to think, reflect, maintain one's concentration, make an effort, control language beyond its rudimentary bases, hierarchize the broad flows of information produced by the digital world or interact with others. Basically it all comes down to a plain and simple question of timing. On the one hand, as long as you spend a minimum amount of time on it, a late conversion to digital won't stop you from becoming as agile as the most seasoned digital natives. On the other hand, premature immersion will inevitably distract you from essential learning which, due to the progressive closing of the 'windows' of brain development, will become increasingly difficult to accomplish.

Political and commercial interests

So, obviously, the idyllic media portrait of digital natives lacks a bit of factual substance. This is a bore; but it's not surprising. Indeed, even if we turn completely away from the facts to stick to a strictly theoretical interpretation, the ludicrousness of this dismal tale continues to be perfectly obvious. Take the quotes presented throughout this chapter. They affirm with the most finger-wagging seriousness that digital natives represent a mutant group that is at the same time hyper-connected, dynamic, impatient, zapping, multitasking, creative, fond of experimentation, gifted for collaborative work, etc. But 'mutant' also means 'different'. Therefore, what is implicitly reflected here is also the image of a previous generation that was miserably lonely, amorphous, slow, patient, single-task, devoid of creativity, unfit for experimentation, resistant to collective work, etc. This is an odd picture; at a minimum, it suggests two lines of thought. The first questions the efforts made to positively redefine all sorts of psychological attributes that have long been known to be highly detrimental to one's intellectual performance: dispersion, zapping, multitasking, impulsiveness, impatience, etc. The second questions the anarchic and surreal relentlessness devoted to caricaturing the pre-digital generations as fuddy-duddies. It makes you wonder how the pathetic, individualistic, slug-like cluster of our ancestors survived the throes of Darwinian evolution. As the teacher and researcher in educational theory Daisy Christodoulou writes, in a

15

very well documented book in which she deliciously disassembles the founding myths of the new digital pedagogies, 'it is quite patronising to suggest that no one before the year 2000 ever needed to think critically, solve problems, communicate, collaborate, create, innovate or read'.[64] Likewise, one might add, it is truly ludicrous to suggest that the world 'before' was made up of unsociable hermits. With all due respect to the voracious technogobblers of all stripes, despite the absence of email and social media, baby boomers by no means lived isolated in some ocean of solitude. People who wished to do so easily managed to communicate, exchange, love one another and maintain strong bonds, even from a distance. There was the telephone and there was the postal service. As a child, I spoke every week to my Aunt Marie in Germany. I also wrote to my cousin Hans-Jochen, after each game won by Bayern Munich, the legendary football team of which he was a devoted fan. He always replied, sometimes with a simple card, sometimes with a small package in which I found a key ring, a mug or a club shirt. Those who doubt these realities should also look at the impressive correspondence from writers such as Rainer Maria Rilke, Stefan Zweig, Victor Hugo, Marcel Proust, George Sand and Simone de Beauvoir, and the many letters, often poignant, sent to their families by soldiers at the front during the Great War.[65]

I can obviously understand the marketing interest of the current caricatures. But frankly, they are all singularly lacking in seriousness. Take education, as a final example. When a French parliamentarian, supposedly a specialist in education issues, the author of two official reports on the importance of information technologies for schools,[66,67] allows himself to write such hair-raising statements as 'digital technology allows us to set up pedagogies of self-esteem, experience, and learning',[8] one can only hesitate between laughter, anger and dismay. What does our dear MP mean? That in pre-digital classrooms there was no question of pedagogy, or of experimentation, or of self-esteem? Fortunately, such distinguished educationalists as Rabelais, Rousseau, Montessori, Freinet, La Salle, Wallon, Steiner and Claparède are no longer there to hear the insult. And then, really – what an incredible revolution! Just think: 'a pedagogy of learning'. As if it could be otherwise; as if pedagogy did not intrinsically name a kind of art of teaching (and therefore of learning); as if any pedagogy could set out to produce stiff conformity, stupefaction and stagnation. There is something a little scary about realizing that it is this kind of hollow and ridiculous rhetoric that drives education policy in our schools.

'A more developed brain'

The myth of the digital native often comes, as we have just pointed out, with that astonishing chimera, the mutant child. According to this strange view, the human lineage today can look forward to bright new prospects. Current evolution, certain specialists inform us, 'may represent one of the most unexpected yet pivotal advances in human history. Perhaps not since Early Man first discovered how to use a tool has the human brain been affected so quickly and so dramatically.'[68] Oh yes: what you need to know is that 'our brains are evolving right now – at a speed like never before'.[68] Besides, make no mistake, our children are no longer truly human; they have become 'extraterrestrials',[69] 'mutants'.[69,70] 'They don't have the same brains anymore.'[71] They 'think and process information fundamentally differently from their predecessors'.[7] This generation 'is smarter and quicker'[4] and its neural circuitry is 'wiring up for rapid-fire cyber-searches'.[72] Subjected to the beneficial action of screens of all kinds, our children's brains have 'developed differently'.[4] They no longer have 'the same architecture'[73] and have been 'improved, extended, enhanced, amplified (and liberated) by technology'.[74] These changes are so deep and fundamental 'that there is absolutely no going back'.[7]

All these ideas are supported mainly by evidence from the field of video games. Indeed, several brain imaging studies have convincingly demonstrated that the brain of gamers exhibited certain localized morphological disparities compared to the brain of the man or woman in the street.[75-9] This has been a godsend for our valiant journalists, some of whom probably have no compunction about reaching for the joystick when necessary. Throughout the world, they gave these studies a triumphant reception, and splashed out on flashy headlines. Examples include: 'playing video games can boost brain volume';[80] 'video game enthusiasts have more grey matter and better brain connectivity';[81] 'the surprising connection between playing video games and a thicker brain';[82] 'video gaming can increase brain size and connectivity';[83] etc. Nothing less. It makes you wonder how sane adults can still deprive their children of such a windfall. Indeed, even if the idea is not precisely formulated, behind these titles we find a clear affirmation of competence: dear parents, thanks to video games, your children will have more developed and better connected brains, and this – as everyone will have understood – will increase their intellectual efficiency.

17

A pleasing fiction

Unfortunately, the myth, yet again, does not stand up to scrutiny for long. To get a sense of how much empty media nonsense this is, you have merely to understand that any persistent state and/or any repetitive activity changes the brain's architecture.[84] In other words, everything we do or experience changes both the structure and function of our brains. Some areas become thicker, others thinner; some connections develop, others become more tenuous. This is a characteristic of brain plasticity. In this context, it becomes obvious that the preceding titles can apply indiscriminately to any specific activity or recurring condition: juggling,[85] playing music,[86] consuming cannabis,[87] having a limb amputated,[88] driving a taxi,[89] watching television,[90] reading,[91] playing sports,[92] etc. However, to my surprise, I have never seen headlines in the press explaining, for example, that 'watching television can boost brain volume', that 'smoking cannabis can increase brain size and connectivity' or that there is a 'surprising connection between limb amputation and a thicker brain'. Yet again, these headlines would have exactly the same relevance as those commonly put forward when it comes to video games. So frankly, to say that gamers have a different brain architecture is to go into raptures over a truism. You might as well trumpet the fact that water is wet. Of course, it is easy to understand the CEO of Ubisoft entering the fray to explain, in a documentary broadcast on a French public TV channel, that thanks to video games 'we have more developed brains'.[a,93] What is more difficult to admit is that supposedly well-trained and independent journalists continue to repeat, without the least critical distance, this kind of grotesque propaganda.

This crass sham seems even more blatant when we realize that the link between cognitive performance and brain thickness is far from unequivocal. Indeed, when it comes to brain function, bigger does not necessarily mean more efficient. In many cases, a thinner cortex is functionally more efficient, with the observed thinning reflecting a pruning of supernumerary or unnecessary connections between neurons.[94] Take intelligence quotient (IQ). In adolescents and young adults, its development is associated with a gradual thinning of the cortex in a number of areas, especially the prefrontal area, that studies of the influence of video games have found to be thicker.[95-7] Specific studies of these prefrontal areas have even linked the extra

---

[a] Ubisoft is a major French company for the creation and distribution of video games.

18

cortical thickness observed in gamers with a decrease in IQ.[98] This negative relationship has also been described in frequent television viewers[90] and pathological Internet users.[99] So now is the time to face the facts: 'a bigger brain' is not a reliable marker of intelligence. In many cases, a cortex that is locally a bit on the plump side is the sign, not of any wonderful functional optimization, but of a sad lack of maturation.

Dubious shortcuts

The above-mentioned attention-grabbing 'headlines' are sometimes accompanied, it is true, by some specific assertions about the nature of the anatomical adaptations observed. So we are told, for example, that one study[76] has just reported that the brain plasticity associated with the sustained use of *Super Mario* can be observed 'in the right hippocampus, right prefrontal cortex and the cerebellum. These brain regions are involved in functions such as spatial navigation, memory formation, strategic planning and fine motor skills of the hands.'[100,101] Basically, this kind of publishers' gold dust is careful not to assert that a causal link exists between the anatomical changes observed and the functional aptitudes postulated, but the turn of the sentence strongly invites us to believe in the existence of such a link. Thus, the average reader will understand that the thickening of the right hippocampus improves spatial navigation and memorization potential; the thickening of the right prefrontal cortex signals the development of strategic thinking skills; and the thickening of the cerebellum marks an improvement in dexterity. This is impressive – but unfortunately unfounded.

Take the hippocampus. This structure is indeed central in the memorization process. But not in a uniform way. The posterior part of the right hippocampus, which thickens in gamers, is primarily involved in spatial memory. This means, as the authors of the study themselves admit, that what *Super Mario* users learn is to find their way around the game.[76] In other words, the modifications observed here at the hippocampus level simply reflect the construction of a spatial map of the available paths and objects of interest inherent in this particular video game. The same type of transformation can be observed among taxi drivers when they gradually build up a mental map of their city.[89] This poses two problems. First, this type of knowledge is highly specific, and therefore non-transferable: being able to orient yourself in the topographical tangle of *Super Mario* is of little use when it comes to finding your way on a road map or navigating your way through the spatial twists and turns of the real world.[102] Second, and more fundamentally, this navigational memory has functionally and anatomically nothing to do with 'memory' as the term is generally understood. Playing *Super Mario* in no way increases the ability of practitioners to retain a pleasant memory, an English or history lesson, a foreign language, a multiplication table or any other knowledge whatsoever. Therefore, to imply that playing *Super Mario* has a positive effect on 'memory formation' is at best a category mistake, at worst gross bad faith. Let us add, for the sake of completeness, that recent work has reported that what was true for *Super Mario* was not necessarily true for first-person shooter games (where the player sees the action through the eyes of his or her avatar) that did not involve spatial learning.[103] These games entail a reduction of grey matter in the hippocampus. However, as the authors of the study explicitly point out, 'lower grey matter in the hippocampus is a risk factor for developing numerous neuropsychiatric illnesses'.[103]

The same is true of the right prefrontal cortex. This area supports a large number of cognitive functions, from attention to decision making, through the learning of symbolic rules, behavioural inhibition and spatial navigation.[104-6] But, here again, there is no way of precisely linking any of these functions to the anatomical changes identified – something that the authors of the study readily acknowledge.[76] In fact, when we look closely at the data, we see that the prefrontal adaptations resulting from heavy use of *Super Mario* are related solely to the desire to play! As the authors put it, 'the reported desire to play the game leads to DLPFC [dorsolateral prefrontal cortex] growth'.[76] In other words, this anatomical change could reflect a perfectly ordinary inducement of the reward system[a] of which the dorsolateral prefrontal cortex is a key element.[104,107] Of course, the term 'ordinary' may seem ill-chosen when we know that the hypersensitivity of reward circuits, as developed by action video games, is closely associated with impulsivity and the risk of addiction.[108-11] In fact, several studies have linked the thickening of the prefrontal areas considered here to a pathological use of the Internet and video games.[99,112] These data are far from trivial when

---

[a] The reward system can be described as a set of brain structures that induce the reproduction of pleasurable experiences. Basically, the pleasant (or positive) experience leads to the release of biochemical substances (neurotransmitters) which activate the pleasure circuits; this promotes the reproduction of the associated behaviour.

we remember that adolescence is a highly significant period in the maturation of the prefrontal cortex[113-17] and, what is more, a time of extreme vulnerability for the acquisition and development of addictive, psychiatric and behavioural disorders.[118-20] In this context, the anatomical changes gloated over by certain media could very well lay, not the foundations for a bright intellectual future, but the bases for a behavioural disaster yet to come; a hypothesis to which I will return in detail in the third part of this book (below).

That being said, even if all of the above reservations were rejected, the problem of generalization would still have to be considered. To imply that the prefrontal thickening seen in *Super Mario* users improves 'strategic thinking' skills is one thing; to show how this improvement can exist and be useful outside the specificities of the game is another, and very different, matter. Indeed, once the semantic syncretism of this catch-all concept has been removed, who can reasonably believe that 'strategic thinking' is a general skill, independent of the contexts and types of knowledge that have given it shape? So, for example, who can believe that there is something in common between the process of 'strategic thinking' entailed by *Super Mario* and the process required to play chess, complete a business negotiation, solve a maths problem, optimize a schedule or organize the arguments of an essay? The idea is not only absurd but also contrary to the most recent research reporting that there is hardly any transfer from video games to 'real life'.[121-9] In other words, playing Super Mario mainly teaches one how to play *Super Mario*. The skills thereby acquired are non-transferable. At best, they may extend to certain analogous activities subject to the same constraints as those imposed by the game.[127,130]

That leaves the cerebellum and the supposed improvement in dexterity. Here too there are obvious problems of interpretation and generalization. First, many other mechanisms could account for the anatomical adaptation observed (controlling postural stability and eye movement, learning to make connections between stimulus and response, etc.).[131,132] Then, even if we accept the dexterity hypothesis, it is unlikely that the skill then acquired will be transferred beyond certain specific tasks that require us to control, via a joystick, the movement of an object we have located (for example, piloting a drone, or handling a computer mouse or a remote manipulator in surgery).[133] Who can reasonably believe that playing *Super Mario* can promote the overall learning of fine visual skills such as playing the violin, writing, drawing, painting, hitting the ball in table tennis or building a Lego house? If there is one area where the extreme specificity of learning is now firmly established, it is that of sensori-motor skills.[a,134]

In conclusion

The main lesson of this part of the book is that digital natives do not exist. The digital mutant child, whose aptitude for tickling the smartphone has transformed him or her into a brilliant general practitioner of the most complex new technologies; whom Google Search has rendered infinitely more curious, agile and knowledgeable than any teachers of the pre-digital age could have done; who, thanks to video games, has gained a stronger and bigger brain; who, thanks to the filters of Snapchat and Instagram, has achieved the highest levels of creativity, and so on – this child is just a legend that can be found nowhere in the scientific literature. But such a child's image, nonetheless, continues to haunt collective beliefs. And this is positively stupefying. Indeed, that such an absurdity could have emerged is, in itself, nothing out of the ordinary. After all, the idea deserved to be scrutinized. No, what is extraordinary is that such an absurdity persists through thick and thin, and, in addition, helps guide our public policies, especially in the educational field.

Beyond its folklore aspects, this myth obviously comes with ulterior motives.[22] At the domestic level, first of all, it reassures parents by making them believe that their offspring are real geniuses of digital technology and complex thinking, even if, in fact, they only know how to use a few trivial (and expensive) apps. On the educational level, it also makes it possible – to the delight of a flourishing industry – to support the frenzied digitization of the system, despite what are, to say the least, worrying performances (I will come back to this in the third part). In short, everyone wins ... except our children. But this is a problem that, quite clearly, nobody seems to care about.

---

[a] This expression refers to all the activities that involve both sensory functions (seeing, hearing, etc.) and motor functions. These include writing, drawing, grabbing or manipulating an object, playing tennis, football, basketball, etc. Typically, in common parlance we simply refer to 'motor' functions, but the idea is the same.

22

— PART TWO —

USES
An incredible frenzy of screens for recreation

Wasting time is the most irreparable vice, and it is the one that causes people the least worry.

Count Axel Oxenstierna[1]

In terms of the use of digital technology by the younger generations, three additional questions need to be explored: what, how much and who?

What? To avoid any misunderstanding, let's start by restating the obvious: in many areas, digital technology constitutes clear progress, and there is no question here of saying that the influence of screens is unambiguously negative. Undoubtedly, the impact depends on usage. This is why it is essential to determine precisely what this usage involves: what screens do our children use, in what way and for what purposes? Therefore, it will not be a question here of how screens could be employed in some idealized, fantasized absolute realm (the propagandist guilds are perfectly well able to produce this kind of bullshit), but of how they are actually used on a daily basis.

How much? This question will be approached from two complementary angles relating to (i) the duration of specific consumption (television, video games, school activities, etc.) and (ii) total recreational time. Regarding this second point, it should undoubtedly be emphasized that beyond their undeniable specificities, the digital practices of gaming present strong similarities both structural (e.g. sensory saturation linked to an influx of sounds, images or notifications) and functional (e.g. time stolen from other occupations more favourable to development – interactions with other family members, reading, creative games, school homework, physical activity, sleep, etc.). These similarities explain the capacity of screens used for recreation to act

23

in a convergent manner. In other words, when we focus on practices devolved to entertainment (television, video games, etc.), talking about 'screens' in this general way is far from misleading. On the contrary: it is especially interesting as it allows us, ultimately, to address the fundamental problem of 'excess', i.e. the temporal threshold beyond which developmental disorders or delays are to be feared.

Who? This question is undoubtedly the main one that gets forgotten in the media debate. However, as we have already briefly pointed out, the use of screens is far from homogeneous among the younger generations. It varies in particular with age, sex and socio-economic background. Taking into account these heterogeneous factors turns out to be crucial when addressing questions of academic success, invalidating the idea that any attempt to control the time spent on screens for recreation by our offspring is henceforth in vain. This is a piece of astonishing defeatism which the French Academy of Sciences seems to have turned into its credo, unhesitatingly affirming that 'in the younger generations born "in the digital" era, only a marginal reduction in exposure time to screens will be possible'.[2]

Estimates that are necessarily approximate

Before getting to the heart of the matter, one remark is in order: identifying the ways any population uses digital platforms is not easy.[3] In practice, of course, the ideal would be to ask an army of researchers to scrutinize, for twenty hours a day, over a month or two, an army of young users and obsessively note their digital activity. This would be ideal but ... infeasible. An alternative would be to place tracking software in the digital devices used by each individual (smartphone, tablets, TV, consoles, etc.) and then aggregate the data obtained over several weeks. This is technically possible, no doubt, but delicate in terms of the protection of privacy (Nathan won't necessarily want to reveal that he's a fan of YouPorn), and complicated for shared devices (how are we to know, for example, who is watching TV: Peter, Jane, everyone or no one?). In any case, to my knowledge, no such comprehensive study is yet available.

To date, the most common approach relies on interviews or surveys. However, these methods are far from perfect.[3] First of all, people often get the facts wrong and often tend to underestimate their personal consumption and that of their children.[4-9] Also, many of the most frequently cited studies[10-14] add up the uses (TV + smartphone + video games, etc.) without worrying about possible overlaps

(Celia often watches TV while chatting on social networks via her smartphone), which artificially increase the total consumption time. Finally, important variables are not always taken into account, such as the season (the same survey carried out in winter or summer will not necessarily give the same result)[15] or the geographical origin of the sample observed (a survey carried out on children living mainly in urban areas[16] may lead to an underestimation of screen time).[17]

In spite of these reservations, the fact remains that the works presented here, by way of example, have been chosen from among the most meticulously conducted studies. They involve large populations and are based on rigorous interview protocols. Unfortunately, this does not solve all the problems. In particular, self-evaluation biases (we underestimate our own consumption and that of our children) and parallel uses (we neglect simultaneous consumption) remain frequent. However, quantitative analyses have suggested that these factors could have roughly comparable impacts in absolute terms; we need to scale by around 20–50% upwards for self-assessment and downwards for parallel uses.[4,8,9,18,19] We can assume therefore that these factors will, at least in part, cancel out their effects. But obviously, these studies are far from having an impeccable surgical rigour. However, it would be absurd to reject all of them out of hand. Indeed, even if they are neither perfect nor blameless, they are unlikely to be absurd. In other words, while the findings presented in this section should not be taken literally, overall they provide a credible basis for reflection.

It is undoubtedly important to underline that in terms of digital uses, the most complete and rigorous studies have been conducted in the United States.[10,11,20,21] Consequently, one might feel that the figures and habits of consumption obtained have no general validity. This would be a mistake. Indeed, when we compare the American data with observations acquired in other economically comparable countries such as France,[13,14,22] England,[23] Norway[24] or Australia,[25] we find a very high degree of convergence. In other words, in terms of digital practices, there is no longer any country that sticks out as different, and the habits of young Westerners are now very similar. Is this for better or worse? Everyone can decide for themselves.

Childhood: exposure

The study of early digital uses is particularly important, for at least two reasons.

First, it is on the basis of these consumptions that later usage is largely organized. The earlier that children are confronted with screens, the more likely they are subsequently to become persistent and assiduous users.[5,26-31] This is not surprising. We are creatures of habit and, as with the routines of eating, school and social life, and reading,[6,27,32,33] later digital practices are deeply rooted in the practices of childhood.

Second, the first years of life are fundamental to learning and brain maturation. As I will be illustrating in more detail, what is 'missed out' because screens deprive the child of a certain number of essential stimuli and experiences turns out to be very difficult to catch up afterwards.[34-43] This is all the more unfortunate as digital abilities (or a lack of them) are easily compensated for at any age. Thus, as I underlined in the first part, any normally constituted adult or teenager can soon learn to use social networks, office software, commercial sites, download platforms, touch tablets, smartphones, cyber-clouds and other such wonderful toys. This is not the case for the essential knowledge of childhood. Indeed, what was not put in place during the early years of development in terms of language, motor coordination, mathematical prerequisites, social customs, emotional management, etc. proves increasingly more expensive to acquire over time.

To understand this, we can think of the brain as a kind of plasticine whose texture gradually hardens over the years. Of course, adults still learn, but not in the same way as children. Schematically, we could say that *adults learn mainly by rearranging the neural circuits available, while children build up new circuits*. A simple analogy will illustrate this fundamental divergence. Say someone has to get from Boston to Dallas. To achieve this, a child will take her JCB digger and create an optimal route in her neural field. An adult no longer has a digger. She now has just a small trowel. Armed with the latter, she will manage, at best, to make her way modestly to the nearby station. Then, to reach her destination, she will have to take the paths already built, and check their reliability. So, for example, given her past experiences, she can launch out on a Boston–Cleveland route, then Cleveland-Atlanta, then Atlanta–San Antonio and finally San Antonio–Dallas. At first, despite these detours, she will do better than the child; building a road takes time. But very soon the child will surpass her older sister and make her look helplessly ridiculous. If you doubt this, take up the violin at the same time as your 5-year-old daughter. Take advantage of your initial superiority: it may be brief. If you don't like the violin, go to a train station and try running next to a train that's just setting off. The experience will turn out to be similar. At the beginning you will go much faster than the machine; but incrementally it will catch up with you, before leaving you far behind.

While the child is in full development, the time taken up by early digital consumption turns out to be quite extravagant. Two periods need to be considered. One, roughly encompassing the first 24 months, primes the pump, so to speak. The other, lasting from the ages of 2 to 8, marks a clear phase of stabilization before the onset of pre-adolescence.

Getting your foot in the stirrup: 0–1 years

Children under the age of 2 spend, on average, about 50 minutes each day on screens. This duration, which has remained surprisingly stable over the last decade,[11,20,21] probably seems reasonable at first glance. But it isn't. It represents 8% of the child's waking time;[a,44] and 15% of its 'leisure' time, i.e. of the time available once one has removed 'constrained' activities such as eating (seven times a day on average before the age of 2),[45,46] dressing, washing and nappy changing.[47-9] Obviously, these restricted activities play a major role in the child's development (in particular because they are accompanied by social, emotional and language interactions with the adult); but the experiences are not the same as during leisure time. This is mainly structured around active observation of the world, spontaneous games, sensorimotor explorations or other unpredictable activities. The child is sometimes alone, sometimes with another person. In the latter case, the exchanges that take place with her mum or dad are all the more essential as they are very different from those that occur during bathing or meals.

The problem here refers to the gulf between the fruitfulness of these episodes of unconstrained learning and the appalling destructiveness of times of digital usage. It is against this gap that the 'mere' 50 minutes that very young children give to screens every day must be measured. Cumulating over 24 months, these minutes add up to more than 600 hours. This is roughly equivalent to the duration of a year of kindergarten.[b] In terms of language, this means 200,000 lost utter-

---

[a] Waking time is defined in line with the low norm of the optimal recommended duration of sleep.
[b] The number of hours of instruction required in kindergarten obviously varies from country to country and state to state, with, for example, 864 hours in France,[50] 600 hours in California, 522 hours in Missouri, and 952 hours in North Dakota.[51]

ances, or roughly 850,000 words not heard.[52] And those who want to directly measure the magnitude of the figures here being manipulated can just sit quietly in front of their flat screens and watch all the episodes of *Desperate Housewives*, *House*, *The Mentalist*, *Lost*, *Friends* and *Mad Men*. This will deprive their existence of exactly ... 600 hours.

And don't let anyone tell you that digital tools are great vectors of sharing, especially for language. Before the age of 2, only half of the parents report being present 'all the time' or 'most of the time' when the child is in front of a screen.[53] And here again, being present doesn't mean interacting! A study has reported, for 6-month-old toddlers, that approximately 85% of screen time was silent, i.e. without any adult language intervening.[54] This result is compatible with the data of another study of children from 6 to 18 months; this established, as regards television, that the concept of shared use came down in almost 90% of cases to plonking the child next to the parent as the latter watched his or her own programmes for the 'general public'.[55]

When it comes to the fine details, it appears that television swallows up 70% of the screen time of very young children.[11] When other media, particularly mobile devices, are used, they mainly function as auxiliary TVs for viewing DVDs or videos. Year in and year out, more than 95% of screen time for 0- to 1-year-olds is devoted to audiovisual consumption of this kind. However, this figure masks a great disparity of situations: 29% of children are never exposed; 34% are exposed every day; 37% fall somewhere between these two extremes. For the subset of daily users alone, the average consumption is almost 90 minutes. In other words, more than a third of children under the age of 1 are exposed to an hour and a half of screens per day. These heavy users are found mainly in the less privileged socio-cultural backgrounds.

Some studies focus specifically on digital practices in these environments. The result is overwhelming. Depending on the groups studied, it varies between 1 hour 30 minutes and 3 hours 30 minutes of daily use.[54,56,57] The main reasons given by parents to explain this incredible orgy include keeping the kids quiet in public places (65%), while shopping (70%) and/or while performing household chores (58%). In 28% of cases, the screen is used to put the child to sleep. Every day, nearly 90% of underprivileged 12-month-old toddlers watch TV; 65% use mobile tools (tablets or smartphones); 15% are exposed to video game consoles. For 6- to 12-month-olds, these figures are around 85% (TV), 45% (mobile tools) and 5% (consoles).[57] These figures are scary.

The first level: 2–8 years

It is not until the second year that the child moves on, so to speak, to serious matters. Its digital consumption then increases sharply: between 2 and 4 years, it reaches 2 hours 45 minutes per day. The explosion then settles down to peak at around 3 hours. These figures are phenomenal. Over the past decade, they have increased by more than 50%.[11,21] They represent a fifth of a child's normal waking time.[44] Over a year, their cumulative duration merrily exceeds 1,000 hours. This means that between the ages of 2 and 8, an 'average' child spends the equivalent of 6 to 7 full school years[50,51] on screens for recreation: this is 460 days of waking life (a year and a quarter), or the exact amount of personal working time required to become a decent violinist.[58]

Over 90% of the digital time of children aged 2 to 8 is devoted to absorbing audiovisual programmes (TV, videos and DVDs) and playing video games. We can, however, note a small difference related to age: among 2- to 4-year-olds, the audiovisual sector exceeds video games a little more (77% as against 13%) than among 5- to 8-year-olds (65% as against 24%).[11] Obviously, these figures must be weighted with regard to the socio-cultural characteristics of the household. It appears, not surprisingly, that children from under-privileged backgrounds register a recreational digital consumption almost twice as high as their more favoured counterparts (3 hours 30 minutes as against 1 hour 50 minutes).[11] However, the latter would be wrong to gloat too quickly. Indeed, several studies relating to academic success report that screens do not exert their damaging action in a uniform manner. The more the child comes from a privileged socio-cultural home, the more the time wasted watching television,[5,59–61] or on video games,[62] acts as a drawback. In other words, in privileged circles, the total screen time is certainly less, but the hours lost are more expensive because they take place to the detriment of richer and more formative experiences (reading, verbal interactions, musical practices, sports or arts, cultural outings, etc.). A simple analogy will help to illustrate this mechanism: if you deprive a child of two litres of a clear soup that is 25% wilted vegetable, the nutritional impact will be less than if you deprive the same child of a litre of a thick soup that is 60% fresh vegetables. The same goes for screens: advantaged children waste less 'soup', but each fraction of that lost 'soup' would have contributed more to individual development.

It should be noted that the digital consumption described here mainly takes place, as for 0- to 1-year-olds, far from parental scrutiny. Thus, for 2- to 5-year-olds, regardless of the type of screen, only a small minority of parents (around 30%) say that they are present 'all of the time' or 'most of the time'.[11,53] For 6- to 8-year-olds, the situation is more diverse. Television enjoys the highest level of control with just under 25% of parents reporting being present 'all of the time' or 'most of the time'. This falls to around 10% for mobile tools and video games.

Pre-adolescence: amplification

During pre-adolescence, which I will here consider as between 8 and 12 years, children see their daily sleep needs decrease significantly. Compared to earlier periods of childhood, they gain 60 to 90 minutes awake each day.[44] They dedicate the time they have 'won', in its entirety, to their digital trinkets. Thus, between 8 and 12 years old, daily screen time rises to 4 hours 45 minutes, as compared to 3 hours previously.[63] Four hours forty-five minutes! This is pretty significant: it represents about a third of normal waking time.[44] Over a year, that adds up to over 1,700 hours, the equivalent of roughly two school years[50,51,64] or, alternatively, one year of full-time paid employment.[65] This is surprising – but not necessarily surprising for anyone willing to consider the incredible state of 'digital saturation' in which pre-teens find themselves today: 52% have their own tablets, 23% have a laptop, 5% have a connected watch, 84% consume audiovisual content (TV/videos) every day, 64% play video games daily, etc. From the age of 8, 19% have a smartphone. The percentage then increases almost linearly to reach 69% at 12 years. This is doubtless enough to delight the moguls of the new economy – but it fails to feed the minds of tomorrow.

In terms of activities, the change is undoubtedly less drastic.[63] Roughly speaking, it is in line with previous practices: nearly 85% of screen time devoted to audiovisual materials (2 hours 30 minutes) and video games (1 hour 28 minutes). The use of social networks is still, at this age, relatively marginal (4%; 10 minutes), as is the time spent surfing the Internet (5%; 14 minutes). Topping the list of their favourite digital activities, pre-teens mention watching videos online (67%), playing video games on a mobile device (55%) or console (52%), listening to music (55%) and watching TV (50%). These average trends, of course, mask important individual disparities. Some pre-teens (but this is also true of adolescents, as we will see later) prefer to gorge on TV while others prefer to binge on video games or social networks; yet others, finally, prefer to mix up these practices.[10] This variability is found in the time given up to screens for recreation (figure 1, p. 11). Among 8- to 12-year-olds, we can identify 41% of 'heavy consumers' (more than 4 hours per day), as against 35% of 'light users' (less than 2 hours per day). Of these, 8% have zero exposure.[63] Interestingly, we often hear that these screenless children run the risk of being excluded from their peer group – so it is dangerous to deprive our offspring of this 'common culture' and of access to modern communication tools such as social networks. Two objections can be made to this fairy tale. First, to date, no study has reported any social, emotional, cognitive or academic harm in children without access to screens for recreation. Second, although conflicting data exist,[66,67] a large body of research, reports, meta-analyses and overviews has found that pre-teens who spend the least amount of time in the wonderful world of cyber-entertainment are also those who are in the best health.[10,68–86] The conclusion has to be that our kids can do without screens for recreation; this abstinence does not compromise their emotional balance or their social integration. Quite the contrary!

Unsurprisingly, the above heterogeneous findings depend to a large extent on the socio-economic characteristics of the household.[63] Thus, pre-teens from disadvantaged backgrounds devote 1 hour 50 minutes more to screens for recreation each day than their more privileged counterparts (5 hours 49 minutes as against 3 hours 59 minutes). This difference is mainly due to increased consumption of audiovisual content (+ 1 hour 15 minutes) and social networks (+ 30 minutes).[10] There is no difference for video games, which are used in a comparable way regardless of the social background. This last point is interesting. It is tempting to associate it with the media campaigns stubbornly waged for years to defend the positive influence of these games (especially action games) on attention, decision-making skills and academic performance; campaigns which I will be discussing in more detail and which were probably not without some effect on parental trade-offs. It can be noted, however, that these campaigns had little influence on gender differences. Indeed, between the ages of 8 and 12, the excess screen time observed in boys compared to girls (1 hour 6 minutes, i.e. 5 hours 16 minutes as against 4 hours 10 minutes) can be explained to a large extent by an increased exposure to video games.[63]

Adolescence: submersion

In adolescence, which I will here take as between 13 and 18 years of age, screen time still increases significantly, particularly as a result of the spread of smartphones. The daily consumption of digital resources then reaches 7 hours 22 minutes.[63] Is it necessary to underline how stratospheric this figure is? It equals 30% of the day and 45% of normal waking time.[44] Over one year, this amounts to more than 2,680 hours, 112 days, 3 school years, or all of the time spent by French pupils in secondary schools, in the most selective academic fields, in French, mathematics and biology. In other words, over a single year, screens for recreation absorb as much time as the total number of hours of French, maths and biology throughout secondary school. But that doesn't stop the endless ruminations about the busy schedules of schoolchildren.[87] Ah, the poor little privileged martyrs of our affluent societies, overwhelmed by work and deprived of leisure! Ayoub, a young schoolboy, is one of these children; when questioned by a major national daily paper, he said: 'If they shortened my school days, I'd take the opportunity to play more on my Playstation, or to watch TV.'[88] This is what we call a win-win-win project: Ayoub is having a whale of a time, Sony is lining its pockets, and the Ministry of National Education is saving money (fewer hours of lessons means fewer teachers needing to be paid). The success of some private non-profit school programmes, particularly in the United States, shows that this is the exact opposite of what needs to be done to win the educational battle, especially in disadvantaged communities![89–91] But it would be foolish to worry about it. These data, after all, go back to the world 'before' – before our children became rapid-fire cyber-research mutants!

But back to the issue of usage. In this regard, adolescence does not change previously established habits very much.[63] Slightly more audiovisual content (2 hours 52 minutes as against 2 hours 30 minutes), the same number of video games (1 hour 36 minutes as against 1 hour 28 minutes), much more in the way of social networks (1 hour 10 minutes as against 10 minutes) and a little more time to surf on the Web (37 minutes as against 14 minutes) and video chat (19 minutes as against 5 minutes). Year in and year out, these activities absorb 90% of teenagers' digital time. Of course, the socio-cultural characteristics of the household play an important role here too. Members of underprivileged backgrounds spend 1 hour 45 minutes more on screens each day than their more privileged counterparts.

This only confirms the trends observed at earlier ages. The same goes for the gender effect. Between the ages of 13 and 18, boys continue to consume more than girls, but only a little (29 minutes). This relative convergence, however, masks a certain difference in practice. In adolescence, girls prefer social networks (1 hour 30 minutes as against 51 minutes) while boys devote themselves more to video games (2 hours 17 minutes as against 47 minutes).

Family environment: aggravating factors

So it appears that the use of screens for recreation varies greatly depending on the social background, age and gender of the subjects. But important as they are, these factors are far from telling the whole story. Other characteristics, more 'environmental', are also to be considered when we want to define the behaviour of younger generations vis-à-vis digital technology. The advantage of these characteristics is that they are, unlike socio-demographic markers, quite easily controllable. In this sense, they offer parents a potentially effective mechanism with which to curb their children's consumption.

Limiting access and setting an example

Not surprisingly, the number one factor that can boost usage is the physical availability of the screen. Having several TVs, consoles, smartphones or tablets at home clearly favours consumption, especially where the bedroom is concerned.[92-101] In other words, if you want to boost your offspring's digital exposure, make sure they have their own smartphones and tablets and equip their bedrooms with TVs and consoles. This last attention will spoil their sleep,[96,98,102-7] their health[92,96,100] and their school results,[6,93,105] but at least they'll be quiet and give you some peace.[53] On this subject, one study looked at the behaviour of more than three thousand 5-year-old children.[108] Those who had a TV in their room were almost three times more likely to have a daily consumption of more than 2 hours. Ditto for the game console. Children who had one in their room were three times more likely to have a daily use of more than 30 minutes. Comparable results have been reported in older subjects, whether pre-teens or adolescents.[94,95,97,100] In short, to curb the digital exposure of children, one excellent solution is to remove screens from their bedrooms and to delay for as long as possible the time when they are equipped with various mobile tools. In this area, if it is simply a question, as parents often say, of 'being able to keep in touch with the kids to make sure that everything's OK', a basic laptop without Internet access is quite suitable; there's no need for an interstellar smartphone.

As well as these questions of access, we need to think – unsurprisingly enough – about the weight of family habits. Many studies have reported that children's consumption increased with that of their parents.[28,95,99,109-14] A threefold mechanism explains this link: (i) shared screen times (video or TV games, for example) generally increase exposure times (because shared uses, for the most part, do not exclude solitary practices but simply get added to them);[115] (ii) children tend to imitate their parents' excessive behaviour (according to a well-known social learning mechanism);[116,117] (iii) heavy adult consumers have a more positive view of the impact of screens on development,[53] which leads them to impose less restrictive rules of use on their offspring. Indeed, on this last point, several studies have reported that the absence of restrictive rules promotes access to unsuitable content and increases the duration of use.[28,95,97,108,113,115] Thus, as regards television, one experimental study has compared three parental 'styles' in children aged 10–11: permissive (no rules), authoritarian (rigidly imposed rules) and persuasive (rules that are explained).[118] For each of these styles, the proportion of children likely to watch TV for more than 4 hours per day was 20%, 13% and 7% respectively.

This last result underscores the importance of explaining, from childhood, the rationale for imposed limits. Clearly, to be fully effective in the long term, the restrictive framework should be seen not as an arbitrary punishment, but as a positive requirement. It is important that the child should agree with the process and internalize the benefits. When she asks why she isn't 'allowed', when her friends do 'whatever they want', you have to explain that her friends' parents may not have studied the matter sufficiently; she must be told that screens have significant negative influences on her brain, her intelligence, her concentration, her school results, her health, etc.; and you have to tell her why: less sleep; less time spent on more rewarding activities, including reading, playing a musical instrument, practising a sport or talking to other people; less time doing homework; etc. But all of this, of course, is only credible if you yourself aren't constantly glued to a recreational screen. At worst, you must then try to explain to the child that what's bad for her isn't necessarily bad for an adult, because the latter's brain is 'finished' while the child's is still 'in the process of being built'.

Making rules is effective!

In the end, all these factors bluntly give the lie to the doomsters of inevitability. Indeed, pointing out that exposure to screens depends on environmental factors on which it is possible to act means insisting that there is nothing inevitable about the present. A big swathe of studies clearly demonstrates this. In this context, researchers are no longer content to observe their flock. They set up experimental protocols aimed at reducing exposure to screens for recreation. One recent meta-analysis combined the results of a dozen properly conducted studies under the umbrella of this single objective.[119,120] The result is that when parents (and children in some of these studies) are made aware of the harmful influences of digital recreation and when, on this basis, they are offered precise restrictive rules (maximum weekly or daily duration, no screens in the bedroom, no screens in the morning before school, no TV on when no one is watching, etc.), the level of consumption drops substantially; on average, by half. For the twelve studies considered, which mainly involved subjects 13 years of age and under, this intervention reduced the daily time of use from a little over 2 hours 30 minutes to just under 1 hour 15 minutes. The decline, far from being ephemeral, was found to be remarkably stable over follow-up periods of up to 2 years (the average being just over 6 months).

So getting the younger generations to reduce their digital recreational consumption is not impossible. The available studies report that impressive results can be obtained by enacting precise rules of use and by limiting access opportunities. Again, however, in order for the process to work in the long term, the agreement of children and adolescents must be constantly sought. Contrary to what many people seem to believe, this explanatory tenacity in no way precludes the existence of a binding framework. On the contrary! Constraint and empowerment are the twin factors of success. Indeed, it is because children can rely on a set of explicitly defined rules that they will gradually succeed in building up their self-regulatory capacities; capacities which, in turn, will prove to be all the more effective if they are supported by an enabling environment. Basically, the guiding idea here is quite simple: it is easier to resist a desire when the means of its satisfaction are absent, locked away and/or expensive to implement.[121,122] For example, it's much easier to comply with the formal decision not to watch TV during meals when there is no screen in the kitchen. Likewise, it's much easier not to let yourself be dominated by your smartphone when you don't have one (does a 10-, 12- or 15-year-old child *really* need a smartphone?), when precise rules for use exist (for example, after 8 p.m. and while doing homework the smartphone must be left off, on the chest of drawers in the living room) and/or when software aids are used to reinforce willpower (a number of simple apps can define, on a daily basis, the duration and times of use). And, above all, don't start talking about playing Big Brother or disempowering your children. On the one hand, the power of objectification of these tools really helps individuals to become aware of their excessive consumption. On the other hand, accepting help when it's become difficult to avoid the pangs of excessive use, in whatever area (alcohol, gambling, screens, etc.), turns out to be a rather reassuring sign of intelligence and psychological maturity. Ultimately, these initial 'crutches' promote the development of lasting positive habits.

Reorienting activities

In practice, therefore, acting on the family environment effectively reduces screen time. But that's not all; it's not even the most interesting result. Indeed, this approach also makes it possible, more generally, to orient children's fields of activity. Say a schoolboy has a choice between reading a book or watching TV. In almost all cases, he chooses this second option.[26,123] But what happens if we remove the TV? Well, even if he doesn't really like it that much, the kid will start reading. Too good to be true? Not at all! Several recent studies have indeed reported that our doughty brains find it very difficult to stay idle.[124,125] It has been observed, for example, that 20 minutes spent doing nothing resulted in a greater level of mental fatigue than 20 minutes spent doing a complex number task (adding 3 to each digit of a 4-digit number: $6243 \Rightarrow 9576$).[126] Therefore, rather than being bored, the majority of people prefer to leap on the first occupation that comes along, even if it seems at first glance to be off-putting or, worse, involves inflicting a series of painful electric shocks on oneself.[127,128] The American journalist Susan Maushart observed this prescriptive power of empty time for herself on the day she decided to disconnect her three teenage zombies.[129] Deprived of their electronic gadgets, these lucky people first bridled; then they gradually adapted and started (or recommenced) reading, playing the sax, taking the dog for a walk on the beach, cooking, eating with the family, talking with their mum, getting more sleep, etc.; in short, they started living again.

What are the limits to the use of screens?

The central question remains: 'what constitutes excessive use?' When the subject is discussed publicly, the words used are often vague and nebulous. We frequently read and hear, for example, that 'too much screen time damages the brain',[130] that 'excessive screen time is harmful to mental health',[131] or '[that] we must promote a reasonable use of screens'.[132] But, in practice, what does all this mean? 'Reasonable' means how much? Where does 'excess' begin? When does usage last 'too long'? These questions rarely get the answers they deserve. And yet the scientific literature is full of data.

Whether you're an addict or not, enough is enough

Addiction is, of course, a first topic for reflection. Dozens of studies, both behavioural and neurophysiological, have now clearly established the reality of the phenomenon.[133–43] In spite of everything, the criteria for describing a practice as pathological are still fluid and the various classification scales often do not map onto one another, beyond the general principle according to which addiction to screens characterizes a compulsive use detrimental to daily functioning, in particular in the social and professional fields.[144–7] In proportion, the estimated average values remain (still?) relatively low, around 3% to 10% of users, even though a great variability can be observed here too.[134,140,141,145,148–51] In view of the modesty of these figures, it is tempting to conclude that 'excessive use' ultimately affects only a fairly small fraction of the population. This is a reassuring idea, but it calls for two comments. First, a small percentage of a large population actually means a lot of people: in France, 5% of 14- to 24-year-olds represents nearly 400,000 individuals;[152] in the United States, it's six times more, or around 2.5 million souls.[153] Second, a behaviour does not have to be pathological to be harmful. In other words, even if a kid isn't, in the clinical sense, 'addicted' to her smartphone, her social network platforms or her game console, this doesn't mean that she's immune to all kinds of negative influences. If we think that the opposite is true, we risk making a dangerous mistake, since the collective imagination equates the 'addict' with a sort of broken wreck, exemplified by the erratic drug addict and the repellent alcoholic depicted in television series. It's difficult for parents to identify their children with these grim models. It's also difficult for the children to recognize themselves in the proposed archetypes.[154] All the more difficult, in fact, as the digital domain is subject to the same problem as other addictions: denial is deep-rooted and frequent.[155-7]

The importance of age

The problem therefore remains: where are we to set the boundaries of excess? The answer depends on age. To understand this, we must realize that human beings do not develop like a long, quiet river. In terms of brain construction, certain so-called 'sensitive' periods are, as we have already mentioned, much more important than others.[34-42] If neurons are offered 'food' that is inadequate in quality and/or quantity, they cannot 'learn' in an optimal way; and the longer the deficiency lasts, the more difficult it becomes to fill the gap. For example, kittens subjected to occlusion of one eye during the first three months of their life never regain normal binocular vision.[158] Likewise, rats exposed to a particular sound frequency during the second week of their existence experience a persistent expansion of the brain region associated with deciphering this frequency (to the detriment of others, of course).[159] It is tempting to compare this result with clinical observations on children born deaf, reporting that the long-term effectiveness of cochlear prostheses varies greatly with the age of implantation. The deployment of sound discrimination capacities, particularly in the field of language, is excellent up to age 3 or 4 years. It then gradually deteriorates until it becomes very unsatisfactory after 8–10 years.[160,161] In the same way, in adult musicians, the extent of the reorganizations of the cerebral cortex caused by practising an instrument assiduously depends much more on learning to play early (before 7 years) than on total training time.[162,163] Similarly, in immigrant populations, mastery of the language of the adopted country depends less on the number of years spent there than on age at arrival. When this exceeds 7 years, the difficulty becomes notable (apart from acquiring vocabulary, which seems capable of developing without age limit).[164,165] Thus, in the end, after years of living in their host country, twins will display a higher degree of language proficiency if they arrived when they were both 4 years old than they would if they were both 8. That being said, compared to natives, early immigrants may also present long-term deficits if they are subjected to sufficiently precise tests. Indeed, for many linguistic abilities, brain 'crystallization' begins well before the 7-year barrier.[166-8] In the phonetic field, for example, 'native' English speakers are able, when they pay enough attention, to distinguish the existence of a slight accent in adult immigrants who arrived in North America at the age of 3 years.[169] The same goes for grammar. Chinese adults who move to the United States during their early childhood, between the ages of 1 and 3, display syntactic abilities that are less developed than in their native counterparts.[170] Admittedly, the impact turns out to be slight, but it is detectable.

We could fill dozens of pages with observations of this kind. The message, however, would remain unchanged: early experiences are of paramount importance. This doesn't mean that *it's all decided by the age of 6*, as the French title (*Tout se joue avant 6 ans*) of an American bestseller first published in the 1970s (*How to Parent*, by Fitzhugh Dodson) misleadingly proclaims.

But it certainly means that what happens between the ages of 0 and 6 profoundly influences the child's future life. Basically, this is simply to state a truism – to stipulate that learning does not come out of nowhere. It proceeds gradually by transforming, combining and enriching the skills already acquired.[171] Therefore, lessening the impact of early reinforcements, especially during 'sensitive periods', means compromising all later deployments. Statisticians call this the 'Matthew effect', in reference to a memorable biblical sentence: 'for to everyone who has will be given more, and he will have more than enough; but anyone who has not, will be deprived even of what he has'.[172] The idea is quite simple. It states that the cumulative nature of knowledge automatically leads to a gradual exacerbation of initial delays. This phenomenon has been documented in many fields ranging from language to sport, from economics to professional trajectories.[89,173-8] Of course, in many cases the trend can be reversed, at least partially.[179] But, yet again, this becomes more and more difficult as we move away from optimal periods of brain plasticity. The efforts then required turn out to be far greater than if the right steps had been taken to begin with. Again, as the saying goes, 'prevention is better than cure'. For those who still doubt it, the work of James Heckman could prove interesting.[180] Indeed, this Nobel laureate in economics is mainly known for demonstrating that the impact of educational investments decreases very sharply with children's age. In short, the message is clear: when it comes to development, it's better to avoid wasting the incomparable potential of the first years!

No screens for recreation before (at least) 6 years

No doubt nothing expresses this notion of a 'sensitive period' better than the daunting scale of the learning accumulated by the child during its first years of life. No other phase of existence concentrates such a density of transformations. Over 6 years, quite apart from learning a swathe of social conventions, and from taking part in 'optional' activities such as dance, tennis or the violin, the child learns to sit, to stand, to walk, to run, to control her excretions, to eat alone, to control and coordinate her hands (to draw, tie shoelaces or manipulate objects), to talk, think, master the basics of numbers and the written code, to discipline her outbursts of emotions and her impulses, etc. In this context, every minute counts. Of course, this doesn't mean that we have to over-stimulate the child and turn her life into a hell of compulsions. This means 'just' that the child should be placed in an enabling environment, where the necessary 'food' is generously available. However, screens are not part of this environment. As we will see later in this book, their structuring power is much lower than that offered by any standard living conditions, provided, of course, that these are not an abusive environment. Several studies, to which I will also be returning, have reported that, in young children, an average daily screen exposure of 10 to 30 minutes was sufficient to cause significant damage in health (e.g. obesity) and cognitive areas (e.g. language).[181–4] What a child needs in order to grow properly is people and action. She needs words, smiles, hugs, encouragement. She needs to experiment, to move her body about, to run, to jump, to touch, to play, to manipulate rich forms. She needs to look at the world around her, to interact with other children. But she certainly doesn't need Disney Junior, Cartoon Network, Baby Einstein or BabyFirst.

At the heart of a child's first years, screens are like a glacial stream. Not only do they steal precious development time, not only do they lay the foundations for subsequent overuse, but they also intimately damage the construction of the self through the state of sensory saturation they impose. Literally (I will come back to this in more detail in the next section), this state places inattention and impulsiveness at the heart of neuronal organization;[185,186] and this at a time (it is worth repeating) when the brain is going through its most acute period of plasticity. The early use of screens is all the less under-standable since, as we have already pointed out, the cost of abstinence is zero! In other words, there are only advantages to keeping young children away from all these predatory digital tools. This is the simple application of a reasonable precautionary principle, nicely defined as follows by an expert from the American Academy of Pediatrics: 'if we don't know that it's good, and there's any reason to believe it's bad, why do it?'[187] Therefore, the bar of excess is quite easy to define. It starts at the first minute. For kids aged 6 and under (or even 7, if we include the basic preparatory schooling devoted to laying the founda-tions of reading and numbers), the only sensible recommendation can therefore be summed up in two words: no screens! Obviously, this doesn't mean that you can't, from time to time, take your child to the cinema or watch a cartoon with him. It just means that chronic exposure should be avoided as much as possible.

Those who will see this recommendation as exaggerated can consult the recent statement of the WHO.[188] For this institution, 'quality sedentary time spent in interactive non-screen-based activ-ities with a caregiver, such as reading, storytelling, singing and puzzles, is very important for child development'. Therefore, 'for 1-year-olds, sedentary screen time (such as watching TV or videos, playing computer games) is not recommended'. Then, up to the age of 5, 'sedentary screen time should be no more than 1 hour; less is better'. In other words, when it comes to infancy as a whole, less seems better – and less actually means zero. If they make just one more little effort, our international specialists will be able to say it clearly, without feeling obliged to drown the clarities of reality in the smoky fog of a cutesy paraphrase.

Of course, these elements raise the question of so-called 'educa-tional' content. In very young children, the matter seems to have been sorted: the overwhelming majority of competent institutions worldwide now recognize, as the American Academy of Pediatrics indicated in 1999,[189] that before 2 or 3 years of age, screens are uniformly harmful.[190-3] A recent synthesis of the literature on the impact of television (the almost sole screen for toddlers) clearly confirms this. As this work concludes: 'in fact, studies that measured exposure in infancy (both with and without content analysis) consist-ently demonstrated that television viewing is associated with negative developmental outcomes. This is seen with attention, educational achievement and executive functions and language outcomes.'[194] The result is not surprising. It merely reflects the chronic inability of young children to learn from a video – even the simplest things

41

they learn without difficulty through human interaction. But I will be coming back to this point in the next part.

In slightly older children, things seem less straightforward. Indeed, a number of studies indicate that educational programmes, correctly thought out and formatted (a slow pace, a linear narration, the designation of concrete objects, etc.) can, in some children, have a positive developmental impact, above all in terms of vocabulary – especially as these programmes serve as a support for the establishment of verbal interactions with adults.[194,195] On this basis, many institutions have gone further than looking at the question of time in the strict sense and insisted on the nature of the content consumed. The American Academy of Pediatrics provides a particularly representative example. In its most recent report, it stated:

> for children 2 to 5 years of age, limit screen use to 1 hour per day of high-quality programming, coview with your children, help children understand what they are seeing, and help them apply what they learn to the world around them. Avoid fast-paced programmes (young children do not understand them as well), apps with lots of distracting content, and any violent content.[191]

These are recommendations which, beyond their restrictive and limiting nature, to put it mildly, call for some comments.

Let's start with co-viewing, or more generally co-use. On the one hand, as we have seen, the latter has some drawbacks, in the sense that it significantly increases the total duration of consumption. On the other hand, as we have also pointed out, it is more the exception than the rule. Between the ages of 2 and 5, only half of parents say they are present 'all or most of the time' when the child watches TV (32%), plays a video game on a console (28%) or uses a smartphone (34%).[53] These figures drop to 23%, 9% and 13% respectively among 6- to 8-year-olds. This is easily explained, if we consider that screens play the role of babysitter much more frequently than acting as a medium for communication. Also, the fact that the parent is present does not mean that there is any dialogue with the child. It's not easy to talk while watching a cartoon or playing a video game! Books[175,196,197] and free interactions lend themselves much better to this kind of sharing. The position of the Canadian Paediatric Society is particularly interesting from this point of view. Its experts organize their recommendations along two axes: 'minimize screen time [and] mitigate (reduce) the risks associated with screen time'.[192] Regarding the first point, they write: 'for children 2 to 5 years, limit routine or regular screen time to less than 1 hour per day'. Regarding the second, they advise: 'be present and engaged when screens are used and, whenever possible, co-view with children. Be aware of content and prioritize educational, age-appropriate and interactive programming.' And this is where things get interesting. Indeed, in the body of the text, we can read the following more specific points: 'however, while screens may help with language learning when quality content is co-viewed and discussed with a parent or caregiver, preschoolers learn best (i.e., in expressive and vocabulary terms) from live, direct and dynamic interactions with caring adults'. In other words, high-quality 'educational' content can have positive effects on language development if it is a medium for discussion with adults, but these effects remain significantly greater when screens are not there. Clearly, dialogues organized around a screen are possible, but less rich and nourishing than the same dialogues established without screens.

These reservations seem all the more credible as the content labelled 'educational' is on the whole astonishingly poor in culture, creativity and language. Let's look at this last area (by far the best-documented) and consider, as an example, so-called rare words, i.e. the words which do not belong to the list of the 10,000 most frequent words of the English language. There are eight times more of these in preschool books and common verbal exchanges than in emblematic educational programmes such as *Sesame Street* or *Mr Rogers* (16/1,000 and 17/1,000 as against 2/1,000).[198,199] I will come back later to the reasons for this rareness. But before we discuss this, we probably need to note that, in lexical matters, 'rare' does not mean 'unusual'. *The Three Little Pigs* is a nice testimony to this. This well-known children's story is stuffed with words which, although they may be infrequently used, are nonetheless fundamental; for example: huff, puff, chimney, straw, growl, squeak, yell, shout, etc. This lack clearly extends to mobile tools and all those supposedly interactive applications which are meant to teach children a wide range of enviable skills. As recently pointed out by the American Academy of Pediatrics, 'reviews of hundreds of toddler/preschooler apps labeled as educational have demonstrated that most apps show low educational potential, target only rote academic skills (e.g. ABCs, colors), are not based on established curricula, and include almost no input from developmental specialists or educators'.[200] In short, here too, the child will undoubtedly be able to learn 'something', but he will learn infinitely less than what a human interaction, either spontaneous or mediated by a book, could offer him.

43

So, to sum up, before 2–3 years screens provide nothing, whatever their nature or the content offered. Beyond that, during the preschool ages, certain pompously named 'educational' programmes can aid the development of certain basic cognitive skills, in particular in language. But what is learned is always much less than what 'real life' makes possible. Therefore, while it is undoubtedly better to place a child in front of some educational digital content than to abandon her alone in a desert of relational neglect,[201] the best thing is undoubtedly to immerse her in a world of human interactions. Taken together, these elements make it possible to reformulate the previously established recommendation: before 6 years old, no screens. However, after 2–3 years, if this ideal turns out to be truly impossible to maintain, then the less the better, and only slow, linearly structured, non-violent and educational content should be selected.

But, yet again, to avoid any ambiguity, allow me to insist that – although they are undoubtedly practical, when it comes to keeping a child busy – screens are by no means an existential necessity. In the 'old days' too (I know – I was born then!) parents sometimes needed peace and quiet. To do this, they did not hesitate to let their offspring take care of themselves, within a secure environment, with cubes, jigsaw puzzles, books, balls, various disguises and toys of all kinds. The child then learned to extract herself from the solicitations of the world and to focus on her interior universe. From this retreat was born, in particular, a symbolic space for playing ('pretend play') that many studies have linked to the fostering of capacities for narrative, creativity and emotional regulation.[202-4] In other words, early development does not stem solely from human relationships (although these are absolutely essential). To build himself up, the young child also needs to be bored, to dream, to imagine, to create, to act rather than to react. It is crucial to let him sometimes build his activities by offering him the possibility of exploring the world rather than constantly being subjected to its overwhelming, over-exciting frenzy.

Above the age of 6 years, less than an hour a day

It now remains to specify the threshold for harmful use after the first six years of life. The question is less complicated than it seems. Indeed, statistical studies often take 'the hour per day' as the unit of reference. By compiling the results obtained, we observe that a number of problems emerge from the very first hour of each day. In other words, for all ages after infancy, screens for recreation (of all kinds: TV, video games, tablets, etc.) have measurable harmful impacts after 60 minutes of daily use. This concerns, for example, family relationships,[205] academic success,[206] concentration,[207] obesity,[208] sleep,[209] development of the cardiovascular system[210] and life expectancy.[a,211] Unfortunately, it is impossible to determine exactly whether the detrimental effects kick in as early as 30 minutes, or not until after three-quarters of an hour or a full hour. So, first of all, let's be hyper-cautious and choose the 'higher' version. This can be formulated as follows: after early childhood, any exposure to screens for recreation for more than one hour per day results in quantitatively detectable harm and can therefore be considered excessive. In light of the evidence presented, however, formulating an alternative, 'cautious' 30-minute threshold would not be out of order. We can therefore, in the final analysis, recommend keeping the daily exposure of individuals 6 years of age and over to screens at between under 30 minutes (conservative limit) and 60 minutes (tolerant limit). It should be noted, however, that these limits can be organized on a weekly rather than a daily basis. For example, a child who isn't exposed to any screens for recreation on school days and watches a cartoon or plays video games for 90 minutes on Wednesdays and Saturdays would still be pretty much on track. However, it should be noted that time, of course, isn't everything and that the limits defined here are intended for content that is suitable and/or consumed at acceptable times. Thus, *Grand Theft Auto*, a hyperviolent video game full of scenes of torture and explicit sexual content (blowjobs, sexual intercourse, etc.), should be banned to children 12, 14 or even 16 years old, whatever the hourly rate.[b] Likewise, TV until 11 p.m. on Sunday night for a kid of 6, 8 or 10 who has to get up the next day to go to school is out of the question, even when watching the most innocuous family comedies.

One final point must be underlined: it is not because the contents and contexts of usage have an indisputable, even fundamental importance in certain psychosocial fields (aggressiveness, anxiety, smoking or alcohol initiation, etc.)[5,212,213] that we can afford to say, as the journalist of a major English national daily recently did, that 'screen time, in and of itself, is not harmful'.[214] In fact, as this video game specialist tells us,[215] based on a widely used food analogy, 'rather

---

[a] The areas and references mentioned here are given just as illustrations; a more detailed picture of the situation will of course be presented in the next part.
[b] To get an idea, I suggest that any sceptics go onto YouTube and type in expressions such as 'GTA porn', 'GTA sex', 'GTA torture' or 'GTA violence'.

than counting calories (or screen time), think about what you're eating'. The problem is that calories count, and eating right doesn't stop you from overeating![121,216] This point has been made clear by the US Departments of Health and Agriculture. In a joint report, these two institutions write: 'the critical issue is not the relative proportion of macronutrients in the diet, but whether or not the eating pattern is reduced in calories and the individual is able to maintain a reduced-calorie intake over time. The total number of calories consumed is the essential dietary factor relevant to body weight.'[217] In other words, 'quantity, in and of itself, is harmful', even if the meal conforms in all respects to the ultimate qualitative rules of food distribution!

The same goes for screens for recreation. Devoting 3, 4, 5 or 6 hours a day to this kind of activity is too much, simply too much; even if the individual is not pathologically 'dependent' and his consumption remains confined to supposedly 'suitable' content. To state, as our journalist does, on the basis of an astounding bit of cherry-picking, that such a temporal tidal wave will have no impact is plain insulting (especially when anyone has the gall to claim that this nonsense is now a 'consensus'). A large number of studies, as we have reported (more on this later), identify harmful effects as early as 60 minutes a day, regardless of the content consumed.[5,206–11] In part, this influence is linked to a now well-identified process of 'stolen time'. In this context, the impact is completely independent of the nature of the pre-emptive digital activities involved. The only thing that matters, in the end, is that the digital usage comes at the expense of other occupations, much more essential and/or 'nurturing' for the developing organism. Furthermore, the effect of the 'content', when it exists, does not operate independently of the immersion time. These two factors combine their effects so that the degree of harmfulness of unsuitable content increases with the duration of exposure.[5,212] Starting to smoke,[218–22] and the emergence of risky sexual behaviour,[223–6] are excellent examples of this. But they are not enough to disturb the argument of the esteemed hack whom we are citing. Thinking, perhaps, that she is treating her readers to a wonderful joke, she rapidly refers to the vexing conclusions of a group of renowned researchers in the field, only to sweep them aside with startling contempt. For our reporter, their 'suggestion of one hour of daily screen time for teenagers is laughable to anyone trying to parent one'.[214]

After the first feeling of consternation, there are three ways we can respond to this nonsense. First, the elements presented above show that some children/adolescents succeed (by themselves and/or with the help of their parents) in respecting this threshold,[10,63] and that these young people are far from being the unhappiest or the most retarded (I will come back to this in the next part). Second, when added up between the ages of 6 and 18, this 'laughable' little one hour per day represents the modest sum of five school years[50,51,64] or, in other words, two and a half years of full-time paid employment.[65] Third and finally, human history is rich in 'laughable' suggestions (the idea that Black people and White people, or men and women, are equal in intelligence; teaching sign language to deaf children; the fact that tobacco causes cancer; continental drift; etc.) which have become solid truths because a few 'morons' one day decided to stick to the facts rather than kowtow to the inertia of worldly opinions and supposedly 'established' pseudo-dogmas. Neil Postman was one of the 'morons' in question. In the mid-1980s, this professor of culture and communication at New York University was alarmed by the colossal impact of television on our ways of seeing and thinking about the world. He then undertook, in some two hundred remarkably documented pages, to show that the content ultimately mattered much less than the container or, more precisely, that the container intimately shaped the content. In Postman's words,

> we rarely talk about television, only about what is *on* television – that is, about its content. Its ecology, which includes not only its physical characteristics and symbolic code but the conditions in which we normally attend to it, is taken for granted, accepted as natural [...]. To enter the great television conversation, one American cultural institution after another is learning to speak its terms. Television, in other words, is transforming our culture into one vast arena for show business. It is entirely possible, of course, that in the end we shall find that delightful, and decide we like it just fine. That is exactly what Aldous Huxley feared was coming, fifty years ago.[227]

In conclusion

Three main points should be remembered from this part of the book.

First, our children devote not only a phenomenal but an ever-increasing amount of time to their digital recreational activities.

Second, contrary to the usual nonsense purveyed by marketing strategists, these behaviours and trends are not inevitable. They can be effectively combated by laying down clear rules of use (no screens for recreation before school, or in the evening before going to sleep, or during homework, etc.) and by minimizing ambient demands (no TV or games console in the room, a basic phone rather than a smartphone, etc.). One point, however, is important: to be fully effective, these rules and provisions should not be brutally imposed. They must be explained and justified, always, from an early age. It must be hammered out in simple words that screens undermine intelligence, disrupt brain development, damage health, promote obesity, disrupt sleep, etc.

Third, the detrimental impact of screens for recreation on health and cognitive development appears well before we reach the average usage thresholds. Based on the available scientific literature, two formal recommendations can be formulated: (i) no screens for recreation before 6 years old, even if they are pompously labelled 'educational'; (ii) after 6 years, no more than 60 minutes daily, all uses included (no more than 30 minutes, indeed, if a conservative reading of the available data is favoured).

Taken as a whole, these elements are obviously not of a nature to support the soothing words of the devotees of the digital domain. You really have to be a dreamer, naive, foolish, irresponsible or bribed to suggest that the orgy of screens for recreation to which the younger generations are subjected can take place without major consequences. For the record, let us repeat, we are talking here, as a daily average, of almost 3 hours in children between 2 and 4 years old, and more than 7 hours in adolescents – hours that are spent mainly consuming audiovisual streams (films, series, music videos, etc.), playing video games and, in the case of older children, displaying themselves and chatting on social networks with lols, likes, tweets, yolos, posts and selfies. These are arid hours, devoid of developmental fertility – destroyed hours that cannot be made up for once the great periods of brain plasticity specific to childhood and adolescence have closed.

— PART THREE —

IMPACTS
Chronicles of a disaster foretold

— 1 —

PREAMBLE
Multiple and intricate impacts

So we're free of the myth. But what about the reality? All those 'digital natives' in the making, nurtured within the digital world – what do they really look like? What is their present? What can we say about their future? What about their school careers, their intellectual development, their emotional balance and their health? Are they happy? How do they compare with the small fraction of 'survivor' children whom their parents strictly protect from screens for recreation? And what do these screens actually offer our children – and what do they steal from them?

Through these questions, it is the impact of screens on the behaviour and development of the child that I will be examining in this part. The problem is far from trivial. Indeed, beyond the classic methodological difficulties (sampling, causality, statistical models, etc.) it comes up against two major epistemological obstacles.

First, the diversity of the fields concerned. The digital tools considered here affect the four pillars that make up our identity: the cognitive, emotional, social and health components. However, academic work tends to approach these different spaces in an analytical and compartmentalized manner. Therefore, the scientific literature looks more like a dislocated landscape than a homogeneous panorama. This fragmentation goes a long way to obscure the vastness of the problem. However, when you take the time to put the pieces of the puzzle together, the illusion of relative benignity quickly evaporates and the scale of the disaster becomes clearer.

Second, the complexity of the mechanisms of action. These are rarely simple and straightforward. They frequently act in secret and synergistic ways, with knock-on and long-term effects. It's a bore. First, for researchers, in the sense that certain impacts are proving

51

difficult not only to identify, but also, secondarily, to explain. Then, for the general public, insofar as many assertions seem so extravagant in their primitive starkness that they are spontaneously rejected by the proponents of sacrosanct 'common sense'. The influence of screens on academic success, due to impaired sleep, provides an excellent illustration of this. It's now firmly established (I will come back to this in more detail in the final chapter of this part) that screens have a profoundly damaging impact on the length and quality of our nights. Then, regarding academic success:

- *Some influences appear to be relatively direct*; for example, when sleep is impaired, memorization, learning abilities and daytime intellectual functioning are disrupted,[1-4] which automatically erodes academic performance.[5-8]
- *Some influences are more indirect*; for example, when sleep is impaired, the immune system is weakened,[9-11] the child is more likely to be ill and therefore absent, which contributes to increasing school difficulties.[12-14]
- *Some influences emerge late*; for example, when sleep is impaired, brain maturation is affected,[4,15-17] which, in the long term, restricts individual potential (especially cognitive) and therefore, automatically, academic performance.
- *Some influences have a knock-on effect* following certain rather counter-intuitive processes; for example, lack of sleep is a major contributor to obesity.[18-21] But then, obesity is associated with a decrease in school performance, in particular due to increased absenteeism and the destructive nature of the stereotypes (often implicit) associated with this state of health (weakness, abulia, uncleanliness, disloyalty, clumsiness, laziness, rudeness, etc.).[22-8] These stereotypes are largely linked to the portrayal of 'fat' people in the media sphere, whether it be films, series, TV shows, music videos or newspaper articles.[29] The stereotypes work along two main lines.[24-6,30] On the one hand, they foster aggression by peers, which does not make for an easy life in the classroom. On the other hand, they significantly change the grading standards, with teachers tending to be more severe in their assessments, remarks and evaluations with obese or overweight schoolchildren.
- *Most of the influences are multiple* and it is evident that the negative impact of screens for recreation on academic success is not based exclusively on deterioration of sleep. This last factor operates in synergy with other agents, including (I will come back to this at length) a reduction in the time spent on homework or

a collapse in language and attention skills. At the same time, however, it is also clear that the negative influence of screens for recreation on sleep goes well beyond the purely academic field. Getting enough sleep is essential for lowering the risk of accidents, regulating mood and emotions, safeguarding health, protecting the brain from premature ageing, etc.[4,31-6]

- *Most of the influences are partial* and it would be absurd to blame screens for the academic difficulties that more and more children are encountering. Indeed, there is no doubt that academic achievement also depends on non-numerical, demographic, social and family factors (factors that studies on the influence of screens try to note as much as possible).

In short, the question of the impact of digital technology is far from trivial, as the complexity and interactivity of the functional chains involved favour the concealment of the impacts produced. But that's not all. The matter is further complicated when one takes into account the existence of possible 'hidden factors', acting in secret, unrecognized by the established forms of knowledge. By way of example, let's return to the question of brain ageing. In adults, a study showed that the risk of developing Alzheimer's disease increased by 30% for each additional hour of television per day (after taking into account the covariates known to be linked to the development of this pathology: socio-demographic features, degree of cognitive stimulation and level of physical activity).[37] Of course, this result does not mean that TV 'inoculates' the patient with Alzheimer's disease. It simply indicates the existence of a 'hidden' mechanism, both predictive of the development of the disease and subject to the action of the small screen. In other words, the TV effect here reveals a secondary mode of action that can lead to disease, a mode of action that further studies will have to identify. In the present case, among the potential explanatory hypotheses, we can mention sleep; disturbances in this generate, as a number of recent results have reported, certain biochemical disturbances favourable to the appearance of degenerative dementias.[36,38-42] We could also mention a sedentary lifestyle, obesity and smoking;[43] factors both predictive of the disease and dependent on the exposure to screens (I will come back to this in the last chapter). All this means that a result may seem obscure from the point of view of its causality, without being faulty.

To sum up, there are three essential points to remember here. First, just because an observation turns out to be counter-intuitive and/ or difficult to understand does not mean that it should be rejected:

certain mechanisms operate well beyond the obvious. Second, to say that screens have a given impact does not mean that they are the only things that act or even that their action is the most significant: crazy exaggerations such as 'to hear the author speak, screens are responsible for all ailments, etc.' are as grotesque as they are unfair.[44] And third, the impact of digital uses on younger generations can only appear in the light of an integrative and panoramic vision; it does not matter if there are occasional rough patches or counterexamples. What matters in the end is the overall balance; and it is therefore this assessment that I will try to capture in this section. Three fields will be successively covered: (i) academic success (the most general parameter of impact available); (ii) development (especially in its cognitive and emotional dimensions); (iii) somatic health (from sedentary lifestyle, to obesity, via violence and the issue of risky behaviour – smoking, sexuality, etc.).

— 2 —

ACADEMIC SUCCESS
A powerful prejudice

One of my students works in the evenings for a private tutoring company. This allows him to make ends meet. Not long ago, I ran into him in the corridors of his company building. He'd heard me on the radio talking about the harmful influence of screens on child development. He explained to me with a laugh that it wasn't very nice and he could quickly find himself unemployed if parents decided to deprive their children of smartphones, tablets, TVs and video game consoles. A joke certainly, but one that deserves attention. This is all the more true as academic success is a relatively general parameter of aptitude. Indeed, even if it doesn't tell us everything about children, of course, it does say a lot about their intellectual, social and emotional functioning.

For the sake of clarity, I will here focus on two questions relating respectively to the exposure to screens at home[a] and in schools.

Home screens mean poorer academic performance

Taken as a whole, the scientific literature clearly and convergently demonstrates that time spent on home screens significantly weakens academic success. Regardless of gender, age, background and/or testing protocols, duration of consumption is negatively associated with academic performance. In other words, the more time children, adolescents and students spend with their digital soft toys, the more

---

[a] This term defines all screens accessible outside the school, whether they are for 'personal' use (smartphone, TV in the bedroom, games console, computer, etc.) or 'family' use (TV in the living room, family tablet, shared computer, etc.).

their grades drop. This isn't surprising in light of the work carried out over the years in sociology to identify 'the family construction of educational dispositions'.[1] Indeed, the results then show quite clearly that the strict supervision of recreational digital uses, in favour of extracurricular practices deemed to be more positive (homework, reading, music, physical activity, etc.), is an almost universal feature of households whose offspring have a high level of academic performance.[1,2] This finding is itself compatible with the observation, broadly developed above, that recreational digital uses are much more constrained in socio-culturally advantaged children,[3-5] who tend to have a much better level of academic achievement (although other factors must then be considered).

The more screen time increases, the more marks drop

Most general research considers screen time as a whole. This typically includes television, video games, mobile phones, tablets and computers. As indicated in part two, these supports are mainly used for recreational purposes. A number of studies report, not surprisingly, that cumulative digital use predicts a significant decrease in academic performance.[6-18] For example, one piece of research carried out in the UK focuses on GCSEs.[6] These exams take place around 16 years old. Success is rated in eight grades ranging from excellent (A*) to inadequate (G). Insofar as the 'instantaneous' negative effect of screens is no longer in doubt, the authors looked into the existence of possible 'distant' influences (after taking into account, of course, the usual covariates: age, gender, weight status, depression, type of school, socio-economic status, etc.).[a] The results showed that the digital consumption displayed 18 months before the exam very seriously affected the final result. Thus, for each hour of screen exposure at 14.5 years old, the score obtained dropped by nine points. As shown in figure 3, this represents more than one level of scoring. Suppose, for example, that Paul landed an A* with zero digital consumption; 1 hour daily would have brought it down to a B and 2 hours to a C.

Of course, these 'average' data do not take account of inter-individual variability. Clearly, not all screenless teens produce

---

[a] For the sake of readability, I will leave out this clarification in the rest of my text and tacitly assume that it applies to the studies under discussion. If a study did omit this kind of check, I will note this.

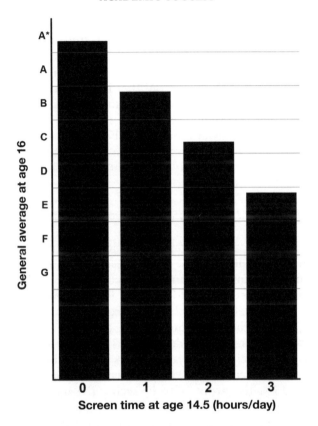

Figure 3. Impact of total screen time on school performance. What is measured is the 'distant' influence (18 months before the test) of digital consumption on success in GCSEs, at age 16.[6] For details, see the text.

excellent results. Likewise, it is obvious that some pupils who clock up 2, 3 or even 4 hours of daily use get very good marks. In fact, it's not uncommon to come across parents who tell you that their hyper-connected teenager is showing satisfactory results. Two things can be said in response to this. First, even if some are doing well despite significant digital use, it is clear that the societal cost is major and that, collectively, the performance of a group of pupils exposed to an hour of screens per day will be significantly worse than the performance of a socio-demographically comparable group not exposed to screens. Second, just because an average, hyper-connected teen's grades are good doesn't mean they wouldn't be significantly better without screens. In other words, if we can't predict Paul's performance 'with screens' (A, B or C), we can safely say that he would do better 'without screens'. A German study of pupils aged 10 to 17 illustrates this idea quite well.[15] The scores were grouped into four levels (here designated from A to D to remain consistent with the previous study). The results showed that the performance in mathematics one year after the start of the study decreased in proportion to the screen time observed at the start of the study. By increasing the duration of use of pupils in group A by 17%, they fell into group B; with an increase of 50%, they came down to C, and with 57%, to D. The impact, it goes without saying, is quite significant.

A broad and long-standing consensus on television

Besides the general studies which have just been mentioned, there are also many specific works. The oldest relate to television. The result cannot be gainsaid: it shows, in a convergent and indisputable manner, that the more time children and adolescents devote to screens, the worse their school results.[19-37] For example, in one particularly interesting study, the same individuals (nearly a thousand) were followed for more than two decades.[26] The latest analyses, carried out when the participants were 26 years old, established that each hour of television consumed daily between the ages of 5 and 15 reduced by 15% the probability of seeing the individual obtain a university degree, and increased by more than a third the risk of seeing her leaving the school system without qualifications. Another study extended these results to an earlier cohort by reporting that consuming an hour of television daily at the age of 2.5 resulted in a more than 40% decrease in maths performance a few years later, at the age of 10.[31] This impact, of course, may seem 'heavy', but it's not in the least unexpected. When a young child groups her cubes by colour, sorts her Lego blocks by shape, orders her miniature figures from the smallest to the largest, deforms, reforms, splits and reconstructs her plasticine ball, etc. she is developing essential mathematical concepts (identity, conservation, etc.) and skills (creating series, groups, etc.). She develops them all the better when an adult is there to guide her path ('look, we've got "the same" number of sweeties!', etc.) or to introduce her to counting ('ooh, you've got "two books" ... what if I take "one" away from you?', etc.). However, as we have said, these interpersonal exchanges and playful explorations carried out on reality are among the first victims of early digital uses (especially television). Consequently, in children subjected to these uses, certain fundamental logical-mathematical prerequisites are not properly formed; and without this foundation, it is difficult to build solidly afterwards. People simply blame the genetic lottery and close down a whole potential future by decreeing that this pupil really isn't very good at maths.

In another study, it was the impact of television in the bedroom that was analysed in primary schoolchildren.[25] The data reported that those who were protected from TV had, compared to their counterparts with televisions, better scores in mathematics (+ 19%), written expression (+ 17%) and reading comprehension (+ 15%). These results are compatible with the conclusions of another study carried out on pupils aged 9 to 15. The analyses revealed that the number of pupils obtaining excellent grades (A on a decreasing scale from A to D) diminished almost linearly according to the time spent in front of the television, on weekdays, and went from 49% for the group without television to 24% for the group showing uses greater than 4 hours per day.[29]

In the end, it seems very difficult to find all these influences benign. This is all the more true as one of the long-term studies mentioned above[26] has recently been extended to the professional field.[38] It was then shown that, for boys, each additional daily hour of television consumed between the ages of 5 and 15 more than doubled the risk of experiencing a period of unemployment of more than 24 months between the ages of 18 and 32. The same trend was identified in girls (risk multiplied by 1.6), without, however, reaching the threshold of statistical significance.

There is also no doubt about video games

The researchers also looked, of course, at video games. Here again, the data are amazingly clear: the more time spent playing, the more marks drop.[29,30,33,37,39–48] Particularly interesting is a study carried out in the United States.[49] Families were recruited through a press advertisement looking for volunteers to participate in an 'ongoing study of boys' academic and behavioral development'.[a] As a reward, the participants were promised a console (PlayStation) and video games (classified suitable for all audiences). Only boys with satisfactory

---

[a]This choice was made not because girls do not deserve any attention from researchers, but to avoid gender effects, and in consideration of the fact that boys play more (and are therefore a priori more 'at risk' than girls).

school results, no behavioural problems and no game consoles in their homes were selected. Half of the families received their 'reward' immediately; the other half had to wait until the end of the study (four months). This protocol is terribly ingenious. It makes it possible to study, without bias, the evolution of academic success after the acquisition of a game console, by comparing two initially homogeneous groups. Unsurprisingly, the children of the 'console' group did not leave it in its box, but used it for an average of 40 minutes a day; that's 30 minutes longer than those in the 'control' group (whose members probably spent some time playing outside the home, especially with their friends on weekends or after school). Half of the extra gaming time was taken away from homework, which dropped, roughly, from 30 to 15 minutes per day. This 'capturing' of attention was bound to have an adverse impact on school performance. At the end of the study, the 'control' group reported better results than the 'console' group in the three academic fields considered: written language (+ 7%), reading (+ 5%) and mathematics (+ 2%, though the difference observed did not reach the threshold of significance in this last case). Interestingly, the researchers also asked teachers to fill in a standard psychometric scale, indicative of possible academic difficulties (especially in learning and attention). The results showed a significant increase (+ 9%) in these difficulties for the pupils of the 'console' group compared to the 'control' group. All these effects speak volumes, especially as they result, we need to remember, from a relatively short duration of exposure (four months) and from a very moderate increase in use (30 minutes per day).

In another study, also conducted in the United States, economists confirmed these results for an older population, made up of young adults entering university.[48] The 'quasi-experimental' protocol was astute, to say the least. Upon arrival in the first year, students were randomly assigned a room-mate. In some cases, this companion brought a games console. The authors then compared the academic results of students whose companion had or did not have a console (with the idea that the room-mate's console would be shared and/ or loaned). The results showed a significant decrease in performance in individuals sharing a room with console owners (− 10%). After taking into account a large list of possible explanatory factors (sleep, alcoholism, absenteeism, salaried employment, etc.), the analyses highlighted the dominant impact of personal working time. Students whose room-mate did not have a console spent almost three-quarters of an hour more per day studying than those whose room-mate did have a console. Unsurprisingly, this difference was reflected in the increase in gaming times. For example, members of the 'console' group spent almost 30 more minutes at the joystick each day than their counterparts in the 'control' group; 30 minutes for a final academic differential of 10%. Here again, this is very far from a marginal effect, especially if we remember, as previously indicated, that the average daily consumption of teens and pre-teens is around 1 hour 30 minutes.

Ditto for the smartphone

Recently, researchers have also started to take an interest in mobile tools, including, of course, the ubiquitous smartphone. This mass entertainment platform concentrates all (or almost all) digital recreational functions in itself. It allows you to access all kinds of audiovisual content, play video games, surf the Internet, exchange photos, images and messages, connect to social networks, etc.; and it allows all of this without the slightest constraint of time or place. The smartphone follows us everywhere, remorselessly and relentlessly. It is the holy grail of brain gobblers, the ultimate Trojan horse of our decerebration. The more 'intelligent' its applications become, the more they replace our thinking and the more they allow us to become idiots. They are already choosing our restaurants, sorting the information available to us, selecting the advertisements sent out to us, determining the routes we must take, offering automatic responses to some of our verbal questions and to the emails sent to us, training our children from kindergarten onwards, etc. One more effort and they will end up really thinking for us.[50]

The negative impact of smartphone use on academic success comes across clearly: the more consumption increases, the more results fall.[32,51–62] One recent study is very interesting from this point of view.[62] Indeed, the experimental protocol did more than just ask participants (in this case students on management courses) about their grades and the use they made of their phones. It also involved objective measurement of the data. Thus, with the written consent of each participant and with the cover of a strict commitment to confidentiality and anonymity, the authors got the administration to send them the results of the exams, and participants to permit, for a limited period of two weeks, the installation of 'spy' software on their smartphones to objectively record, without interference, actual usage times. According to the actual findings of the study, 'the magnitude of the effect found is alarming'.[62] First, it was confirmed that participants spent much more time handling their smartphones (3 hours 50 minutes per day on average) than they thought (2 hours 55 minutes per day on average). Then, it appeared that greater usage time entailed a fall in academic results.

To facilitate the quantitative assessment of the phenomenon, the authors reduced their data to a normalized population of 100 individuals. They then reported that each hour per day dedicated to the smartphone led to a drop of almost four places in the ranking. That's not a big deal, no doubt, when it comes to just getting a qualification such as a non-competitive degree. It is much more of a problem, however, in the brutal world of competitive courses. Medical studies provide a good illustration of this. In France, the entrance examination admits, on average, eighteen candidates out of a hundred.[63] At this level of demand, the smartphone quickly becomes an insurmountable handicap. Take, for example, a student without a smartphone who ranks 240th out of 2,000 and passes his exam. Two hours of smartphone daily would bring him down to 400th place in the elimination round. And of course, things get even worse if you allow yourself, as so many students do, to manipulate your device during actual lectures. The 'punishment' then amounts, on average, to your dropping almost eight places per hour of use.

Note, one last time, that we are only talking about population averages here. We can always find individuals who challenge the rule in an egotistical way, saying, for example: 'yes but take my son, he's always on his smartphone and he's passed his medical exams'. This kind of example does exist, it is true – especially as almost all students today own a smartphone. The problems have to be tackled no longer in terms of absolute values, but in relative gaps: in other words, when the average usage is close to 4 hours per day, 120 minutes can prove to be 'reasonable' enough for you to reach your goal – but that doesn't mean (far from it!) that these 120 minutes were without impact. Basically, to be perfectly clear, we could reformulate the previous observations as follows: academic performance deteriorates in proportion to the time offered to the despotism of Sir Smartphone; the more a student yields to this, the further her results fall.

A usage effect for computers and social networks

To all these studies, we could add even more specific research on, for example, the use of social networks. Again, the results are as consistent as they are stubbornly negative. The more time pupils (mainly adolescents and students) devote to these tools, the more their academic and intellectual performance deteriorates.[32,52,64-72] There is one fly in the ointment of this argument, however: it relates to certain educational experiences involving, via the creation of closed discussion groups, the sharing of targeted academic resources and information. In this context, a marginally positive increase in grades has been reported among mathematics students.[73] However, one recent large-scale study failed to generalize this observation.[71] Despite everything, the data obtained confirmed that the strictly academic use of social networks had at least the good taste not to turn out to be damaging. But, basically, even if we admit the possibility of a modestly positive impact, that would not change much, since purely academic consumption is drowned in the flood of debilitating recreational operations (figure 2, p. 13). That's why the studies of overall consumption cited at the beginning of the chapter lead, in the final analysis, to such a negative assessment.

The same problem arises for home computers. On the one hand, these offer almost unlimited access to all kinds of recreational content, whose harmful impact on school performance we have just mentioned (television, series, video games, etc.). At the same time, however, no one can reasonably dispute that these tools also allow access to an inexhaustible space of educational resources, even if we must not then confuse availability and usability: it's one thing to be able to follow, online, a course from Harvard University or MIT; it is another to have the attentional, motivational and academic skills necessary to assimilate the knowledge provided.[74-6] I'll be coming back to this later. In the meantime, what about those wonderful computers and their overall impact? In the end, what weighs the most in the balance: their brain-deadening uses, or the nourishing practices they foster? The answer depends, in part, on the studies consulted. If we stick to well-conducted, large-scale research, the impacts range from zero[77,78] to negative.[79-81] In other words, the favourable inputs from home computers are just enough, at best, to offset the damaging influences.[82] And yet, this is the most accommodating interpretation. Indeed, the studies that have failed to report any overall negative influence[77,78] are based on the distribution protocols of computers to severely disadvantaged school pupils. However, the vast majority of the latter do not have an Internet connection at home and spend very little time with the device they have been given. The increased use (about 20 minutes per day) has no impact on the amount of time devoted to homework, which is already not very great. But that could change once the computer comes with an Internet connection. The kids will then see the wonderful promise of relentless dumbing-down open before them: video games, films, series, music videos, social networks, porn sites, shopping platforms, etc. The few studies that have concluded that home computers have no impact on academic success can then quickly join the large cohort of negative studies; and Aldous Huxley will re-emerge from his long silence; for, nearly eighty years ago, he had already foreseen what has been described as 'the perfect dictatorship – a prison without walls from which prisoners would never dream of escaping; a system of slavery in which consumption and entertainment would lead to the slaves loving their servitude'.[83] And we will finally remember, no doubt rather belatedly, the bitterly prophetic title of Neil Postman's book: *Amusing Ourselves to Death*.[84]

And in the end, it's always the dumbing-down use that wins

Nothing better illustrates the way entertainment trumps effort than the question of homework. This is an important ingredient of academic performance.[85-9] In the short term, it operates mainly by promoting the assimilation and memorization of interesting content. In the longer term, it also permits the development of certain skills of self-discipline and self-regulation[90-3] which are absolutely essential for academic success.[94-9] After all, in practice, to put it simply, we are not born conscientious, studious and/or able to do the essential things (such as finishing our essay) instead of the contingent things (for example, playing video games or chatting on Facebook); we *become* conscientious (etc.),[100,101] and homework is an essential element of this evolution. However, as pointed out previously, personal academic work pays a heavy tribute to digital recreation. The damage is due to both a shortening of the time dedicated to homework[23,48,49,102-6] and a tendency to multitasking, which is not very favourable to the understanding and memorization of the content learned.[52,107-14] This attack on the quantity and quality of homework is a direct and obvious explanation for the negative impact of screens for recreation on academic success. It is obviously not the only one (see the next chapter, where I will be discussing the question of development).

Ultimately, what all these data confirm is that when you put a screen (computer, tablet, smartphone, etc.) in the hands of a child or teenager, it's almost always the most debilitating recreation that prevails, winning out over virtuous practices. This conclusion is confirmed, if this were still necessary, by the data of the famous international programme 'one laptop per child'. The aim was to provide underprivileged children with low-cost computers (then tablets) in the hope that this would have a positive impact on their academic and intellectual skills. All over the world, the media praised this formidable initiative, launched by an American NGO; its first results were described with great enthusiasm.[115-22] We learned, for example, from the very mouth of the programme's founder, Nicholas Negroponte, that 'some children manage to learn to read without going to school in Ethiopia, while in New York others can't reach this level despite going to school. What should we conclude from this?'[119] Good question! As French president Jacques Chirac said once, 'promises are binding only on those who receive them'. Because, unfortunately, the objectively measured impact of the programme did not live up to the expectations announced – to put it mildly. In evaluation after evaluation, researchers had to recognize the futility of this costly project[123] on children's academic and cognitive skills.[124-9] In many cases, the results were actually negative, with the beneficiaries preferring (no surprise here) to use their computers for fun (games, music, TV, etc.) rather than work. In Catalonia, for example, 'this programme had a negative impact on student performance in Catalan, Spanish, English and mathematics. Test scores fell by 0.20–0.22 standardised points, which represent 3.8–6.2% of the average test score.'[129] This fall isn't drastic, but it is still substantial. As one review article concluded: 'One laptop per child represents the latest in a long line of technologically Utopian development schemes that have unsuccessfully attempted to solve complex social problems with overly simplistic solutions.'[130] This is a very gloomy observation – and one which, it should be noted, received very little attention in the media, especially on the part of those who initially showed themselves to be the most fervent defenders of the project. This 'oversight' undoubtedly explains why so many people still believe today, as was initially proclaimed loud and clear, without the slightest critical distance, on the basis of anecdotes cleverly distilled by the promoters of the operation, that, thanks to their tablets, illiterate kids 'educate themselves alone'[131] and are 'teaching themselves to read without teachers'.[122] What is striking here is the frenzy with which this fable was taken up wholeheartedly by journalists the world over, while, without any such fanfares, other much more promising interventions were totally neglected, such as a programme that had shown, in developing countries, that the distribution of books to mothers of young children had a strong positive effect on the development of language, attention and social interaction skills.[132,133] After all, why deal with a simple, effective and inexpensive intervention when you can praise a complex, ineffective and expensive project?

Contradictory data?

Obviously, it is always possible to quote the conclusions of a few isolated studies that go against the above findings. This is not surprising. All scientific fields, however consensual, contain discordant observations within them. The trouble is that many media tend to pounce blindly on these observations, without the slightest critical hindsight; and a major consequence of this is that they lead public opinion to mistrust the most established experimental realities. This is an important point and it deserves further reflection. With this in mind, I will proceed in three steps. First, I will (briefly) present some basic statistical principles so that everyone can understand why the existence of studies that disagree with the consensus is mathematically inevitable. Second, I will offer a concrete illustration of the media's propensity to pounce on perfectly 'aberrant' studies for the sole reason that these are likely to generate a widespread buzz. Finally, I will return to the subject of academic success by looking at some recent research that contradicts the idea that screens are harmful and that has, despite some appalling conceptual and methodological deficiencies, aroused incredible journalistic enthusiasm.

An inevitable statistical variability

Statistics are useful – but imperfect. You could say they are the science of reasonable doubt. Thus, researchers typically consider a difference between two experimental groups to be statistically significant (i.e. actually existing) when it has less than a five-in-one chance of occurring 'by chance'. This means that if 100 studies are done, it will always be found that about 5 of them conclude that a difference exists when it doesn't. The opposite is also true: you will always find some studies which claim that there is no difference when there is.

Consider one brief digital example. Take two perfectly balanced coins, toss them each 200 times and count the number of 'heads'. If 100 researchers do the experiment, 95 will confirm that there are as many 'heads' as there are 'tails' and that, in the end, the coins are indeed identical. Five, however, will lead to the opposite result on the grounds that the difference between the number of 'heads' and 'tails' is statistically significant (that is, it has less than 5 out of 100 chances of occurring 'at random').

Now let's repeat the experiment with two mechanically biased pieces coming up 'heads' in 40% (P1) and 60% (P2) of cases respectively.[a] Let's toss them each 200 times and compare the number of 'heads'. If 100 researchers do the experiment, 98 will identify a difference; 2 will not detect any. This number of 'false negatives' (not finding a difference when there is one) will, however, vary with the number of tosses. The greater this number, the lower the chances of making a mistake. Thus, in the context of our example, if we go up to 300 tosses, the error rate will drop to around 1 per 1,000. On the other hand, if we go down to 20 tosses, the degree of inaccuracy will rise to almost 70% (that is, a majority of researchers will conclude that the coins are similar). Indeed, 1 in 1,000 will state that the first coin (P1) is more likely to come up heads than the second (P2).

In short, when a scientific field generates a large number of studies, it is inevitable that erroneous results will emerge. Some studies will then describe effects that do not exist, while others will fail to identify proven impacts. Therefore, the publication of contradictory research in the midst of a solidly homogeneous field of experimentation should always be greeted with great caution. Unfortunately, this is far from the case – even when the research under consideration displays a staggering level of methodological weakness. The following section provides an edifying illustration of this.

When the buzz trumps information

A 'scientific' study recently caused a worldwide media stir: we learned, despite the conclusions of hundreds of well-conducted studies, that eating chocolate (fat + sugar) made you lose weight. *Bild*, Europe's highest-circulation daily (of German origin), went so far as to put the news on the front page! Behind this work was the American John Bohannon, holder of a doctorate in molecular

---

[a] The data in this paragraph were obtained on the basis of a simple mathematical simulation. The idea is to 'perform' the experiment virtually, using calculation software. Each coin is then 'tossed' n times (with a random calculation function) and the proportion of 'heads' for the two coins is compared. We do this many times and we can thus estimate the probability of obtaining a similar result for the two coins. Here we have chosen three values of n (20, 200, 500) and 100,000 replications of the experiment.

biology, and at the time a writer for the prestigious magazine *Science*. His aim was clear: to produce an absurd study but one that would be sufficiently popular to interest the media and demonstrate 'how easy it is to turn bad science into the big headlines behind diet fads'.[134] Bohannon didn't cheat. He just used a few big, well-known statistical tricks to make sure he would find something where there was nothing.[a] He then invented a fictitious academic affiliation for himself (The Institute of Diet and Health – 'nothing more than a website') and sent his article to a pseudo-scientific journal willing to publish just about anything in return for a cheque: *The International Archives of Medicine*. Once the paper came out, 'it was time to make some noise'. For this, Bohannon sought the advice of a specialist in press relations. The result was quite impressive. The information was relayed in six languages, in more than twenty countries, often by leading media. This finding was all the more alarming in that everything in the presented study was decidedly dodgy (the source, the iconoclastic conclusion, the author's affiliation, his lack of past productions in the field, etc.). This work should have been treated with the utmost suspicion. Instead, it easily reached a huge readership and was internationally celebrated. In fact, most journalists simply did a 'copy and paste' job on the press kit written by Bohannon.

The conclusion? Any pseudo-study, no matter how inept, can end up making the headlines of the world's mainstream media, as long as it's flashy enough and capable of creating a buzz.

'Digital entertainment does not affect school performance'

What is true of chocolate that makes you lose weight is also, unfortunately, true of screens that make you smart. One piece of French research illustrates this in a sadly representative way. Involving more than 27,000 school pupils, it appeared more or less simultaneously in two places: (i) in exhaustive form,[135] in a minor French-language newspaper classified at the bottom of the hierarchy of academic psychology journals;[136] (ii) in abbreviated form,[137] in an activist, non-scientific association magazine. It was this last source that started the tidal wave. Almost all of the mainstream media pounced

---

[a] For example, by measuring a lot of variables (eight in the study: weight, cholesterol, sleep, etc.) in a small number of subjects (fifteen in the study), you have every chance of finding something – especially if the variables considered have a natural tendency to fluctuate (such as weight).

on the information.[138-46] It must be said that this work, which, in the opinion of the authors themselves, was simply 'an investigation and not an experimental plan' (in other words: it was in no way a scientific study worthy of the name),[135] was bound to please the parochial digital world. Admittedly, the conclusions weren't kind to reality TV. 'Reality TV lowers teenage test scores' was the attention-grabbing headline of one national weekly.[143] But that wasn't the point. Indeed, the issue of reality TV today seems not only secondary in terms of what you can see on your screens, but also largely outdated, now that the harmful potential of this type of programme has been admitted.[19,147-53] The controversy is now focused on other, apparently more 'open' subjects (TV in general, social networks, video games, etc.). And from this point of view the 'survey' we are considering proved to be rich in stimulating news. So when a reporter asked if 'the television medium, in itself, is not at issue', the lead author firmly replied in the negative: 'No. Other programmes, such as action films or documentaries, have very little effect on academic performance.'[141] Likewise, as one major free daily paper explained,

> Video games are less harmful than they say. 'Playing video games (action, combat, platform) does not have a negative impact,' write the researchers, which will not help some of those parents who have run out of arguments to use against their teenage addicts [...]. Other activities generally accused of leading to every evil, such as the very frequent use of mobiles (78% of the panel) and social networks (73%) apparently have only a 'minimal influence' on their results.[138]

In short, according to the authors of the survey, 'on the whole, the majority of leisure activities, such as video games, have little or no influence on academic and cognitive performance; they are leisure activities that allow relaxation, or the expression of the affective and social dimensions of the pupils (telephone, texts)'.[137]

This is indeed enough to soothe parental worries. Unfortunately, parents would be wrong to feel reassured: the methodology of the survey was deeply flawed. It was so dubious, in fact, that the chances of identifying a general harmful effect of TV, video games or undue mobile phone use were, from the start, almost nil. First there is the question of time. In the introductory paragraph of the more 'popular' version of their work, the authors list some questions such as 'does the time spent on the phone and exchanging text messages have negative consequences on reading and comprehension?'[137] Surprisingly, in total contradiction to this attractive objective, they admit in the academic version of their survey that 'we did not measure the time occupied by the activity per day';[135] and there's the rub. In this study, there is never any question of duration. Participants are not asked about the number of daily hours they spend with a particular tool. They are simply asked if they do the activity 'every day (or almost); about once or twice a week; about once or twice a month; 1 or 2 times per term; never after the start of the school year'.[135] However, contrary to what is then implicitly admitted, these categories do not say much about the actual usage times. So it doesn't matter whether a pupil's daily digital use lasts 15 minutes, 2 hours or 6 hours: she will be labelled a 'heavy consumer'. Likewise, a child who is deprived of a console or TV on school days but gorges himself for hours at weekends will appear in the list of 'minor users'. Added to this is the danger of significant social heterogeneity within each group. The mass of heavy consumers, for example (around 80% of the sample), certainly includes children from more and less privileged families. Any epidemiological investigation, since that is what is at stake here, can be credible only if it takes into account this kind of covariate. However, this is not done here. On the contrary, all the elements of risk are mixed together in an inextricable factorial mush. Deriving any solid conclusions from this kind of mess is just impossible. Researchers and statisticians have known this for a long time. Thus, for example, nearly fifteen years ago, German economists reported, using PISA data, that school pupils who had a computer at home had better grades than their non-equipped counterparts.[79] The performance differential was not negligible as it roughly equated to one school year.[a] 'Eureka!' shouted the crowds – except that when they took their analyses further, the authors revealed that this lovely fairy tale did not hold water. The observed positive influence was in fact completely reversed and became damaging when one took into account, in particular, the socio-economic characteristics of the household. The authors soon came to the conclusion: 'Mere availability of computers at home seems to distract students from effective learning.'[79]

Of course we can admit, ultimately, that these methodological 'subtleties' have escaped the attention of non-specialized journalists. But what about the mass of contradictory studies already published and the abysmal absurdity of the hypotheses put forward by

---

[a] This means that while the group of children who own a computer has a 'start-of-fourth-year' level at secondary school, the group of children who do not own a computer have a 'start-of-third-year' level.

the authors to justify their results? According to the study's first signatory, 'Pupils who watch too much reality TV obviously don't have enough time to work on their school subjects. But above all, this kind of programme contributes to an impoverishment of culture and vocabulary.'[141] And of course, such inconveniences should not affect children who, for example, play action, combat and platform video games. The linguistic richness of this content is undoubtedly exuberant and the many studies (previously cited) which report a significant impact of these games on the time and quality of schoolwork are necessarily at fault. Really, this is all hardly serious – but, at the cost of an incredible misunderstanding on the part of the media, it keeps alive the idea that school pupils' digital use has no impact on their level of academic performance. And in the end, we can without blushing explain to parents that 'video games have almost no impact on results in class' and that indulging in this kind of practice 'is the same as when playing golf'.[144] It really is appalling!

'Playing video games improves school results'

It is clear that not all the flawed research displays a level of methodological poverty comparable to that of the survey presented above. In most cases, the most glaring experimental weaknesses are masked under a reassuring glaze of statistical respectability. Thus, for example, today it is very rare for a study to be published in an international scientific journal, even a third-rank one, without taking into account the main significant covariates (sex, age, socio-economic level, etc.). Undoubtedly, this varnish makes it more complicated to identify inadequate work. However, certain warning signals are easily detectable: a second-rate publication medium or, worse, an unscientific one; an iconoclastic conclusion that contradicts, without plausible explanation, dozens of convergent works; a result that opportunely establishes the harmlessness or interest of an industrial product that has come in for severe criticism (pesticides, sweeteners, etc.); etc. This does not mean, as we have said before, that these indicators are infallible. But clearly, they should call for the utmost caution from those in the journalistic trade. This is far from always being the case, and a number of 'studies' hampered by these flaws continue to be publicized with strange fervour.

The latest example of this is an Australian study, published in a minor journal, on the influence of digital consumption on academic success.[154] The impact was global. Two results particularly caught the attention of journalists: regular online video game play has a positive impact on grades; conversely, the use of social networks exerts a negative influence. Most 'headlines' emphasized the first point, noting, for example, that 'Teens who play online have better grades.'[155] Certain less frequent headlines adopted a more general approach and also mentioned the question of social networks: 'playing video games could boost children's intelligence (but Facebook will ruin their school grades)',[156] or 'teen gamers do better at math than social media stars, study says'.[157]

Beyond these initial attention-grabbing ploys, most press articles chose to entrust the study's author with the task of interpreting the results obtained.[a] An economist by training, he explained that the 'students who play online games almost every day score 15 points above the average in math and reading and 17 points above the average in science'.[154,156,158-61] This connection, apparently, stems from the fact that 'when you play online games you're solving puzzles to move to the next level and that involves using some of the general knowledge and skills in maths, reading and science that you've been taught during the day'.[155,156,159-61] From these data, it follows that 'teachers should consider incorporating popular video games into teaching – so long as they're not violent ones'.[156,160,161]

Faced with this information, many major media outlets were singularly laudatory. 'Video games and education: both fighting on the same side', enthused one of them.[158] 'Video games' bad reputation may be unfair', gushed his colleague. And what about the 'specialist' interviewed by a major French national daily, who presented us with an incredible balancing act in which he succeeded on the one hand in glorifying the positive influence of video games and on the other hand refuting the negative impact of social networks? We learned that 'certain video games linked to conquest, discovery or construction promote certain skills such as anticipatory reasoning, logic and strategy', while for social networks 'it all depends on the context. We must not generalize. [...]. Social networks are never just classroom chatter. Young people [...] need to flourish socially in order to do so at school.'[162] The author of the study himself refused to suggest that it would be good to limit pupils' use of social networks. Worse, our man went so far as to assert that it was necessary to reinforce the use of these tools at school.[156,161] According to him, 'given that 78%

---

[a] This is why several references appear for the citations in this paragraph. It is interesting to see how many of these have been repeated, without any critical distance, in identical (or almost identical) terms throughout the world.

of the adolescents in our study all use social networks every day or almost every day, schools should take a more proactive approach to using social networks for educational purposes.'[163]

Amidst this concert of praise, a single journalist (!) had the foresight to relate the observed differences to the average.[a] These differences then appeared 'significant but minimal [...] among regular online video game players, the scores are 3% higher than the average'.[163] Curiously, this quantitative weakness was largely emphasized in the case of social networks.[155,157] One example:

> students who played online games almost every day scored 15 points above average in maths and reading tests and 17 points above average in science [...] [The author] also looked at the correlation between social media use and Pisa scores. He concluded that users of sites such as Facebook and Twitter were more likely to score 4% lower on average,[159]

all without it being specified anywhere that this percentage represents, compared to the average, an absolute drop of 20 points, so that it is therefore impossible to compare with the positive effect of video games, whose impact is given only as an absolute value.

Therefore, the research in question reports, at best, a modest negative influence of social networks and a weak positive impact of online video games on school performance. A very meagre record, let's face it, given the media hubbub it generated. But hey, at a pinch, let's admit the hype and consider exaggeration to be just part of the media ballet. The real problem, in fact, is that even reduced to its correct quantitative proportions, this study remains woefully flawed. From a methodological point of view, even if its statistical model is of better quality, it contains many of the faults displayed by the survey mentioned above (in particular the failure to take into account actual durations in favour of a frequency classification: 'every day', 'every day or almost', etc.). That's not all. Two other shortcomings are particularly significant. They concern the consistency of the various results produced (do they agree with each other, are they credible, are they compatible with existing data and if not, why not, etc.?), and the author's ability to provide a plausible explanatory framework for his observations.

Let's start with the consistency problem. Beyond the two elements 'selected' by the media (video games and social networks), the

---

[a] About 515 points for PISA studies (the average always hovers around 500 points).

original publication considers a large number of variables: the time devoted to homework, the use of the Internet for academic purposes, school attendance, the pupil's sex, the family's socio-economic level, etc. If our journalist friends had deigned to take a look at these variables, they could have produced all kinds of captivating headlines.[a] Examples:

- 'To get good grades, it's better to play video games than to do your homework': playing video games 'almost every day' gets you 15 points on average; spending an hour a day doing homework only gets you 12.
- 'To get good grades, you don't have to go to school': pupils who do their homework using the Internet 'once or twice a month' see their average increase by 24 points; or a little more than what absentees lose who skip school '2 to 3 times a week' (– 21 points). It could also be pointed out that one to two monthly homework sessions on the Internet (+ 24 points) improve the average twice as much as one daily hour of old-fashioned homework, done without the Internet (+ 12 points). What magic! The spirit of the Web penetrates, no doubt by capillary action, the brains of our young learners, like some didactic demiurge. But, as the author says, you have to be careful and remember that there are other factors to consider. Indeed, 'the results also reveal that skipping school every day [sic] is approximately twice as bad for performance as using Facebook or chatting on a daily basis'.[154] How reassuring!
- 'To obtain good grades, it's better to have poor parents': for decades, doubtless deceived by the original works of sociologist Pierre Bourdieu,[3] specialists believed that children from the most economically advantaged backgrounds did better at school than their less privileged counterparts.[4,5] The present study indicates that this is not the case: the average of the most economically disadvantaged children is about 40 points higher than the average of the most outrageously privileged children. This is a joke that even the USSR in its prime did not dare to use on its flocks!

We could continue with this litany of wacky titles for a long time. But this would be of little interest. The few examples cited are enough, we hope, to demonstrate the eminently 'fragile' character

---

[a] The following figures are based on results in 'reading'. We could just as well have used 'maths' or 'science' data (except for a few units, the values are the same).

of the work presented, even if the absolute good faith of its author is beyond doubt. When a study indicates that, if you want to get good grades, you're better off playing video games than doing your homework, you may well be surprised. When the same study adds that you can, without adverse effect, miss two to three days of school per week if you commit to a monthly session of homework on the Internet, you may start to wonder. But when this study concludes that children from the most disadvantaged backgrounds perform better at school than their more privileged counterparts, some psychedelic aberration seems the only real explanation.

These results are all the weirder as no plausible hypothesis can explain them – apart, of course, from the usual torrent of commercial puffery about the capacity of video games to develop all kinds of wonderful and universally generalizable skills. But, as we will see below, these skills do not exist. What is learned by playing a video game is not transposed beyond this game and a very small number of structurally similar activities.[164–72] In other words, there is nothing to explain how online video games could, as a whole, independently of any individual specificity (strategy, war, action, sport, role-playing games, etc.), improve the overall nature of school performance in reading, maths or science. The converse is not true. As I will show in the next chapter, a number of general mechanisms easily account for the harmful effect of video games (of all types) on the various factors likely to affect school performance (impaired sleep, ability to concentrate, language skills, time spent on homework, etc.).

One study among many?

Certainly, some will argue that the previous study is far from isolated and that several other studies point to the existence of a positive link between video games and academic success. This is true, except for one detail. Almost all of this research is based on the same data sets (PISA). Once for Australia,[154] another for the average in twenty-two countries,[173] yet another for the average in twenty-six countries, etc.[174] Starting from the same data, hampered by the same congenital defects (for example, taking into account not the actual times but the frequencies of use), it is not surprising that we arrive at roughly the same conclusions, with no one, obviously, bothering to mention the bias. 'Wow!', they then exclaim, to soothe any cold fish who dares to cast doubt on the results: 'that still makes a lot of convergent positive studies'.

Take, as a final example, the original source, the PISA report itself, as published by the OECD.[175] On the media side, the text contains few surprises: 'playing video games can boost exam performance, OECD claims',[176] 'gaming has been found to improve teenagers' performance in math, science, reading and problem solving',[177] etc. Admirable, but, again, unfortunately, lacking any foundation. A quick glance at the PISA report is enough to be convinced of this. Overall, this shows, in fact, that the supposed influence of video games on school performance is not favourable, but nil. Thus, according to the terms of the document,

> students who play one-player video games between once a month and almost every day perform better in mathematics, reading, science and problem solving, on average, than students who play one-player games every day. They also perform better than students who never or hardly ever play such games. By contrast, collaborative online games appear to be associated with lower performance, regardless of the frequency of play.[175]

In other words, the supposedly positive action of 'one-player' games is offset by the negative action of 'collaborative network' games. Some media did not even bother to mention this discrepancy and contented themselves with stating without a blush that 'according to an OECD study, playing video games "moderately" can be useful for achieving better school results [...] A ban on video games is therefore not recommended.'[178] This negative effect of network games is all the more noticeable, however, as the study discussed above,[154] focused on a single country (Australia), reports exactly the opposite, namely a positive effect of online games (first and foremost multiplayer games) on the academic performance of children.

Such a level of consistency, undoubtedly, is reassuring. But never mind that: let's go back to the PISA report. Interestingly, the negative impact of network games can be observed regardless of the frequency of use (on average, the deficit is even greater among students who play infrequently rather than frequently).[174] The same goes for the positive influence of individual games. This emerges from a single monthly session (and, again, on average, the gain is greater for pupils who play infrequently rather than frequently).[174] Quantitatively, one monthly session of individual video games has the same effect on grades as 20 minutes per day of homework, which some media could not help pointing out in very charming terms, as with this alluring soundbite: 'why spending time playing video games instead of doing homework could help boost teenagers' grades'.[179] Effective – but not easy to justify, especially as we must also consider the negative influence of network games. On this issue, the author of the PISA assessment programme has an idea. He notes: 'playing collaborative online games seems to be consistently negatively associated with performance. One explanation is that these online games you have to play with other players are typically late at night, and take up large chunks of time.'[179] But in this case, how are we to explain that these network games are harmful even when usage is minimal (once a month)? And above all, how can we account for the fact that they are, on average, more harmful for infrequent than for frequent players?[174] And, once this hypothesis has been rejected, how can we explain the diametrically opposite effect of monthly, weekly or daily sessions of the same game played alone on a console or with several other players on a network? Clearly, none of this makes any sense.

Unreliable data

Recently, a new PISA study confirmed and generalized the previous observations.[180] In contradiction with almost all the scientific work available, this work shows that the beneficial influence of screens on school performance is not limited to video games, but extends to all recreational digital activities: the more school pupils busy themselves with these entertainments, the better their marks. Remarkable! Yet this study received no notable media coverage. But one hypothesis could explain this curious lack of interest. It involves the 'gluttony' of the authors, who, not content with focusing on the recreational uses of digital technology, also looked at consumption in schools (educational ICT);[a] and the least we can say is that the results are hardly encouraging. In agreement with a large body of scientific observations, they report that the academic use of screens (both at home and in college) weakens academic performance: the more school pupils are force-fed with ICT, the more their grades drop. It's a bore, and rather awkward at a time when the digitization of the school system is progressing rapidly (I'll come back to this in the next section). Of course, the study's authors attempt (alas, not very convincingly) to come up with scholarly interpretations for this anomaly: when used for fun, screens increase academic performance; when used

---

[a] ICTs are information and communication technologies for education – in short, all the digital tools used in a school setting.

for learning, they decrease it! Strangely enough, this explanatory endeavour omits the only truly plausible interpretation, which is that the data used are simply unreliable. And unfortunately, regardless of the validity of a statistical treatment, if the input variables are flawed, the output data will be useless.

However, it would be unfair to dismiss the entire PISA study considered here. Of course, not all the elements analysed in it have the same degree of credibility.[181] On the one hand, indeed, many of the variables turn out to be questionable. It isn't easy, for example, in a long, boring questionnaire to give precise answers to questions as nebulous as: 'During a typical weekday, for how long do you use the Internet at school?'; or, 'During a typical weekday, for how long do you use the Internet outside of school?'[182] Neither is it easy, as has already been pointed out, to carry out accurate quantitative analyses based on crude measures such as: 'How often do you use digital devices for the following activities outside of school?'; activities including, for example: 'Using email' or 'Obtaining practical information from the Internet (e.g. locations, dates of events)'; with the possible choices: 'Never or hardly ever; Once or twice a month; Once or twice a week; Almost every day; Every day.'

Other questions, however, are more precisely defined and thus ipso facto less problematic. It is easy for a school head to answer such questions as: 'At your school, what is the total number of students in the [national modal grade for 15-year-olds]?' (this is the age of school students taking part in the PISA assessments); 'Approximately, how many computers are available for these students for educational purposes?'; 'Approximately, how many of these computers are connected to the Internet/World Wide Web?', etc. Likewise, for school pupils, it seems fairly simple to answer questions such as: 'Are any of these devices available for you to use at home [Desktop computer, Portable laptop, or notebook, Video games console, Cell phone with internet access, Cell phone without internet access, etc.]?'; or 'Which of the following are in your home [A desk to study at, A room of your own, A link to the Internet, etc.]?'; etc. When we focus on these easy (and thus, in principle, most robust) questions, the original anomalies quickly vanish. We then observe that school performance declines with the availability of digital tools at home, and does not vary significantly with the availability of these same tools in the classroom. Two conclusions, let's face it, that are not very consistent with the prevailing discourse and the blithe fable of the digital native. Perhaps this is ultimately why the mainstream media chose to ignore the study discussed here: too anxiety-provoking, too critical, too hostile, too pessimistic. In this case, what a pity, and what a lack of boldness! Imagine what beautiful headlines we could have had! 'Zero points for digital tools at school', 'Screens are bad for grades', 'Failure at school: don't waste any more money on private tuition, just get rid of the console', etc.

But let's take a closer look.

The wonderful world of digital tools at school

'Books will soon be obsolete in the schools [...]. Our school system will be completely changed in ten years.'[183] A wonderful quotation, and, it has to be admitted, highly relevant – except that it dates from 1913, and stems from American inventor and industrialist Thomas Edison's amazement at the countless educational possibilities of cinema. At the time, this medium was indeed 'destined to revolutionize our educational system'[184] and we were promised that, with its help, it would be 'possible to teach every branch of human knowledge'.[183] We are still waiting for this lovely dream to come true. But that did not prevent the same kind of discourse from appearing in the 1930s about radio, supposedly 'bringing the world to the classroom, to make universally available the services of the finest teachers'.[185]

More recently, in the 1960s, it was television's turn to have its praises sung. Thanks to this superb invention, its devotees then told us, 'it is possible to multiply our best instructors, that is, to select a single best instructor and give all students the benefits to be derived from superior instruction [...]. TV makes every living room, den, attic, etc., a potential classroom.'[186] This vision was widely shared by Lyndon Johnson, then US president, famous for having launched (together with the Vietnam War, and without much more success) a war on poverty in which television was to be one of the spearheads. While travelling in the Pacific, this distinguished visitor declared, in 1968, that thanks to the small screen, 'Samoan children are learning twice as fast as they once did, and retaining what they learn [...]. Unhappily, the world has only a fraction of the teachers it needs. Samoa has met this problem through educational television.'[187] It is perhaps worth pointing out that, here too, the results did not live up to the original expectations.[19] But in spite of this, the hydra wasn't ready to die. As French poet Nicolas Boileau put it in his *Art poétique*, 'Revise your work a full score of times.'[188]

What are we talking about?

And so it was that TV was replaced by 'information and communication technologies for education'; that famous ICTE, which, as a French parliamentarian told us in 2011, seemed

> an appropriate response to the challenges of education in the 21st century: fighting against school failure; promoting equal opportunities; giving back to pupils the pleasure of going to school and learning; boosting the profession of the teacher, who needs to assume his or her proper place by playing the role of 'stage director of knowledge' [...]. It is not on the education of yesterday that we will build the talents of tomorrow.[189]

Let's face it, the promise was sweeping and the words inspiring; and then, reducing the teacher to the status of a simple 'stage director' was rather piquant. I will come back to this. But before we do, let us ask ourselves if these wonderful ICTEs have finally confirmed their eminent promise.

Let's start, to avoid any ambiguity, with a little clarification. Many people seem to confuse (sometimes deliberately) learning 'about' digital tools with learning 'through' digital tools. The latter depends partially on the former because one obviously needs to have a minimum command of computer tools to be able to learn 'through' digital media. But, beyond this partial overlap, it would be misleading to amalgamate these two issues. Regarding the first, there are many questions that need to be asked. For example, apart from the small amount of basic knowledge that may be necessary for learning 'through' digital tools (turning on a computer or a tablet, launching and using the required software, etc.), what needs to be taught 'about' the digital? Do all pupils need to know how to use standard office suites (Word, Excel, PowerPoint, etc.)? Are all pupils required to learn certain programming languages (Python, C++, etc.)? Do all pupils have to master the use of a digital camera and associated post-processing software (Adobe Photoshop or Premiere, etc.)? If so, at what ages should this knowledge be introduced, and what then is their priority level compared to more 'traditional' knowledge (English, mathematics, history, foreign languages, etc.)? These questions are legitimate and deserve to be addressed.

From a practical point of view, it is obvious that certain digital tools can facilitate the pupil's work. Those who, like myself, have lived through the old days of scientific research know better than anyone the 'technical' contribution made by the recent digital revolution. But that's the problem: by definition, the tools and software that make our life easier de facto remove part of the brain's nourishing substrates. The more we abandon an important part of our cognitive activities to the machine, the less our neurons need to structure, organize and wire themselves.[50,190] It then becomes essential not to confiscate the foundational elements of the child's cognitive deployment and therefore to separate the expert from the learner (in the sense that what is useful for the first can be harmful for the second). So, for example, just because a calculating machine saves time for a final-year high school pupil who already knows how to count does not mean that it helps a junior school pupil to master numbers, the subtleties of base ten arithmetic, or the principle of subtraction with carrying. Likewise, just because Word makes the life of researchers, secretaries, writers, clerks and journalists so much easier does not mean that the use of word-processing software promotes learning to write. The opposite is true, if we are to believe the available studies. These clearly show that children who learn to write on a computer, with a keyboard, have a much harder time remembering and recognizing letters than those who learn with their hand, a pencil and a sheet of paper.[191-3] They also have more difficulty learning to read,[194] which is hardly surprising to those who have concluded that the development of writing strongly supports that of reading – and vice versa.[195-200] In the end, once they have become accustomed to the keyboard, these children also have, compared to the users of good old pens, a deficit in understanding and memorizing their lessons.[201] In short, if you want to make it as difficult as possible for a pupil to gain access first to the world of writing, then to the world of academic success, be modern and (the word is so fashionable) 'progressive'. Use 'common sense', forget the pen; go straight from kindergarten to Twitter and word processing.[202]

Thus, no one disputes the importance of asking what should be taught 'about' digital tools and, correlatively – knowing that time is not infinitely extendable – what aspects of old-style knowledge should be erased. But this is only a (small) part of the problem, because the real question relates, more basically, to the more general subject of digital learning. In other words, it is one thing to question the digital skills that each pupil must have; it is quite another to wonder whether it is possible, desirable and efficient to entrust part or all of the teaching of non-digital knowledge to digital mediation (French, mathematics, history, foreign languages, etc.).

Again, let's be clear. I am not out to demonize the digital approach on principle. That would be idiotic if not senseless. Everyone agrees that certain digital tools, whether linked to the Internet or not, can constitute relevant learning supports, within the framework of targeted educational projects, set up by qualified teachers. But is this really what is at stake? One can doubt as much, as the ideal model defined here is in sharp contrast with actual fact. More precisely, the idea of occasional use, conceptually controlled and strictly subject to pedagogical needs, seems far removed from the crazed and all-encompassing techno-frenzy, one that tends to set 'the' digital up as the ultimate educational grail and sees in the stubborn distribution of tablets, computers, interactive whiteboards and Internet connections the pinnacle of educational excellence. In other words, what is being challenged here is the theoretical and experimental foundations of the unbridled policies of digitization of the school system, from kindergarten to college. What is being disputed is the crazy idea that 'pedagogy must adapt to the [digital] tool'[203] and not the other way around.

Of course, it is extremely easy to show that a pupil can learn more with some lame program or another than with nothing at all. Even the most pathetic software or online course in maths, English or French teaches a child 'something'. But that is not the point. To be convincing, we must go further and meet a twofold requirement. First, we must guarantee that what is being learned has a general value; this amounts to showing that the acquisitions made are transferred beyond the specific characteristics of the tools used (i.e. that they positively affect academic performance and/or success on the usual standardized tests). Second, it must be established that digital investment offers real educational added value. In this context, two forms of use must be distinguished. There is an exclusive use, implying that digital technology takes the place of the teacher: it therefore appears essential to quantitatively compare the respective impacts of digital technology and a well-trained teacher. And there is a combined use, where it is assumed that digital technology is used as a 'simple' teaching aid: it therefore appears fundamental to show that the results produced are significantly superior to those recorded when the teacher acts 'alone' (here, the response obtained obviously leads on to the question of whether the resources committed could not be better allocated). For the moment, the defenders of digital education are still very far from having provided these various prerequisites with any credible support.[82,204–8] This flaw seriously undermines the claim that the frenzied digitization of the school system is scientifically founded, experimentally validated and, therefore, ultimately, carried out for the benefit of pupils (and even, incidentally, teachers).

Disappointing results, to say the least

Let's begin by looking at the impact studies carried out over the past twenty years in a number of industrialized and developing countries. Overall, despite massive investments, the results have been terribly disappointing. At best, the expense appeared unnecessary;[79,209-16] at worst, it proved to be harmful.[209,217] The most recent survey, conducted by the OECD in the framework of the PISA programme,[a] is in this respect interesting.[218] You don't have to read much of the document to appreciate the extent of the debacle. To avoid any suspicion, I will quote the report's own words. The data in the chapter devoted to the influence of ICTE on academic performance are first recapped in a summary box: 'Despite considerable investments in computers, Internet connections and software for educational use, there is little solid evidence that greater computer use among students leads to better scores in mathematics and reading.' Reading the text, we learn that 'for a given level of per capita GDP and after accounting for initial levels of performance, countries that have invested less in introducing computers in school have improved faster, on average, than countries that have invested more. Results are similar across reading, mathematics and science' (figure 4). These sad findings could indicate that the digital resources offered 'were, in fact, not used for learning. But overall, even measures of ICT use in classrooms and schools show often negative associations with student performance.' So, for example, 'in countries where it is more common for students to use the Internet at school for schoolwork, students' performance in reading declined, on average. Similarly, mathematics proficiency tends to be lower in countries/economies where the share of students who use computers in mathematics lessons is larger'. It could of course be 'that resources invested in equipping schools with digital technology may have benefitted other learning outcomes, such as "digital" skills, transitions into the labor market, or other

---

[a] In the previous part, we questioned the quality of some PISA measurements. We should therefore specify, to avoid any ambiguity, that the data discussed here are among those that can be considered a priori as robust: test results, transnational digital investments, digital penetration rate in schools (number of computers per student, Internet connections), etc.

skills different from reading, mathematics and science. However, the associations with ICT access/use are weak, and sometimes negative, even when results in digital reading or computer-based mathematics are examined, rather than results in paper-based tests. In addition, even specific digital reading competencies do not appear to be higher in countries where browsing the Internet for schoolwork is more frequent.' Another observation is far removed from the dominant promises: 'perhaps the most disappointing finding of the report', says Andreas Schleicher, a collaborator on the PISA programme, in his foreword, is that 'technology is of little help in bridging the skills divide between advantaged and disadvantaged students. Put simply, ensuring that every child attains a baseline level of proficiency in reading and mathematics seems to do more to create equal opportunities in a digital world than can be achieved by expanding or subsidizing access to high tech devices and services.'

The (somewhat obvious) conclusion: 'Technology can make it possible to optimize excellent quality education, but it can never, however advanced it may be, compensate for poor quality education.'[219] Nothing supports this finding better than two studies conducted around the same time under the aegis of the US Department of Education. In the first, undertaken at the request of Congress,

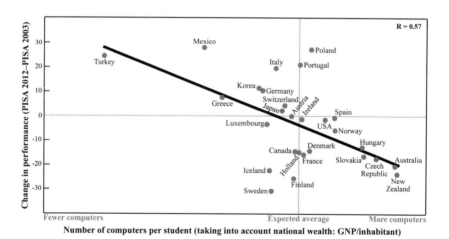

Figure 4. Impact of digital investments on school performance. The figure considers the results in mathematics, for OECD countries (the trends are the same for reading and science). It shows that the countries which have invested the most are those which have seen their pupils' performance decline the most severely.[218]

the authors questioned whether the use of educational software in primary school (reading, mathematics) had an effect on pupil performance.[220] The result was that, although all teachers were trained in the use of this software – satisfactorily, in their own words – no positive influence on the pupils could be detected.[a] In the second study, the role of around fifty hours of pedagogical training for teachers was assessed based on a major review of the scientific literature.[221] The result was a strongly positive impact representing, for pupils, a performance improvement of slightly more than 20%. This means that if a pupil turns out to be 'average' and you stick her in front of some kind of 'educational' software, at best she will remain average, at worst she will become fragile. But if you put her in front of competent, well-trained teachers, she will progress significantly and end up in the top third of her class. This 'teacher' factor is hardly a surprise. Indeed, beyond the differences in rhythms, approaches and methods, the quality of the teaching staff constitutes the fundamental trait common to the most efficient education systems in the world.[222-6] The summary of the last PISA report dedicated to this question explicitly underlines this. In the terms of this work, 'teachers are the most important resource in today's schools [...]. Contrary to what is often assumed, high-performing systems do not enjoy a natural privilege simply due to a traditional respect for teachers; they have also built a high-quality teaching force as a result of deliberate policy choices, carefully implemented over time'[227] – and, once again, to be clear, let's remember that these 'high-performing systems' are also those which (what a coincidence!) invest the least in the digital equipping of their schools.[218] We cannot fail to think, yet again, of Bill Joy, a co-founder of Sun Microsystems and a genius programmer, concluding a discussion on the educational virtues of digital technology as follows: 'this all, for me, for high school students sounds like a gigantic waste of time. If I was competing with the United States, I would love to have the students I'm competing with spending their time on this kind of crap.'[228] The language is a little rough, but it is deliciously clear.

In the light of these elements and comments, one might have hoped that current digital policies would have been called into question. Not at all – quite the contrary. Rather than confronting the aridity of the facts, the dominant institutional discourses continue to claim,

---

[a] All this is rather good news in view of the PISA data which show, for their part, that the use of this type of software has a negative impact on the performance of students.[218]

without a blush, that the problem does not come from digital technology itself but from those responsible for using it: the teachers. Still mothballed in the past, unfit for new technologies, trained in a rigid form of knowledge delivered face to face, these outdated fossils use the tools of the new world so badly that any hope of profit is illusory. This is stated, for example, in a nicely civilized manner, by a report from the European Commission: 'the lack of adequate teacher education relating to digital learning and digital pedagogies is a challenge that is widely acknowledged and documented throughout Europe. A number of countries are working to update their teacher education programmes to include techniques and strategies for digital learning, but there is still much to be done.'[229] Andreas Schleicher also refers to this hypothesis, in fairly similar terms. For this specialist in education policies, if the results are not more encouraging, this is perhaps because 'we have not yet become good enough at the kind of pedagogies that make the most of technology; that adding 21st-century technologies to 20th-century teaching practices will just dilute the effectiveness of teaching'.[218] However, this is not really what a detailed analysis of the PISA data presented above shows. Also, Schleicher puts forward another hypothesis according to which 'building deep, conceptual understanding and higher-order thinking requires intensive teacher–student interactions, and technology sometimes distracts from this valuable human engagement'.[218] This last idea is definitely worth considering.

Above all, a source of distraction

Let's start with a brief anecdote. Recently, the management team of a large French university was concerned about the congestion of its IT infrastructures. A message addressed to students read: 'We have noticed for some time a significant saturation on the WiFi network. A more in-depth analysis of the flows shows that the bandwidth is used in great part for external applications such as Facebook, Netflix, Snapchat, YouTube or Instagram and very marginally for university resources.'[230] In other words, the educational materials made available to students generate ridiculously little traffic compared to social network platforms and video-on-demand sites.[231] There is nothing unusual about this finding; it is the rule much more than the exception. In this area more than in any other, it is now clear that the fiction of virtuous use cruelly collides with the objective reality of harmful practices. An ever-increasing number of studies report that the introduction of digital technology in classrooms is above all a source of distraction for pupils and, consequently, a significant factor in academic difficulties.[62,232-47] The drop in grades is the result of a twofold movement: the sterility of strictly academic uses and the harmfulness of use for entertainment;[241] and as the preceding anecdote might suggest, the latter is considerable.[234,248-54] One study, for example, examined the use that students made of their computers in a geography class.[253] This lasted 2 hours 45 minutes and included the dynamic projection of images, graphics and videos in order to solicit the active participation of the pupils. The lucky owners of laptops spent almost two-thirds of their time on distracting, non-academic tasks. Other studies, however, have suggested that this 'interference' decreases somewhat when the lesson is shorter. Thus, for example, in a study carried out at the University of Vermont, for a class lasting 1 hour 15 minutes, the time stolen by distracting activities totalled 42%.[254] This is roughly the 'lower' average from the studies available. Is it really necessary to stress the astronomical nature of this value?

Obviously, the researchers were not satisfied with these 'field' results. Anxious to specify the nature and extent of their observations, they also undertook to carry out formal, rigorously controlled studies. With a few local variations, these were all carried out in a similar way: to assess the understanding/retention of a given academic content in two comparable populations, only one of which was exposed to a distracting digital source. The results were clear: any digital derivative (text messages, social networks, emails, etc.) results in a significant drop in the level of comprehension and memorization of the elements presented.[114,255-64] For example, in one recent study, pupils attended a 45-minute lesson, after which they were asked to answer around forty questions.[262] Half of the participants used their computers only for note taking; the other half also used them for entertainment. The pupils from the first group presented an appreciably higher percentage of correct answers than those of the second group (+ 11%). More surprisingly, for students focused on note taking alone, the mere fact of being placed behind an easily distracted peer (one whose screen was visible) caused a substantial drop in performance (– 17%). Interestingly, a comparable study had previously reported that the use of the computer was harmful even when it was used to access academic content related to the lesson in progress.[255] The message was quite simple: if you take your attention away from what's being taught, you lose information, and ultimately you understand less well what is being explained to you. In other words, learning about the circumstances of the Siege of Bastogne via the Internet is a great idea as part of a history lesson on the Battle of the Bulge – but after the lesson, not during it!

Of course, what is true of the computer also goes for the smartphone. Thus, in another work representative of the existing literature, the authors discovered that students who exchanged text messages during a course understood and remembered the content of the course less well. When subjected to a final test, they displayed 60% correct answers, compared to 80% for subjects in a non-distracted control group.[263] A previous study had also indicated that it wasn't even necessary to respond to the messages received to be distracted.[258] The retention of information can be disrupted even by a phone ringing in the room (or vibrating in your pocket). To show this, two experimental conditions were compared. In the first, the class, recorded on video, took place without disturbance. In the second, that same lesson was interrupted twice by the ringing of a mobile phone. The comprehension and memorization of the elements presented at the time of the interruptions were, not surprisingly, severely affected: the number of correct answers to a final test fell by about 30% compared to when no phones rang. But, more surprisingly, recent work has found that simply asking pupils to put their phones on their desks during a class preoccupied their attention enough to disrupt cognitive performance; and this was true even when the telephone remained perfectly inert and silent.[264]

To be sure, all of this directly contradicts the glorious mythology of the digital native and, more specifically, the idea that younger generations have different brains, brains that are faster, more agile and more suited to parallel cognitive processing. The annoying thing is that this pseudo-scientific hoax is now so widespread that our descendants themselves have come to believe it. Thus, the majority of current pupils think that they can, without detriment, take a class or do their homework while watching music videos or TV series, surfing on social networks and/or exchanging text messages.[242,243,265,266] This is unfortunately not the case, as we have just pointed out.

A logic that is more economic than educational

So, to sum up, the available studies report at best the ineptitude and at worst the pedagogical harmfulness of the policies of digitization of the school system. A fairly simple question therefore arises: why? Why such a frenzy? Why so much enthusiasm for digitizing the school system, from kindergarten to university, when the results are so unconvincing? Why such an avalanche of laudatory language when the available evidence would lead to real scepticism? An article from 1996 published by a French economist sheds interesting light on these questions.[267] Assessing the political risk of various budget-saving measures set up in some developing countries, this former senior OECD executive adopted a few 'low-risk' approaches; approaches that 'do not create any political difficulty'. For example,

> if we decrease operating expenses, care must be taken not to decrease the quantity of service, even if the quality decreases. We can, for example, reduce the operating funds given to schools or universities, but it would be dangerous to restrict the number of pupils or students. Families will react violently to a refusal to enrol their children, but not to a gradual decline in the quality of education.

This is exactly what is happening with the current digitization of the school system. Indeed, while the first studies had generally reported no convincing influence of this digitization on pupil success, the most recent data, notably from the PISA programme, reveal a strong negative impact. Oddly enough, nothing is being done to stop or slow down the process – on the contrary. There is only one rational explanation for this absurd situation. It is of an economic nature: by replacing human beings with digital tools, more or less completely, it is possible, in the long term, to envisage a significant reduction in teaching costs. Of course, the approach is accompanied by a marketing tidal wave aimed at persuading parents and, more broadly, civil society as a whole that the forced digitization of the school system not only does not constitute an educational renunciation, but represents tremendous educational progress. US President Lyndon Johnson, at least, as we have seen, had the honesty (or naivety) to recognize that educational television was a remarkable opportunity for children on the sole ground that 'the world has only a fraction of the teachers it needs'. Because the heart of the problem is there. Forced to provide ever more school and university facilities, almost all developed countries today are struggling to pay their teachers a decent wage, hence the intense shortfall in recruitment.[268-71] To break the deadlock, it is difficult to imagine a better solution than the famous 'digital revolution'. Indeed, this de facto authorizes the recruitment of poorly qualified teachers, reduced to the rank of simple 'mediators' or 'stage directors' of knowledge delivered by pre-installed software tools. The 'teacher' then becomes a sort of anthropomorphic serving hatch whose activity essentially boils down to directing pupils to their daily digital program while ensuring that our brave digital natives don't fidget about too much in their seats. Of course, it's easy to continue to giving the name 'teachers' to simple 'prison wardens 2.0', underqualified and underpaid; and thereby, as noted above by our economist, to lower operating costs without risking a parental revolution. One can of course, as an additional precaution, dress the whole business up in a nice empty rhetoric by talking of 'blended learning'.

However, one can also (especially when there is no choice) recognize the real for what it is and acknowledge the havoc that is being created. This is what several American states have done, including Idaho[272] and Florida.[273] For the latter, for example, the administrative authorities have proved unable to recruit enough teachers to meet a legislative constraint limiting the number of pupils per class (twenty-five in high school). The authorities therefore decided to create digital classes, without teachers. In this context, pupils learn on their own, in front of a computer, with the sole human support of a 'facilitator'[273] whose role is limited to solving small technical problems and ensuring that the pupils are working efficiently. This is a 'nearly criminal' approach according to one teacher, but a 'necessary' approach according to the school authorities. For them, the change is all the more interesting as there is hardly any limit to the number of pupils (thirty, forty or even fifty) that a facilitator can supervise. In other words, the digitization of classes makes it possible to save in terms of both quality and quantity. Fewer teachers/facilitators (whatever they may be called), paid less: it's not easy to resist the beauty of the equation when you're holding a calculator – especially if you yourself can afford to put your offspring in a private, fee-paying school with 'real' qualified teachers. Teachers in Idaho understood this well, and have protested in droves against the cutting of their salaries and social protection; a measure intended to finance a digitization plan even though it would mean all those dusty, talk-and-chalk teachers being promoted to the remarkable rank of 'guide helping students through lessons delivered on computers'.[272] It would obviously be inappropriate to establish any link between these elements and the results of a recent study reporting that Florida and Idaho are among the American states which pay their teachers the least well, have the lowest rates of graduation from high school and spend the least on the education of each child.[274]

Classes without teachers?

Many digital aficionados readily recognize the relevance of these economic considerations. In one recent book, a French journalist, supposedly an 'expert' on the educational issue, stressed that

> education is above all an industry with a significant workforce. 95% of the national education budget goes into salaries! [...] One of the major contributions of digital technology, particularly in the form of MOOCs, is to allow significant savings in this item.[a] Where today you have to pay teachers every year to deliver lectures to lecture halls of a few hundred students, tomorrow you will be able to deliver these lectures to a potentially infinite number of students for the same price. The cost of raw materials will drop.[275]

The argument is compelling and it should, in theory, stand on its own. Most of the time, however, this is not the case; it's as if the economic argument by itself could not win social support. To make MOOCs (like all 'educational' software) presentable, it seems necessary to adorn them with solid educational virtues. Thus, for our journalist, these virtual courses make it possible to move 'from the school that teaches to the school where people learn'.[276] Delivered on screen, the courses come 'in a much more attractive form than the handouts of yesteryear'. In addition, they

> are accompanied by extremely rich complementary resources – links to other courses, reference texts, etc. At every step of the course, a series of exercises is offered, in order to check that you have acquired the concepts presented – we do not allow those little gaps in under-standing to build up which, put end to end, finally block the process of learning. The student community is now connected and they can help each other in real time, which makes it possible to limit the numbers dropping out and save considerable supervision and tutoring time.[275]

---

[a] MOOC: massive open online course. The MOOC is a course (or a series of courses), on a given subject, delivered via the Internet. However, this definition covers extremely disparate realities. The most rudimentary versions boil down to simple course videos. The more mature versions include successive assessment tests, a discussion forum for participants and the final award of a certificate of competence.

Are we to understand that before the 'MOOC revolution',[276] teaching was not about learning? Are we to understand that teachers did not assess pupils' understanding and did not offer them, if necessary, additional content, exercises and/or explanations? Likewise, are we to understand that, before the advent of digital tools, pupils wandered about in a vacuum like a torpid mass, never talking to each other, interacting, helping each other or asking their teachers questions? Seriously, who can give credence to these grotesque caricatures? And then, what are we to say about this fable of the attractiveness of MOOCs? Of course, it's easy to recognize that they can be potential learning tools. What is difficult is to understand how their disembodied nature could prove to be more stimulating, motivating and effective than a real human presence. In other words, no one doubts that a MOOC can make it possible to understand the proof of the Pythagorean theorem by the method of similar triangles;[277] what is problematic is the constantly reaffirmed idea that it can do it universally, more effectively and in a more motivational way than a qualified teacher. This hesitation seems all the more justified as the hypothesis that MOOCs are more motivational does not agree well with the available experimental results. Take, for example, the course in microeconomics produced by the American University of Pennsylvania. Out of 35,819 registrants, only 886 candidates (2.5%) had enough perseverance to reach the final exam, of which 740 (2.1%) obtained their certificate.[278] This is a quantitative disaster – one that, alas, is far from isolated. The dropout rate observed for similar supposedly fun, engaging, motivating online courses typically exceeds 90–5%,[279–81] with peaks greater than 99% for the most demanding courses.[75] And what about the immense effectiveness of these MOOCs? After all, in 2013, after only a few months of experimentation, the American University of San José, in California, brutally chose to interrupt its cooperation with a specialized platform (Udacity) due to a staggering failure rate that ranged, depending on the course, from 49% to 71%.[76] In an article in the *New York Times*, the co-founder of this platform recognized, after leaving academia to focus on vocational training, that 'the basic MOOC is a great thing for the top 5 percent of the student body, but not a great thing for the bottom 95 percent'.[282] This finding is consistent with the conclusions of a large experimental study on the effectiveness of a MOOC in physics. In the words of the authors,

the MOOC is like a drug targeted at a very specific population. When it works, it works well, but it works for very few [...]. MOOCs are effective learning environments only for a small, select demographic – older, well-educated students, with a strong physics background and who possess a combination of self-discipline and motivation. This population is a very different group than our college freshmen.[283]

In short, these fine MOOCs clearly do not arouse, in most of their users, the enthusiasm one might expect. To make matters worse, it also appears, as a bonus, that these instruments dangerously reinforce social inequalities by favouring pupils from the most privileged backgrounds. For example, a study of sixty-eight courses offered by Harvard University and MIT in the United States reported that a teenager with at least one parent with a university degree was, all things considered, almost twice as likely to obtain his final certificate as a teenager neither of whose parents had this diploma.[74] This differential largely reflected the better quality of academic and motivational support offered to pupils favoured by their socio-family background.

All this confirms that MOOCs are not, for the majority of students, an easy, motivational or effective solution. They require time, effort, work, solid prior knowledge and a (very) solid intellectual maturity if they are to be assimilated. In other words, despite the songs of praise they elicit, it is infinitely more demanding to learn with a MOOC than with a qualified teacher. Fortunately, it seems that this obvious fact is slowly gaining ground in the media; as this recent article in *Le Monde* puts it, 'MOOCs are going pooof!'[284] This headline resonates nicely with an earlier text, in the columns of the *New York Times*, on 'demystifying the MOOC'.[282] Apparently, the bubble has burst, as happened in their time with the glorious educational revolutions promised by film, radio and television.

The Internet, or the illusion of available knowledge

Beyond just the issue of MOOCs, it is the didactic potential of the Internet that should be questioned. For many, it now seems to be an open-and-shut case, and it would appear, as one director of a management school explains, 'that the pure vertical knowledge typical of the lecture course is disappearing and that we can learn a lot more, and a lot more quickly, by going on the Web'.[285] This kind of statement is simply surreal.

Certainly the Web contains (in theory) all the knowledge in the world. But at the same time it also unfortunately contains all the nonsense in the universe. Even supposedly serious sites, of an academic, institutional, journalistic or encyclopaedic nature (including Wikipedia), are far from always reliable, honest and complete; witness numerous academic studies[286-91] and other surveys mentioned so far. How, then, are we to isolate credible documents from idiotic writings, fallacious positions, venal allegations and other fanciful information? How, then, are we to select, organize, prioritize and synthesize the knowledge obtained? These questions are all the more crucial as search algorithms care not a jot about the validity of the data returned. When responding to a query, they do not question the factual rigour of the content identified. Typically, they look for a few keywords and analyse various technical elements such as the age of the domain name, the size and traffic of the site, its adaptation to mobile media, the page-load time, the date of publication of the link, etc. In the end, it is not surprising that the results delivered are often somewhat biased and unfair; especially if we add the potential problem of more deeply hidden criteria of a political or commercial nature.[292-5] So, for example, when Michael Lynch, professor of philosophy at the University of Connecticut, asked Google 'What happened to the dinosaurs?', the first link sent him to a creationist site.[296] Feeling doubtful, I tried the same query in French ('Qu'est-il arrivé aux dinosaures?'). The winning combination: (i) a creationist blog, in which we read that 'the testimony of fossils does not, therefore, confirm the theory of evolution';[297] (ii) a creationist site explaining '[that] there is no evidence of any kind to claim that the world and its fossil layers are millions of years old';[298] (iii) a news site about the end of Nortel, a telecommunications 'dinosaur';[299] (iv) the home page of a proselytizing Christian site with an article explaining that 'dinosaurs and the Bible go together, but dinosaurs and evolution do not'.[300]

In short, when it comes to documentary research, it is better not to place too much trust in Google and its ilk when it comes to sorting out the wheat from the chaff. This is all the more true as the example reported here is neither isolated nor surprising. It's part of the organization and 'structural stupidity' of search engines. Indeed, in order to assess the credibility of a source, we need not only to analyse it in detail, but also to compare it with other available factual elements. This means that the assessor must understand and weigh all of the arguments presented. No machine can do this, at least not yet.[a] And

---

[a] If a search engine were one day to acquire this ability, should it be allowed to decide for us what to believe and what not to believe? Wouldn't the risk of manipulation then be absolutely huge?

what is true for the machine is also, alas, true for the naive subject, in the sense that there can be no factual understanding, critical thinking, ability to prioritize data or power of synthesis without close disciplinary control.[301-3] In other words, in these matters, 'general' competence does not exist.[304] Besides, the attempts made to teach such universal abilities to teenagers, in the framework of undifferentiated media education programmes, have turned out to be quite inconclusive.[305,306] One study of reading speaks volumes.[307] American school pupils were presented with a text describing a baseball game. Two experimental factors were explored: knowledge of baseball (yes/no) and reading skills (high/low, gauged on the basis of a standardized psychometric test). Combining these factors, the authors created four interest groups: (i) good baseball knowledge and good readers; (ii) good baseball knowledge and poor readers; (iii) poor baseball knowledge and good readers; (iv) poor baseball knowledge and poor readers. The results showed that poor readers with prior knowledge of baseball understood the text much better and then recalled the reported factual details much more precisely than good readers with no knowledge of the sport. No difference was observed between good and bad readers who knew nothing about baseball.

So understanding inevitably relies on the availability of internalized knowledge, and this largely explains the previously described inability of the younger generations to use the Internet for documentary purposes.[308-14] Indeed, how could individuals devoid of precise disciplinary knowledge assess and criticize the relevance of statements such as: 'smoking improves endurance capacities by increasing the concentration of haemoglobin in the blood'; 'dark chocolate makes you lose weight thanks to its appetite-suppressant properties'; 'action video games boost brain volume and promote academic success'; etc.? More generally, how can school pupils or college students cope effectively when each of their requests generates an endless stream of cacophonous, disparate and contradictory links? It's simply impossible. Moreover, it is now established that non-experts learn much better when informational content is presented in a linear, hierarchically arranged form (which is typically the case with books, lectures and practical work programmes, which force the teacher to be responsible for all the selection, coordination and structuring of knowledge). Things get much more complicated when the data appear in a reticular, anarchically fragmented form (as happens in response to Internet searches, when you are suddenly deluged by all the mass of accessible data, without any background or context, without any concern for hierarchy, relevance or credibility).[315-20]

Therefore, in educational matters, the question isn't whether the elements of knowledge are available. The question is whether the information is presented in such a way that it can be understood and assimilated. By this yardstick, the Web's maze-like and labyrinthine architecture is less than optimal. A qualified teacher is far preferable because it is precisely the function of the 'teacher' to organize and arrange her field of knowledge so as to make it accessible to the pupil. It is because the teacher knows her subject (and the pedagogical tools for its transmission) that she can guide others by methodically organizing the succession of courses, exercises and activities that will ensure the gradual acquisition of the knowledge and skills that are sought.

In this context, it must be clear, contrary to a deeply rooted belief in the media establishment, that all knowledge is not equal. The knowledge of a pupil being taught can in no way be compared to that of a qualified teacher. Some knowledge is made up of scattered, inconsistent and incomplete islands, while other knowledge forms the basis of an orderly, coherent and structured universe. This implacable asymmetry obviously does not prevent certain 'experts' who dwell in the depths of some sort of relativistic delirium from stating that

> you [the teachers] have clearly realized that providing digital terminals to pupils inevitably leads to them contesting your teaching. You have realized what they do with this: they read, they search, they cross-check the information, they criticize your magisterial message, and they thereby challenge your authority and force you to come down from your podium ... It's extremely unsettling. Was it really worth studying for all those years to get to this point?[321]

As if studying were pointless, as if knowing what you're talking about were irrelevant to teaching. As if, indeed, anybody could become a teacher as long as their pupils were offered an Internet connection. Always the same kind of language. Always the same empty proselytism, shaped by thaumaturgical verbiage rather than by the spadework of experience.

In conclusion

From this chapter, two main points should be remembered.

The first relates to domestic screens. In this area, apart from a few iconoclastic (and most often lame) studies, the conclusions of the scientific literature could not be clearer, more coherent or more indisputable: the more pupils watch television, the more they play video games, the more they use their smartphones, the more active they are on social media, the more their grades collapse. Even the home computer, whose educational power is endlessly touted to us, has no positive effect on school performance. This does not mean that the tool is devoid of potential virtues. It just means that when you gift a computer to a child (or teenager), the unfavourable recreational uses very quickly swallow up the formative educational uses.

The second concerns screens for school use. Here again the scientific literature is definitive. The more countries invest in 'information and communication technologies for education' (ICTEs), the more pupil performance falls. Simultaneously, the more time pupils spend with these technologies, the more their grades drop. Collectively, these data suggest that the current movement to digitize the school system follows a logic that is much more economic than educational. In fact, contrary to the official opinion, 'digital' tools are not just an educational resource made available to qualified teachers and usable by them, if they deem it relevant, within the framework of targeted educational projects (nobody would complain in this case, and the only possible axis of divergence might then be how to use the invested subsidies more effectively). No; in fact, digital technology is above all a means of reducing the scale of educational expenditure by replacing, more or less completely, humans with machines. This transfer puts the qualified teacher on the long list of endangered species. Indeed, a teacher is expensive, very expensive – maybe *too* expensive? In addition, a teacher is hard to train and, due to competitive pressure from more advantaged economic sectors, very difficult to recruit. Digital technology provides a very elegant solution to the problem. Of course, the fact that this solution comes at the expense of educational quality makes this a sore point and thus one that is difficult to admit. Therefore, in order to pass the buck and avoid parental fury, the whole business must be dressed up in elegant pedagogical verbiage. The cauterization effected by digital tools must be transformed into an 'educational revolution', a 'didactic tidal wave' produced, of course, for the sole benefit of the pupils. We must camouflage the intellectual impoverishment of the teaching body and praise the mutation of those old pre-digital dinosaurs into sparkling guides, mediators, facilitators, stage directors or conveyors of knowledge – one can choose whatever term suits! The catastrophic impact of this 'revolution' on the perpetuation and deepening of social inequalities must be concealed. Finally, the reality of the essentially distracting uses that pupils make of these tools needs to be disguised. In short, to pass the buck, we must deliberately conceal the reality. But, in spite of everything, in spite of these small soothing compromises, the uneasiness remains. As one female teacher from Idaho, a former military police officer in the Marines, put it, 'I fought for my country. Now I'm fighting for my kids [...]. I'm teaching them to think deeply, to *think*. A computer can't do that.'[272] Nor can a computer smile, help, guide, console, encourage, stimulate, reassure, show empathy or move you. But these are essential elements in the transmission of knowledge and of the desire to learn.[322] 'Without you', wrote Albert Camus to his former schoolteacher, after being awarded the Nobel Prize for literature,

> without that affectionate hand that you extended to me, a small child from a poor background, without your teaching, and your example, none of this would have happened. I don't want to blow up the importance of this sort of honour, but at least it's an opportunity to tell you what you were and still are to me, and to make sure that your efforts, your work and the generous heart you put into them are still alive in one of your little scholars who, despite his age, has not ceased to be your grateful pupil.[323]

Judging by these words, it perhaps becomes easier to realize the exorbitant cost of the so-called 'digital revolution'.

— 3 —

DEVELOPMENT
A damaging environment

If the use of screens so heavily affects academic success, it is obviously because their action extends far beyond the academic sphere alone. Grades are, then, the symptom of more serious damage, blindly inflicted on the cardinal pillars of our development. What is under attack here is the very essence of the developing human edifice, from language to concentration, memory, IQ, sociability and emotional control. A silent aggression, carried out without qualms or any sense of restraint, for the benefit of a few people and to the detriment of almost all.

Amputated human interactions

We know today that the newborn baby is not a tabula rasa. From birth, the little human displays great social, cognitive and language skills.[1-4] Many marvel at this fact, and rightly so. However, these original skills should not hide the forest of the faculties that are still latent and unformed. Indeed, impressive as it is, the essential baggage of our offspring remains very incomplete. Ultimately, it could be represented as a sort of minimal operating programme from which future deployments will take place. What then needs to be understood and emphasized is that this primitive immaturity is by no means a deficiency: quite the contrary. It is the essential foundation of our adaptive capacities, that is to say, in the final analysis, of our intelligence, in the sense in which Jean Piaget understood it.[5] From a strictly physiological point of view, one could say that immaturity imposes plasticity. Obviously, the developmental wonder then implemented is not without cost. It means that a large part of cerebral structuring relies on the outside world. Therefore, if the environment proves to be faulty, the individual can only express a fraction of its possibilities. This point has been discussed above, through the concept of 'sensitive period'.

The primordial baggage of the newborn, however, is not like some ecumenical assembly; it is methodically and obsessively human-oriented. From conception, the child is wired for social interactions. Thus, as a recent overview explains, 'at birth, infants exhibit a number of biases that preferentially orient them to socially relevant stimuli. In particular, it has been shown that newborns prefer faces over other kinds of visual stimuli, voices over other kinds of auditory stimuli and biological motion over other kinds of motion.'[4] This primitive equipment is gradually built up by the baby in response to the demands of her environment, especially within the family. The interactions promoted (or hindered) will then shape, in a decisive way, the whole of the baby's development, cognitive, social and emotional.[6-12] In this regard, however, three points should be emphasized, to avoid any ambiguity.

First, even if they are then particularly essential, the importance of intra-family relationships is not limited to the infantile stage alone; they continue to play a major role throughout adolescence, particularly in academic success, emotional stability and the prevention of risky behaviour.[6,13-17]

Second, even seemingly 'modest' levels of stimulation (or deficiency) can have significant impacts, especially if they accumulate over time. In the baby monkey, for example, during the first four weeks of existence, a few minutes of daily facial interactions with the animal are enough to promote, in the long term, the animal's social integration into the group of its peers.[18] Likewise, in young humans, the fact that parents take some time each evening to share a picture book or a story greatly favours the development of language, the acquisition of writing and academic success.[19,20] This observation is corroborated in an indirect but fascinating way by sibling studies. These start from an observation that is as simple as it is disturbing: on average, in families with several children, the eldest does better than his younger siblings in terms of IQ, academic performance, salary and legal risk.[21-4] As a recent study reports, the 'prejudice' suffered by the youngest children essentially reflects the progressive saturation of parental commitment (especially maternal) when the number of siblings increases.[24] In other words, to the extent that the firstborn has his parents 'to himself', he benefits from richer interactions than his future brothers and sisters, and therefore enjoys an improved developmental trajectory. Of course, again, that doesn't mean that all seniors fare better in all families. It simply means that there is, at the population level, a significant success bias in favour of the oldest child and that this bias is mainly associated with a greater level of parental stimulation at early ages.

A human being is not the same 'on video' as 'in real life'

This brings us to our third point, the human dimension. In order for the relational magic to work, one element is fundamental: the 'other' must be physically present. For our brain, a 'real' human is not at all the same as a 'video' human. Pier Francesco Ferrari provided one of the most glaring demonstrations of this, to his great disappointment. This researcher is one of the world's leading specialists in social development in primates. In particular, he studies the role of the famous 'mirror neurons'. These owe their name to the fact that they are activated in a similar way when the subject herself produces or sees a third party performing a particular action (for example, a facial expression of anger). This concomitance allows the behaviour of others to resonate with our own feelings and, in so doing, it places mirror neurons at the heart of our social behaviour.[25-7] To study the perceptual side of these amazing cells, researchers typically measure the brain activity generated by observing physical movement. However, in one animal study, Ferrari decided, in order to save time and better control the experimental parameters, to replace motion with a video of motion.[28] He was taken aback by the results! Indeed, 'mirror neurons that, during naturalistic testing, showed good responses to a hand action made by the experimenter, showed weak or no response when the same action, previously recorded, was shown on the screen'. This lack of responsiveness to the screen has since been reported in humans too, where it affects both children and adults.[29-33] This confirms that we are indeed social animals and that our brains respond much more acutely to the real presence of a human than to the indirect image of this human on a video. Everyone, I think, has been able to experience this for themselves. For my part, many years ago I was lucky enough to be invited to the opera. What a delight! A few weeks later, noting that Verdi's *Nabucco* was on TV, I decided to watch. What a disappointment! The boredom was abysmal. It was lucky I hadn't started with this sad experience. I think it would have cured me of opera forever.

In short, the human brain turns out, whatever its age, to be much less sensitive to a video representation than to an actual human presence. It is for this reason, in particular, that the educational power of a flesh-and-blood being so irrevocably surpasses that of the machine. The data on the subject are now so convincing that researchers have decided to give the phenomenon a name: the 'video deficit'. We came across many examples of this in the last chapter, when we talked about the pitiful achievements of digital education, MOOCs and many types of audiovisual programme and supposedly educational software. This last field provides an impressive number of experimental studies reporting that the child learns, understands, uses and retains better the information presented when it is delivered by a human being rather than by a video of the same human.[34–41] For example, in an often-cited work, children aged 12 to 18 months saw the experimenter handling a doll.[42] At the end of her right hand, fastened with Velcro, the doll wore a mitten into which a bell had been inserted. The presentation took place live or on video. It consisted of three steps: (i) removing the mitten; (ii) ringing the bell; (iii) replacing the mitten. The doll was then placed in front of the children, either immediately or after 24 hours. The result was that the participants' ability to reproduce what they saw was consistently poorer in the 'video condition'. The same results were reported in a study involving subjects aged 24 and 30 months.[43] Figure 5 illustrates these observations.

In another study, it was short educational sketches, comparable to those found in educational audiovisual programmes, that were used with kindergarten children (3–6 years).[44] Unsurprisingly, the 'video condition' revealed a much lower level of comprehension and memorization than direct presentation. Finally, in yet another study, children aged 6 to 24 months, from privileged families, were exposed on a smartphone to YouTube videos.[45] The authors tested different types of learning that involved, in particular, recognizing the same person when she appeared in several different videos (a skill that, in real life, humans are able to develop well before the age of 2). A related goal was to find out if children really understood what they were doing when interacting with the touch buttons controlling the video stream. The study concluded: 'Children up to two years of age could be entertained and kept busy by showing them YouTube clips on smartphones, but did not learn anything from the videos.' Moreover, 'the children did not understand the use of the different buttons and kept pressing them randomly'.

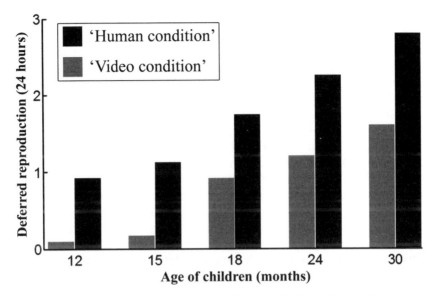

Figure 5. The phenomenon of 'video deficit'. Children 12 to 30 months old see an adult use an object. The demonstration always consists of three steps (e.g. removing a glove containing a bell from a doll's hand; shaking the glove to make the bell jingle; putting the glove back on). It is performed either live (the adult is in front of the child; 'Human condition', black bars) or on video (the child sees the adult perform the action on a screen; 'Video condition', grey bars). Twenty-four hours after the demonstration, the child is put in contact with the object. Each step reproduced gives a point to the child (3 is therefore the maximum possible, for perfect reproduction). The scores obtained are systematically higher in the 'Human condition'. The figure aggregates data from two similar studies: children 12 to 18 months;[42] and children 24 to 30 months.[43]

More screens means less communication and sharing

Ultimately, the finding can be summarized quite simply: to promote the development of a child, it is better to give time to human inter-actions, especially within the family, than to screens. This lesson was recently confirmed by a study reporting the negative effect of overall screen time on children's motor, social and cognitive development.[46] The authors commented: 'One of the most effective methods for enhancing child development is through high-quality caregiver–child interactions without the distraction of screens.' Unfortunately, as we have seen, this is not the current trend. Digital activities are colonizing an increasingly important part of our daily life; and since there are only twenty-four hours in each day, time surrendered to the digital orgy must be taken from 'somewhere' else. Some of the main contributing sources are homework (as already discussed), sleep, creative play, reading (I'll come back to this) and, of course, intra-family interactions. Regarding the last of these, the data in the literature are as predictable as they are convergent: the more time children and parents spend on their screens, the more the extent and the richness of their reciprocal relations are reduced.[47-59]

A study often cited in support of this observation concerns television (but basically, this isn't important: the impacts described here are independent of the media used and the content consumed).[59] It involves children from 0 to 12 years old and considers weekly and weekend consumption separately. The results show that the time given up to television inevitably reduces the duration of parent–child interactions. For example, for every hour spent in front of the small screen during the week, a 4-year-old child loses 45 minutes of inter-action with her parents; an 18-month-old baby gives up 52 minutes, and a 10-year-old pre-teen 23 minutes. For those who would deem the case to be not all that serious, let's think in cumulative terms again. It then appears that the total interaction time stolen by 60 minutes of television a day over the first 12 years of a child's life is 2,500 hours. This represents almost 180 days of waking (6 months),[a] 3 school years and 18 months of full-time paid employment. Not insignificant, especially if we relate these data to consumption amounting not to one, but to two or three hours a day. This disaster is made even worse by the deterioration in relations engendered by the displays in the background. In other words, even when children and parents are talking to each other, TV has an effect. This is what the following study demonstrates.

In a large number of households (from 35% to 45% according to the surveys),[61-4] the small screen is always or almost always on, even when no one is looking at it. In order to assess the impact of this presence on intra-family relationships, a group of researchers from the University of Massachusetts observed parents (mainly mothers) playing with their children (aged 1, 2 or 3) for an hour.[56] There was a TV in the room and it was switched on, at random, for the first or last 30 minutes of the experiment. The analyses revealed a strong

---

[a] Considering, over this period, an average of 10 hours per night,[60] i.e. 14 hours of daytime activity.

interference effect. Parent and child spent significantly less time communicating and playing when the TV was on. For example, one parent spent 33% of the time actively playing with his 24-month-old child when the TV was off. This value dropped by half (17%) when the set was turned on. This result will not surprise those who have been out to a restaurant for dinner where a TV was turned on and spewing out its programmes into the room. Even when we 'don't want to', we usually end up watching, if only furtively; and, irrevocably, we lose the thread of the dialogue with those around us. Our brain, in fact, is programmed to respond to obtrusive, sudden and unexpected external stimuli (sound or vision).[65-70] Of course, one can choose to 'resist'. But, in this case, the effort is such that it diverts a large fraction of our cognitive potential, and this leads to the same result as unwanted glances: it degrades the exchange.

A recent study has confirmed and generalized these data.[49] It concerns mobile phones and is based on a fairly simple protocol. Mother–child pairs were observed for four consecutive 4-minute periods. At the beginning of each period the experimenter brought a different food. Mother and child were then invited, if they wished, to taste and evaluate these foods, some of which were familiar (e.g. cupcakes) and others new (e.g. halva). During the experiment, a quarter of the mothers spontaneously used their mobile phones. This led to a sharp drop in both verbal and non-verbal exchanges. This impoverishment turned out to be particularly clear for so-called 'encouraging' interactions (verbal example: 'try a bite'; non-verbal example: the mother brings the food closer to the child or offers him a bite) and for unknown foods which, in mothers without mobiles, generated the highest levels of interaction. Thus, in the case of the halva, the presence of the telephone led to a 72% drop in maternal encouragement and a 33% drop in all verbal interactions. These data are consistent with other observations made by the same research group at several restaurants in the Boston area – observations showing that smartphone use results in less parental engagement and a more mechanical mode of interaction. Thus, as the authors write,

> caregivers absorbed in devices frequently ignored the child's behaviour for a while and then reacted with a scolding tone of voice, gave repeated instructions in a somewhat robotic manner (e.g., without looking at the child or relevant to child behaviour), seemed insensitive to the child's expressed needs, or used physical responses (e.g., [...] one female caregiver pushed a young boy's hands away when he was trying to repeatedly lift her face up from looking at a tablet screen).[50]

This is hardly surprising, in fact, because humans cannot be attentive to both their digital tools and the environment. In other words, when a parent or child is preoccupied by their smartphone, they can only give a distracted attention to others.[47,52]

Besides, the device doesn't even have to be used to be disturbing. Its very presence monopolizes enough attention (most frequently without our knowledge) to affect the quality of the exchange, especially when the subject matter of the conversation is considered important by the protagonists.[71] This power to distract explains, moreover, to a large extent, the remarkable ability of our smartphones to provoke serious conflicts when they are handled within the home (by parents and children together, or by the two parents).[47,50,72-5] No one likes to feel that they are, in the eyes of those close to them, less important and worthy of attention than a mobile phone. The tensions then generated favour the emergence of relational dissatisfaction, aggressive behaviour, even depressive states and a certain existential discomfort.[51,72-5] Similar results were reported for TV and game consoles.[76-8] These considerations are far from being trivial when we consider the major influence of the family 'climate' on a child's social, emotional and cognitive development.[79-81]

A mutilated language

Language is the cornerstone of our humanity. It is the final frontier that separates us from the animals. It is mainly thanks to language that we think, communicate and safeguard important knowledge. A close link exists between language development and intellectual performance.[12] As Robert Sternberg, professor of cognitive psychology at Yale University, explains, 'vocabulary [which reflects the general state of language development fairly well] is probably the best single indicator of a person's overall level of intelligence'.[82] And a large number of studies now report that exposure to screens for recreation significantly disrupts language development.[83-91] This conclusion has recently been validated in a large meta-analysis: 'greater quantity of screen use (i.e., duration of use and background television) is associated with lower language skills'.[92]

Early influences

Unsurprisingly, the influence of screens on language deployment begins early, which seems to support the previously advanced idea

106

that it is better to avoid exposure during the first years of life. For example, in 18-month-old children, each additional half-hour per day spent with a mobile device has been reported to increase almost 2.5 times the likelihood of experiencing delays in language acquisition.[90] Likewise, in children aged 24 to 30 months, the risk of language deficit has been reported to increase in proportion to the duration of television exposure.[83] Thus, compared to small consumers (less than 1 hour per day), moderate (1 to 2 hours per day), medium (2 to 3 hours per day) and significant users (more than 3 hours per day) saw the probability of a delay in language acquisition multiplied by 1.45, 2.75 and 3.05 respectively. This result was confirmed in another study that established, again for television, that the risk of deficit was quadrupled, in children from 15 to 48 months, when consumption exceeded 2 hours per day. This quadrupling even turned into sextupling when these children had been introduced to the joys of the small screen before 12 months (regardless of duration).[89] In older subjects, from 3.5 to 6.5 years old, another study has reported that the fact of being placed in front of a screen of any kind in the morning, before going to school or to the crèche (i.e. at a potentially privileged time for intra-family interactions), multiplied the risk of slowing down language acquisition by 3.5.[91] These results are consistent with those of a large-scale epidemiological study showing, in children aged 8 to 11, that individuals who exceeded the use threshold recommended by the Canadian Society for Exercise Physiology (2 hours per day)[93] presented an overall impairment in their intellectual functioning (language, attention, memory, etc.).[94] This conclusion is itself compatible with the observations of two longitudinal studies[a] indicating, for television[95] and video games,[96] the existence of a negative correlation between time of use and verbal IQ in children aged 6 to 18 years. In other words, the more the participants increased their screen exposure, the more their language intelligence decreased. Note that the link then identified was comparable, in terms of its magnitude, to the association observed between the level of lead poisoning (lead is a powerful endocrine disruptor)[97] and verbal IQ.[98] This means that if you hate your horrible neighbours' insufferable brat and dream of ruining his life as much as possible, there's no need to put lead in his water bottle. Instead, give him a TV, tablet or game console. The cognitive impact will be just as devastating – and you will run zero legal risk.

---

[a] Longitudinal studies study the joint evolution of one or more variables, within the same population, over several months or years (for example, IQ and screen time).

In recent years, researchers have set out to go beyond these behavioural findings to try and identify the neural correlates of the damage observed. The results obtained indicate that recreational digital exposure disrupts the organization and development of brain networks supporting language, reading and more generally cognitive functioning.[95,96,99,100] For example, recent work has reported that the more the child (3–5 years) strayed from the recommendations of the American Academy of Pediatrics (usage time, content, etc.), the more the risk of language deficits increased, and the more the microstructural anomalies worsened in white-matter pathways involved with language, executive functions and emergent literacy skills.[101]

A clearly identified causality

Interesting as they are, these neurophysiological data are not surprising. With a touch of impertinence, one could almost say that they go without saying. Indeed, hundreds of studies carried out over more than a century report, in humans and animals, that brain networks need to be actively engaged if they are to organize themselves. Therefore, any lack of functional stimulation results in a deficit of biological maturation.[102-4] And this is the whole problem with screens: they brutally impoverish the number and the quality of verbal interactions. In other words, the more time household members spend with their digital gadgets, the fewer words they exchange.[49,50,56,58,59,89] For example, in one frequently cited study, researchers equipped children aged 2 to 48 months with a tape recorder, whose recordings were then automatically decoded.[55] On average, during the day, children heard 925 words per hour. When television was present, that count dropped to 155 words, a drop of 85%. Likewise, the children's daily vocalization time was 22 minutes. Each hour of television took away five units from that total, or almost a quarter.

These early verbal exchanges are absolutely essential not only for language development, but also, more generally, for intellectual development.[12,105-11] One longitudinal study recently confirmed this by reporting that the extent of early verbal interactions (18–24 months) accounted for a significant portion (between 14% and 27%) of the variance in IQ and verbal skills scores measured in adolescence (9–13 years).[112] These conclusions are perfectly consistent with the founding observations of psychologists Betty Hart and Todd Risley.[12,113] Moreover, not surprisingly, in agreement with all these data, a neuroimaging study has recently reported, in young children (4–6 years), that the higher the level of verbal solicitation (especially in the context of dialogical exchanges with adults), the more structural connectivity was reinforced within the neural networks of language.[114]

For sceptics, we can cite a recent longitudinal study involving more than 2,400 preschool children.[46] In the words of the authors, the study's aim was to determine 'what comes first: delays in development or excessive screen time viewing?' To do this, participants' digital consumption as well as their performance on a standard developmental test were assessed three times (at 24, 36 and 60 months).[a] The analyses showed, on the one hand, that more screen time at 24 months was associated with lower developmental performance at 36 months and, on the other hand, that more screen time at 36 months was associated with lower developmental performance at 60 months. This means that the increase in screen time preceded the emergence of developmental delays or, more prosaically, 'that screen time is likely the initial factor'.[46] In other words, it is not developmental delays that cause children to spend more time in front of screens, but screens that cause developmental delays in children. It can be noted that the value of this study has sometimes been downplayed on the grounds that the observed causal effect was of modest magnitude.[115,116] Even if the point is correct, it is misleading. Indeed, the statistical tools captured only a fraction of the total causality – the part linked to intra-individual evolutions (i.e. to what changed for the same child over time). The proportion of causality attributable to systematic differences (that is, to what remained stable over time) could not be estimated. But that does not mean that this part is zero or negligible. Let us imagine that between 36 and 60 months, Mark goes from 15 minutes to 40 minutes per day, while Peter goes from 3 hours 15 minutes to 3 hours 40 minutes. The 'intra' effect will not take into account the 3 hours of systematic difference between these two children. However, when we place a child for 3 hours a day in front of various screens for recreation, we obviously activate all kinds of damaging causal chains: we talk to him less, he moves less, he reads less, he is subjected to more intense sensory bombardment, his sleep is affected, etc. Therefore, the fact that the causal part of the 'stable' effects could not be irrefutably quantified does not mean

---

[a] This was the third edition of the Ages & Stages Questionnaires (ASQ-3). This test measures children's progress in five developmental areas: Communication, Gross Motor, Fine Motor, Problem Solving and Personal-Social.

that it must be erased. To be clear, in the study considered here, the overall magnitude of the association observed between screen time and development was by no means modest: one hour of screen daily was associated with a decrease of 20 points in behavioural test results (averaging 55 points at 60 months).

The sad illusion of 'educational' programmes

If only screens had something positive to offer. But, that's not really the case. In language too, the 'video deficit'[a] prevails and digital technology cannot replace humans. Take, for example, one study on the ability to discriminate between sounds.[36] The ability of children to recognize sounds foreign to their language deteriorates rapidly between 6 and 12 months.[9] Based on this observation, Patricia Kuhl and her colleagues exposed 9-month-old American babies to Mandarin, under two conditions: one real (an experimenter was present in front of the child), the other indirect (the face of the same experimenter was presented, in close-up, on a video facing the child). As a result, while the 'real' condition made it possible to preserve the discriminatory capacities of babies, the 'video' condition proved to be totally sterile. This means that if you hope to cure your children's English, German, Chinese or Japanese accent by stuffing them early on with programmes in the original language, you may be sorely disappointed.

Obviously, this 'video deficit' does not only concern phonetics. It also applies, in particular, to vocabulary. Thus, before age 3, the ability of supposedly educational programmes to increase children's vocabulary is at worst negative, at best non-existent.[87,117-20] In one oft-cited representative study, children aged 12 to 18 months were exposed to viewing a successful 39-minute commercial DVD purported to develop language.[121] Twenty-five simple words describing common objects (table, clock, tree, etc.) were then presented three times in a non-consecutive manner (each repetition of the same word occurred several minutes apart). The children watched the DVD five times a week for four weeks, for a total of sixty presentations; an extravagant scale with regard to the few repetitions typically necessary for a child (or a dog!)[122] to memorize this kind of words in a 'real' situation.[110] In the end, and contrary to what many parents thought, no learning

---

[a] See above, p. 102.

was observed even when the viewing took place in the presence of an adult. The authors' conclusion:

> children who viewed the DVD did not learn any more words from their month-long exposure to it than did a control group. The highest level of learning occurred in a no-video condition in which parents tried to teach their children the same target words during everyday activities. Another important result was that parents who liked the DVD tended to overestimate how much their children had learned from it.

These results were, however, contradicted by a subsequent study involving a similar but much denser, more 'compact' experimental protocol.[124] The DVD this time lasted 20 minutes and consisted of only three words, each presented nine times. After 15 days, the children had seen the DVD six times, on average – for each word, that is, 40 minutes of 'bombardment' and 54 repetitions. Before the age of 17 months, this avalanche produced no effect. Beyond that, however, in the author's words, the children 'benefited from repeat exposure to the DVD'. Unfortunately, it is impossible to say from the reported averages how many children had learned how many words. But this isn't important: what is striking here, even if we place ourselves in the most favourable position (all the children have learned the three words), is the incredible gap between the enormity of the time allowed and the blatant insignificance of the acquisitions observed. Fortunately, real life is not so voracious and, when it comes to learning vocabulary, it can be satisfied with a few scattered encounters; sometimes even just one.[110,123] The day we replace human beings with digital tools, it will no longer be 30 months (as at present) but 10 years that our children will need to reach a lexical volume of 750 to 1,000 words.[12,110]

To this grim prediction, one could obviously object that what fails at 18 or 30 months can succeed perfectly well at 4 years. True enough. Syntheses and meta-analyses of the literature, moreover, confirm quite clearly that educational audiovisual programmes allow certain linguistic acquisitions.[92,117] A detailed analysis of the data emphasizes, however, that learning then essentially relates to fairly basic lexical content, mainly in kindergarten children.[117] Things take a turn for the worse when this preschool period is passed and more complex skills are considered,[117] for example grammatical skills[125] – a limitation that is also found in experiments involving the use of subtitled films for the learning of foreign languages in adolescents.[126]

However, it is precisely these complex skills that constitute the heart of language and are most subject to the constraints imposed by the sensitive windows of development. Vocabulary can be learned at any age, but syntax cannot![9] In other words, once again, the apparent superficial benefit hides the invisible sacrifice on a more fundamental level, in the sense that what is learned is of paltry significance when compared to what is lost. One thing needs to be made clear here: just because a child manages to shout 'yellow', 'pear' or 'lemon' in front of her TV (or any junk app) when a puppet shows her a pear or a lemon, this doesn't mean that she is learning to speak. One recent study demonstrates this nicely.[127] This time, the authors were interested not in nouns but in verbs, these 'angels of movement who [give] movement to the sentence', as the poet Charles Baudelaire said.[128] Two major results were reported. Before age 3, children using an educational video were found to be unable to learn simple verbs (such as 'to shake' or 'to swing') that they easily acquired through human interaction. Between 36 and 42 months, these same children were able to learn the meaning of the proposed verbs, but without being able to generalize the acquisition to new characters or new situations, as they easily did when the learning involved a human being. In other words, even when they seemed to learn something, children learned less well and less deeply with the screen. This was a predictable finding, and one which only confirms the phenomenon, already widely mentioned, of 'video deficit' and could be summarized as follows: in terms of language learning, it is better to put the child in front of a so-called 'educational' application than to abandon her to a complete absence of relation; but the optimum still consists (by far) in speaking to her, in naming things to her, in telling her stories (or reading to her), asking for her reactions, etc.

But basically, when you take time to think about the problem, this inability of so-called 'educational' programmes to significantly enrich the language of young children is not unexpected; and this for at least three reasons. First, as we have said, our brains pay much less attention to video stimuli than to human incarnations. However, attention greatly promotes memorization.[129] It's no wonder, then, that mum and dad prove to be infinitely more effective teachers than any supposedly educational audiovisual content. Second, no learning can take place if the viewer is looking at his feet when the video points to glass, for example. However, unlike parents, the screen never checks the child's visual anchorage before naming an object. So it should come as no surprise that the child experiences some learning difficulties if, when the word 'glass' sounds out, he is staring at the fly that's just landed on the table or at the funny puppet that's pointing to the glass, rather than at the glass itself. Added to this is the fact that lexical acquisition is more efficient when the child hears the name of an object on which his attention is already fixed than when he must first focus this attention on the object of interest.[130] Finally, third, and above all, human interaction is irrevocably necessary for initial language learning. On the one hand, it encourages the active repetition of the words heard – a repetition which itself, in turn, greatly favours memorization.[131,132] On the other hand, it alone embodies language in its communicational dimension.[130] Unlike parents, the video never responds when the child is talking or pointing. It does not adapt to her level of knowledge or to any bodily messages of incomprehension. It does not smile or hand out the apple when the child says 'apple'. It does not kindly correct the child when she pronounces it 'happle' rather than 'apple'. It does not turn each phonetic approximation into a fertile game of imitation ('now you, now me'). Later, it does not reformulate the child's expressions, it does not enrich them with new words, and it does not correct haphazard syntax.

In short, in terms of language, the poor performance of educational audiovisual programmes is not only experimentally demonstrated, but also theoretically predictable. Maybe this won't last. Perhaps in a few years or decades, mobile applications will be able to compensate for the deficiencies described here. Maybe even anthropomorphic robots will one day be able to educate our children for us, interpret their babbling, feed their curiosity, watch over their sleep, smile at their mimicry, change their nappies, bring them what they ask for or point to, hug them, etc. No more need for dad, mum, babysitter, teacher, tutor, friend, family, siblings. You can have a child without all the hassle, produce offspring without the burden of raising them. Google and its algorithms will take care of everything; a true 'digital best of all worlds'! Certainly, we are still far from this, as current apps remain, according to a recent observation of the American Academy of Pediatrics that we have already mentioned, pathetically primitive.[133] But ultimately, who knows? All nightmare scenarios are possible.

After the early years, reading is a sine qua non

That being said, even if these nightmares did come true, that wouldn't solve everything – far from it. Indeed, after the early years,

113

language requires much more than words to ensure its deployment; it requires books.[19,134] In this respect, one of my speech therapist friends used to say that her daughters were bilingual – in the oral and written languages. The idea may make one smile. Yet it is remarkably relevant. If you need convincing, just take a look at the studies which have compared the respective complexity of different oral and written language corpora.[19,135,136] Typically, these studies are based on normative scales allowing all the existing words to be ordered according to their frequency of use. We then observe that 'the' is number 1 (that is to say that 'the' is the most frequently used word), that 'it' is number 10 (that is, 'it' is the tenth most frequently used word), that 'know' is number 100, that 'vibrate' is number 5,000, and so on. From this classification, it is easy to determine the 'average' complexity of a text (for example, by ordering all the words of this text and taking the rank of the median word) and, consequently, the average complexity of a large number of similar texts (novels, films, cartoons for children, etc.). When they did this, the researchers observed the extreme poverty of the oral corpora compared to their written counterparts. As shown in figure 6, on average, language is more complex, and 'rare' words (words above the 10,000th rank)[a] more frequent, in children's books than in any television programmes or ordinary conversations between adults. This is not to say, however, that children's texts are riddled with esoteric, hyper-specialized jargon. Far from it; rather, it means that the oral space generally provides relatively little lexical and syntactic richness. In other words, our daily exchanges use a singularly modest language. Words like 'equation', 'relinquish', 'exposure', 'legitimate' or 'literal', for example, an understanding of which hardly seems superfluous, are encountered far less often orally than in writing.[136] The same applies to terms such as 'infernal' or 'xenophobia', which, respectively, are not used by 40% of fourth-year high school pupils[137] and 25% of sixth-formers.[138]

In short, all this means that beyond a fundamental basis, orally constructed during the first years of life, it is from books and only from books that the child will be able to enrich and fully develop her language. One study is particularly interesting in this respect.[139] It reports the excellent 'value for money' of books for children in the middle years of school. On average, they would read for 10 minutes a day, 'for pleasure'[b] – a thirteenth of the time they spent watching

---

[a] For examples, see p. 43 above.
[b] That is, personal reading with no direct relation to schoolwork.

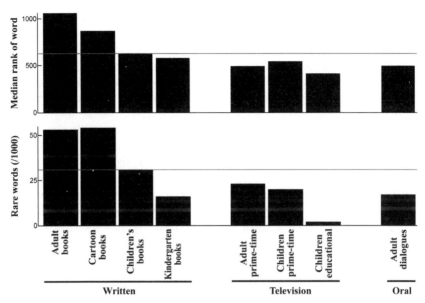

Figure 6. The richness of language is concentrated in the written word. The linguistic complexity of different media is measured in two ways: by determining the rank of the median word; and by evaluating the proportion of rare words (per 1,000 words). It can be seen that, on average, television programmes and ordinary conversations between adults contain fewer words than children's books (grey horizontal line). The linguistic poverty of so-called educational television programmes (*Sesame Street* and *Mr Rogers*) is particularly striking.[135,136] For details, see the text.

television. Over the course of a year, those meagre 10 minutes represented almost 600,000 words. Only 2% of children spent more than an hour reading each day. For these, the annual total was close to 5 million words (!); and once again, a large fraction of these fell outside the impoverished paths of verbal communication. These figures unmistakably echo the observations of Anne Cunningham and Keith Stanovich. For these two American researchers, who have devoted their entire academic career to the study of reading:

> First, it is difficult to overstate the importance of getting children off to an early successful start in reading [...]. Second, we should provide all children, regardless of their achievement levels, with as many reading experiences as possible [...]. An encouraging message for teachers [and parents!] of low-achieving students is implicit here. We often

despair of changing our students' abilities, but there is at least one partially malleable habit that will itself develop abilities – reading![136]

In line with this last remark, a number of studies have demonstrated the positive influence of reading 'for pleasure' on school performance.[140-5] This result makes for an interesting contrast with the strongly negative impact of screens for recreation.

The problem, clearly, is that the more time they give to their screens, the less exposed children will be to the benefits of the written word. Two mechanisms are involved. First, a decrease in the time spent reading with parents.[57] Second, a decrease in the time spent in solitary reading.[140,144,146-52] For example, an oft-cited study reported that the frequency with which parents read stories to their kindergarten children fell by a third when the latter were exposed to more than 2 hours of screen daily.[57] Likewise, another study established, for a teenage population, that each daily hour of video games led to a drop of 30% in the time spent reading alone.[153] These facts explain, at least in part, the negative impact of screens for recreation on the acquisition of the written code[154-6] – an impact that compromises, in return, the deployment of language. Everything is then in place for a pernicious self-sustaining loop to develop: since he is less exposed to writing, the child has more difficulty learning to read; since he has more difficulty reading, he tends to avoid writing and therefore to read less; as he reads less, his language skills do not develop to the expected level and he finds it increasingly difficult to cope with the expectations for his age. This is a remarkable illustration of the famous 'Matthew effect' already mentioned (the rich get richer) or, if you prefer, of the famous popular adage according to which 'you only lend to the rich'.

In line with these considerations, recent large-scale surveys confirm the marked lack of interest of the younger generations in reading.[157-9] Only 35% of 8- to 12-year-olds and 22% of 13- to 18-year-olds say they read 'for pleasure' every day.[160] The investment devoted to the book (print and e-books) then amounts to 26 and 20 minutes respectively. This means that our teens spend 22 times more time with their screens for recreation than with their books. For pre-teens it's 11 times more. Of course, a plethora of specialists will explain to us that it is useless to worry because 'young people have never read as much as they do today [...] but they read on the Internet, not in books, looking for what will be useful to them'.[161] For our digital experts, 'to say that "young people read less than before" no longer makes sense in this age of the Internet'.[162] This supposed tidal wave of online reading, however, seems quite modest: on average 1 minute per day among pre-teens; 7 minutes for teens (including 'articles, stories, poems or blogs on a computer, tablet, or smartphone').[160] This is, indeed, something to be excited about. However, as one sociologist who has produced a well-documented study of the cultural practices of the younger generations[163] puts it, 'the reading sequences of young people are shorter, often linked to their written exchanges on the Internet, and are therefore closely linked to sociability'.[164] The problem is that these activities do not have anything like the same structuring potential as the good old books so dear to the dinosaurs of pre-digital ages. In line with this assertion, two recent studies have reported the existence of a clear educative hierarchy between 'traditional' books and digital content. The former have a strong positive influence on the acquisition of vocabulary and the development of reading comprehension skills; the impact of the latter oscillates between zero and negative.[165,166] Three complementary hypotheses explain this result. First, the content commonly produced, exchanged and consulted by the younger generations on the Internet presents too limited a linguistic range for it to compete with the traditional book. Second, on the Web, the fragmented format of the information and the constant distractions (emails, hypertext links, ads, etc.) disrupt the development of the concentration skills necessary for understanding complex written documents. Third, for our brain, the 'book' format is easier to handle and understand than the 'screen' format.[167] Many studies have reported that a given text is generally understood more precisely in its paper form than in its screen version; and this regardless of the age of the readers.[168,169] In other words, when it comes to reading and understanding a document, even supposed digital natives are more comfortable with the book than with the screen – though this does not prevent a majority of them from asserting the contrary![170] This is another illustration, if necessary, of the structural weakness of our subjective feelings.

Fighting dyslexia with video games

Obviously, the media will tell us, the picture painted here is far too negative. Beyond the 'educational' content we have talked about, recreational digital programmes definitely bring all kinds of indirect positive effects. Video games, again, are seen as being at the forefront. In particular, we are told, they promote learning to read and the treatment of dyslexia. That's all that's needed!

Thus, for example, following two apparently converging scientific studies, journalists around the world have embarked on an incredible semantic one-upmanship, with wonderful headlines: 'Video games to fight against dyslexia';[171] 'Video games "help reading in children with dyslexia"';[172] 'A day of video games tops a year of therapy for dyslexic readers';[173] 'Video games may treat dyslexia';[174] etc. This is mind-boggling – and goes completely against the facts. Indeed, nothing in the research that it was supposed to report on could justify such a sycophantic flood. A few details should allow it to be dismantled, without it being necessary to go into overly technical discussions.

Let's start with the most recent study.[175] Performed on adult subjects, this has nothing to do with video games. It simply confirms that there are specific difficulties in integrating audiovisual information in some dyslexics. The question of video games appears very allusively, at the end of the article, when the authors suggest that these tools could perhaps help to resolve the audiovisual disorder identified by the study. Given such rudimentary speculation, one may still feel indignant when a major daily paper has the gall to headline: 'Action video games recommended for dyslexics'.[176] Likewise, a reporter trumpets on prime-time national radio that 'a recent Oxford University study shows action video games could help fight dyslexia by accustoming the brain to link images to sound'.[177] If this kind of hallucination is to be granted a seal of approval as a contribution to the popularization of science, then Rudyard Kipling will soon have to be awarded the Nobel Prize in medicine for his tale of the origin of the camel's hump.[178]

The problem posed by the second study is more subtle, but just as fundamental. In this work, conducted at the University of Padua, Italy, the authors measured the speed of reading in dyslexic children aged 10 years.[179] For 12 hours, spread over 2 weeks, two similar populations (incredibly small: ten subjects only) were exposed to different sequences of the same video game (*Rayman Raving Rabbids*): for the 'experimental' group, rapid ('action') sequences, and for the 'control' group, slow ('neutral') sequences. At the end of this exposure, only the children in the experimental group reported a significant improvement in their decoding ability: they read the words a little faster without making more mistakes. The gain reached 23 syllables per minute, or about ten words. To understand what this means, you have to know that a 10-year-old Italian dyslexic child reads approximately 95 syllables per minute (roughly 45 words).[180,181] A non-dyslexic child reaches 290 syllables (approximately 140 words). In other words, after exposure to play, children with dyslexia still had a terrible deficit: they had gone, roughly, from 45 to 55 words per minute, which was 2.5 times less than children without dyslexia. Therefore, to suggest that 'Video games "teach dyslexic children to read"'[182] seems exaggerated to say the least. This is all the more true as there is also a serious difference between decoding and reading. Just because a child with dyslexia decodes words marginally faster does not mean that she will better understand what she is reading; and it is still, in the final analysis, this understanding that defines reading! The problem is obviously mentioned by the authors of the study and it is a real shame that the army of digital lackeys missed the clarification: 'considering that children with dyslexia could present reading comprehension problems as a consequence of the core reading decoding deficit [they aren't even sure!], further studies could directly investigate the possible effect of action video games on this higher level reading parameter'. In other words, it is not known whether the modest improvement seen in decoding skills in a very small group of dyslexic children influences the reading itself, but it would be nice to test it one of these days. It seems that there is still a long way to go from this cautious scientific reality to the media emphasis previously described. But this little compromise with reality is nothing, let's face it, compared with the startling inaccuracy of other statements like: 'playing fast-paced video games helped improve dyslexic children's reading speed more than a year of intense, traditional therapies could'.[173] Actually, it's not a year of therapy that is at stake in the study but, according to the words of the authors, '1 year of spontaneous reading development [i.e. of development without therapy]'[179] – rather a different matter. But hey, even if it means talking nonsense, you might as well go for it.

The worst part is that even if one admitted that the game *Rayman Ravid Rabbids* really improves the reading ability of dyslexic children (and we are far from doing so!), the press articles mentioned above would mostly still be quite misleading. In fact, in many cases the formulas used suggest, through their generalizations, that the beneficial influence of action video games on learning to read concerns, in fact, all children and video games. For example, according to some journalists, 'honing visual attention boosts reading ability',[174] or 'a study from the University of Padua throws cold water on the idea that video games are bad for the brains of young children',[183] or

video games are often accused of making children aggressive, but what is less well known is that they have medical benefits

119

[...] Researchers had dyslexic children play video games, such as *Rayman*, for 9 sessions of 80 minutes per day. They realized that in just 12 hours, the children had gained a reading speed similar to that acquired after a year of conventional treatment [*sic*], while having fun. This is very good news, therefore, especially for children, who finally have a valid excuse to skip homework and play at the console![177]

These extrapolations are certainly unfounded. Indeed, not all video games have the same structure, and what is true for *Rayman* may not be true for *Minecraft*, *Fortnite*, *Super Mario* or *Grand Theft Auto* (*GTA*). And even if we admit that the supposed positive effect can be generalized to all types of play, how can we be sure of a benefit in children without dyslexia? And again, even if we accept this point, how do we know that the final risk–benefit ratio will turn out to be positive and that the negative influences will not outweigh the few positive effects observed – especially if the exposure exceeds 12 hours and becomes chronic? Many studies establish, as we shall see, that action video games do not have only positive virtues in terms of sleep, addiction, concentration or academic success: far from it. But why needlessly worry parents, readers and listeners with these kinds of secondary details?

In short, the scientific studies mentioned here are undoubtedly interesting. But in view of their methodological weaknesses and the questions they leave open, one can wonder about their formidable media impact and the total lack of perspective shown by journalists. We can also notice that, once again, the bias relates to video games which really do seem to have some very enviable qualities – it is time to say a few words about these.

Optimized visual attention (and other alleged virtues of action video games)

In the digital realm, with the exception of questions of violence, which I will come back to in detail in the next chapter, the most accomplished propagandist work undoubtedly concerns the supposed benefits of so-called 'action' video games for attention. This is not a recent case. It began in 2003, with the publication of a study reporting that these games could have a favourable influence on certain components of visual attention.[184] This result triggered an avalanche of studies, many of which, as I will show below, confirmed the phenomenon. The result was a persistent stream of approving media allegations: 'first-person-shooter video games sharply improve visual attention skills';[185] 'They are accused of developing aggression, but action games are above all very effective in improving attention, vision and reaction speed';[186] 'Various studies have shown that the practice of shooting games rapidly and lastingly improves the concentration and visual acuity of players';[187] 'Video games can help develop greater mental focus';[188] etc. The enthusiasm reached its peak in 2013, in the context of an astounding opinion from the French Academy of Sciences.[189] The impact was phenomenal (and remains lasting). It must be said that the message was far-reaching. It said that 'some action video games aimed at children and adolescents improve their visual attention and concentration skills and thereby facilitate rapid decision-making'. In other words, 'the strategies that the player is invited to put into play can stimulate the learning of skills: the ability to concentrate, innovate, make quick decisions and resolve problems and tasks collectively'. Unfortunately, the only support the authors provided was one reference[190] – and one which, strangely enough, said nothing about the majority of the assertions presented. We are still there today. The media fable so perfectly synthesized by the French Academy of Sciences remains as ubiquitous as it is ill-founded.

Gamers more creative?

There is no doubt that the video games industry is highly innovative; but it would be utterly specious to extend this capability from designer to user. To date, there is no scientific evidence, even of an embryonic kind, capable of validating such an extrapolation. There is also no plausible theoretical hypothesis to explain how *Fortnite*, *Super Mario*, *Call of Duty* or *GTA* could boost the inventiveness of those who play them. Conversely, there are many reasons to conclude that such an idea is fundamentally inept. Indeed, the capacities for creativity and innovation do not exist in absolute terms. They are articulated and organized on the basis of all the knowledge acquired in a discipline. In other words, to cross a border, you must first reach it. This is why, contrary to some popular beliefs, innovators never come out of nowhere; before producing anything of note, they spent a considerable amount of time mastering their field in depth.[191-3] As Anders Ericsson, one of the foremost international specialists on the subject, explains,

One thing we do know about these innovators is that they, almost without exception, have worked to become expert performers in their fields before they started breaking new ground. It makes sense that this should be so: After all, how are you going to come up with a valuable new theory in science or a useful new technique on the violin if you are not intimately familiar with – and able to reproduce – the accomplishments of those who preceded you?[194]

In other words, innovation is not some kind of disembodied general skill that some video game could miraculously instil in us. No; innovation is first and foremost, for any given field, time, work and sweat. Therefore, it seems completely wrong to dare to assert that action video games promote 'innovation'.

Players better equipped to work in groups?

This is yet another perfectly unfounded statement. First, it can be noted that many action video games are played alone. Then, of course, a multitude is not always a guarantee of high performance – far from it. Several studies have reported that creativity is, in the overwhelming majority of cases, the work of solitary minds.[195] As a rule, the group tends to be far less fertile and intelligent than the sum of its individualities. You have a problem? Brainstorm collectively. You'll get far less interesting results than if you had first asked everyone to think by themselves, in their own corner.[196-8]

Moreover, the fundamental question of transfer arises in this case too. Let's say that the players learn to talk to each other, organize and coordinate to solve the problems posed by the game: shooting a mega-zombie, demolishing a tank, etc. In what and how can this 'knowledge' be useful in the real world (apart from – possibly! – some circumstances structurally close to game situations – for example, carrying out security operations in urban war zones)? Where are the studies showing that the skills developed by manipulating the joystick extend to situations unrelated to gaming? Where is the work suggesting that playing action games helps an individual work more effectively in a surgical team? Where are the studies suggesting that *Fortnite* and its associates optimize a player's cooperative performance in a symphony orchestra, football team, sales team or restaurant kitchen? Nowhere, of course. Can this come as any surprise when we realize, yet again, that the ability to cooperate and work in a group depends mainly on a specific disciplinary competence? For the collective to be effective, each individual must know how to blend into the kinetic melody of the whole. But to do this, everyone must be able to effectively carry out their unique part of the work, to interpret the group's actions, to decipher the state of progress of their aims and objectives, etc. How could such specific skills be learned by playing an action video game with a few pals? In short, the claim that playing an action video game improves ability to work together appears to be at best a fairy tale, at worst a piece of propagandist hypocrisy.

Gamers more attentive and faster?

At last: a statement based on concrete data! We're making progress – but this doesn't conceal the lack of precise definition of the terms and concepts being manipulated. Indeed, behind the words used there lurk skills that are, to put it mildly, rather limited. There is no question here, for example, of any ability to pay attention for longer and more effectively to the content of a text. Nor is it a question of a general improvement in decision-making skills. No; what we are talking about is only a slight optimization in the processing time of the visual information received by the brain. In other words, the gamer can respond a little faster than the average layabout to certain visual elements in his environment.[190,199] Thus, when compared to his inexperienced counterparts, the gamer manages to take into account a greater number of visual elements (figure 7, row 1); exhibits a more widely scattered visual attention (figure 7, row 2); identifies more quickly the presence (or absence) of a target element in the visual field (figure 7, row 3); and turns out to be able to detect a little more quickly the preferred direction of movement of a group of interspersed points (figure 7, row 4). Note that the previously mentioned opinion of the French Academy of Sciences referred, on the basis of this last result, but without ever describing it, to 'a generalizable capacity (beyond the game) of probabilistic inference'.[189] This is indeed enough to impress the unconvinced reader.

No one is denying that these studies are interesting. What is problematic is the incredible way the value of their findings is exaggerated. The point calls for two remarks. First, it is necessary to underline the existence of methodological reservations and contradictory observations, likely to cast doubt on the solidity and the generality of the results presented.[202-6] These are doubts that several recent studies have failed to remove – far from it.[207-11] Second, the

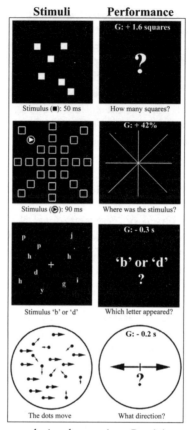

Figure 7. Video games and visual attention. Participants stare at the screen. *Row 1*: squares appear briefly (between 1 and 10; 50 ms). The subject must say how many squares she saw. Gamers (G) show a superior performance. On average, they detect up to 4.9 squares without error, as against only 3.3 for non-gamers.[184] *Row 2*: 'distractors' (squares) and a 'target' object (the triangle in the circle) appear briefly (90 ms). The subject must say on which of the 8 rays the target object appeared. The average success of gamers is higher than that of non-gamers (81% as against 39%).[200] *Row 3*: 'distractors' (letters apart from b and d) and a 'target' letter (b or d) appear. The subject must identify the target letter. Gamers are faster than non-gamers (1.2 s versus 1.5 s).[201] *Row 4*: Dots moving in a more or less coherent way suddenly appear on a screen: between 1 and 50% of the dots go in the same direction (to the right or to the left); the rest move randomly. The subject must determine the preferred direction of movement. On average, gamers respond in 0.6 s, non-gamers in 0.8 s.[201] The superiority of the gamers is real for all tasks. However, it concerns very modest skills; all the more so as the superiorities observed do not transfer, with rare exceptions, to real-life situations. For details, see the text.

124

issue of skill transfer (from attention gained through play to 'real-life' situations) should in fact have been addressed. Obviously, it is easy to argue that playing action games positively impacts on all kinds of motor skills requiring rapid and precise processing of visual flows; for example, playing football.[190] The difficulty lies in proving it. It's especially difficult as the available research is hardly favourable. Indeed, it is now clearly known, with regard to complex visuo-motor skills, that the degree of expertise is in no way linked to the efficiency of the basic functions of attention (supposedly developed by action video games). Take one study on handball, for example: no significant relationship was found between the gamers' skill and their performance in standard tests on visual attention.[212] The authors' conclusion: 'sports expertise effects are unrelated to basic differences in attention – expertise does not appear to produce differences in basic attention and basic differences in attention do not appear to predict eventual expertise'. The same goes for baseball. Professional batters, whose response speed is astounding, are no better than the average person when subjected to attention tasks requiring them, for example, to press a button as quickly as possible in response to the appearance of a visual stimulus.[194,213] This is hardly surprising. In fact, the batter does not react 'after the fact' to adverse behaviours; he anticipates them, that is, he begins to organize his strike long before the ball is pitched. To do this, he focuses his attention early on, looking for the revealing clues in the pitcher's gesture (the axis of his shoulders, the trajectory of his arm, etc.). This kind of talent is not innate. It is built during learning, based on failures, successes, repetitions and, it is important to point out, the specific nature of the discipline. In this regard, the available studies show that visual exploration strategies clearly vary with the task.[214–18] This means that the information collected by the brains of a tennis player, footballer, basketball player, skier, baseball player or racing driver are fundamentally different. In other words, each complex visuomotor skill constructs and mobilizes a unique type of attentional functioning.[194,218,219]

Therefore, the lack of transfer from action video games to complex visuomotor skills is hardly surprising, and you have to be a total joker to assert, as we still hear all too often in the leading media, that the skills potentially acquired by gamers at the cost of intensive practice 'aren't just virtual: they can help you do better in real-life situations, like driving your car'.[220] Let's consider this last activity, as a final example. Research suggests two things: (i) playing action games has no positive influence on driving;[221,222] (ii) on the contrary, the often frantic and euphoric nature of these games favours the emergence of risky and reckless behaviours which lead gamers to drive more frequently without a licence, to have more accidents and to be more often fined or stopped by the police.[223–8]

Obviously, these negative results do not agree with a number of recent newspaper headlines suggesting that 'Playing Mario Kart makes you a better driver, it's been scientifically proven!';[229–31] that a 'Study confirms "Mario Kart" really does make you a better driver: see, mom!';[232] or that 'Playing Mario Kart CAN make you a better driver.'[233] Behind these noisy headlines is a study that unfortunately has nothing to do with a credible driving situation (real or simulated).[234] Experimentally, the case has three stages. First, subjects play a rudimentary video driving game (a sort of very simplistic *Mario Kart*). They are placed in front of a computer screen symbolizing a road opening up before them (they see this road as if they were in the passenger seat of a car). They are asked, using a small steering wheel, to stay in the middle of this road without being 'caught out' by random disturbances (sudden lateral thrusts that make the car deviate from its straight path). The visual environment is as bare as one can imagine: it includes no obstacles, no vehicles, no pedestrians, no trees, no traffic signs, no turns, no intersections – nothing. The screen just shows a horizon (black), a ground (brown) and two red dotted lines (the road). The results show that fans of action video games are somewhat more successful than non-gamers at staying between the two lines. In other words, when regular video action gamers are subjected to a rudimentary new driving video game, they perform better than their novice cronies. Big deal!

In the second phase of the study, participants are subjected to a slightly edited version of the initial game. In the presence of random disturbing forces (this time vertical), they have to use a joystick to control the trajectory of a small red ball moving on a black screen, keeping it horizontal. Here again (what a surprise!), the aficionados of the joystick do better than their inexperienced counterparts. In the third step, finally, two groups of non-gamer participants are formed. For 10 hours, some play *Mario Kart* while others indulge in *Roller Coaster Tycoon III* (a strategy game). At the end of the training period, only members of the *Mario Kart* group have improved their performance of the previous task (keeping the trajectory of a small red ball horizontal on a black screen). It is on the basis of this amazing result, we must admit, that our journalist friends were able to tell their readers that 'Playing the video game *Mario Kart* really does prepare you for the real-world driver's seat'[232] and that 'spending hours in front of *Mario Kart* seems to have unexpected benefits'.[235] From now on, 'you no longer need to spend hours learning the Highway Code to become an outstanding driver'.[230] Indeed, 'Hours of video game training improved players' real-world driving skills. It could be used as a cost-effective way of training drivers in the future.'[233] Quite obviously, as everyone will have understood, a 'better driver' is not an individual who has deciphered the environment better, adapts his speed more flexibly to external constraints, interprets the rules of the road more aptly, gauges the stopping distances more accurately, anticipates the behaviour of other users (pedestrians, motorcyclists, cyclists, motorists) more precisely, etc. No! A 'better driver' is someone who performs better when asked to keep the movement of a red ball horizontal on a black screen, in the presence of random disturbing forces.

To conclude from the study discussed here that *Mario Kart* makes us 'better drivers' is just surreal. Scientifically, the only use of this work is to show that frequently playing action video games makes our life a little easier when we have to pick up a game that we don't know. The result is undoubtedly interesting, but basically it turns out to be quite foreign to the extravagant messages transmitted by the media to their users. As noted above, when considering real driving situations, the supposedly better ability of gamers not only disappears, but turns into a negative (mainly due to a greater risk-taking propensity). And really, you have to be completely talking through your hat to say, on the basis of the study described here (carried out, remember, in an absolute environmental desert), that action video games make us better drivers because they 'help motorists spot hazards in the real world'.[233] The author of this glorious tirade is omitting just one little practical detail: to spot the dangers of the road, you have to know where to find them; that is, you have to know where to look, and when! However, this type of knowledge can be acquired only through real and repeated experience of the road. For those who (still!) doubt this, one recent study recorded the eye scans of 'real' drivers and the users of driving video games. Result: 'gamers without real driving experience do not have a pattern of visual exploration of the road that is functional for real driving [...]. Virtual driving in video games does not aid in the development of an adequate exploration of road patterns.'[222]

In short, it is therefore possible (and undoubtedly probable,[236] although the matter is still up for debate),[237] that action video games improve, not our attention or our decision-making abilities in general, but certain characteristics of our visual attention. The problem is that these improvements remain 'local' in the overwhelming majority of cases; they do not extend to 'real-life' situations. This means, in plain language, that playing a video action game essentially teaches us to ... play that game and similar ones. Of course, some skills may be generalizable when reality imposes the same demands as the game. This is the case, for example, with the handling of a surgical endoscope[238,239] or the distant piloting of combat drones.[240] But apart from these particular situations, it is quite illusory, as numerous studies confirm, to hope for a significant transfer of aptitudes from video games to reality.[194,241-7] Thus, in the words of one recent large-scale meta-analysis:

> We found no evidence of a causal relationship between playing video games and enhanced cognitive ability. Video game training thus represents no exception to the general difficulty of obtaining far transfer [i.e. generalizations on the basis of a particular area, such as learning chess, to another area, such as memorizing a poem] [...]. Our results support the hypothesis according to which expertise acquisition relies to a large extent on domain-specific, and hence nontransferable, information. By contrast, those theories predicting the occurrence of far transfer after video game training (e.g., 'learning to learn') and cognitive training in general are not supported.[248]

Players with better focus?

This is yet another made-up story. This may seem surprising, as the assertion is repeated so often in the mainstream media, but there are no data in the scientific literature that could support it. It is based only on a fallacious extrapolation of the aforementioned elements relating to visual attention. It's so easy to go from this latter to attention as a general faculty, and then, quite simply, to concentration. Such a trend, of course, is not specific to the aforementioned opinion of the French Academy of Sciences.[189] It is common for our journalist friends to indulge in the hastiest simplifications, explaining, for example, in an article soberly entitled 'These video games that do you good', that 'virtual armed struggle has another interesting virtue: it improves attentional control, i.e. the ability to concentrate on a task without being distracted';[249] or, in a documentary for the general public modestly titled 'Video games: the new masters of the world', claiming that experiments are carried out 'to measure the attentional capacity of players, that is to say their faculty of concentration'.[250] Recently Stanislas Dehaene himself, an eminent

128

French neuroscientist, president of the Scientific Council of National Education and member of the French Academy of Sciences, told the millions of listeners of a major national radio station that we should not 'demonize video games [...]. Even action video games, "shooters", have a positive effect on education because they increase children's concentration and attention span.'[251]

The problem, as everyone will understand, is that behind the generic terms 'attention' or 'concentration' lie very disparate functional and neurophysiological realities.[252–4] In the first sense, the dictionaries tell us, concentration means 'the action of bringing together in a centre or at a point what was originally dispersed'; applied to the cognitive domain, it means 'the action of gathering the forces of one's mind and bringing them to bear on a single object'. Likewise, attention characterizes 'a tension of the mind towards one object to the exclusion of all others'. These definitions reflect the brain mechanics of focused attention quite well.[70,252] Indeed, when the brain 'concentrates', two things happen. First, the activity of regions important for the task concerned increases. Second, the activity of unnecessary regions, especially those related to processing disruptive external sensory flows, subsides.[a] This second mechanism plays an essential role in our ability to ignore unwelcome information and therefore, ultimately, to stay focused on the objective pursued.

When worried parents are told that action video games improve their child's 'attention' or 'concentration', it is this hyper-focusing of cognitive resources that they spontaneously think of; an absolutely essential process, we must emphasize, in intellectual functioning and, consequently, in academic success.[256–64] Basically, for the general public, to be attentive is to be 'in your zone', focused on the sole task at hand. Attention can then be seen as a mechanism that concentrates all light at one point, and actively leaves everywhere else in the dark. The problem is that video games have the very opposite effect. They suppress the focused light beam and light up the whole room. This is because of the intimate nature of these games and the fact that they are structurally oriented to the outside world. In so doing, they require a generously scattered attention. To be effective, the player must constantly sweep the visual space. She must be able to spot without delay, in the succession of the scenes presented, the

---

[a] For example, if someone strokes your fingertip while you are focused on a task in mental arithmetic, the information that travels to sensory brain areas is significantly attenuated compared to a condition where your finger is being stroked without you being focused on arithmetic.[255]

appearance of any threatening stimulus or relevant visual configuration – even at the extreme periphery of the field.

Some mischievous spirits might be amused, no doubt, that the aptitude of our chimpanzee cousins is, in these areas, far superior to that of a standard human being;[265] and that if the goal is to provide our children with the attentional baggage of a laboratory primate, then video games are indeed a very suitable teaching tool. But let's not wax too sardonic, and simply note that, in terms of action video games, an optimal achievement can be obtained only through the development of a scattered exogenous attention, i.e. one that is vigilant to the slightest movement in the outside world. It means an attention whose properties are, by nature, exactly opposite to those of concentration. In one case, we spread out and try not to miss any external environmental signals; in the other, we focus and try to ignore as much as possible the disturbing influence of these same signals. To amalgamate these different types of attention merely because the word 'attention' is used in both cases is inappropriate, to say the least. All the more so since it has been clearly shown that the process of dispersing attention causes serious damage to concentration: when we train the subject's capacities for rapid visual processing, we also increase, as the other side of the coin, her tendency to be distracted by agitations in her environment.[266] In other words, it is then literally *distractibility* that will become part and parcel of our individual functioning.

In practice, the emergence of increased distractibility, actively learned and diligently implemented at the heart of the brain structure, explains why video games have, beyond their potentially positive effects on visual attention, a notoriously damaging impact on focused attention, i.e. concentration.[267–75] We will have the opportunity to come back to this in detail in the next section. Even the researchers most involved in demonstrating the positive influences of action video games on visual attention admit the reality of this dissociation. Daphné Bavelier, for example, stated in a leading scientific journal, a few months before being interviewed by the editors of the aforementioned report of the French Academy of Sciences, that:

> If one means the ability to rapidly and efficiently filter visual distractors that are quickly presented (that is, visual attention), then clearly playing action games greatly enhances this ability. However, if one means the ability to sustain focus on a slowly evolving stream of information, such as paying attention in class, there is recent work that suggests that total screen time, and video game playing time in particular, may have negative effects.[276]

Another researcher also explained, in the same article, that, in his view,

> the same attentional skills that are learned by playing action games (such as a wider field of view and attention to the periphery) are part of the problem. Although these are good skills in a computer-mediated environment, they are a liability in school when the child is supposed to ignore the kid fidgeting in the chair next to him and focus on only one thing.

It's a real shame (and it causes real harm) that this kind of distinction is so often overlooked because, by lumping together the concepts of visual attention, attention as such and concentration, we end up making scientific data say the complete opposite of what they really say.

That being said, here is one last little point – a secondary one, no doubt, but revealing. A journalist who found that her curiosity was piqued by the case took a closer look at the above-mentioned text by the French Academy of Sciences. The article, originally titled 'Video games: the academy is partial',[a] suggests that this document was not concerned only with science. Ultimately, it turned out to be very useful, the journalist tells us, to 'lift a legislative lock which, since 2007, has prevented the video game industry from benefiting from tax credits for the development of PEGI 18 games, that is to say games intended for adults and containing violent or pornographic scenes likely to arouse a feeling of disgust in the viewer'.[277] This was a helping hand extended to our industrialists because, as one senator stated, 'To tell the truth, I was most surprised that this amendment passed [...] We had to make a gesture to prevent the brain drain towards North America, where significant tax credits facilitate the complex and costly development of PEGI 18 games.'[277] The argument is worth hearing. But did it need further support? Was it necessary to back it up with such a partisan 'scientific' report – a report that, even today, feeds into the worst demago-geeky propaganda? Was it necessary to inflict such heavy damage on the credibility of a centuries-old official institution, supposed to guarantee the integrity of science? These questions are not trivial at a time when, through the unleashing of the most furious conspiracy theories, a generalized suspicion of public discourse is developing.

---

[a] It was later given the title 'When the Academy of Sciences inclines towards a favourable view of video games'.[277]

131

A ruined capacity for concentration

So behind the seemingly unitary concept of 'attention' lie disparate behavioural and neurophysiological realities. Certain activities, such as action video games, demand 'distributed' attention, extrinsically stimulated and wide open to the hustle and bustle of the world. Conversely, other practices, such as reading a book, writing an overview or solving a mathematical problem, require 'focused' attention, intrinsically maintained and not very permeable to outside disturbances or parasitic thoughts. In the rest of this text, I will use the qualifiers 'exogenous' or 'visual' to characterize the type of attention developed by action video games. At the same time, in keeping with common usage, I will simply speak of 'attention' or 'concentration' to characterize the 'focused' attention mobilized by reflective activities such as reading a book.

Overwhelming evidence

To date, almost all of the available studies converge to show that screens for recreation have, overall,[274,278,279] a profoundly damaging impact on the ability to concentrate. In other words, in this respect, video games[267-73,275,280] prove to be just as harmful as television[261,271,272,279-85] and mobile media.[286-9] A meta-analysis of this topic confirmed, without the slightest doubt, the existence of a positive correlation between the exposure to screens for recreation (video games and/or television) and attention disorders.[279] The relationship measured had a strength comparable to that observed between IQ and academic performance[290,291] or, alternatively, between smoking and lung cancer.[292] The individual impact of video games turned out to be exactly the same as that of television. Likewise, non-violent content appeared to be just as harmful as violent content.

By way of illustration, let us mention one long-term study that established that each hour per day spent in front of the small screen when the child was at primary school increased by almost 50% the probability of attention deficit disorder in primary school.[282] An identical result was reported in a subsequent study[261] showing that spending between 1 and 3 hours in front of the television daily at 14 years old increased by a multiple of 1.4 the risk of observing attention difficulties at 16 years old. Beyond 3 hours, the figures were almost triple (figure 8). These are disturbing figures in the light of a complementary result showing that the existence of attention deficit disorder at 16 almost quadrupled the risk of failure at college at 22. Many studies have in fact, as we have already pointed out, confirmed the fundamental importance of endogenous attention for academic success.[256–60,262–4] In another study, the authors directly compared the effect of video games and television in two populations, one of children (6 to 12 years old), the other of young adults (18 to 32 years old).[271] The results showed that the two activities affected attention in a quantitatively equivalent manner, regardless of age. On average, participants who exceeded two hours of daily use (TV and/or video games) were twice as likely to experience attention difficulties. Interestingly, the analyses indicated that initial screen exposure (TV and video games) predicted a worsening of attention deficit disorder during the follow-up period (13 months). In yet another study, comparable results were obtained for mobile use in subjects aged 12 to 20 years.[289] Those who owned a smartphone were, compared to their non-equipped counterparts, almost three times more likely to have attention deficit disorders. Recreational consumption (games, videos, etc.) turned out to be particularly harmful. In fact, individuals who spent more than 1 hour per day on this type of activity had a near-doubling of their attentional risk compared to those who stayed below 20 minutes. These observations are worrying, but could almost seem 'reasonable' in view of recent research, carried out on 5-year-old children.[293] It was then the total screen time that was considered (TV, consoles, mobile devices, etc.). As a result, subjects with a digital consumption greater than 2 hours per day were six times more likely than those who did not exceed 30 minutes to have attention deficit disorder.

For sceptics, one final study is undoubtedly worth mentioning here. It comes not from an academic group, but from Microsoft Canada's marketing department.[294] This work, curiously made public, begins by explaining that the attention capacities of our fair species have continued to deteriorate for 15 years; they have now reached an all-time low and are lower than those of ... a goldfish. This decline is directly linked to the development of digital technologies. Thus, in the words of the document, 'Digital lifestyles affect the ability to remain focused for extended periods of time. Canadians with more digital lifestyles (those who consume more media, are multi-screeners, social media enthusiasts, or earlier adopters of technology) struggle to focus in environments where prolonged attention is needed [....] They're suckers for novelty.' The conclusions for the use of advertising networks are clear: 'Hook consumers right off the

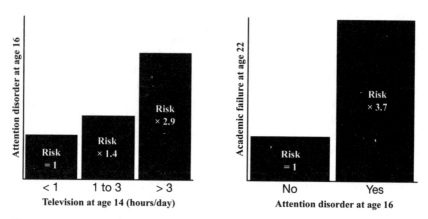

Figure 8. Impact of screens on attention. The risk of observing attention deficit disorder at age 16 increases with time spent watching television at age 14 (left panel); at the same time, the risk of failure at college at age 22 increases significantly in adolescents with attention deficit disorder at age 16 (right panel).[261] For details, see the text.

bat with clear and concise messaging that's communicated as early as possible [...] Be different. Stand out and challenge the norm.' In ordinary language, this could be translated as: 'dear partners, for your marketing campaigns, don't extend them for more than a few seconds if you want to stay within the attention span of your dear goldfish consumers; and opt for incisive, touting, provocative, shocking, earthy messages if you don't want your communication to be drowned anonymously in the raging ocean of digital stimulation'. An entire programme!

Learning to disperse attention

The negative impact of screens on concentration involves many complementary mechanisms. These act in a more or less direct way, depending on the time taken. Take sleep, for example. We now know that there is a strong link between daytime attentional functioning and the effectiveness of shutting things down completely at night.[295-8] In other words, when the brain is not getting enough and/or not the right quality of sleep, it cannot concentrate effectively on its daily tasks. However, it is clearly established (I will be coming back to this in the next chapter) that the greater the digital consumption, the more the quality and duration of sleep are affected. This is a major

134

source of inattention. In this regard, I quite often talk about screens to primary and secondary school pupils. I am systematically struck by the number of drowsy pupils struggling to keep their eyes open and yawning their heads off. Whatever their desire to learn, these children are physiologically incapable of absorbing the slightest knowledge. This is all the more true as many of them see their exogenous attention being overtaxed every morning, before school, by video games or exciting audiovisual programmes.[91] However, it is now established that, over the long term, this practice impairs the ability to concentrate and, as a result, intellectual performance.[299-302] One frequently cited study illustrates this nicely. Children aged 4 to 5 were subjected to various cognitive tests after being exposed, for 9 minutes, to a fantastic, quickly paced cartoon (*SpongeBob SquarePants*).[303] The results were significantly worse than those obtained under two 'control' conditions (9 minutes of colouring or watching a slow-paced educational cartoon). In an 'impulsivity' test, for example, children had in front of them a bell and two plates: one plate contained two sweets, the other ten. The instructions were as follows: if you wait for me to come back (after 5.5 minutes), you can eat the ten sweets; if you don't want to wait, you can ring the bell at any time and eat the two sweets. Participants resisted for 146 seconds in the 'SpongeBob condition', compared to 250 seconds, on average, in the 'control conditions' (+ 71%). In another 'concentration' task, the experimenter said to the child: 'When I say touch your head, I want you to touch your toes, but when I say touch your toes, I want you to touch your head.' After ten attempts, the instruction changed (shoulder/knee); and after ten new attempts, it changed again, one last time (head/shoulder). The child got two points for a successful attempt and one point for a wrong but corrected attempt (the child first went to the wrong target, then returned to the correct one). Participants totalled 20 points in the 'SpongeBob condition', compared to 32, on average, in 'control conditions' (+ 60%). In short, exciting the exogenous circuits of attention before asking a child to bring his concentration to bear on all kinds of reflective tasks is not a good idea; in the same way, to use an analogy, it is not particularly wise to treat yourself to a shot of caffeine in the evening before going to sleep.

In addition to these occasional damaging effects, there is obviously, in the long term, the conditioning action of an increasingly distracting environment. Mobile tools are then on the front line. In this area, even if we admit the extreme variability of usage studies (mainly polls), we cannot help but be struck by the magnitude of the problem. Every day, on average, smartphone owners, whether adults or adolescents, experience between fifty and one hundred and fifty interruptions, or one every 10 to 30 minutes; even one every 7 to 20 minutes if we remove 7 hours of sleep from our days.[252,294,304,305] Half of these interruptions are linked to the occurrence of intrusive external requests (messages, texts, phone calls, etc.).[306,307] The other half come from a compulsive endogenous movement. This latter seems to be innate. It reflects the progressive selection, during the biological process of evolution, of the most 'curious' individuals, i.e. those most quick to collect and analyse information coming from their environment (in terms of opportunities or dangers). This curiosity is itself fuelled by the activation of the brain's reward system.[a,252,308-10] In other words, if we also frantically consult our mobile devices, without any objective necessity, this is on the one hand because we are (unconsciously) afraid of missing vital information, and on the other hand because the fulfilment of the verification process gives us a little dopamine shot – all very pleasant (and addictive). This dual mechanism is now frequently called by its acronym FoMO: Fear of Missing Out.[311-13]

In keeping with this idea, recent research has reported how difficult it is to resist 'the call of the mobile phone'.[314] A diverse population of pupils (from school to university) was observed during a quarter-hour work session. On average, participants only spent 10 minutes studying. Despite the inquisitive presence of an experimenter, they couldn't manage to exceed 6 minutes of concentration before pouncing as though they were starving on their electronic gadgets. Six minutes is arguably better than Microsoft's standard goldfish;[294] but it's still not huge! This finding echoes another previously cited study, showing that just having a laptop close by occupies one's attention enough to disrupt intellectual performance – even if the device remains perfectly inert. We can associate this observation with the existence of a bitter internal fight waged against the impulsive need to 'check' the environment, i.e. to make sure that we have not missed some important information. The process is similar to that which takes place when an external summons arises (beep, ringing, vibration, etc.), the only difference having to do with the nature of the trigger stimulus (exogenous versus endogenous). In both cases, the result is the same: cognitive functioning is disturbed, concentration suffers and intellectual performance declines.[315,316]

What needs to be realized here is that an interruption doesn't have to be persistent to be damaging. In the words of a recent

---

[a] See above, p. 20, note a.

study, 2 to 3 seconds of inattention are more than enough to 'derail the train of thought'[317] – probably because the latter is surprisingly fragile and, once destabilized, it does not recover easily. Suppose, for example, that you are asked to write a report. You're ordering your arguments, selecting them, sorting them, structuring them – and suddenly your phone vibrates or beeps. Whether you like it or not, your attention is immediately directed to the incoming message. Several questions follow: should I look, should I wait, should I answer, who can it be, etc.? The problem is that, even if you quickly decide to ignore the disturbance, the damage is done: it is no longer, as one might think, a matter of retrieving the thread of a momentarily interrupted reflection faithfully stored somewhere in your brain, a reflection that you just need to 'recharge' at the heart of the neural machinery. No, after the interruption, you have to rebuild the reflective flow, find its constituent parts and reassemble them to return to the original state before the interruption. The time and energy spent doing this obviously affect cognitive reliability and productivity significantly.[318–21] And this is just the most favourable case. The detriment is automatically worse when one's thought is activated by information offered as a flow, in a class, during a conference or in a simple dialogue. In these situations, a suspension of attention creates a double breach in one's access to information and the thinking process; and this obviously proves not very conducive to understanding the content presented. This point was discussed at length in the previous chapter when the impacts of digital education on cognitive development were discussed. Then there are the numerous experimental data showing, in the case of driving a car, the incredible way mobile notifications and uses can occupy one's attention and, therefore, massively increase the risk of accidents.[322,323] For text messages, for example, this risk is twenty-three times higher, according to the results of a large study by the US Department of Transportation.[324] This doesn't prevent 50% of parents from checking their messages while driving, in the presence of their children; 30% even allow themselves to actively text![325] By saying this, my goal is not to make anyone feel guilty, but to underline the incredibly compulsive power of our mobile tools.

Multitasking

Beyond these problems of interruption, it is the general subject of multitasking that must be addressed. Of course, we are told that young people have changed, that their brains are now different, sharper, faster, more suited to the fragmented structure of digital spaces. We are told that after millennia of being held back, the neural organization of the younger generations has finally broken free from the shackles of sequential accomplishment (task after task) to achieve the nirvana of simultaneous operations (multitasking). It's a nice story. But it's absurd. Young or old, modern or old, the human brain is completely incapable of doing two things at the same time without losing precision, accuracy and productivity.[321,326–8] Our brain is not a computer processor. All it can do when faced with multiple issues at the same time is juggle.[329–32] Roughly speaking, what then happens is: (i) we deal with the first task (like reading a text), then we decide to move on to the second; (ii) we then suspend the processing linked to task 1 and store the elements acquired in a temporary memory; (iii) then we tackle task 2 (for example, replying to Rachel's messages on Snapchat); (iv) until we decide it's time to return to task 1; (v) we then interrupt task 2 and store the relevant elements in a temporary memory; (vi) then we retrieve the data relating to the first task (hoping that nothing has been forgotten and/or corrupted) and resume our work where (supposedly) we left off; (vii) and so on. Each transition takes time and leads to errors, omissions and loss of information. Moreover, for each task, cognitive engagement can only be partial and mutilated. Indeed, just to operate at all, the juggling process mobilizes a very important portion of the brain's resources. The target tasks must then be processed with the neural residue still available. In the end, the understanding of the text read and the quality of the answers given to poor Rachel are likely to end up very far from the desirable optimum.

But that's not all. It's also probable that the multitasking process will affect the storage of the operations carried out.[333–5] Indeed, there is a strong link between the retention of a given content and the level of attention that has been given to the processing of that content – a level which, in energy terms, reflects the extent of the cognitive effort made.[129] In multitasking, however, attention skims over tasks more than it penetrates them. It's no wonder, then, that memorization, too, is adversely affected when we do multiple things at once.

The same mechanism accounts for the considerable superiority of the pencil to the computer for note-taking tasks.[336,337] In this regard, researchers have reported that it is faster and less painful to type than to write (in individuals who have at least some practice in typing, obviously). Therefore, while the keyboard allows relatively fluid and exhaustive note taking, the hand forces one to be parsimonious. In doing so, it imposes an effort of synthesis and reformulation which is very favourable to the memorization process. This link between memorization and cognitive effort is also quite easy to isolate experimentally. It has thus been shown, for example, that the same written information is better retained when it is presented in a less easily readable format.[338] Likewise, it has been established that the memorization of lexical lists was significantly higher when the target words had a few letters left off (which made them more difficult to decipher).[339]

Making inattention a core aspect of the brain

The distracting potential of digital worlds is therefore considerable. Resisting this surge of temptation is difficult; and all the more so since the lure of our beloved digital tools activates, as we have seen, the most intimate flaws in our neuronal organization. Our children are young, it is true; but their brain is ancestral. It is genetically programmed to acquire information and receive a 'reward' – in the form of a shot of dopamine – whenever it succeeds.[252,308–10] This reality is one that the economic protagonists of the Internet have mastered perfectly.[340,341] Not long ago, Sean Parker, the former president of Facebook, admitted that social networks had been conceived, in all lucidity, to 'exploit a vulnerability in human psychology'.[342] For him, the issue that motivates the people who create and manage these networks is: 'How do we consume as much of your time and conscious attention as possible?'[342,343] In this context, to keep you captive,

> we have to release a little dopamine to you, on a sufficiently regular basis. Hence the likes or the comments you receive on a photo, a post ... This will impel you to contribute more and more and therefore to receive more and more comments and likes, etc. It's a form of endless loop in which you are judged by the number of responses.[343]

This idea can be found almost word for word coming from Chamath Palihapitiya, former vice-president of user growth at Facebook.[344,345] This penitent executive now declares he feels a 'tremendous guilt' for having worked on 'tools that are ripping apart the social fabric of how society works'.[344] His conclusion is clear: 'I can't control them [his former Facebook employers]. I can control my decision, which is that I don't use that shit. I can control my kids' decisions, which is that they're not allowed to use that shit.'[344] Athena Chavarria, who has also worked for Facebook, says more or less the same thing: 'I am convinced the devil lives in our phones and is wreaking havoc on our children.'[346] Is this an exaggerated conclusion? Not if we look at the growing number of studies showing that multitasking behaviours associated with the incessant demands of the digital world (especially social networks) foster cognitive inattention and impulsivity at the heart not only of our behavioural habits,[335,347–53] but also, more intimately, of our brain functioning.[354]

In the light of these results, it is of course legitimate to consider the existence of an inverse causality. As indicated in one key article, the question then arises as follows: 'Does heavier media multi-tasking cause cognitive and neural differences, or do individuals with such pre-existing differences tend toward more media multitasking behavior?'[355] The answer is now known: it is multitasking which, at least in part, is the source of the above-mentioned adaptations. A first piece of evidence comes from a recent experimental study in which a group of unequipped young adults were given a smartphone for three months.[356] At the end of this (relatively short) period, participants showed a very significant decline in performance on a rapid arith-metic test that required close attention. In addition, they saw their level of cognitive impulsivity increase in proportion to the time spent on the smartphone.

A second and more decisive evidence of causation can be found in the rather gloomy conclusions of several recent animal studies. The underlying idea is quite simple: what you can't do with humans, sometimes you can do with animals. In particular, you can set up protocols for stimulating exogenous attention similar to those produced by the digital environments to which children are exposed, and assess the developmental impact that ensues. One remark is in order, however. It is not a question here of putting the animals in an enriched environment, i.e. in a physical and social environment favourable to explorations, interactions and active learning.[a] Rather, it is a matter of subjecting them to a repetition of exogenous sound, visual and/or olfactory sensory stimulation. Simply put, we could say that this difference between protocols of enrichment on the one hand and sensory solicitation on the other covers the semantic duality of the verb 'stimulate'. Indeed, this means both 'to put someone or something in the conditions suitable for making her act

[a] Typically, in this case, animals are reared in groups, in spacious cages, with attractive physical features favourable to exploration (balls, ramps, wheels, tunnels, etc.) and regularly replaced.

or react' and 'to submit someone to an excitation, to the action of a stimulus'.[357] Enrichment involves the first meaning; sensory stimulation the second. The impact of these two approaches on the social, emotional, cognitive and brain development of animals is obviously very different: the enrichment situations turn out to be extremely positive,[103,104,358] while the protocols of sensory stimulation are seriously harmful.[359] It is this second point that concerns us here. It was first investigated in mice, by Dimitri Christakis's team at the University of Washington.[360] The animals were subjected to audiovisual stimulation reproducing the effects of television. A 6-hour daily exposure was maintained over a 42-day period spanning the infancy and adolescence of the rodents. The latter heard cartoon soundtracks for young people (for example *Pokemon* or *Bakugan*). This sound flow, of moderate intensity (equivalent to what a child typically hears watching TV), was associated with the operation of coloured light sources (green, red, blue and yellow). In adulthood, compared to standard mice, the stimulated mice were found to be hyperactive, as well as less stressed by risks and more prone to taking them (for example, in moving away from cage walls or dark spaces). They also showed significant learning and memorization difficulties. The same experimental protocol was used in a subsequent study.[361] The authors confirmed the emergence of hyperactive behaviours without an increase in stress level (the latter parameter this time being measured directly on the basis of blood samples of the stress hormone corticosterone). However, and this is an essential point, the study also showed that the stimulated animals were more vulnerable to addiction – a vulnerability itself associated with profound changes in the brain reward circuit. In humans, this circuit plays a major role in addiction pathologies and attention deficit hyperactivity disorder (ADHD), two problems that are often linked.[362-4]

However, these results are not specific to audiovisual stimulation. They are expressed in a similar way in the context of olfactory manipulations.[365] Recent research has studied two populations of rats. The first (experimental group) was subjected daily, for 1 hour, over a period of 5 weeks (roughly corresponding to the animal's adolescence), to a succession of different odours (one every 5 minutes). The second (control group) was for its part exposed to a single odour (resulting from the mixture of all the odours presented to the rats of the first group). In adulthood, the animals in the experimental group had significant disturbances in attention, compared to their counterparts in the control group.

Obviously, as pointed out above, it is impossible, for obvious ethical reasons, to conduct this kind of experiment in humans. However, several old studies, carried out in crèches or in socially disadvantaged families, have confirmed the conclusions of the animal studies reported here. This work shows that the magnitude of ambient noise and, more generally, of the level of sensory stimulation has a significant negative impact on cognitive development,[366-8] and in particular on attention skills.[369]

Taken together, all these data therefore strongly suggest that an excess of sensory stimulation during childhood and adolescence has a negative effect on brain deployment. Too many images, sounds and various other stimuli seem to create conditions favourable to the occurrence of concentration deficits, learning disabilities, symptoms of hyperactivity and addictive behaviour. It is certainly tempting to reconcile these findings with epidemiological observations showing a sharp increase in ADHD diagnoses (and associated drug prescriptions) over the past two decades.[370-2] It is also tempting to recall that the exposure to screens for recreation is, apart from its previously documented effects on concentration, significantly associated with the risk of ADHD in children and adolescents.[279,293,373,374]

In conclusion

The main lesson of this chapter is that screens undermine the three most essential pillars of child development.

The first concerns human interactions. The more time the child spends with his smartphone, TV, computer, tablet or game console, the more intra-family exchanges deteriorate in quantity and quality. Likewise, the more mum and dad immerse themselves in the digital labyrinth, the less available they are for their children. This twofold trend would be harmless if the screens provided the child with adequate brain 'nourishment', with a nutritional value equal to or greater than that of living and embodied intercourse. But this is not the case. When it comes to development, the screen is a furnace while humans are a forge.

The second concerns language. In this area, the action of screens operates along two complementary axes. First, by affecting the volume and quality of early verbal exchanges. Second, by hindering entry into the world of writing. Of course, beyond the age of 3, certain forms of so-called 'educational' audiovisual content can teach a child some lexical elements. What is thereby gained is, however, infinitely more time-consuming, fragmented and superficial than what is offered by 'real life'. In other words, in terms of language development, it's not because it is preferable to put the child in front of a screen rather than lock her up alone in the darkness of a broom closet[375] that we can, in the absence of a cupboard, replace the human by the screen and not cause any damage. This is because, yet again, the child does not need videos or mobile applications to deploy her language; she needs to be spoken to, she needs language to be elicited from her, she needs to be encouraged to name objects, to organize her responses, to be told stories and urged to read.

The third point concerns concentration. Without it there is no way to motivate thought towards a goal. However, the younger generations are immersed in a dangerously distracting digital environment. The influence of video games is therefore no less harmful than that of TV, or mobile tools. Besides, it matters little what the medium or the content are; the reality is that the human brain was simply not designed for such a density of exogenous stresses. Subject to a constant sensory flow, it 'suffers' and cannot build itself properly. In a few tens or hundreds of thousands of years, things will perhaps have changed, if our brilliant species has not by then vanished from the planet. In the meantime, it is real cognitive devastation that we are witnessing.

— 4 —

HEALTH
A silent aggression

The scientific community has affirmed for years that '[electronic] media need to be recognized as a major public health issue'.[1] It must be said that the body of research associating recreational digital consumption and health risks is huge. The list of affected fields seems endless: obesity, eating disorders (anorexia/bulimia), smoking, alcoholism, drug addiction, violence, unprotected sex, depression, sedentary lifestyle, etc.[2-4] One can assert, without blinking, that screens are among the worst causes of disease of our time (doctors would say the most 'morbid' factors). However, the subject is still largely ignored in popular articles and books. There is no doubt it's high time to bring it out of the shadows and devote a few lines to it. Once again, there will be no question of claiming to be exhaustive here, as the potentially relevant research is so varied and profuse. I will limit myself to the essentials and focus on three well-studied issues relating to the impact on health of sleep disorders, sedentary lifestyle and 'risky' content (sex, violence, smoking, etc.).

Harsh impact on sleep

On the subject of screens, many books and reports address the issue of sleep. However, in most cases this takes the form of a simple and brief mention. It is not the subject of any specific and documented discussion.[5-9] And yet the matter is of primary importance, and far from being a relatively secondary difficulty. Parents themselves seem to share this vision, if I am to believe my own personal experience. In fact, I have never been asked about sleep after the many talks I have given on the digital issue. This is due, I believe, to the popular belief that we sleep in order to rest; and if we don't get quite enough rest, it's no big deal. We're just a little tired, we yawn a bit more than usual – but we still manage to get by.

While we sleep, the brain is working

The problem is that we don't sleep to rest. We sleep because there are tasks our brain cannot perform when we are active. A (schematic) analogy will help to clarify this point. Imagine a supermarket on the first day of the sales. As soon as they open, a compact mass of customers invades the aisles. Products are taken, others moved around, others broken. Rubbish, mess and sweepings litter the ground. Overwhelmed, the employees try to deal with the problem as fast as they can. They busily replenish the shelves, remove litter, keep the customers informed, run the checkouts, etc. But despite their efforts, the situation deteriorates inexorably. Then evening falls: time to close. The customers leave. Calm returns. The employees can finally repair the damage. They carry out the necessary repairs, sweep the floors, refill the shelves, inventory the stocks, count the receipts from the cash registers, prepare for the next day, etc. Our organization is a bit like this supermarket. During the day, 'neural workers' are busy controlling the ongoing frenzy. All essential work turns out to be unfeasible. Then comes 'closing' time, when sleep breaks through. The brain is conveniently freed of much of its burden. It can devote itself to its essential maintenance tasks. The body is repaired. Memories are sorted and stored, learning stabilized, growth stimulated, infections and diseases fought, etc. At the end of the night, the machine is back on its feet, ready to face the challenges of the dawning day with zest. The curtain rises and sleep fades.

Now imagine that the 'closure' period is just a little too short or too disrupted to allow the necessary maintenance operations to be carried out completely. If this incident is rare, it won't be a major problem. However, if it becomes chronic, it will eventually cause significant damage. Indeed, when the body is no longer properly maintained, its functioning deteriorates. As table 1 shows, it is the integrity of the whole individual that is then shaken, in its most critical cognitive, emotional and health dimensions. Basically, the message conveyed by the enormous field of research available on the subject can be summed up quite simply: a human (child, adolescent or adult) who does not sleep well and/or enough cannot function properly.[10–12] A few representative studies demonstrate this.

Health, emotions, intelligence: sleep controls everything

Let's start with emotions and a study carried out on a large adolescent population (approximately 16,000 young people). The authors set out to analyse the role of parental instructions and, more precisely, of the time they told their children to go to sleep. The results showed a substantial increase in the risk of depression (+ 25%) and suicidal thoughts (+ 20%) in adolescents allowed to go to bed after midnight (adolescents who, in fact, had a reduced sleep time).[13] These findings echo several recent studies suggesting that sleep deprivation disrupts the responsiveness and connectivity of brain circuits involved in the management of emotions.[14-16]

In the area of health, a number of studies have focused on the question of obesity.[17,18] One study has established that subjects of normal weight tripled their risk of becoming obese after 6 years of age when they did not get enough sleep (less than 6 hours per day).[19] Again, this is not surprising if we consider that the lack of sleep (notably through the biochemical and in particular hormonal disturbances that it induces) stimulates hunger,[20] directs the brain towards the most fattening and pleasurable foods[21] and decreases diurnal energy expenditure.[22]

Finally, as regards the cognitive sphere, one recent study is particularly interesting.[23] The authors followed almost 1,200 children from the start of kindergarten to the end of primary school (between 2.5 and 10 years old). The results revealed a relatively stable sleep duration over time for most participants. Strikingly, at the age of 10, the group of those who slept less (between 8 hours 30 minutes and 9 hours of sleep per night) were, compared to the reference group (11 hours of sleep per night), 2.7 times more likely to show delays in language acquisition. This increase was 'only' 1.7 for average sleepers (10 hours of sleep per night). Again, these data are not surprising when we consider the importance of sleep for the functioning of memory, the efficiency of attention and the process of brain maturation (see table 1).

Let's finish with a somewhat lighter piece of research suggesting that even the best-tuned mechanisms don't work well when sleep is lacking.[24] The authors focused on basketball players from the American professional league (NBA) who maintained an active Twitter account over the period 2009–16. One hundred and twelve players were identified. For each of them, two pieces of information were collected: (i) performance statistics; (ii) the posting (or not) of

146

Table 1. Impact of lack of sleep on the individual. When sleep is chronically impaired, all of our cognitive, emotional and health functioning suffers (the arrows ↘ – decrease – and ↗ – increase – highlight the effect of chronically disturbed and/or insufficient sleep on the function considered; for example, ↘ decreased attention span and ↗ increased risk of obesity).

Cognition	↘ Decision making, especially in complex tasks[25-7]
	↘ Attention[28-34]
	↘ Memorization[31,35-7]
	↘ Brain maturation and cognitive development[23,38-43]
	↘ Creativity (solving complex problems)[44]
	↘ Academic results[45-50]
	↘ Productivity at work[51,52]
Emotion	↗ Emotional disorders (depression, suicide, anxiety, etc.)[13-16,53-9]
	↗ Impulsivity, hyperactivity, behavioural disorders[32,34,43,49,50,60-3]
	↗ Aggressiveness[48,55,64]
Health	↗ Obesity[17-19,65-70]
	↗ Type 2 diabetes[71,72]
	↗ Cardio-metabolic risk (hypertension, diabetes, heart attack, etc.)[73-7]
	↘ Immune response[78-80]
	↘ Cellular integrity (in particular, correction of damage inflicted on DNA by cellular activity)[81]
	↗ Mortality[82,83]
	↗ Road and work accidents[84-6]
	↗ Risk of dementia[87-92]

late tweets (after 11 p.m.) the day before matches. This information was then cross-referenced to determine if performance changed when the player went to bed later the night before the game (the latter parameter being inferred from observed activity on Twitter). Unsurprisingly, our basketball friends performed better when they took care to get enough sleep. They then scored more points (+ 12%) and won more rebounds (+ 12%).

Sleeping less and less well because of screens

We could provide an endless list of similar examples. But that wouldn't change the overall picture, namely that sleep is the key to our health, and our emotional and cognitive integrity. This is especially true in children and adolescents, when the body and brain are actively developing. That being said, we must be careful not to believe that only major disturbances count here. For fifty years, in fact, many studies have reported that apparently modest modulations of sleep time can have major influences on the functioning of the individual. It is thus possible to very significantly improve (or worsen) the latter by lengthening (or shortening) the nights of our offspring by between 30 and 60 minutes.[93-8]

It is certainly tempting to relate these figures to the digital orgy experienced every day by the younger generations. This parallel seems all the more valid as it refers to two widely established facts. First, a large number of children and adolescents (between 30% and 90% depending on age, country and thresholds used) sleep for much less than the recommended minima.[11,99-104] Second, to a significant degree, this sleep debt, which has been on the rise for twenty years,[100,103,105] is linked to increasingly massive digital consumption.[4,104,106-8] All media and uses are involved, from TV to video games, including smartphones, tablets and social networks.[103,109-17] Likewise, all sleep parameters are affected, whether they are qualitative (split nights, difficulty falling asleep, parasomnias, etc.) or quantitative (duration).

For example, one large meta-analysis involving more than 125,000 individuals aged 6 to 19 recently identified 'a strong and consistent association between bedtime media device use and inadequate sleep quantity (odds ratio, 2.17), poor sleep quality (odds ratio, 1.46), and excessive daytime sleepiness (odds ratio, 2.72)'.[107] These are results compatible with those of another study that showed, in subjects aged 11 to 13, that the frequent use of various digital tools before bedtime significantly increased the probability of seeing the child endure incomplete nights of sleep several times a week, due to waking early without any chance of falling asleep again.[109] The risk was multiplied by a factor of 4.1 for television; 2.7 for video games; 2.9 for the mobile phone; and 3.5 for social networks. In yet another study, it was established that adolescents who were exposed to more than 4 hours of screens per day were 3.6 times more likely to get very little sleep (less than 5 hours), 2.7 times more likely to get little sleep (5–6 hours) and 2.1 times more likely to get insufficient sleep (6–7 hours).[113] This observation was confirmed by subsequent research suggesting that more than half of those with heavy screen exposure (more than 5 hours per day) slept less than 7 hours per night. This proportion was only a third among small-scale users (less than 1 hour per day).[103] In other research, it is the need to protect the personal space of our offspring from digital intrusions that has been particularly emphasized.[118-22] It has been observed, for example, that the risk of sleep disorders almost triples in children (5–11 years old) who have a television in their bedroom.[116]

As well as school-age populations, researchers have also looked at babies and young children. It has been established, for bouncing babies aged 6 to 36 months, that each daily hour spent on the tablet or smartphone reduced nightly sleep time by almost 30 minutes.[111] These results are consistent with the findings of other work showing that children aged 2 to 5 who spent more than 2 hours per day on a mobile screen were, compared to their more parsimonious counterparts (less than 1 hour per day), almost twice as likely to have insufficient sleep. For 0- to 1-year-olds, this risk was cheerfully quadrupled.[115] Again, the impact of screens in the bedroom proved particularly problematic.[123] It was reported, for example, that 3-year-old children with a television in their bedroom were, when compared to their unequipped peers, almost 2.5 times more likely to suffer from a disturbed and not very restorative sleep (nightmares, night terrors, fatigue upon waking up, etc.).[117]

We could quote many more examples. But that wouldn't change the overall message: recreational digital consumption has a major damaging impact on the sleep of children and adolescents. In terms of causality, this association is by no means a mystery. It relies on four major mechanisms.[4,104,106-8] First, screens delay bedtime. In doing so, they shorten the duration of sleep, especially on weekdays, when wake-up time is imposed by the school rhythm. In connection with this, it has also been reported that delaying the start of lessons positively affects sleep time and, consequently, academic performance.[11,124,125] Second, screens increase the sleep onset latency period (i.e. the time that elapses between going to bed and the moment when Morpheus enfolds you in his arms). The problem is then due, in particular, to the disruptive action of modern visual terminals on the secretion of melatonin.[a,126-8] Third, screens (especially mobile screens) interrupt the continuity of our nights. In doing so, they lower both the duration and the quality of sleep. A recent study has reported that nearly 50% of young adults respond to incoming requests (texts, emails) and consult their smartphone (for purposes other than checking the time) at least once a night.[129] In another study, almost

---

[a] Melatonin, known as the 'sleep hormone', is involved in controlling the sleeping–waking cycle. Its secretion depends on the characteristics of luminosity. However, when evening falls, certain components of the light emitted by screens make the brain 'believe' that it is still daylight, which inhibits the secretion of melatonin and, ultimately, delays the process of falling asleep.

20% of adolescents declared that they were woken up by their smartphone several nights a week.[130] These discontinuities imposed on sleep obviously have a heavy impact on users' cognitive and emotional functioning.[131-5] And fourth, certain particularly exciting, stressful and/or anxiety-inducing contents delay falling asleep and affect the quality of sleep. Researchers have studied the impact of television on the sleep of young children (5–6 years).[136] Those who were regularly exposed to programmes not intended for them were three times more likely to experience severely disturbed sleep (difficulty falling asleep, nocturnal awakenings, etc.). It does not matter, then, whether the exposure is active (the child watches TV) or passive (the child does something else while the TV is switched on nearby). In another study,[137] 13-year-old school pupils were subjected to verbal learning (remembering words, names and numbers). Immediately after this exposure, a memorization test was performed. Then, approximately 60 minutes later, participants were assigned one of three experimental conditions:[a] (a) 1 hour of a video action game ('video game condition'); (b) 1 hour of an 'exciting' film ('film condition'); (c) 1 hour of free activity excluding video games and television ('control condition'). Between 2 and 3 hours later, the subjects went to bed. During the night, the brain parameters of sleep were recorded. The next day, the level of memorization was again assessed. The results showed that: (i) the retention of verbal material was significantly affected in the 'video game condition' as compared to the 'control condition' (figure 9); (ii) the same negative trend arose for the 'film condition', without, however, reaching the statistical significance threshold compared to the 'control condition' – but also without it being possible to statistically distinguish the 'film condition' from the 'video game condition' (figure 9);[b] (iii) sleep was disturbed under both experimental conditions. For the 'film condition' the data showed a significant decrease in sleep efficiency (ratio 'total time spent in bed'/'sleep time': 90.7% as against 94.8% for the 'control condition'). The same reduction was identified for the 'video game condition', but in addition to two other, more fundamental impairments. First, a sharp increase in the time it took to fall asleep (time spent between bedtime and falling asleep: + 22 minutes compared to the 'control

---

[a] Participants experienced all three conditions, at random, one week apart.
[b] As shown in figure 9, the memorization level for the 'film condition' lay between the 'control condition' and the 'video game condition'. In fact, this condition could not be distinguished statistically from either the 'control condition' or the 'video game condition'.

condition'). Then, a greater difficulty in entering deep sleep (involved in particular in memorization processes):[138,139] this represented 34% of total sleep time in the 'control condition', as against only 29% in the 'video game condition'. On the basis of these data, the authors proposed a twofold explanation for the decline in memorization. The first was deferred, and linked to sleep; the second was immediate, and associated with an excess of psychological excitement (states of strong psychological tension lead, in fact, to the massive release of certain neuromediators[a] known to interfere with memorization processes). In the light of these two hypotheses, the greater negative influence of video games on retention could be explained by a greater impairment of sleep and/or by the fact that the players manifested a state of arousal greater than that of the spectators (and therefore an increased release of interfering neurotransmitters). A recent study seems rather to favour the first hypothesis.[140]

Is it really necessary to stress the quantitative importance of these observations? By playing a video action game for 60 minutes, 1 hour after doing homework and 2 hours before going to bed, the child's retention rate on awakening is cut by almost 30%! Add up this deficit over several years, for screen times well in excess of an hour, often as close as possible to bedtime, and you will conclude, like the European Commission in one of its reports: 'Allow video games, but only after homework.'[141] Note that this will always be a better conclusion than the one reached by another expert, a co-signer of the aforementioned report of the French Academy of Sciences, who is forever popping up in the media declaring, with regard to the study described here, that it has been reported 'that teenagers who spend two hours in the evening watching TV will learn their lesson better the next day than teens who have played video games. TV can be a learning tool.'[142] Mind-boggling!

Of course, when a child goes to bed at night at abnormal hours, when she frequently suffers from nightmares and nocturnal awakenings, when she falls asleep at her desk at school, when she shows exaggerated irritability, it is easy for others to understand, and for the child herself to feel, that something isn't working in the land of Morpheus. The case becomes more complicated when the effects turn out to be less severe. For example, when a child who goes to bed reasonably early takes just a little too long to fall asleep, when a teenager who seems to be functioning properly appears a bit too lazy, when a perfectly respectable amount of sleep changes just a tiny

---

[a] These are biochemical compounds that affect the brain's functioning.

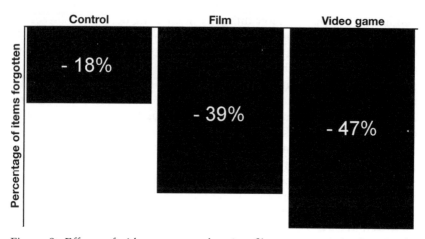

Figure 9. Effects of video games and action films on memorization. In the late afternoon, 13-year-old school pupils learn a word list. After learning this, they are subjected to an exciting activity for an hour (video games or film on television) or do what they want outside of these activities (control group). The next day, the level of memorization is assessed (the percentages represent the number of items forgotten).[137]

little bit, to the detriment of the phases of deep sleep, the problem can easily escape the vigilance of the sleeper and those around him. This blindness is not without its consequences. In addition to its damaging effect, mentioned above, on individual functioning, it also explains why many parents deny the negative effect of television on sleep (90%) and make the small screen a regular element in the young child's sleep routines (77%).[116] A third of adults who place a TV in their offspring's bedroom go so far as to say that it helps them get to sleep.[143] The data synthesized here show how bizarre this type of belief is. Certainly, if you stay in front of a screen at night, of whatever kind, you end up getting tired. So it's tempting to think that it's the screen that sends you to sleep. In reality, unfortunately, the reverse is true: digital nocturnal activities do not induce sleepiness, they ward it off until the feeling of fatigue becomes too overwhelming to be dismissed. In other words, we think that the screen has patiently sent us to sleep when it has unduly delayed our plunge into sleep. If one needed final proof of this, it could be found in a study designed to measure, in an adolescent population, the 'sleep potential' of four common activities: TV, video games, music and books.[144] As a result, participants who used electronic media to fall asleep (TV, video games and/or music) went to bed later and had a significantly reduced sleep time (by approximately 30 minutes). An opposite influence was observed for books whose action on sleep time was found, via the expectation of bedtime, to be slightly positive (of the order of 20 minutes).

Basically, these data simply reveal, yet again, the total inadequacy of our ancestral physiology when faced with the sacrosanct injunctions of digital modernity. The organism can do without Instagram, Facebook, Netflix or *GTA*; it cannot deprive itself of optimal sleep, or at least not without major consequences. To disrupt such a vital function in order to satisfy such trivial distractions is madness. But this madness cannot be blamed on its victims. It is part of us, fostered by the weaknesses of our brain reward system, a system that digital activities are uncommonly good at engaging with. In terms of hedonic susceptibility, our children's brains are hardly different from those of all those lovely lab rats – rats that are capable of sacrificing their most primitive needs (food, reproduction, etc.) when given the opportunity to electrically stimulate, using a pedal, certain key cells of their reward system.[145] It's really not easy for a child or a teenager to fight against this physiological priority – especially when armies of researchers and engineers are shamelessly selling to the industrial world all the keys necessary to turn every potential biological weakness into hard currency.

If only this digital orgy made our children happy, we could undoubtedly accept the situation. But this is not the case! For a few years now, more and more studies have been demonstrating the existence of a close link, within the younger generations, between digital consumption[a] and psychological suffering (depression, anxiety, malaise, suicide, etc.).[146–65] The impact of screens on sleep provides a direct and solid explanatory basis for this disastrous state of affairs.

A 'minor' impact?

The damaging impact of screens for recreation on sleep is now the subject of such a scientific consensus that it has become almost impossible to deny the problem. In fact, no one dares to assert, as was the case even a decade ago, that no studies prove that screens interfere with sleep. 'People have fallen asleep in front of the TV for years', people dared to tell us, 'and if it was bad we'd have heard

---

[a] The effect is typically seen for uses lasting longer than 2–3 hours daily, although studies have reported an effect from as little as 60 minutes.[146]

about it'.[166] No, the argument is now more subtle: it no longer denies, it minimizes. The recent words of one professor of developmental psychology provide an excellent and representative illustration of this. During a general public programme devoted to the impact of screens, he began by recognizing the impact of the latter on sleep (while rejecting the existence – you can never be too careful – of a possible consensus in other fields).[167] He said: 'this is perhaps one of the only factors on which we still have data that are somewhat convergent'. This apparently painful confession was quickly tempered by an important clarification: 'The absolute difference in sleep time for a teenager is 8 minutes, for an average of 8 hours 30 minutes. Yes, it has an effect – do you need a public health policy on this issue, is it a real question? You're only 8 minutes out.' One is tempted to say that the answer is more or less contained in the question, but let's not be too negative. Eight minutes out of 8 hours 30 minutes of sleep, that's 1.6% – indeed, a mere trifle. The problem is, these figures are grossly misleading. Regarding sleep time, one recent study has established, it is true, that the average daily length of sleep on weekdays for middle school pupils is 8 hours 30 minutes.[168] However, this overall value masks large disparities. Indeed, we go from almost 9 hours at age 11 to 7.25 at age 14. This figure is consistent with data from a survey published by the French Institute for Sleep and Vigilance which established the sleep time of young people aged 15 to 24 as 7 hours 17 minutes.[169] This figure is itself confirmed by an international meta-analysis involving nearly eighty studies carried out in seventeen countries and establishing average sleep times of 8 hours 3 minutes for 12- to 14-year-olds and 7 hours 24 minutes for 15- to 18-year-olds.[170] Is it necessary to specify that these times fall well outside the recommended optimal intervals (respectively 9–11 hours and 8–10 hours)?[171] Concerning the impact of screens on sleep, the study[172] mentioned by our specialist does not say that the effect is '8 minutes', but '8 minutes per daily hour of screen', which is significantly different. Furthermore, this figure is in no way representative of existing data. As early as the 1950s, American psychology professor Eleanor Maccoby noted that children's bedtime was 30 minutes later in families that had bought a TV.[173] More recently, in 2007, a Japanese team showed that pupils' sleep time increased from 7 hours 4 minutes to 8 hours 13 minutes when their television consumption was experimentally reduced to a daily maximum of 30 minutes.[174] Recently, one large Norwegian study found that adolescents who played computer video games for more than 4 hours a day had a sleep deficit of around 40 minutes, compared to those who played 30 minutes or less.[113] For users of social networks, the deficit exceeded 1 hour. Another study, conducted in England on 11- to 13-year-old school pupils, showed that frequent mobile phone use on weekdays before going to sleep reduced sleep time by 45 minutes.[109] The figure was almost half an hour for video games. For social networks, it exceeded 50 minutes. In addition, as noted above, it should be clear that the impact of screens on sleep is not just a question of duration. Quality is also important, and we need to remember that this is very sensitive to both the content viewed (exciting, anxiety-provoking, violent, etc.) and the frequency of nocturnal digital uses. In short, concerning our expert's question (one that is representative of a general trend towards minimizing impacts that have actually become indisputable), we can clearly state that the answer is *no*, the influence of screens on sleep is not minor, and *yes*, this question does indeed require a vigorous public health policy.

A devastating sedentary lifestyle

Apart from sleep, if we were to draw up a list of the little-known problems of digital technology, a sedentary lifestyle would undoubtedly end up the winner. The question is far from trivial, and it took a long time for it to escape from the preoccupation with obesity (which I will come back to later).

Typically, a sedentary lifestyle is defined negatively, by the prolonged absence of physical activity. In this context, a sedentary person is one who remains sitting or lying without moving for long periods (excluding sleep). Beneath its mundane appearance, it's important to get this definition right: it indicates, in fact, that one can be both sedentary and active. A postman, for example, may walk for miles during the day as part of his work, and binge on television shows every night while relaxing in his armchair. Likewise, a high school pupil can run or play football regularly and sit for hours behind the joystick of his game console. To account for this disso-ciation, researchers have recently proposed the concept of the 'active couch potato'.[175] Apart from its provocative side, the expression carries a twofold message. First, the (positive) influences of physical activity and the (damaging) impacts of a sedentary lifestyle must be studied independently. Second, a high level of physical activity does not protect the individual (or at least not completely) from the harmful effects of a sedentary lifestyle. Note that we cannot offer a general view of the problem here (at work, at school, in transport, etc.). I will focus just on sedentary behaviours relating to recreational digital consumption.

Sitting down damages your health

As a preamble, we undoubtedly need to remember that the human mechanism wasn't designed to sit chronically for long periods of time. A sedentary lifestyle damages our body. Worse, it ends up killing us prematurely.[176] In part, this sad observation is based on the study of a very common behaviour: watching television. In this area, one of the first studies[177] followed a large adult population for seven years (nearly 9,000 people; age over 25). The results showed that each additional hour spent daily in front of the small screen increased the risk of death by 11% (all causes included).[a] For cardiovascular pathologies alone, the 'punishment' reached 18%. In another study, a large group of young adults (approximately 13,500 people; average age 37) was followed for eight years.[178] The results revealed a doubling of the lethal risk when the daily level of audio-visual consumption increased from less than 1 hour to more than 3 hours. More recent research (4,500 participants; over 35 years old) extended these data to all uses of digital entertainment.[b,179] The risk of death increased 1.5 times when daily screen time increased from less than 2 hours to more than 4 hours. The probability of occurrence of a cardiovascular disease (fatal or not) was doubled.

Lately, several teams have been reformulating all these data in a less austere way. Their work has revealed that in the United States life expectancy increased by almost a year and a half if average television consumption fell below the 2-hour mark per day.[180] A comparable result was reported by an Australian team, but the other way around.[181] The authors showed that a sedentary lifestyle in front of the television reduced the life expectancy of the inhabitants of their country by almost two years. Formulated differently, this means that 'on average, every single hour of TV viewed after the age of 25 reduces the viewer's life expectancy by 21.8 min'. In other words, advertising included, each episode of *Mad Men, House* or *Game of*

---

[a] Even if this detail has been omitted throughout the book for the sake of readability (see note, p. 59), perhaps it is not unnecessary to recall that all the data described here are obtained after taking into account potentially important covariates. In this case, for example, this includes, for the standard statistical model: gender, age, abdominal circumference and level of physical activity.

[b] Professional or school usage time was explicitly excluded from the study.

Thrones lops almost 22 minutes off your existence (and much more without doubt if you factor into the sedentary lifestyle other aspects such as the impact of TV on smoking, food, alcohol, etc.; I will come back to this later). Recently, a meta-analysis corroborated these data and extended them to the risk of diabetes (type 2).[182] Other studies, albeit less stringent, have also associated excess screen time and sitting with the emergence of emotional disorders (depression, anxiety, suicide).[183-6] In the elderly, an impact has also been observed on cognitive decline and the onset of neurodegenerative disorders (including Alzheimer's disease).[187]

Unfortunately, the mechanisms that might account for all these observations are still poorly understood. The most promising avenue lies in biochemistry. It suggests that sitting causes significant metabolic disturbances at the muscular level, the accumulation of which is dangerous in the long term.[a,175,188-90]

Immobility threatens development

In short, it emerges from these data that the sedentary lifestyle caused by digital consumption is, in itself, an important health risk factor and (potentially) a source of emotional and neurodegenerative pathologies. In other words, just because Lucy does a lot of sport, this doesn't mean that her health won't suffer from the hours she devotes daily to Netflix and her games console. That being said, the potential impacts on her body will probably be much more moderate than those suffered by the general population. Indeed, the 'active couch potatoes' are by no means part of the majority group. They're the exception, not the rule. This is easy to understand if we include time in the equation. We can see that it's really not easy to keep a window open for physical activity when we devote 4, 5, 6 or even 7 hours each day to screens for recreation. A large number of studies have confirmed the existence, in children, adolescents and adults, of a negative relationship between screen time and physical activity.[191-9] This link is reflected indirectly in the gradual decline that has been observed over the past forty years in the cardiovascular capacities of

---

[a] Schematically speaking, a sedentary lifestyle leads to a reduction in the activity of an enzyme (lipoprotein lipase, or LPL) involved in lipid metabolism and, more specifically, in the uptake of fatty acids circulating in the blood. In this way, a sedentary lifestyle especially causes an accumulation of non-uptake fats in the organs (liver, heart) and blood vessels. This increases the cardiovascular risk.

our children.[200-2] A recent press release from the French Federation of Cardiology sums up the situation well: 'In 1971 [or roughly at the time when television started to be a universal consumer of time], a child could run 800 meters in 3 minutes; in 2013 for the same distance, she needed 4 minutes.'[203]

Of course, screens are not the only cause. The development of an urbanization ever more favourable to physical inactivity, for example, also plays an indisputable role.[204,205] But this role, and the involvement of other potential factors, cannot absolve the 'digital revolution' of its responsibility. A number of studies confirm the existence of a significant damaging link between exposure to screens and weakening of physical capacities, particularly in terms of endurance.[155,206-10] We can also point to recent research suggesting that, in a large sample of children (approximately 1,500 children aged 6), 1 hour of screens per day was sufficient to disrupt the development of the cardiovascular system.[211] Although there is as yet no long-term longitudinal research in this area, converging evidence indicates that the anomalies observed could be associated with an increased risk of disease at an older age.[212-15] This remote impact could explain, in part, the significant increase in the number of cerebrovascular accidents (strokes) over the past 30 years in young adults.[216,217]

However, the benefits of physical activity are not limited to the cardiovascular system alone. Like sleep, activity has a profound positive effect on all individual functioning, from obesity to the risk of depression, including memory, attention and brain development.[218-23] These benefits come at a 'cost', however. For children and adolescents, there is relative unanimity in placing this at 60 minutes a day of moderate and/or vigorous physical activity – with the idea, however, that this is a lower limit just begging to be passed.[224-6] However, all the available research indicates, whatever the country concerned, that our dear digital natives find it immensely difficult to reach this minimum milestone.[227] In France, for example, only 20% of children (under the age of 11) and 33% of adolescents (11–17 years) pass the fateful bar.[228] In the United States, these figures are 43% for 6- to 11-year-olds, 8% for 12- to 15-year-olds and 5% for 16- to 19-year-olds.[229] One recent study showed that an 18-year-old teenager now has about the same level of physical activity as a 60-year-old senior.[230] It is therefore easy to understand that this 'epidemic of inactivity', to use the words of a report by the American Academy of Pediatrics,[231] has dramatic consequences for the development of both children and adolescents. Clearly, limiting screen time alone will not solve the whole problem. But it is also clear that the implementation of such a limit would go a long way in reducing the attacks.

Unconscious but deep influences

The evidence presented so far indicates that the damaging impact of screens for recreation is largely non-specific, i.e. independent of the tools used and the programmes consumed. This does not mean, of course, that the issue of content is unimportant; quite the contrary. This is what we would like to show here. For this purpose, it is important to identify the neurophysiological mechanisms that allow the image to shape our representations of the world and, in so doing, to constrain our behaviour – most often without our knowledge.

Memory: a machine for creating links

In a famous work by Antoine de Saint-Exupéry, a solitary fox crosses the path of a melancholy little prince.[232] 'Come and play with me', suggests the latter. 'I can't play with you', the animal replies, 'I'm not tame.' 'Ah! sorry', the child continues before asking, his curiosity aroused: 'What does "to tame" mean?' 'That's too often been forgotten', replied the fox. 'It means "to create links."'

Forming bonds to tame the world and give it meaning is exactly what our memory does. Contrary to what one might hastily believe, memory is not just a data bank. It is a real organizing intelligence, i.e. an intelligence capable of connecting our different forms of knowledge with each other.[233-5] The process is beneficial because, once these forms of knowledge have been associated, they exhibit a strong tendency to 'co-activate'. This means that if you stimulate a particular node in the neural network involved in memorization, the whole web starts to vibrate and is thus placed at the service of thought or action. This propagative tendency explains, for example, that the word 'doctor' is recognized more quickly after the word 'nurse' than after the word 'bread'.[236,237] Likewise, it explains why subjects can be persuaded that they have heard the verb 'sleep' when they were in fact exposed only to certain semantic neighbours such as 'bed', 'rest', 'dream' or 'yawn'.[238,239]

The problem, unfortunately, is that our memory isn't always very careful about the links it weaves between things. The remark is especially valid for associations operated by 'temporal contiguity'.

The process involved here is quite simple. It can be summed up as follows: if two elements are presented together frequently enough they end up connecting to each other in the networks of memory.[240,241] Take wine, for example. In this area, 'experience' tends to teach us that quality has to be paid for and that the more expensive a bottle, the better the product. This implies that the notions of price and pleasure will gradually be bound together within our neural mazes, until they are activated reciprocally. A study by researchers at the California Institute of Technology shows this nicely.[242] Three results were reported: (i) the same wine is valued as better when its price is higher; (ii) this appreciation effect is based on the activation of a particular area of the cortex (the median orbitofrontal cortex) linked to the emergence of pleasant feelings; (iii) whatever the price of the wine, the response of the brain areas involved in the processing of taste sensory information is identical. In other words, the idea that 'it's expensive' on the one hand leads to the recruitment of populations of neurons controlling the feeling of pleasure, and on the other hand has no detectable impact on the actual sensory feeling. In everyday language we could translate this as: when it hurts the wallet, the brain tells us that it's better even when it's actually the same.

Interestingly, a similar bias is observed for some major food brands. An oft-cited study, for example, evaluated the respective virtues of Coca-Cola and Pepsi-Cola. In a first 'blind' test, healthy subjects had to compare these two fizzy drinks presented in two identical glasses.[243] A majority preferred Pepsi (55%). In a second, semi-blind test, subjects did much the same thing, with two differences: (i) one of the two glasses was explicitly identified as Coke; (ii) both glasses contained Coke (but the subjects were unaware of this). A clear reversal of preference was measured. Sixty per cent of the participants rated the fizzy drink in the branded Coke glass better than the fizzy drink in the unmarked glass.

The entire study was then replicated with patients with damage to the ventromedial prefrontal cortex (a region at the front and bottom of the brain that includes the orbitofrontal area discussed above in connection with wine). The results confirmed the majority inclination for Pepsi in the blind condition (63%), but failed to validate the effect of the logo in the semi-blind condition. In other words, the association 'Coke/best', arbitrarily set up by the manufacturers at the cost of intense marketing campaigns, had broken down in these patients due to their brain damage. Several neuroimaging studies confirm this observation, showing that the preference generally displayed for Coca-Cola is linked not to the better taste of the product, but to the advertising which makes it possible to create artificial connections in the brain's mnesic networks (the neuronal networks involved in the process of memorization) between this brand of fizzy drink and various positive emotional attributes.[244,245]

This kind of bias is obviously not specific to Coca-Cola or adult populations. It affects the youngest brains and concerns other consumer giants such as Nike, Apple and McDonald's. Take the last of these, for example: in a now well-known study, researchers asked 4-year-olds to rate identical foods, presented in plain packaging or bearing the McDonald's logo.[246] Seventy-seven per cent of participants thought McDonald's fries were better, compared to 13% who favoured fries without labels and 10% who saw no difference. For nuggets, these percentages were 59%, 18% and 23%, respectively. Although no neurophysiological studies could be conducted, due to the young age of the children, the preference biases displayed here were clearly based on the establishment, within nascent neural networks, of an aberrant relationship between the McDonald's brand and various positive emotional attributes – a relationship sparked by intense and overhyped campaigns.

Behaviour: the weight of unconscious representations

Undoubtedly, the associative power of 'temporal contiguity' stretches far beyond the sphere of marketing manipulations. The mechanism is universal. To a large extent, for example, it constructs our social stereotypes related to gender, disability, age, ethnicity, sexual orientation, etc.[247] Of course, these stereotypes are often implicit, i.e. nestled in the heart of our most unconscious functioning.[248,249] But that does not prevent them from being able to dangerously bias our supposedly 'deliberate' and 'enlightened' behaviours.[250-3] Gender representations are an excellent illustration of this. Most often acting without our knowledge, they can profoundly affect not only the way we look at others, but also the image we have of ourselves. Two studies show this nicely. In the first, subjects had to hire a candidate to carry out a scientific study.[254] A strong selection bias was observed in favour of males. When the information available was limited to gender (based on photos), recruiting subjects (whether male or female) chose a male candidate twice as often as a female candidate. When objective skills data were added to the table, the bias against women decreased but did not disappear. Interestingly, these arbitrary choices directly reflected the existence of implicit gender stereotypes (such as 'women are no good at maths') identified in participants through a standard item association test.[a]

The second study is even more striking. It shows that we are sometimes the victim of our own preconceptions.[255] Female Asian students from a major American university were first divided into three groups, each having to answer a questionnaire skilfully constructed to activate specific memory networks (the term used is 'priming'): (i) the 'neutral' version (indicating, for example, whether they used the university telephone service, whether they would consider subscribing to cable television, etc.); (ii) the 'gender' version, activating the 'I'm a girl, girls are no good at maths' stereotype (for example, whether their floors were co-ed or single-sex, whether they had a room-mate, etc.); (iii) the 'ethnic' version, activating the stereotype 'I'm Asian, Asians are good at maths' (for example, what languages they spoke at home, how many generations of their family had lived in America, etc.). The same maths test was then submitted to all three groups. The results revealed a very significant effect of the questionnaire on test success, obviously unbeknownst to the participants. The number of problems answered successfully was 49% for the 'neutral condition', 43% for the 'girl condition' and 54% for the 'Asian condition'. In other words, the links slowly forged by contiguity in the participants' memory banks between 'girl/no good at maths' and 'Asian/good at maths' interfered very noticeably with cognitive performance.

However striking, this last result comes as no surprise, as so many similar observations are made these days, even going beyond social stereotypes. For example, pupils take longer to leave an experiment room to get to the lift when they have just been constructing sentences from words related to the concept of old age (grey, wrinkles, old, etc.).[256] Likewise, individuals eat a quarter less chocolate from a bowl placed in front of them when a computer screen placed nearby (but generally not consciously detected by the participants) conveys ideas of thinness, weight and diet by displaying the images of certain extremely threadlike humanoid sculptures by Alberto Giacometti.[257] Likewise, students who are asked to turn a doorknob, without any

---

[a] Schematically, the subjects are presented with an item (image or word) belonging to the 'male' or 'female' categories, and the time taken to identify another item belonging to the 'scientific' categories (for example, calculation, engineer, etc.) or to the 'human sciences' (such as literature, the arts, etc.) is measured. The underlying assumption, already discussed in the text, is that functionally related items within memory networks will be more quickly and easily retrieved.

instructions as to the force to be used, produce significantly greater pressure if they have previously been subliminally (i.e. too fast for a conscious reading) exposed to words such as 'power' or 'vigour'.[258] Again, what emerges from these data is the remarkable power of 'memory co-activation' processes to influence our thoughts and behaviours unconsciously.

To avoid any misunderstanding,[259] we should point out that this is not, strictly speaking, a question of 'learning things', i.e. of building up a skill (for example, playing the violin) or of memorizing knowledge (for example, a poem). It is just a matter of linking together already constructed representations. This is why the necessary effort is minimal, especially at the level of attention. To take an analogy, you could say that writing a book and producing a marble sculpture are two activities that require patience, work and energy. However, once these items are made, it is very easy to store them in the same cabinet. There is therefore no paradox between children's difficulty in 'learning' with a screen and the ease with which they manage to artificially link elements already stored within their memory (for example, connecting the McDonald's brand to concepts such as cool, nice, parties, etc.).

In short, our memory is not a simple storage organ, but a machine for creating links. To do this, it mainly uses rules of temporal contiguity. However, the latter sometimes lack perspicacity: their automatic nature favours the formation of potentially harmful artificial connections; connections which, once established, strongly bias our perceptions, representations, decisions and actions.

Selling death in the name of 'culture'

The weaknesses in our memory described here obviously open up immense, lucrative horizons for all the 'available brain time'[a] merchants on the planet and other mercenaries in neuromarketing. These people have no compunction. Based on the digital uses of our

---

[a] In a now famous interview, Patrick Le Lay, CEO of the TF1 group (a major player in the European audiovisual landscape), explained that his work was aimed at 'helping Coca-Cola, for example, to sell its product'. The description of the method had shocked people at the time (it is the most honest thing ever said about the raison d'être of commercial television). 'For an advertising message to be perceived,' explained Le Lay, 'the viewer's brain must be available. Our programmes aim to make it available: that is to say to entertain it, to relax it in order to get it prepared, between two messages. What we sell to Coca-Cola is available human brain time.'[260]

offspring, they do not hesitate, in the name of their profits, to feed three of the biggest killers on the planet: smoking, alcoholism and obesity.

Smoking

First some general points so that everyone will understand the full extent of the problem. Cigarettes kill more than 7 million people per year,[261] including nearly 500,000 in the United States[262] and 80,000 in France.[263] In sum, it's the population of a country like Paraguay[264] or a state like Arizona[265] that disappears from the planet every 365 days. For the community, the annual economic cost is around 1,250 billion euros,[266] which represents 165 euros per human being. For a developed country like France, which offers excellent social coverage, the price of smoking rises to nearly 1,800 euros per capita each year. And please do not come telling us, as I sometimes hear, that the state has nothing to complain about, as it gorges itself on taxes and stuffs its pockets with them. In France, tax revenues barely cover 40% of the health costs caused by smoking.[267]

Of course, the question posed here is by no means a moral one. It's not a matter of denouncing or blaming the user. It's just a matter of understanding the conversion mechanisms that make a non-smoker child fall one day into the hands of Philip Morris and the like. As the WHO nicely puts it, 'to sell a product that kills up to half of all its users requires extraordinary marketing savvy. Tobacco manufacturers are some of the best marketers in the world.'[268] It must be said that our tobacco-making friends have behind them more than sixty years of experience in trickery, deceit and various forms of tampering with the truth. Their propaganda skills became so sharp that even the cautious WHO eventually lost its temper. In a document entitled 'Tobacco industry interference', this organization brutally denounced 'an industry that has much money and no qualms about using it in the most devious ways imaginable'.[269] Among the deceptive strategies listed, we find in particular: 'discrediting proven science', 'manipulating public opinion to gain the appearance of respectability', 'intimidating governments with litigation or the threat of litigation', 'manoeuvring to hijack the political and legislative process', etc.

However, we need to recognize that the position of the industrialists isn't easy, for at least three reasons. First, they face regulations, which, though not perfect in many countries, are nevertheless tending to become more and more drastic and rigorous.[270] Second, they rapidly lose their clients to the funeral service companies.[271] Third, they only have an extremely limited window of time to recruit replacements. Regarding this last point, we now know that the risk of conversion to smoking weighs disproportionately on minors and, basically, hardly affects adults. Thus, 98% of smokers started before the age of 26, 90% of them before the age of 18;[272] and, as the WHO once again emphasizes, 'the younger children are when they first try smoking, the more likely they are to become regular smokers and the less likely they are to quit'.[268]

In short, for tobacco companies, recruiting large cohorts of children and adolescents is a vital necessity. This is where the unexpected support of the audiovisual industries comes in. Under the guise of creative freedom and artistic grandeur, they pour out onto our offspring, day after day, an avalanche of pro-tobacco stereotypes. In films and on television, cigarettes and cigars have become wonderfully convenient symbols of virility (Sylvester Stallone in *Rocky*); sensuality (Sharon Stone in *Basic Instinct*); the adolescent spirit of rebellion (James Dean in *Rebel Without a Cause*); the visionary scientist (Sigourney Weaver in *Avatar*); power and sex (Jon Hamm in *Mad Men*); freedom (Eric Lawson, and several other Marlboro cowboys – who died from their tobacco consumption);[273,274] etc. What inventiveness! The worst thing is that in many countries, including France, the United States, Germany and Italy, many of these films and programmes receive generous public subsidies.[275,276]

It all started in the 1960s and 1970s with cinema and television.[277,278] For tobacco companies, these 'new technologies' were a weapon in an intense campaign to normalize tobacco consumption. The goal was simple: to take people's minds off morality and to associate tobacco with as many positive virtues as possible. So, for example, Sylvester Stallone was among the first to agree to a $500,000 contract guaranteeing he would smoke in five of his upcoming films (including *Rambo* and *Rocky IV*). This was a first step 'to link smoking with power and strength, rather than sickness and death'.[278]

It would be a mistake to think that the problem has been solved today. Indeed, in the fifty years that this infamy has lasted, nothing has really changed and no collective awareness has emerged. Worse, merely bringing up the question[279] exposes you to all kinds of abysmally stupid comments like 'you have to die of something' or 'I don't understand: I'm a real movie buff and yet I don't smoke.'[280] Frankly, should we abstain from any prophylactic measures on the grounds that there are many ways of falling sick and dying? Should we give up the fight against the scourge of tobacco morbidity on the pretext that it's much more dangerous to jump out of a plane without a parachute than to smoke? Should we ignore all epidemiological reality because there are statistical flying pigs, and the risk isn't as high as 100%? If you go skiing, you're more likely to fall than if you're walking. This doesn't mean that no one falls while walking, or that everyone breaks their legs while skiing! Likewise, just because there were survivors of the great plague epidemic that hit Europe in the fourteenth century doesn't mean that the disease wasn't fatal! All of these pseudo-arguments are overwhelming in their inanity. Not long ago, an American journalist summed up the problem superbly: 'There's a game I like to play sometimes. It's called "How many Internet comments do I have to read until I lose faith in humanity?" All too often, the answer is: *one comment.*'[281]

For those who doubt the reality of the problem, one recent study has analysed the 2,429 most lucrative films that came onto the North American market (United States and Canada) between 2002 and 2018.[a,282] This represents more than 95% of cinema admissions for the period considered. The analyses identified an overall rate of tobacco 'penetration' in these films close to 60%. However, strong disparities were identified, depending on the classification of the films. For the year 2018, 70% of films rated 'restricted' (R; prohibited for unaccompanied under-17s) contained scenes showing actors smoking, with an average of 42 episodes per work. For films rated as '13 and over' (PG-13; warning that some content may be inappropriate for children under 13), these figures were 38% and 54 episodes. For films classified as 'general audience' (G; open to all audiences), they were 13% and 6 episodes. As table 2 shows, if we consider the percentage of feature films affected, the data show an overall decrease from 2002 to 2010, then a phase of stabilization. On the other hand, if we look at the number of episodes per work, the trend is upwards, especially for films directly targeting adolescents ('13 years and over'). In other words, since 2002, people smoke in fewer films (which is positive), but they smoke more in each film where the presence of tobacco is important (which is a little discouraging). Comparable results were reported for television[283] with the prevalence of smoking reaching 0% (excellent news), 43%, 25% and 64% respectively for the TV-Y7, TV-PG, TV-14 and TV-MA programmes.[b]

---

[a] These are all the films that were in the top ten in terms of box office takings, on their release, for at least a week.

[b] These are, respectively, 'Designed for children age 7 and above', 'Parental guidance suggested; This program contains material that parents may find unsuitable for

Table 2. Prevalence of smoking scenes in the cinema. All films on the North American market classified in the top ten for at least one week after release are taken into account.

Ranking		2002	2010	2014	2018
'Restricted'	%	79%	72%	59%	70%
	Episodes	47	35	54	42
'13 years and over'	%	77%	43%	39%	38%
	Episodes	23	25	42	54
'General audience'	%	29%	11%	5%	13%
	Episodes	8	7	9	6

% = percentage of films showing actors smoking. Episodes = number of times an actor is seen smoking.[282]

Beyond this handful of digital subtleties, what should be remembered is that smoking is still heavily present in North American productions, including, unsurprisingly, in films classified as 'Restricted' and '13 years and over'. This is all the more annoying in that these productions are widely exported and that the classification system used in the United States is, on the whole, much more protective than that implemented in other countries including France[275] – where it is common to see films that in North America are classified as 'Restricted' or '13 years and over' placed in the 'All audiences' category.[a] Note that American producers tend to be well behaved here – although, once again, their performance is far from excellent. Other countries do worse, including Germany, Italy, Argentina, Iceland, Mexico and France.[275,285] For the last of these, one study analysed the 180 French-made films with the most cinema admissions over a 5-year period, 2005–10.[286] The result was that 80% of the works contained images of actors smoking for an average duration of 2.5 minutes per film.

We must obviously be careful not to think that the cinema is the only medium concerned with this issue of smoking. Recent work has looked at the most popular series broadcast via cable networks and

younger children', 'This program contains some material that many parents would find unsuitable for children under 14 years of age' and 'This program is specifically designed to be viewed by adults and therefore may be unsuitable for children under 17.'[284]
[a] Examples: 'Under 13': *Avatar, Titanic, Forrest Gump, The Lord of the Rings*[1], *Independence Day, Gravity*, etc.; 'Restricted': *Beverly Hills Cop (1, 2 & 3), Pretty Woman, Wedding Crashers, Bad Moms, Air Force One, Letters from Iwo Jima*, etc.

streaming sites.[287] The authors observed, in the majority of cases, a veritable orgy of tobacco consumption affecting productions such as *Stranger Things, The Walking Dead, Orange is the New Black* and *House of Cards* – the worthy successors, no doubt, of the acclaimed *Mad Men.*

Of course, for twenty years smoking has been massively taking over all the new digital media available,[288–92] from social networks,[293–7] to video games,[298–303] via hosting sites such as YouTube.[304–9] For example, almost half of the most viewed hip-hop music videos on various Internet platforms (YouTube, iTunes, Vimeo, etc.) between 2013 and 2017 contain scenes of smoking.[310] The same goes for 42% of the video games most played by adolescents;[311] in this case, however, as for television, there are wide divergences, related to the classification of the works. The presence of tobacco thus reaches 75% for products marked 'mature' (17 years and over), 30% for products marked 'adolescents' (13 years and over) and 22% for products marked 'children' (10 years and over). Note, however, that these labels are far from being truly protective: 22% of 8- to 11-year-olds, 41% of 12- to 14-year-olds and 56% of 15- to 18-year-olds play games classified as 'mature'.[312] And again, this picture is largely tempered by the merging of the sexes: if we only look at boys, we find an exposure level much higher than 50% among 8- to 18-year-olds.

The *GTA* video game series perfectly illustrates this disturbing reality. This economic juggernaut[313,314] is both violent and drenched in pornography[a] and incitement to tobacco use.[301] However, 70% of boys aged 8 to 18 say they have played it, including 38% of 8- to 10-year-olds, 74% of 11- to 14-year-olds and 85% of 15- to 18-year-olds.[315] Allow me to rephrase this point: four out of ten middle-school kids are involved, through their virtual avatars, in hyper-violent behaviour, most often completely gratuitous; unimaginable acts of torture worthy of the worst hours of the Vietnam or Algerian Wars; and explicit sexual practices that would be at home in the seediest of porn films.

In short, the digital world of children and adolescents appears to be saturated with images wreathed in smoking: television, video games, social networks, streaming sites, etc.; no space is free from the flood of these pictures. This wouldn't be a problem, of course, if the impact of smoking on health were honestly presented. Unfortunately, this is not the case. All these actors, singers, rappers,

---

[a] See p. 45, n. b, above.

influencers, Instagrammers and game characters who show off their pleasure in smoking are rarely afflicted by cancer, and they are not aphasic or hemiplegic following a stroke; they do not suffer from cataracts or age-related macular degeneration, or from erectile dysfunction; their foetuses are not born malformed, their immune systems do not seem to be weakened, etc.[a] Quite the contrary. Smokers are shown in an incredibly favourable light.[4,297,301-3,316-19] In the overwhelming majority of cases, these people are beautiful, intelligent, socially dominant, cool, fun, daring, rebellious, manly (for men), sensual (for women), etc. And this, of course, is where the flaws in our memory come in. Indeed, by dint of judicious temporal coincidences, the vision of tobacco connects to all kinds of positive attributes within our neural networks; and ultimately, when the 'smoking' node is stimulated by an image (of someone smoking) and/or an opportunity (for smoking), it's the whole web of associated actions and representations which is activated (cool, sexy, rebellious, manly, etc.), to the detriment of the decision-making process.

It's no longer a question of whether repeated exposure to positive images of smoking increases the likelihood of initiation in adolescents. This debate is now settled, as indicated by various reports recently issued by the largest health institutions in the world.[275,320-2] As summarized in one monograph from the National Cancer Institute, 'the total weight of evidence from cross-sectional, longitudinal, and experimental studies, combined with the high theoretical plausibility from the perspective of social influences, indicates a causal relationship between exposure to film smoking depictions and youth smoking initiation'.[323] This assertion is based on dozens of studies, rigorously conducted using various protocols, in a large number of countries.[3,4,275,288] Overall, this extensive corpus shows that the most exposed adolescents are two to three times more likely to smoke than their least exposed counterparts.[324-32] For example, one frequently cited study followed 1,800 children aged 10 to 14, for eight years.[333] As a first step, all subjects were asked to identify, from a large list, the films they had seen. This allowed the experimenters to assess each participant's degree of exposure to tobacco. The results showed that a quarter of the most exposed children between the ages of 10 and 14 were twice as likely to have become

---

[a] Again, let me be clear. I'm not out to judge smokers. I simply wish to understand how the child becomes a user of a substance whose terrible side effects are listed here (not exhaustively).

chronic smokers eight years later than were the quarter of the least exposed children.[a] Put differently, this observation means that 35% of smokers succumbed to tobacco addiction through an early process of audiovisual imbibition.

In another similar piece of research, nearly 5,000 adolescents, on average 12 years old, were followed for 24 months.[334] The results indicated two things: (i) removing scenes showing people smoking in films intended for adolescents (classified as '13 years and over') would reduce the number of smoking initiations by 18%; (ii) rigorous respect for age labelling ('Restricted' classification) would further significantly improve things and obtain a total reduction of 26%. In another study, researchers followed a cohort of 1,000 children for more than twenty years.[335] The results showed that the taking up of tobacco by 17% of adult smokers (26 years) could be attributed to television consumption of more than 2 hours per day between 5 and 15 years (and therefore to an overall increased exposure to images promoting tobacco). For those who find these percentages harmless, a reformulation may be interesting. Consider a 20% decrease in the number of smokers (roughly the average estimated from previous studies). This represents one and a half million deaths averted annually globally – the equivalent of the city of Philadelphia. For the United States, based on figures provided by the Department of Health and Human Services,[320] this means that one million children under the age of 18 today will not smoke and will not die prematurely from a cigarette-related illness. Yet, once again, the mere fact of highlighting the ubiquity of tobacco in digital content accessible to young people, or suggesting that protective legislative measures for minors would be a justified step, triggers torrents of outrage. Perhaps the obtuse fanatics of free speech will one day wonder if their high opinion of themselves and their sacrosanct art justifies the present butchery.

However, it should not be believed that only non-smokers are victims of the plethora of smoking images produced by our digital worlds. Indeed, users are also heavily affected. This is due to the phenomenon of priming which we spoke about above. The idea, remember, is quite simple: when the brain is confronted with smoking

---

[a] Perhaps it is useful to reiterate, to avoid any misunderstanding, that the data described in this section (and the following ones) are obtained after taking into account many potential covariates. In this case, for example: age; sex; smoking among relatives, friends, siblings; school results; parental attitude towards tobacco; personality tests; etc.

stimuli (cigarette, lighter, smoker, etc.), it activates the desire to smoke and, consequently, significantly increases the risk of putting this desire into practice. This process has two consequences: (i) daily consumption increases, which reinforces the process of addiction[336] and therefore the risk of perpetuation of tobacco consumption in those who are starting to smoke, especially adolescents; (ii) efforts to quit smoking become more haphazard and painful. It has been observed that smokers who spend more time watching television smoke more.[337] Likewise, it has been shown that the presence of smoking stimuli on the screen attracts the attention of smokers more frequently and for a longer period of time,[338] triggering a substantial urge to consume.[339,340] The phenomenon is then sufficiently intense to be detected at the most basic physiological level (increased skin temperature and sweating).[341] Ultimately, all these elements lead, unsurprisingly, to the implementation of gratifying behaviours. Thus, in one representative study, 100 young smokers in their twenties[a] saw an 8-minute video clip containing (in the case of the experimental group) or not (the control group) images related to tobacco. Members of the experimental group were four times more likely to allow themselves a cigarette within 30 minutes of the end of the screening.[342] Recently, neuroimaging work has identified a clear impact of such images on the brain.[343] Two populations of smokers and non-smokers, again in their twenties, were exposed to films containing smoking stimuli. The latter caused in smokers, compared to their non-smoking counterparts, a twofold activation involving the brain areas linked (i) to the emergence of the desire for consumption and (ii) to planning the manual gesture. In other words, everything happened as if the subjects' brains felt a strong urge to smoke and simulated the movements of the actors (or alternatively prepared the hand to light a cigarette).

In short, the omnipresence of images of tobacco consumption in the digital world is of threefold interest for manufacturers: (i) it greatly facilitates the recruitment of new users; (ii) it makes it much more difficult to quit; (iii) by hiding advertising behind the screen of creative freedom it can circumvent legislative restrictions and, ultimately, violate the spirit of the law, without risking any legal action being taken against it.

---

[a] For ethical reasons, researchers are not allowed to conduct this kind of experimental studies (which induce use) in younger subjects not of legal age to consume and/or purchase tobacco.

Alcoholism

The mechanism detailed above obviously does not limit its impact on smoking alone. It also largely affects the field of alcoholic use. This is what we propose to demonstrate below. However, this section will be less detailed than the previous one. Indeed, given the similarity of the mechanisms involved, it seems judicious to simplify the demonstration so as to avoid tedious repetitions. I will therefore focus here mainly on the causal chain between images and alcohol use.

Like tobacco, alcohol is one of the leading preventable killers, with three million annual deaths to its credit.[344] In the case of minors, the scientific community unanimously considers that the only safe consumption is zero consumption.[345,346] This conclusion is consistent with the implementation, in almost all the countries in the world, of a legal age below which any sale of alcohol is strictly prohibited. This age is 18 in France and 21 in the United States.[347] If any justification for this kind of caution were necessary, it could be found in the extreme fragility of the developing brain. Drinking in adolescence (and, a fortiori, before) disrupts brain maturation[346,348,349] and increases the risk of long-term addiction.[346,350]

However, even if it seems to be decreasing slightly in many countries, especially in Europe, alcohol consumption remains very high among young people.[344] In France, a quarter of 16-year-old high school pupils drink regularly and get drunk at least once a month. Sixty per cent of 11-year-olds have already drunk alcohol.[351] Yet again, screens play their part here. Indeed, within digital spaces, alcoholic use is both omnipresent and described in a misleadingly favourable light.[309,332,352-64] For television, for example, one study showed insane prevalence levels of 3%, 75%, 73% and 79% respectively for TV-Y7, TV-PG, TV-14 and TV-MA.[a] This bludgeoning relentlessly feeds into the associative flaws in our memory networks. Subjected to an avalanche of positive representations, these gradually link alcohol to all kinds of enviable traits: cool, party-going, relaxed, rebellious, etc. These connections then encourage early initiations and, once these have taken place, support excessive consumption (chronic drinking or binge-drinking).[b,365-71]

---

[a] See above, p. 166.
[b] Binge-drinking is particularly dangerous. It has strong toxic effects on the brain. It also increases the risk of accidents, unprotected sex, alcoholic coma, violent behaviour and addiction.

For example, one study followed almost 3,000 German adolescents with an average age of 13 who had never ingested alcohol.[372] After one year, the quarter of the participants who had consumed the most films with alcoholic scenes (regardless of the platform) were twice as much at risk as the quarter of the least exposed participants of having drunk alcohol unbeknownst to their parents, and 2.2 times more likely to have engaged in dangerous binge-drinking.

The good news, as with tobacco, is that parental vigilance pays. In often-cited research, 2,400 American school pupils who had never drunk alcohol were followed for an average of 18 months.[373] The likelihood of alcohol initiation was measured as a function of the parental propensity to allow the child to watch films classified as 'Restricted'. And this educational dimension did indeed prove to be strongly associated with the risk incurred. Compared to the baseline decision 'never', the chances of the child starting to drink during the follow-up period were multiplied by factors of 5.1, 5.6 and 7.3 respectively for the decisions to drink 'rarely', 'from time to time' and 'always'. These results confirm those of another recent study which involved more than a thousand English adolescents aged 11 to 17 years.[332] Those who had played video games rich in alcoholic content (labelled 'adult' for the most part – for example, GTA V, Max Payne 3, Sleeping Dogs, etc.) – were three times more likely to consume alcohol than their unexposed counterparts.

Additionally, as has been observed with tobacco, seeing people drinking on the screen also has a significant effect on immediate consumption.[374-6] In other words, when the brain is confronted with alcoholic stimuli, this activates the idea of drinking and, consequently, significantly increases the risk of acting out. The same phenomenon is observed for fizzy drinks.[377]

In short, the omnipresence of alcoholic images in the digital world is of twofold interest for manufacturers: (i) it substantially lowers the age of first initiation; (ii) it appropriately inflates the volume of chronic consumption.

Obesity

After tobacco and alcohol, let's take a look at the weight issue. Here again, I will focus on the essential, and mainly try to shed light on the causal chain from images to being overweight and to obesity.

Worldwide, excess weight affects 2 billion adults and 350 million children.[378] Each year, it kills around 4 million people.[379] Even though the problem has multiple origins, no one now seriously disputes the damaging implication of our digital habits, especially among children and adolescents.[3,4,380-3] Several factors are involved, including sleep and a decrease in the level of physical activity, as we have shown. One possible contribution of the advertising steamroller is, we are told, that it blocks any regulatory legislative measures.[384-6] For fifteen years, in children and adolescents, all major scientific and institutional publications have pointed out the increased risk of obesity entailed by a food marketing as aggressive as it is ubiquitous (television, social networks, video-sharing platforms, etc.).[4,387-96] Study after study, the same conclusions are repeated: 'ample evidence indicates that the obesity epidemic is, at least to a large degree, the result of increased marketing power over the American diet'.[387] In other words, 'the scientific literature documents that food marketing to children is (a) massive; (b) expanding in number of venues (product placements, video games, the Internet, mobile phones, etc.); (c) composed almost entirely of messages for nutrient-poor, calorie-dense foods; (d) having harmful effects; and (e) increasingly global and hence difficult to regulate by individual countries'.[397] Or, to quote a recently published overview, today there is 'a strong body of evidence that exposure to food marketing impacts children's attitudes, preferences and consumption of unhealthy foods, with detrimental consequences to health. Current studies provide valuable insights and provide compelling evidence to support the restriction of food marketing to children.'[395]

Thus, to take a few examples, it has been reported that the risk of obesity increased significantly in children exposed to commercial channels that broadcast many food adverts, but not in children exposed to non-commercial public channels lacking these same adverts.[398] Likewise, it was calculated that a ban on this type of advertising would, depending on the models considered, reduce childhood obesity by between 15% and 33%.[399,400] In line with this conclusion, an international comparison carried out on around ten developed countries (United States, Australia, France, Germany, Sweden, etc.) has established that the rate of childhood obesity increases almost linearly with the frequency of food advertising in youth programmes.[401]

Basically, this is no surprise. These data bring us back to what has already been said for alcohol and tobacco; except, however, that food advertising is not restricted. Advertisers have carte blanche to act and literally imprint their brands and products in the nascent brains of our offspring. Once the memory structures have been infected, all taste preferences are affected – in favour of the most widely promoted high-calorie foods. In this regard, a large number of studies show that the propensity of children to demand, obtain and consume processed, ultra-fattening products (snacks, fast foods, fizzy drinks, etc.) increases with the intensity of the marketing pressures exerted.[400,402-7] Who can seriously think, even for a second, that the excess energy thereby entailed could leave the weight status of these children unscathed?[408,409] One study analysed, for example, the impact of 1 hour of television per day at age 3 on weight, physical activity and eating behaviour found at age 10.[191] The result: more junk food (fizzy drinks, snacks: + 10%), less fruit and vegetables (– 16%), less physical activity at weekends (– 13%) and, unsurprisingly, a significantly higher body mass index (+ 5%).[a] The observation is all the more worrying as the biases identified here tend to spread well beyond childhood. In fact, precociously acquired taste inclinations often persist throughout life.[410-13] This partly explains – beyond potential genetic predispositions, for example – the ability of childhood obesity to pursue its victims for a very long time.[414,415]

Then, obviously, there are the problems of priming mentioned above, because, of course, the fact of seeing people eating on the screen significantly increases our immediate consumption.[390,416] In other words, when the brain is confronted with food stimuli, this activates the idea of eating and, consequently, significantly increases the risk of snacking.[17]

In short, taken as a whole, these elements show that food marketing, ubiquitous on television and on all digital media, greatly increases the risk of obesity in children and adolescents.

The impact of norms

Basically, the preceding elements merely reflect the general capacity of mass audiovisual content to format our social representations. YouTube, series, films, music videos and video games are real machines for creating norms, i.e. rules – often implicit – of conduct, appearance or expectation.

---

[a] The body mass index (BMI) is obtained by dividing the weight (in kilograms) by the square of the height (in metres); it is therefore expressed in kg/m^2. When the BMI is between 18.5 and 25, the subject is at a healthy weight. Below 18.5 she or he is underweight. Between 25 and 30, she or he is overweight. Over 30, she or he is obese.

At the origins of the middle class

The sociologist Juliet Schor, now a professor at Boston University, was one of the first to theorize on this point. In one of her bestsellers, published in 1998 and entitled *The Overspent American*, she brilliantly analysed the role of the small screen in the consumerist frenzy of her compatriots.[417] Although richly documented, the analysis is quite simple to summarize: before, we compared ourselves to our neighbours, our relatives and our friends; now, we confront our television alter egos. For the middle classes, this change led to an incredible feeling of social regression as the audiovisual world offered a distorted image of the 'real world': vast lofts in Manhattan, gigantic houses in the suburbs, spacious cars (one for madam, one for sir), fancy clothes and restaurants, etc. Basically, Schor tells us, 'the story of the eighties and nineties is that millions of Americans ended the period having more but feeling poorer'.[417] Drawing on her own research, she says,

> the more TV a person watches, the more he or she spends. The likely explanation for the link between television and spending is that what we see on TV inflates our sense of what's normal [...] Television viewing results in an upscaling of desire, and that in turns leads people to buy – quite a bit more than they would if they didn't watch. In the Telecom sample,[a] I found that each additional hour of television watched in a week led to an additional $208 of annual spending[b] [equivalent to $360 at present].[c]

Compared to 3 or 4 hours daily of small screen, this puts the total of the additional expenses at between $4,368 and $5,824 [that is, between $7,567 and $10,090 today].[d] This is how a perpetual race for status began in the United States, fuelled by borrowing, stress and professional burnout.[418]

---

[a] This is a reference to an investigation carried out between November 1994 and May 1995 at a telecommunications company in the southeast of the United States, employing more than eighty thousand people.
[b] In a note, Schor, to avoid any ambiguity, points out that 'other factors that influence spending as well as TV watching were controlled for, including income, occupation, education, gender, and age'.
[c] According to the Bureau of Labor Statistics. See https://www.bls.gov/data/inflation_calculator.htm.
[d] Ibid.

Negative body images

Since this original observation, the normative power of audiovisual content has been confirmed in a number of fields and generalized to a wide range of digital media. Take, for example, the issue of weight status. In France, nearly 60% of women and 30% of men with a medically healthy weight want to lose weight.[419] The almost universal way the media, especially the digital media, extol extreme thinness for women and excessive muscularity for men is linked to this craziness. Every day, in fact, in films, series, music videos, video games and Instagram posts, we are confronted with a tidal wave of completely 'abnormal' physical types (in the statistical sense of the term).[18] And the worry is that, by dint of seeing only aberrant bodies, we end up thinking that these are the norms and that we are the exception. Let's consider the female body as a further example. The subject is remarkably well documented today, and the evidence for bias is overwhelming.[18] For example, in just under a century, the weight of Miss America has gone from normal to near anorexic.[420] Ditto for the glamour models and fashion models whose extreme thinness, still problematic,[421–3] was already being singled out almost twenty-five years ago.[424] The stars of our podiums are thinner than 98% of the female population;[425] on average, they are 17 cm taller and weigh 21 kg less than 'normal' women.[a,426–8] In prime-time television series, nearly a third of actresses have a body mass index that qualifies for thinness; 3% are obese.[429] In real life, these figures are rigorously reversed with a third being obese and 2% being thin.[425,430] This set of data is certainly not unrelated to the omnipresence in the media, as we have already noted,[b] of negative stereotypes of obese individuals, seen as prone to weakness, abulia, uncleanliness, disloyalty, clumsiness, laziness, rudeness, etc.[18,431–4]

In many women of the 'real world' this gap causes a real and violent feeling of dissatisfaction, known to open the way to a wide spectrum of psychological suffering (depression, low self-esteem, etc.) and eating disorders (anorexia, bulimia, etc.).[18] A meta-analysis devoted to this issue concludes, moreover,

> that media exposure is linked to women's generalized dissatisfaction with their bodies, increased investment in appearance, and increased

---

[a] Yet again, this term is to be considered in its strictly statistical sense.
[b] See above, p. 175.

endorsement of disordered eating behaviors. These effects appear robust: They are present across multiple outcomes and are demonstrated in both the experimental and correlational literatures. Thus we can see that media exposure appears to be related to women's body image negatively regardless of technical assessment, individual difference variables, media type, age, or other idiosyncratic study characteristics.[435]

One piece of experimental work beautifully demonstrates this point. Researchers at Harvard University have looked at a province in Fiji which did not as yet have television but was due to be connected in the near future.[436] The existence of eating disorders was assessed using a standard test in two comparable populations of teenage girls, one before (a few weeks) and the other after (three years) the arrival of the TV sets. The result: a marked increase in the number of young girls admitting to making themselves vomit in order not to gain weight (0% to 11%) and a quasi-tripling of the number of teenagers considered 'at risk' by the test. Since not all households purchased a television, researchers were able to compare participants who had a set at home with those who did not. The probability of being detected 'at risk' was three times higher in the former than in the latter.

A profound impact on sexual representations

Sexuality provides similar results. In this area, the issue of pornographic content often masks the insidious impact of, say, more 'ordinary' films and series, such as *Mad Men*, *Avatar* and *Desperate Housewives*. Admittedly, the sexual episodes in them are not brutally explicit. But this does not prevent them from being real, frequent and, in many cases, threatening in their propensity to be somewhat 'casual' in manner (that is, they fail to mention the potential risks and desirable prophylactic measures).[3,4437-9] On television, for example, risky sexual behaviour appears in 8%, 65%, 55% and 91% respectively of TV-Y7, TV-PG, TV-14 and TV-MA programmes.[a,283] The problem is that the viewer unconsciously ends up, via the associative tendencies of her memory system, turning this torrent of examples into a standard of conduct. In this case, two corollaries are theoretically expected: a facilitation of turning the image into a reality, and an abandonment of protective conduct. This is exactly what the

---

[a] See above, p. 172.

scientific literature reports.[440-5] One study, for example, looked at television. Nearly 1,800 adolescents aged 13 to 17 were followed for a year.[446] At the end of this period, the probability of having sexual intercourse for the first time was doubled in the 10% of subjects who were initially exposed to the most sexual content, compared to the 10% of subjects who were the least exposed. In another study, also focused on television, 1,700 adolescents aged 12 to 17 were followed for three years.[447] Over this period, the likelihood of enduring an unwanted early pregnancy was doubled among the 10% of participants exposed to the most sexual content, compared to the 10% of participants with the least exposure. In line with this observation, a subsequent study showed the extreme persistence of the impacts identified. Thus, in the words of the authors, 'higher early movie sexual exposure (before age 16) predicted more risky sexual behaviors (i.e., a higher number of lifetime sexual partners and more frequent casual sex without a condom) in adulthood'.[444] In yet another study, it was the impact of rap videos that was analysed.[448] More than 500 African-American teenagers aged 14 to 18 were followed for a year. At the end, the odds of having had more than one partner and of having contracted a sexually transmitted disease were increased by factors of 2.0 and 1.6, respectively, among the most exposed participants.

And what about explicitly pornographic content? In many countries, including France, the access restrictions are just ridiculous. You just press the magic button 'over 18' to access the most explicit images.[a] A simple click and the child is exposed to all kinds of wonderful practices favourable to the development of the worst gender stereotypes and the emergence of risky and violent sexual behaviour:[3,449-55] sadism, humiliation, aggression, orgies, multiple unprotected sexual relationships, etc. We cannot simultaneously put in place the – fundamental – discourses relating to the prevention of rape, the need to use condoms and the unacceptable nature of gender discrimination while tolerating our children being exposed without control to content that endorses and (often) aestheticizes these behaviours, by showing for example (this is a common scenario in pornographic videos) that the woman who is being raped actually wanted it very much because, like all women, she inevitably hides her intimate essence as a 'bitch' beneath a bourgeois veneer and ends up asking for more while enjoying endless climaxes as she is subjected

---

[a] I have just sampled two main streaming sites: PornHub and YouPorn (22 November 2020).

to the assaults of her attacker! This is also a well-known scenario in certain hugely popular 'action' video games – games stuffed with testosterone that promote a virile masculinity which tends to be expressed to the detriment of the secondary feminine characters, often represented as mere foils for the dominant male.[456] These games have a negative role in gender stereotypes and sexist attitudes, as has been increasingly well documented.[456-64] Sceptics can get a more precise idea of the problem by taking a look at *GTA*, which we have already talked about. This blockbuster, generously mixing violence and pornography,[a] is – forgive me for insisting – consumed by 38% of 8- to 10-year-olds, 74% of 11- to 14-year-olds and 85% of 15- to 18-year-olds.[315]

In short, taken as a whole, these data show that audiovisual and digital content is a powerful prescriber of social standards. By changing our view of the world, such content prescribes the way we act; and more often than not it does so surreptitiously, without awakening the radar of conscious defences. At this point, the question is no longer, as some fusty lobbyists still try to suggest, whether these data are reliable. They are. They are all the more so as the effects described are part of the biological intimacy of our neuronal organization. The brain is a wonderful machine, but it is also a deeply vulnerable machine. It processes a lot of information without our knowledge, in a purely automatic way.[248,252,465-7] From a functional point of view, not only is this not a flaw; it's a true evolutionary miracle without which our thinking and decision-making processes would be instantly saturated. Unfortunately, from a commercial point of view, it's a disaster. For the armada of 'spare brain-time merchants', this disaster is a godsend. It constitutes a formidable security gap, thanks to which it becomes possible to orient and manipulate human behaviour. And frankly, without a collective awareness spreading soon, things are unlikely to improve in the years to come. Indeed, what was until now only a rather crude enterprise, scattering its produce at random, is becoming, thanks to the exponential ubiquity of digital surveillance tools, a fundamentally pernicious and immoral work of surgical targeting.[468] Every trace, every piece of data, every purchase, every word, every visit, every click, every 'like' that we leave on the Web is now used against us, with worrying precision. The manipulation orchestrated by the company Cambridge Analytica in several countries, including the United States, to distort various democratic elections by relying on the personal data left on Facebook

---

[a] See above, p. 45.

by millions of wildly overconfident users is probably just the first of a long list of outrages yet to come.[469-72] This scandal – for as such it has now been acknowledged – served to confirm, on a large scale, that it was now possible to identify, reach and influence certain key voters to swing their votes or incite them not to vote. But is there really anything to be shocked about here, when we know that these 'tools' are already being used on a large scale for ad targeting? Indeed, this is the business model of digital giants such as Google or Facebook.

Violence

So the list of content that threatens our children is far from being small or trivial. It extends its generous embrace from tobacco to alcohol, via junk food, pornography, consumerism and various particularly nauseating stereotypes about sex, the body, gender, weight or race (even if the latter field hasn't been mentioned here, it has been extensively studied).[473-5] However, one giant factor is still missing from the discussion: violence. This is so ubiquitous in digital spaces that it is now almost impossible to preserve our offspring from it. As the American Academy of Pediatrics recently recognized: 'exposure to media violence is becoming an inescapable component of children's lives'.[476] However, there is now a very broad scientific consensus, to which I will come back in detail below, that is critical of the profoundly damaging influence of this torrent of images on the development of our children. Generally, three main issues are considered: (i) the accentuation of aggressive thoughts, feelings and behaviours; (ii) the desensitization and weakening of the potential for empathy; (iii) the factually unfounded exacerbation of the subjective feeling of insecurity. Despite everything, as we will also see, the media controversy remains lively, and debate follows debate, regularly fed by iconoclastic studies and opinions. This persistence is totally implausible; even if we were to forget all the experimental evidence accumulated over fifty years, the impact of violent content on children's representations and behaviours could hardly be disputed! Indeed, from a causal point of view, the associative and normative mechanisms involved here are the same as those mentioned in previous pages with regard to tobacco, alcohol, sexuality, body image, etc. By what miracle could violence be set outside the universal field of these evolutionary weaknesses? Basically, from the point of view of brain functioning, the surprise is not that violent content has a profound influence on our behaviour; the surprise would be if it didn't.

PART THREE

A long-standing debate

For over sixty years, the influence of violent media content has been obsessively investigated by scientists in every possible way. Beyond variations in media (films, series, video games, television news, etc.), protocols (experimental, observational, longitudinal, cross-sectional, etc.), populations (age, sex, ethnicity, etc.) and statistical methodologies, the result has never varied: violent content promotes the emergence of aggressive behaviours and feelings, in both the short and the long term, in both children and adults.[476-85] 'Aggressive' does not mean, however, that violent films or games turn all kids into bloodthirsty killers and lead them to perpetrate rapes, killings and mass cruelties. This does not mean, either, that violent content is the only (or even the main) explanatory factor for aggressive behaviour. It does not mean, finally, that the effect is unconditional and uniformly expressed. It means 'simply' that if you take a population of individuals exposed to violent content, their verbal and/or physical aggressive behaviours will be more frequent and more marked than in a comparable population not subjected to such content. The average effect will then increase with the dose, that is, with the intensity of the exposure. Against this background – let's restate the point one last time, to avoid any ambiguity – no one can claim that the increase in the level of aggressiveness inherent in the consumption of violent content is likely to lead, even occasionally, to brutally violent behaviour – but no one can absolutely rule it out, either. For example, without this little surplus of aggressiveness or irritability (and/or without this image of the virile male gradually internalized from exposure to violent and sexist virtual content), Mr X might not have jumped out of his car to have words with the individual who had dangerously cut him up – and the affair would not have degenerated into a brutal and savage fight.

The problem, as the American Academy of Pediatrics points out, is that 'unfortunately, media reports frequently present "both sides" of the media violence and aggression issue by pairing a research scientist with an industry expert or spokesperson or even a contrarian academic, which creates a false equivalency and the misperception that research data and scientific consensus are lacking'.[476] And, indeed, many articles aimed at the general public do not hesitate to draw on what they claim is a lack of scientific unanimity to deny the existence of a causal relationship between an increase in the level of aggressive behaviour and violent media content.[486,487] So as to put paid to this depressing fable, one group of researchers recently undertook to explore the question quantitatively.[488,489] Several hundred scientists working in the digital field, paediatricians and parents were interviewed (figure 10). The result: 'there is broad consensus [...]. Although a few vocal researchers claim there is a "debate" on this issue, the overwhelming majority of researchers believe that violent media increase aggression in children, and that the relationship is causal. Pediatricians are even more convinced, and parents also have little doubt.'[488] These last two observations are hardly surprising when we know that clinicians and parents are actively confronted – much more than researchers – with the effect that massive use of screens, especially those with violent images, can have on the behaviour of children. In fact, the parents' response seems particularly reassuring because it shows that the latter are not totally fooled by the propagandist manipulations to which they are subjected.

Basically, what is most surprising in the light of these data is that the observed consensus within the scientific community isn't greater. One

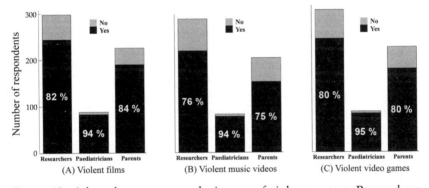

Figure 10. A broad consensus on the impact of violent content. Researchers (in communication and psychology of the media – not necessarily specialists in questions of violence), paediatricians and parents must decide on the validity of three statements: films (A), violent music videos (B) and video games (C) 'can increase aggressive behavior among children'. The figure illustrates the broad supremacy of positive responses ('agree' and 'strongly agree' aggregated as 'yes'; black part of the bar) over negative responses ('disagree' and 'strongly disagree' aggregated as 'no'; grey part of the bar). The figure does not take into account those without an opinion (approx. 15% of respondents) because it is not possible to know whether these non-responses reflect a feeling of incompetence ('I do not know the subject well enough to say') or an admission of uncertainty ('in the current state of knowledge, it is impossible to say').[488,489]

might think that this is due to the lack of specificity of the academic sample examined. Indeed, it is probable that a study centred solely on real experts in the field (i.e. experts who directly conduct research on the effect of violent content) would have delivered a much higher level of unanimity.[490] As a proof of this assertion, we can note that all the hyper-specialized panels brought together under the aegis of major institutions, whether governmental,[491,492] medical,[476,482,493-5] and/or academic[481,496] have drawn similar conclusions:[a] 'extensive research evidence indicates that media violence can contribute to aggressive behavior, desensitization to violence, nightmares, and fear of being harmed'.[494] Then there are, of course, a host of rigorously conducted meta-analyses and syntheses.[477,478,480,483,484,497-501]

In short, when we take the time to seriously analyse the available data as a whole, it just seems bizarre that the artificial controversy over the effects of violent images and video games has not yet ended. Already in 1999, in the *New York Times*, the secretary general of the American Psychological Association declared that 'the evidence is overwhelming. To argue against it is like arguing against gravity.'[502] However, the debate continues and protests expressed in the media remain vociferous. A study of content carried out in the early 2000s puts its finger on the problem. Around this time, two researchers began to seriously question the apparently highly nuanced (not to say very favourable) view that the mainstream American media took of the question of violent images.[503] After being refused by *Newsweek* the right to respond to an article deemed to be lacking in objectivity, our specialists, feeling a little annoyed, decided to study the subject once and for all from its quantitative perspective. To do this, they undertook to compare, based on extensive bibliographic research, the respective development of scientific knowledge and media representations over a quarter of a century. The result was that they had followed strictly opposite paths. Between 1975 and 2000, the more the level of scientific certainty about the toxic effect of audiovisual violence on behaviour had increased, the more cutesy and reassuring the media discourse had become. In other words, the more academic studies agreed to emphasize the reality of the problem, the more journalists explained to their customers that there was nothing to

---

[a]For example, for the United States alone, the American Academy of Pediatrics, the American Psychological Association, the American Psychiatric Association, the American Academy of Child and Adolescent Psychiatry, the Society for the Psychological Study of Social Issues, the American Medical Association, the American Academy of Family Physicians, the International Society for Research on Aggression, the U.S. Surgeon General, the U. S. National Institutes of Health.[490]

panic about; if there was a problem, it could in any case have only marginal consequences in 'real life'. As one might fear, the bias has not gone away since the publication of this original finding. According to the results of a recent study, the timorousness of the media has only increased over time.[504] In the early 2000s, there were 2.2 times more 'affirmative' press articles (recognizing the existence of a significant link between audiovisual violence and aggressive behaviour) than 'neutral' articles (emphasizing that one could not decide). Ten years later, despite, as we have seen, a still strong consensus in the scientific community, the relationship was almost reversed with 1.5 times more 'neutral' articles than 'affirmative' ones. Interestingly, the latter appeared significantly more often when written by women than by men. Men, known to be heavier consumers of video games,[505] may have been less inclined to recognize the problem.[506] (Unsurprisingly, 'affirmative' articles were less frequent when the number of 'non-specific' sources increased – researchers unrelated to the field, members of the media industry, consumers, etc.)

Of course, the protest actions of a few incompetent or hired pseudo-experts cannot, by themselves, explain this slow divergence between scientific knowledge and the media picture. To effectively implant the worm of uncertainty in the bud of knowledge, the rebuttal must come from within the body of researchers as a whole. In the long term, doubt can only be rooted in the intimate impression that the fight is being waged between studies and parties of equal authority. In short, any contradiction must come from an academic. And in this matter, no one performs better than the now famous Christopher Ferguson. For years, this doctor of psychology, a professor at Stetson University in Florida, has been piling up media statements[507-9] and academic publications[510-15] indicating that there is no link between violent audiovisual content and aggressive behaviour. These publications, however, have a bad habit of presenting alarming methodological biases and approximations.[477,478,488,516-18] Let's take just one recent representative example, from a meta-analysis carried out by Ferguson and aimed at settling the debate on the potential impact of video games (in particular, violent games) on cognitive functioning and behaviour.[511] Unsurprisingly, this researcher once again 'finds' that video games have a marginal influence on aggressive behaviour, academic performance and attention disorders. Unfortunately for our iconoclast, Hannah Rothstein happened to come across this study.[519] She is one of the best international specialists in meta-analytical statistics, a difficult subject on which she has co-developed dedicated software[520] and published a number of reference texts in the form of books[521-3] and articles.[524-6] Her conclusions, presented by the journal which had previously accepted Ferguson's article, are caustic (to say the least), as the title of the paper indicates: 'Methodological and reporting errors in meta-analytic reviews make other meta-analysts angry.'[a] After drawing up a long list of methodological and statistical aberrations, the text concludes:

> we have no confidence in the reliability or validity of the coded variables. The partialled and corrected effect sizes are incorrect and cannot be interpreted. Yet, we fear that readers (e.g., parents, pediatricians, policymakers) will assume that because this meta-analysis is published in this prestigious journal – *Perspectives on Psychological Science* – it is a valid synthesis of research on the effects of video games on children. It is not. It is fatally flawed and should not have been published in this journal or any other journal.[519]

When one is familiar with all the intricacies of scientific rhetoric, this kind of comment is singularly clear.

But let's be kind and assume that, despite the scepticism they frequently arouse, the studies Ferguson produces are solid, rigorous and valid. At the end of the day, this doesn't change the problem. Indeed, when they are combined with all the available research, in exhaustive (and correctly conducted!) meta-analyses, it appears that the work (and positions) of this researcher completely fall outside what is acceptable and constitute, with a few other errant productions of the same kind, real statistical anomalies.[477,478] In other words, our iconoclast finds nothing when almost everyone else finds something. Curious ... but practical, because it provides all the merchants of doubt on the planet with solid ammunition, especially as there persists within the mainstream media a deceptive 'fairness doctrine'[90] which requires that all 'camps' be offered overall comparable exposure and thereby makes aberrant works seem more important.[278] In this way, the anomaly is seen as being as worthy of respect as the dozens of studies it contradicts. And so, as one could read almost twenty years ago in the prestigious magazine *Science*, the debate on the influence of violent images persists, 'long after [it] should have been over, much as the cigarette smoking/cancer controversy persisted long after the scientific community knew that smoking

---

[a] Doubtless a reference to the title of Ferguson's paper 'Do Angry Birds make for angry children?'

causes cancer'.[527] But it's probably time to establish the reality of this assertion once and for all, by taking a look at the data.

What the data say

Let's start with studies of content. These show that the biases observed for tobacco, alcohol or sexuality also concern violence. In the digital world, the last of these is not only ubiquitous. It is also valued and associated with all kinds of positive traits, including power, money, stubbornness or (for men) manhood. In many cases, it is presented in a singularly glamorous light and portrayed as a legitimate, if not necessary, remedy. Its traumatic effects are surprisingly underestimated in both the short and long term (what human could endure, without suffering irrevocable neurological consequences, a hundredth of the hammering suffered by Rocky in each of his films?).[3,4,494,528] So yes, obviously, to say it once again, this avalanche of violent content has a significant impact on the behaviour of children and adolescents.[476–48,480–45,491–501] This can be observed in both the short and the long term.

Let's start with the short-term influences. They are based, in particular, on the already mentioned phenomena of priming. The idea is quite simple: exposure to violent stimuli and behaviour promotes hostile behaviour by activating memory networks of aggression. Dozens of studies demonstrate the reality of this mechanism. In one study, for example, young adults had to inflict an electric shock of a freely chosen intensity (between 1 and 10) on a stranger when the latter incorrectly answered a question.[529] Just before the experiment started, a student came into the room explaining that he absolutely had to complete a study to pass his exam, but his subject had just let him down. He begged for help and claimed it was only for a few minutes. The person conducting the first experiment obviously agreed. The new task was to form sentences from scattered words. These were either 'neutral' (e.g. 'the door open fix') or hostile ('hits he her them'). The results showed that participants in the 'hostile' group then used significantly higher electrical intensities than those in the 'neutral' group (+ 50%, 3.3 versus 2.2). In another, comparable study, sentences were formed from words evoking politeness (respect, polite, patiently, etc.) or rudeness (intrude, bother, disrupt, etc.).[256] Once the task was completed, participants had to introduce themselves to the experimenter, who 'unfortunately' happened to be in the middle of a conversation. The members of the 'rudeness' group were almost four times more likely than those of the 'politeness' group to interrupt the discussion (63% versus 17%).

These results have obviously been largely reproduced from audio-visual 'priming'. One study, for example, first exposed young adults to short videos, both violent and non-violent.[530] Second, the participants had to decide as quickly as possible whether a series of letters briefly presented on a screen constituted a real word. Individuals previously exposed to violent videos recognized the terms 'aggressive' (destroy, harm, hurt, etc.) more quickly than their counterparts exposed to non-violent videos. No difference was observed for neutral words. In another study, students were exposed to four films in four days.[531] At the end of each screening, they had to rate these films. On the fifth day they were told that the study was on hold and asked to perform a facial recognition task instead. Then, these students were asked to rate the two experimenters who had supervised the completion of this second task (are they courteous [on a scale of 1 to 10]? Do they deserve a scholarship [yes/no]? Etc.). The students subjected to a series of 'violent' films during the first phase of the experiment showed a much higher level of hostility than their peers exposed to more 'neutral' works. The latter were thus more likely to state that the experimenters had shown greater courtesy (+ 29%; 5.8 versus 4.5) and to conclude that they should be granted financial support (+ 23%; 66% versus 43%). Comparable results were obtained in a population of juvenile delinquents placed in boarding schools.[532] For a week, some were exposed to 'neutral' films, others to 'violent' films. This second condition resulted, unlike the first, in a significant increase in physical attacks.

Unsurprisingly, several studies have made it possible to generalize these behaviours to younger populations. For example, children aged 4 to 6 were invited to play freely with two small automatons.[533] In response to the pressure of a lever, the first released a ball which then circulated through various obstacles and returned to its original position. The second operated a doll which, with the help of a stick, came and hit its neighbour. Before playing, children were exposed to a cartoon with neutral or violent images. This second condition strongly aroused the participants' appetite for the doll that hit its neighbour; its frequency of use rose from 29% (neutral cartoon) to 50% (violent cartoon). Similar results were obtained in a comparable study involving slightly older children (5–9 years). These were first exposed to a violent film or to an athletic programme (jumps, races, etc.).[534] Then they were placed behind a window, in a position to assist or thwart the movement of a lever that another child was supposedly trying to operate. Not surprisingly, the results showed a significant increase in hostile behaviour in the 'violent' condition.

More recently, these observations have been extended to the field of a violence no longer passively observed, but actively perpetrated. In one representative experiment, students were exposed to a video game, violent or non-violent, daily for 20 minutes, over a period of 3 consecutive days.[535] After each session, they were asked to complete an 'ambiguous' story to assess the level of hostility felt (i.e. attributed to the outside world). Then, in a third step, each participant was placed in a situation of direct opposition (this was fictitious, though the players obviously didn't know this). They had, in response to a sudden visual cue, to produce a faster response than their opponent. After each duel, the winner had the right to inflict on the loser, through headphones, a sonic attack of freely configurable intensity (1 to 10) and duration (0 to 5 s). 'As expected', write the authors of the study, 'aggressive behavior and hostile expectations increased over days for violent game players, but not for nonviolent video game players, and the increase in aggressive behavior was partially due to hostile expectations'. Thus, at the end of the third day, the average aggression score (calculated by aggregating the parameters of intensity and duration) was 1.7 times greater in the 'violent' group (6.8) than in the 'neutral' group (4.1). A compatible result was obtained in a more 'ecological' study, carried out on a population of schoolchildren (8–10 years).[536] It was then reported, after a period of 6 months, that the implementation of a protocol to reduce the level of media exposure (video games, television, DVD) had led to a significant reduction in aggressive behaviour. The latter had remained stable in a control group that had not been the subject of any intervention. This result echoed an earlier observation that showed that the arrival of television in a Canadian city had resulted, within 2 years, in a significant increase in behaviours of physical aggression ($\times$ 2.6) and verbal aggression ($\times$ 2.0) observed during school breaks.[537] This progression contrasted with the lack of development identified in two control towns, already connected to television.

Thus, the short- and medium-term impact of violent media content on the emergence of hostile and aggressive behaviour is absolutely indisputable. But what about longer-term influences? Obviously, the question cannot be approached experimentally. It requires the establishment of a cross-sectional or longitudinal epidemiological study. The principle is fairly standard. It consists in determining, after taking into account the relevant covariates, whether the individuals who consume the most violent audiovisual content produce a greater number of aggressive behaviours. The answer is clearly positive. For example, one study showed that every hour spent watching TV in preschool (4 years) increased the risk of bullying in primary school (6–11 years) by 9%.[538] This effect was undoubtedly 'driven' by the pervasiveness of violent content on the small screen. Indeed, other complementary research has established that early exposure (between 2 and 5 years) to violent audiovisual programmes (films, sports, cartoons, etc.) predicted the onset of behavioural disorders five years later.[539] The effect was only significant for boys (the risk was then quadrupled). It was not found with educational or non-violent programmes. In another study, children aged 6 to 10 were followed for 15 years.[540] In adulthood, the frequency of aggressive behaviours among the 20% of individuals who, during childhood, had absorbed the largest number of violent images was compared with the frequency of such behaviours among the 80% who had absorbed the smallest number. For men, the results showed a greater probability of having mistreated their spouse ($\times$ 1.9), of having been convicted ($\times$ 3.5) and/ or of having committed a traffic offence (excluding parking: $\times$ 1.5). Women, for their part, showed an increased risk of having thrown an object at their husband ($\times$ 2.3), of having assaulted another adult ($\times$ 4.8) and of having committed (according to them) a criminal act during the past year ($\times$ 1.9). In yet another study, separate groups of American (9–12 years) and Japanese (12–15 years and 13–18 years) young people were followed for 3 to 6 months.[541] The results showed that being a regular user of violent video games at time T1 (start of the study) doubled or tripled, depending on the groups, the probability of physical aggression at time T2 (end of the study). In another survey, it was the impact of rap videos that was assessed on a panel of African-American adolescents (14 to 18 years old).[448] At the end of a 12-month follow-up period, the participants initially most at risk had a significantly increased risk of having hit a teacher ($\times$ 3.0), having been arrested ($\times$ 2.6) or having taken drugs ($\times$ 1.6).

We could cite more examples and extend these results to different content (e.g. pornographic content)[452] and different groups (by age, culture, socio-economic origin, etc.).[542–5] But that wouldn't add much to the subject, as the data are convergent. The only controversy that can still be considered at this level concerns the existence of a possible causal attribution error. The idea here is that the observed impacts might not go from exposure to behaviour but, rather, from behaviour to exposure. In other words, it may simply be that 'naturally' aggressive individuals are more attracted to violent content. Procedures for controlling the initial level of aggressiveness, as well as various specific statistical tools, made it possible to reject this hypothesis by demonstrating that the causal chain did indeed mainly go from exposure to behaviour and not the other way around.[540,541,543-5] In short, here too it seems to be an open-and-shut case, and it can be concluded that early exposure to violent media content has a lasting effect on the aggressive propensity of the individual. We still need to understand the nature of the mechanisms involved. Two factors seem particularly credible: normative appropriation and desensitization.

Normative appropriation has already been mentioned in the previous sections. It involves the progressive assimilation, by vicarious absorption (most often unconsciously), of a number of social norms.[546] Applied to the questions that concern us here, this model suggests that repeated confrontation with all kinds of brutal content teaches children that violence and aggression can effectively resolve interpersonal conflicts, get what one deserves and, in fact, constitute enviable personality traits.[545,547-50] Ultimately, these beliefs literally end up colonizing the psyche, as one particularly interesting study has reported.[551] Students (age 18) were subjected to a semantic association test to determine the link, within their unconscious memory networks, between the concept of 'me' and various aggressive attributes.[a] The results identified a significantly higher degree of connection among violent video game users.

Desensitization, for its part, is a phenomenon of habituation which leads to a progressive loss of effectiveness of the original stimulus. This is a basic biological process that results in a gradual drop in neuronal responses[552] and explains, for example, that we fairly quickly cease to perceive the presence of the scent we are wearing.[553] Regarding the present chapter, the idea can be summarized through the concept of 'acceptable violence'. From a physiological point of view, this could be defined as the maximum threshold of violence which fails to produce a negative emotion. It is now clearly established that this threshold varies greatly in children, adolescents and adults depending on the degree of exposure to violent media content: the more the individual is impregnated with such content, the more

---

[a] Schematically, subjects are presented with an item taken from one of two categories: me/others (this item can be a family name, a first name, a date of birth, an image, etc.). Then the time taken to identify another item also taken from one of two categories is measured: aggressive/calm (revenge, threat, attack, etc./dialogue, reconciliation, exchange, etc.). The underlying hypothesis, already discussed in a previous note (p. 162), suggests that functionally related items within memory networks will be more quickly and easily retrieved.

her level of insensitivity increases.[554-6] Longitudinal research, for example, followed a group of Singaporean schoolchildren (7–15 years old) for 2 years. The results showed that the use of violent video games at the start of the study causally predicted a lower level of empathy 24 months later.[557] Recently, neuroimaging studies have identified the neuronal substrates of this desensitization.[558] In the short term, the brain has been shown to deactivate its emotional networks when subjected to repeated violent images.[559,560] In the long term, the adolescents most exposed to television violence have been reported to have discrete but significant developmental abnormalities at the level of the prefrontal regions involved in the control of emotions and the inhibition of aggressive behaviour.[561] In line with these observations, various studies based on the electrical conductivity of the epidermis (which changes when we feel a strong emotion) have indicated that children and adolescents accustomed to audiovisual violence displayed a higher tolerance to real images of brawling or aggression than their less exposed peers.[560,562,563] Similar results have been reported for video games in neuroimaging studies showing a lower responsiveness to violence in the emotional brain networks of regular players of violent games.[564-6] Unsurprisingly, several studies have confirmed that this desensitization process promotes the emergence of aggressive and hostile behaviour.[564,567,568]

If only this loss of sensitivity to the pain of others helped us better control our own fear of being victimized. But this is not the case. In other words, we can be less empathetic without being less fearful. A large number of studies thus indicate, for example, in children and adolescents that violent content increases the risk of anxiety, depression and sleep disorders (refusal to go to bed, difficulty falling asleep, nightmares, etc.).[165,494,569-71] The effect is obviously greater for disaster stories and/or extremely violent stories (terrorism, natural disasters, climate change, etc.)[572] than for more 'ordinary' content (detective films, crime series, news, cartoons, etc.).[573] However, a large individual variability seems to emerge in the latter case. Thus, according to the results of one recent meta-analysis,

> there is little to suggest that, at the group level, scary TV has a *severe* impact on children's mental health (in terms of internalizing problems [fear, anxiety, sadness, and sleep problems]). However, such programming does have a consistent effect that is comparable to effects found for externalizing behaviours [aggression, violence, antisocial, etc.] [...] Some individual studies do show extreme reactions in a substantial minority of children.[573]

192

And, to avoid any ambiguity, let's note one last time: 'a substantial minority' means a lot of people when the risk applies to a population of several tens of millions of individuals.

The war of correlations

In the perpetual fight waged by commercialism against the public good, certain ways of spinning the data have been so often exploited that one might have thought they had become stale. This is not the case. The same coarse tricks of the trade, however threadbare, continue to produce the same noisily affirmative statements and the same overhyped, misleading headlines. The most egregious example of these delusional schemes is undoubtedly the 'fallacious correlation'. The concept is quite simple and operates in two stages. First the premise: if A acts on B, then as A increases, B increases. Then comes the fallacy or sophism:[a] if B does not increase when A increases, then A does not act on B. In almost all cases, this pattern is absurd. Indeed, it only works if A is the sole influencing factor on B, which hardly ever happens in 'real life'. Let's take a simple example. I'm riding my little scooter on a flat track. When I pull the throttle grip, the speed increases. So I conclude that the throttle grip controls the speed of the vehicle. Until this point, everything works fine. But suddenly the road begins to climb sharply. I step on the accelerator again, but my speed doesn't increase; worse, it decreases. Am I to conclude that the accelerator is slowing down my scooter? Of course not. If I'm going more slowly, this is because the slope also affects the speed, in a way opposite to that of the accelerator. As this slope effect is heavier than the accelerator effect, the scooter slows down. Anyone who would take advantage of this observation to claim that the throttle grip has no positive influence on speed would be immediately seen as brain-dead. Yet this kind of confusion is pervasive in the media, especially when it comes to denying the impact of violent content on aggressive behaviour. This is especially true in the field of video games. Alongside the general discourses already mentioned (there's no consensus, the data contradict each other, etc.), the 'fallacious correlation' has emerged as a central argument for the

---

[a] This term refers to 'an argument that seems true but is really false and is used to deceive people' (https://dictionary.cambridge.org/dictionary/english/sophism). So here I am referring to a correlation which relies on a sophism: it starts from true premises and leads to false conclusions.

promoters of doubt. This is why it seems important to briefly address the issue here.

In practice, the case takes several forms. The first is transnational and teaches us, as some recent media 'headlines' have loudly asserted, that: 'Countries that play more violent video games such as Grand Theft Auto and Call of Duty have FEWER murders'[574] or that 'Ten-country comparison suggests there's little or no link between video games and gun murders'.[575] After all, one journalist explains,

> if video games were really the root of all evil [which no serious researcher has ever suggested, but let's ignore that], then logic would suggest that there would be more violent gun crimes as at least a partial result. That simply isn't happening [...] In fact, countries where *video game consumption is highest tend to be some of the safest countries in the world.*[576]

No doubt it's better to read this than to be blind, as Madame Vessilier, a wonderful teacher I had in my last year of primary school, liked to say with a gentle smile, after each of my terrible dictations.[a] The 'logic' displayed here is, in fact, perfectly absurd. It would only make sense if video games were the one and only cause of crime and violent assault. This is obviously not the case. Who can think, even for a second, that the potentially facilitating action of violent video games on aggressive behaviour will counterbalance the political, social or religious instability observed in the most dangerous countries on the planet? To reject any possible impact of violent games on aggressive behaviour on the grounds that there are more video games and fewer murders in Japan than in countries as endemically unstable as Honduras, El Salvador or Iraq[574,577] is plain wrong.

Of course, some observers are smart enough to avoid this distressing caricature; they look at seemingly comparable countries like Japan and the United States. It is therefore tempting to argue that there are more murders and fewer video games in the country of Uncle Sam than in the Land of the Rising Sun.[575] This would be to forget that certain factors in violence, the combined action of which weighs much more heavily than the possible impact of video games, are potentially expressed in very different ways in these two countries: access to firearms (on sale almost for nothing in the United States), economic conditions (crime increases, for example, with increasing levels of unemployment and poverty), early exposure to

---

[a] I hope she will forgive me if I've misspelled her name.

certain organic pollutants (there is a significant link between crime and lead poisoning), the age pyramid (the older the population, the lower the level of crime), the police force and its methods, the consumption of psychotropic products (crime increases with the use of alcohol or crack cocaine), etc.[578-83] To assert that there is no relation between the level of penetration of violent video games in a population and the crime rate is impossible if these risk factors are not integrated into the statistical model. Returning to our original analogy, omitting these factors means omitting the effect of a gradient when estimating the role of the scooter's throttle. In other words, while pandering to 'common sense', all of the transnational correlations described here – which some media love to refer to, so as to justify the idea that violent video games are harmless – make absolutely no sense.

In another, more frequent version, the principle of spurious correlation takes a longitudinal form. In this case, for example, we hear that 'the proliferation of violent video games has not coincided with spikes in youth violent crime'.[486] In other words, 'As video game sales climb year over year, violent crime continues to fall'.[584] A recent study supports the veracity of this observation.[585] 'One more study', a major weekly tells us, 'which puts paid once and for all to most common clichés'.[586] Nicely worded – but a little optimistic. Let's briefly take a closer look.

First, the study in question simply shows that in the United States sales of video games are moving in the opposite direction to crime. Thus, since the beginning of the 1990s, the former have sharply increased, while the latter has fallen dramatically. A nice result – which, however, once again, means nothing. Indeed, during the last decades, a number of factors have collaborated to make possible a massive decrease in the level of crime in North America: an explosion in the rate of incarceration, an increase in police numbers, an improvement in the economic situation, a decline in certain major triggers of criminality (alcohol, drugs, lead, etc.), etc.[578,580,582] It's clear that the combined action of these factors weighs much more than the potential influence of video games alone. Therefore, these may very well have a significant negative impact in an overall decrease in the crime curve. This is all the more true since we are not just talking about violent video games here. The correlation presented curiously mixes all types of games, from the most childish games to role-playing games, including strategy, arcade and sports games. This amalgamation obviously minimizes the chances of finding anything significant. You can never be too careful.

No doubt aware of the limitations of their first study, the authors present a second analysis, supposedly 'more precise'.[586] To do this, they seek to link the sales figures of three violent games (*Grand Theft Auto San Andreas*, *Grand Theft Auto IV* and *Call of Duty Black Ops*) to monthly crime statistics. As explained in the article, the idea is quite simple (dare we say simplistic): 'if violent video games are causes of serious violent crimes, it seems probable that serious and deadly assaults would increase following the release of these three popular violent video games'.[585] Except that the suspected increase did not occur. Over the 12 months following the release of each of these games, the number of violent assaults remained stable and, on average, the number of homicides even appeared to decrease slightly in the third and fourth months – a result that the authors are, of course, unable to explain. But so what? The problem is elsewhere. Indeed, if you read the previous sentence correctly, you won't have missed the fact that we are here talking about the release of a *game*; one and the same game (the analysis is simply repeated three times for games released in 2004, 2008 and 2010 respectively). However, violent games come out every month. Take November 2010, for example, and the release of *Call of Duty Black Ops*, taken as a benchmark by the study's authors. The previous 12 months had seen a number of hugely popular hyperviolent video games being released in a staggered fashion;[a] the same was true in the following 12 months. Therefore, there is absolutely no reason why one game on its own could significantly increase the level of crime, unless we assume that the damaging effect of that particular game was significantly greater than that of all the others. In other words, the logic proposed here only works if the singular impact of *Call of Duty Black Ops* significantly outweighed the combined impact of all the other games – a most unlikely hypothesis, to put it mildly.

To illustrate the problem more concretely, let's take a simple example. Each month, a greengrocer organizes one or more special offers depending on arrivals: January (week 1: lychees, week 2: clementines, week 4: apples); February (week 2: avocados, week 4: pineapple); etc. He wants to know if these offers are having an effect on his bottom line. To do this, he chooses a reference (grapefruit – March, week 1) and a duration (6 months; he suspects that the impact of the offer could be spread over time because it might

---

[a] *Battlefield (Bad Company 2)*, *God of War 3*, *Halo (Reach)*, *Dead Rising 2*, *Medal of Honor*, *Fallout (New Vegas)*, *Saw 2*, etc.

make customers want to buy grapefruits even when not on special offer, and/or consumers might find it worth returning to this store as it often has great discounts). The grocer therefore looks at the way his turnover has changed over the 6 months preceding and following the offer. Unsurprisingly, he finds nothing. Yet this failure reflects not the lack of effect, on his sales, of the commercial operations implemented, but the stupidity of the experimental model employed: this model doesn't take into account the impact of previous and subsequent offers.

The study on video games mentioned here suffers from the same methodological weakness. Indeed, once again, the logic deployed to discover whether *Call of Duty* affects crime would only make sense if no product of the same type had arrived on the market in the months and weeks preceding or following the release of the game. Since this is not the case, it is impossible to draw any conclusion from the work presented. All the more impossible since it's hard to believe that gamers weren't playing another game before *Call of Duty* was released. In fact, for the reasoning put forward to hold true, it would also be necessary to ensure that the release of *Call of Duty* did indeed cause a significant increase in playing time and not a simple change of game (with the player quite simply replacing, for example, *Medal of Honor*, released the previous month, with the recently released *Call of Duty*). And even if we assume that players temporarily increase their playing time, what is to say that this increase is enough to bring about a noticeable change in behaviour? On the one hand, the increase may be too small to have a detectable influence; on the other hand, it may also lie beyond the optimal impact threshold. (One can legitimately conclude that the behavioural effect will hardly vary when the duration of daily consumption temporarily rises from 4 hours to 5 hours.)

In short, scientifically, beneath the surface veneer, this kind of study makes absolutely no sense; and it is fascinating that scientific journals can still welcome such calamities into their columns. However, for lobbyists, merchants of doubt and media hungry for a buzz, this 'research' is meat and drink. So some journalists have launched out into incredible flights of lyricism and asserted, for example, that these results certainly

> do not prove with any certainty the beneficial effect of video games on crime but nonetheless destroy [*sic*], incidentally, the eternal assertion that virtual violence encourages real violence [...]. The cliché goes back a long way. Born in puritanical political circles, this simplistic

belief quickly contaminated many strata of a society, fostering its misunderstanding of a phenomenon that went over its head.[587]

Just that. Personally, I don't know if I'm a puritan and mired in misunderstanding, but it seems clear to me that before launching such an idea into the public domain, it would be a good thing to rely on sound and relevant studies. Unless, of course, the intention is not to inform, but to convince. Indeed, the major interest of the bastard correlations discussed here is to provide lobbyists with an argumentative basis for their activities. And the least that can be said is that these good people do not hesitate to exhaust the vein.[385,588] Brainwashing, no doubt, is then fair game. This is no longer the case when the flow of propaganda starts to rely on being taken up by a journalism that supposedly guarantees serious and objective information. One simple rule, however, is to protect against this kind of manoeuvre: if you are told that two phenomena are independent because their variations are apparently not correlated, be *extremely* cautious. Always ask yourself if these phenomena are determined by several causes. When this is the case, and it is almost always the case in the epidemiological field, ask yourself whether these causes are taken into account in the statistical model (i.e. included as covariates). When the answer is no, this is undoubtedly a sign that what has just been said to you is not mighty science, but a sad hoax.

When justice steps in

Of course, there was a judgement handed down in 2011 by the Supreme Court of the United States, in favour of video game manufacturers.[589] A year earlier, the latter had attacked a California law aimed at 'restricting the sale or rental of violent video games to minors [defined as anyone "under 18 years of age"]'. Among the nine members of the Court, seven declared this law to be unconstitutional. Giving judgement, Judge Antonin Scalia devoted two short paragraphs to the question of scientific evidence. For him,

the State's evidence is not compelling. [...] They do not prove that violent video games cause minors to act aggressively (which would at least be a beginning). Instead, '[n]early all of the research is based on correlation, not evidence of causation, and most of the studies suffer from significant, admitted flaws in methodology'. *Video Software Dealers Assn.* 556 F. 3d, at 964.

198

This final statement was, as indicated by the quotation marks and the reference, taken (surprisingly!) from a text produced by manufacturers in the sector.

This was a superb piece of good fortune, of course, for those who believe that video games are harmless. But unfortunately, once again, it seems that the mask of initial appearances fails to tell the whole story. Indeed, contrary to what the preceding lines suggest, the case considered here was assessed not on a scientific basis, but on a political basis.[501,590,591] Thus, the judges did not ask themselves whether violent video games might have a certain negative effect on behaviour; they questioned whether the bill presented respected the First Constitutional Amendment, relating to freedom of expression. The proof – as reported in an academic article written after the judgement – was that 'the justice who wrote the majority opinion (Scalia) admits that he did not read any of the scientific articles offered to support the California law, but simply quoted from the Entertainment Software Industry's briefs in support of his argument that "the evidence was not compelling that video game violence was harmful"'.[501] Indeed, one member of the Supreme Court (Stephen Breyer) recognized, explicitly, in an addendum to the main judgement, the total lack of ability of the members of the Supreme Court to deal with the scientific basis of the dispute: 'I, like most judges, lack the social science expertise to say definitively who is right. But associations of public health professionals who do possess that expertise have reviewed many of these studies and found a significant risk that violent video games, when compared with more passive media, are particularly likely to cause children harm.'[589] With a touch of black humour, he also linked this judgement with an older opinion issued by the same Supreme Court and limiting the sale to minors of products containing images of nudity. He writes:

what sense does it make to forbid selling to a 13-year-old boy a magazine with an image of a nude woman, while protecting a sale to that 13-year-old of an interactive video game in which he actively, but virtually, binds and gags the woman, then tortures and kills her? What kind of First Amendment would permit the government to protect children by restricting sales of that extremely violent video game only when the woman – bound, gagged, tortured, and killed – is also topless? [...] This case is ultimately less about censorship than it is about education.[589]

In fact, the law attacked by the video game industry, the repeal of which delighted all the demago-geeks on the planet, simply set out to prevent the circumvention of parental educational prerogatives. Thus, as another judge (Clarence Thomas) noted:

> all that the law does is prohibit the direct sale or rental of a violent video game to a minor by someone other than the minor's parent, grandparent, aunt, uncle, or legal guardian. Where a minor has a parent or guardian, as is usually true, the law does not prevent that minor from obtaining a violent video game with his parent's or guardian's help.[589]

But that was too much to ask of Judge Scalia. He noted that 'no doubt a State possesses legitimate power to protect children from harm, but that does not include a free-floating power to restrict the ideas to which children may be exposed'[589] – even, therefore, if these ideas come from strictly mercantile institutions and cheerfully circumvent the educational freedom of parents. But hey, again, you have to be sensible: leaving them their freedom of choice could cause a cruel drop in sales, which would be pretty damn annoying. As one senator from the state of California put it: 'the Supreme Court once again put the interests of corporate America before the interests of our children. It is simply wrong that the video game industry can be allowed to put their profit margins over the rights of parents and the well-being of children.'[591]

In short, in the final analysis, it was an argument relating to freedom of expression, and not the validity of scientific bases, on which the Supreme Court ruled. Moreover, for anyone still in doubt, Judge Scalia (who, once again, has not read the studies involved) concludes the main judgement as follows:

> we have no business passing judgment on the view of the California Legislature that violent video games (or, for that matter, any other forms of speech) corrupt the young or harm their moral development. Our task is only to say whether or not such works constitute a 'well-defined and narrowly limited clas[s] of speech, the prevention and punishment of which have never been thought to raise any Constitutional problem' (the answer plainly is no).[589]

A year earlier, the Supreme Court had used arguments of the same nature to bury a federal text criminalizing the creation, sale and possession of images displaying cruel behaviour intentionally inflicted on living animals (mutilations, injuries, torture, murder, etc.).[589] In other words, in the United States, the First Amendment grants the right to purchase videos in which animals are beaten, tortured, burned and butchered alive. It also sells games to 5-, 6- or 8-year-old kids in which, as one of the judges admitted (even though he voted against the State of California),

'the violence is astounding. Victims by the dozens are killed with every imaginable implement, including machine guns, shotguns, clubs, hammers, axes, swords, and chainsaws. Victims are dismembered, decapitated, disemboweled, set on fire, and chopped into little pieces. They cry out in agony and beg for mercy. Blood gushes, splatters, and pools [...] There are games in which a player can take on the identity and reenact the killings carried out by the perpetrators of the murders at Columbine High School and Virginia Tech. The objective of one game is to rape a mother and her daughters; in another, the goal is to rape Native American women. There is a game in which players engage in 'ethnic cleansing' and can choose to gun down African-Americans, Latinos, or Jews. In still another game, players attempt to fire a rifle shot into the head of President Kennedy as his motorcade passes by the Texas School Book Depository.[589]

Yes, in the United States all of this is protected by free speech; and for the judges of the Supreme Court this justifies the right of manufacturers to sell freely to minors. It doesn't matter what impact these contents and practices may have on the social representations and psychological maturation of a nursery or primary school child. And, please, don't come telling us that parental responsibility is at issue here and that the state doesn't need to get involved in the subject: all that this law asked for was precisely that the full expression of this responsibility be allowed.

In conclusion

The point to be taken from this chapter is that exposure to screens for recreation has a very negative impact on the health of our children and adolescents. Three mechanisms then turn out to be particularly damaging.

First, screens seriously affect sleep. However, this is an essential, if not vital, pillar of development. When it goes off the rails, it's one's individual integrity as a whole that is affected, in its physical, emotional and intellectual dimensions. It is quite surprising (and disturbing) how underestimated the magnitude of this problem is today.

201

Second, screens greatly increase the degree of sedentary lifestyle while significantly reducing levels of physical activity. However, to develop optimally and to stay healthy, the body needs to be actively and frequently involved. Sitting down kills us! Exercise builds us up! And not just in our physical dimensions. Moving has a major impact on our emotional and intellectual functioning. Here again, the problem is inexplicably forgotten in the debates relating to the uses of digital technology by our offspring.

Third and last, so-called 'risky' content (with sex, smoking, alcohol, violence, etc., or encouraging obesity) saturates digital space. No platform is free of it. However, for children and adolescents, these contents are important prescribers of standards (often acting unconsciously). They dictate acceptable behaviour (e.g. a 'normal' high school pupil smokes and sleeps around – and ignores condoms). Once learned, these norms have a dramatic effect on behaviour (for example, the likelihood of a high school pupil smoking or having unprotected sex).

— EPILOGUE —

A VERY OLD BRAIN FOR A BRAVE
NEW WORLD

A very old brain for a brave new world
Each of your steps today is your life tomorrow.

Wilhelm Reich[1]

It's said that writing calms you down. I'm afraid this is not always the case. Sometimes words only add to our dismay. We start in good faith, we advance scrupulously, we end up aghast. This book is a good example. At the beginning, supported by a bibliographical knowledge that was still only fragmentary, it expressed merely a vague uncertainty. Then, slowly, confronted on one side by an ever-growing body of disturbing scientific studies and on the other by a barrage of ever-more complacent public discourse, it developed into a genuine anger. What we are doing to our children is inexcusable. Never in the history of mankind has such an experiment in stripping them of their minds been conducted on such a large scale.

I was recently told that I was 'contemptuous' of the younger generations. This is nonsense: nothing could be further from the truth. If I looked down on these kids, I'd wisely flatter their tastes. I'd tell them they're all transcendental brain mutants and suggest all kinds of flawed (but bankable) 'educational' apps they could use. I'd brag about their tremendous creativity, while quietly explaining to my lucrative clientele that these kids have such a crippled attention system that any ad longer than 10 seconds is doomed to fail. I would glorify their digital genius while doing my best to protect my own descendants from this threatening madness. I'd marvel at their prodigious lexical inventiveness so as not to have to deplore the worrying anaemia of their language. Deep down, if I despised these children, I wouldn't have written this book, but a complacent,

203

abjectly unctuous, approving hagiography. I would have sold my pen and my decency to some e-learning industrialist or video game manufacturer in need of scientific legitimation. I would have become a 'consultant' filled with a highly paid zeal, doing the rounds of TV studios and press rooms.

The reality is, I wrote this book not because I despise these kids but because I love and respect them. My life is largely over. Theirs is still a promise, and that promise should be sacred. Yet we're laying it waste on the altar of profit. 'Children are the living messages we send to a time we will not see', wrote Neil Postman almost forty years ago.[2] By the light of this fine image, perhaps we should ask ourselves what kind of witness we want to provide and what kind of society we want to found. The one that today's world promises looks more and more like the dystopian spectre of Huxley's *Brave New World*. On the one hand, the Alphas: a small minority caste of privileged children, preserved from this recreational orgy and endowed with a solid human, linguistic, emotional and cultural capital. On the other hand, the Gammas: a vast majority caste of underprivileged children, deprived of the basic tools of thought and intelligence. A subordinate caste of zealous performers, talking Orwell's 'Newspeak', dulled by inane entertainment and happy with their fate. For those who might be tempted to blindly reject this risk, a brief reminder of the main elements set out in this book might prove salutary.

What are the points to remember?

Four major conclusions need to be remembered.

First, when it comes to digital uses, the information offered to the general public is singularly lacking in rigour and reliability. Subject to implausible productivity imperatives, many journalists simply do not have time to deepen their understanding of the subject enough to speak with relevance, or to distinguish qualified experts from incompetent or corrupt sources.

Second, the recreational digital consumption of younger generations is not just 'excessive' or 'exaggerated'; it's wildly out of control. Among the main victims of this temporal orgy are all kinds of activities essential to development; for example, sleep, reading, intrafamily exchanges, school homework, sports and artistic practices, etc.

Third, this all-consuming digital frenzy is seriously impairing the intellectual, emotional and health development of our offspring. From a strictly epidemiological point of view, the conclusion to be drawn from these data is quite simple: screens for recreation are an absolute disaster. Any disease with the same causes (obesity, sleep disturbances, smoking, violence, attention difficulties, delays in language acquisition, anxiety, memorization, etc.) would see an army of researchers rising to combat it. No such thing happens with regard to our lucrative digital toys. Just here and there, a few timid warnings and calls for 'sensible vigilance'.[3]

Fourth, if the effect of screens for recreation is so damaging, this is in large part because our brains are not adapted to the digital fury that is devastating them. To build itself, it needs sensory temperance, human presence, physical activity, sleep and favourable cognitive nourishment. However, digital ubiquity offers it the complete opposite: constant perceptual bombardment; a collapse of interpersonal exchanges (especially intra-family); both quantitative and qualitative disturbance of sleep; amplification of sedentary behaviour; and chronic intellectual under-stimulation. Subjected to this damaging environmental pressure, the brain suffers and is poorly constructed. In other words, it continues to function – obviously – but well below its full potential. This is all the more tragic as the great periods of brain plasticity characteristic of childhood and adolescence do not last forever. Once closed, they can no longer be resuscitated. What has been spoiled is forever lost. The argument of modernity so often advanced then takes on its full absurdity. 'You have to live with your times', the progressive army tells us. No question about it. But we should warn our brains that the times have changed, because they haven't moved one iota for ages. And, unfortunately, before they can adapt perfectly to their new digital environment (if they ever do), this will take a few tens of millennia! In the meantime, things are not going to get better and reality may well remain just as repellent. No doubt it would be good if the supporters of a forced digitization of the school system were aware of this, too. To date, only one mechanism has demonstrated a truly positive and profound influence on the development of pupils: the qualified and well-trained teacher. She is the one element common to all of the best-performing school systems on the planet.

Writing this, I am aware '[that] nobody loves the person who brings bad news', as Sophocles made Antigone say.[4] I very much wish things were different. I wish the scientific literature were more positive, more encouraging, less disturbing. It isn't. Some people will not fail to deplore the 'alarmist' nature of this work. Fine. But, in all fairness, is there not, in the evidence presented here, some cause for alarm? Let everyone judge for himself.

What should be done?

So what should be done? Two things, I believe. First, don't give up. There is nothing inevitable here. As citizens and parents, we have a choice and nothing is forcing us to surrender our children to the terrible corrosive power of all these digital recreational tools. Of course, resistance isn't easy, but it's always possible; many do resist, especially in privileged circles. Of course I'm aware of that fable of the social pariah, the poor martyr who, because he is deprived of access to social networks, online games and the benefits of a 'common digital culture', finds himself irrevocably isolated and rejected by his peers. Moreover, when negotiating the purchase of a smartphone, a tablet or a game console, children and teenagers have completely grasped all the profit they could derive from this kind of talk. But, in practice, the sales pitch does not hold up. To date, no study has indicated that deprivation of screens for recreation leads to social isolation or any emotional disturbance! On the other hand, a large body of research highlights the severely detrimental impact of these tools on the depressive and anxious symptoms of our offspring. In other words, the presence of these things cripples when their absence does no harm. Between these two options, the choice seems clear – especially as I am not out to prohibit all digital access, but to ensure that the usage times are kept below the threshold of harmfulness.

Once the language of helplessness has been rejected, educational action can take back its rights. For the parents, it will then be a matter of putting in place specific rules for consumption. Based on the evidence set out in this book, we can retain seven essential points. Seven rules that everyone, of course, can adapt to the characteristics of their children and the family context.

Seven fundamental rules

Before 6 years

- *No screens.* To grow properly, a young child doesn't need screens. She needs someone to talk to her, to read her stories, to give her books. She needs to be bored, to play, to do puzzles, to build Lego houses, to run, to jump, to sing. She needs to do drawings, sports, music, etc. All of these activities (and many more like them) build a brain much more safely and efficiently than any recreational screen. This is all the more true as lack of digital exposure during the first years of life has no negative impact in the short or long term. In other words, the child will not become a person with a digital handicap because she has not been exposed to screens during the first 6 years of her life. Quite the contrary. What she has developed away from screens will then help her to make the best use of the more positive aspects of the digital world.

After 6 years

- *No more than 30 minutes to 1 hour per day (all inclusive!)*. It's in this point, without a doubt, that 'the' good news of this text lies! In modest doses, screens are not harmful (obviously subject to the content being suitable and the right amount of sleep being ensured). In particular, when daily consumption remains less than 30 minutes, they do not appear to have detectable negative effects. Between 30 minutes and 1 hour, drawbacks emerge, but they seem small enough to be tolerable. Based on these data, a cautious approach could aim for a gradation by age: a maximum of 30 minutes up to 12 years and 60 minutes beyond. Parents should remember that almost all digital media (tablets, smartphones, game consoles, computers, television, Internet TV boxes, etc.) now offer, in the form of options or downloadable apps, useful and effective time control systems. Once the pre-set daily limit is reached, the device is blocked. That being said, some parents seem to consider 'doing no screen time is almost easier than doing a little', as one mother, a former social computing researcher married to a Facebook engineer, recently reported to the *New York Times*.[5] The option seems all the more interesting as it is both without any drawbacks (as we have already pointed out) and likely to avoid many conflicts. It's a bit like hedonic food consumption. It's often easier to do without chocolate when there's none at home than to have to limit yourself to a single small square.[6]
- *Not in the bedroom*. Screens in the bedroom have a specifically unfavourable impact. They increase usage times (especially at the expense of sleep) and promote access to inappropriate content. The bedroom should be a sanctuary, free from digital presence. And, in answer to one frequently heard objection, there are powerful alarm clocks for 2 or 3 euros. No need for smartphones (these can sleep very well in some cosy corner of the living room).
- *No inappropriate content*. Whether in the form of clips, films,

207

series, video games, etc., content that is violent or sexual, involves smoking or alcohol, etc., has a profound effect on the way in which children and adolescents perceive the world. At the very least, it is important to respect the age ratings (bearing in mind the notable permissiveness of certain classification systems which, like the French system, show a rather surreal tolerance). Here again, apps make it quite easy, for almost all digital media, to block access to inappropriate content. Of course, there is access via a third party – the friend's smartphone, computer or tablet. These can't be controlled. It's essential to talk about this with your children (teenagers included!). It's not perfect, but it's unfortunately the only possible option – at least as long as the public authorities will not deign to seriously regulate the access of minors to hyperviolent, pornographic, racist and other content.

- *Not in the mornings, before the school day.* 'Exciting' content, in particular, lastingly depletes the child's cognitive capacities. In the morning, let the child dream, be bored and have breakfast in a serene environment; listen to her, talk to her, etc. Her academic performance will be greatly improved.
- *Not at night before going to sleep.* 'Evening' screens strongly affect the duration of sleep (we go to bed later) and its quality (we sleep less well). 'Exciting' content is, again, particularly damaging. Unplug everything at least 1 hour 30 minutes before the scheduled bedtime.
- *One thing at a time.* One last point, but it's an important one. Screens should be used alone (one at a time). They should be kept out of reach during meals, homework and family discussions. The more multitasking the developing brain is subjected to, the more permeable it becomes to distraction. In addition, the more things it does at the same time, the less well it performs, the less it learns and the less it memorizes. This is one last demonstration, if one was needed, that our brain is really not made for the practices of the new digital modernity.

Fewer screens means more life

These rules may involve limitations, but they're by no means just a vain fad. They are formidably effective, as we have seen. As for the hours taken back from the hegemony of screens, they must be brought back to life. This is neither simple nor immediate, because it's the whole family ecology that needs to be reorganized. But if enough willpower is brought to bear, children adapt; and 'empty' time can be filled with new activities: talking, exchanging ideas, sleeping, playing sports, playing a musical instrument, drawing, painting, sculpting, dancing, singing, taking acting lessons and, of course, reading. And if books really sound too inhospitable, feel free to look at comic books. Some have an astounding creative and linguistic richness.

In the end, if all this seems difficult, if your children kick up a fuss and drive the red-hot dagger of guilt into you, remember this: when they grow up, many will thank you for giving their lives the liberating fertility of sport, thought and culture, rather than the pernicious sterility of screens. Only recently, one of my most brilliant pupils told me how much screens (especially smartphones and video games) had been a serious subject of tension between him and his parents and how grateful he now was to them in hindsight for not 'giving up'.

A glimmer of hope?

'A fly attacking an elephant': these are the words that Sébastien Castellion is said to have used to define his struggle in Geneva, nearly five hundred years ago, against the fundamentalist and dictatorial madness of Jean Calvin, a major actor of the Protestant reformation.[7] When I began this book a little over four years ago, those are the words I first thought of. The digital wave was at its zenith; so tall and powerful it seemed indestructible. And then things started to change. Imperceptibly, headwinds arose. Childcare professionals in particular have become more hesitant. I was then contacted by unions and associations of teachers, speech therapists, parents of pupils, paediatricians and school nurses. Each time, the same language, the same observations, the same questions and the same admissions of helplessness. There was nothing 'scientific' in this observation, of course, but a stubborn and persistent impression that scepticism was taking hold. It must be said that reality cannot be gainsaid and that the disaster is starting to become apparent.

It is no coincidence that the unease is emerging mainly among the men and women who are in direct contact with the younger generations. Everything that is reported in this book is described by these professionals with startling precision: problems with attention, language, impulsivity, memory, aggressiveness, sleep, academic success, etc. It is both sad for the present and encouraging for the future. Indeed, a healthy awareness seems to be emerging. I sincerely hope this book can help its spread.

NOTES

Introduction

[1] Braque G., *Le Jour et la Nuit*, Gallimard, 1952.

[2] Schleicher A., in 'Une culture qui libère?', round table organized by the newspaper *Libération*, Université catholique de Lyon, 19 September 2016.

[3] Carter C., 'Head teachers to report parents to police and social services if they let their children play Grand Theft Auto or Call of Duty', dailymail.co.uk, 2015.

[4] OECD, 'PISA 2018 results (volume 1)', oecd.org, 2019.

[5] Phillips T., 'Taiwan orders parents to limit children's time with electronic games', telegraph.co.uk, 2015.

[6] Hernandez J. et al., '90 minutes a day, until 10 p.m.: China sets rules for young gamers', nytimes.com, 2019.

[7] Bilton N., 'Steve Jobs was a low-tech parent', nytimes.com, 2014.

[8] Bowles N., 'A dark consensus about screens and kids begins to emerge in Silicon Valley', nytimes.com, 2018.

[9] Richtel M., 'A Silicon Valley school that doesn't compute', nytimes.com, 2011.

[10] Bowles N., 'The digital gap between rich and poor kids is not what we expected', nytimes.com, 2018.

[11] Erner G., 'Les geeks privent leurs enfants d'écran, eux', huffingtonpost.fr, 2014.

[12] Tapscott D., 'New York Times cover story on "growing up digital" misses the mark', huffingtonpost.com, 2011.

[13] Bauerlein M., *The Dumbest Generation*, Tarcher/Penguin, 2009.

[14] Oreskes N. et al., *Merchants of Doubt*, Bloomsbury, 2010.

[15] Petersen A. M. et al., 'Discrepancy in scientific authority and media visibility of climate change scientists and contrarians', *Nat Commun*, 10, 2019.

[16]Glantz S. A. et al., *The Cigarette Papers*, University of California Press, 1998.

[17]Proctor R., *Golden Holocaust*, University of California Press, 2012.

[18]Angell M., *The Truth About the Drug Companies*, Random House, 2004.

[19]Mullard A., 'Mediator scandal rocks French medical community', *Lancet*, 377, 2011.

[20]Healy D., *Pharmageddon*, University of California Press, 2012.

[21]Goldacre B., *Bad Pharma*, Fourth Estate, 2014.

[22]Gotzsche P., *Deadly Psychiatry and Organized Denial*, People's Press, 2015.

[23]Leslie I., 'The sugar conspiracy', theguardian.com, 2016.

[24]Holpuch A., 'Sugar lobby paid scientists to blur sugar's role in heart disease – report', theguardian.com, 2016.

[25]Kearns C. E. et al., 'Sugar industry and coronary heart disease research: a historical analysis of internal industry documents', *JAMA Intern Med*, 176, 2016.

[26]Cunningham A. et al., *Book Smart*, Oxford University Press, 2014.

[27]Cunningham A. et al., 'What reading does for the mind', *Am Educ*, 22, 1998.

Part One

[1]Esquiros A., *L'Esprit des Anglais*, Hachette, s.d.

[2]Kirschner P. et al., 'Do learners really know best? Urban legends in education', *Educ Psychol*, 48, 2013.

[3]Serres M., *Thumbelina: The Culture and Technology of Millennials*, translated by Daniel W. Smith, Rowman & Littlefield International, 2015.

[4]Tapscott D., *Grown Up Digital*, McGraw Hill, 2009.

[5]Veen W. et al., *Homo Zappiens: Growing Up in a Digital Age*, Network Continuum Education, 2006.

[6]Brown J. S., 'Growing up digital', *Change*, 32, 2000.

[7]Prensky M., 'Digital natives, digital immigrants (part 1)', *On the Horizon*, 9, 2001.

[8]Fourgous J., *Réussir à l'École avec le Numérique*, Odile Jacob, 2011.

[9]Ségond V., 'Les "digital natives" changent l'entreprise', lemonde.fr, 2016.

[10]Prensky M., 'Listen to the natives', *Educational Leadership*, 63, 2006.

[11]'Le cerveau des natifs du numérique en 90 secondes', lemonde.fr, 2015.

[12]Davidenkoff E., *Le Tsunami Numérique*, Stock, 2014.

[13]Prensky M., *Teaching Digital Natives*, Corwin, 2010.

[14]Khan S., *The One World Schoolhouse*, Twelve, 2012.

[15]Fourgous J., 'Oser la pédagogie numérique!', lemonde.fr, 2011.

[16]Reynié D., in '"Apprendre autrement" à l'ère numérique: rapport de la mission parlementaire de Jean-Michel Fourgous', La Documentation Française, 2012.

[17] Tapscott D., 'Educating the net generation', *Educational Leadership*, 56, 1999.

[18] Kirschner P. et al., 'The myths of the digital native and the multitasker', *Teach Teach Educ*, 67, 2017.

[19] De Bruyckere P. et al., *Urban Myths about Learning and Education*, Academic Press, 2015.

[20] Gallardo-Echenique E. et al., 'Let's talk about digital learners in the digital era', *Int Rev Res Open Distrib Lear*, 16, 2015.

[21] Jones C., in *Reshaping Learning* (eds. Huang R. et al.), 'The new shape of the student', Springer, 2013.

[22] Jones C. et al., 'The net generation and digital natives', *Higher Education Academy, York*, 2011.

[23] Bullen M. et al., 'Digital learners in higher education', *Can J Learn Tech*, 37, 2011.

[24] Brown C. et al., 'Debunking the "digital native": beyond digital apartheid, towards digital democracy', *J Comput Assist Lear*, 26, 2010.

[25] Bennett S. et al., 'Beyond the "digital natives" debate: towards a more nuanced understanding of students' technology experiences', *J Comput Assist Lear*, 26, 2010.

[26] Bennett S. et al., 'The "digital natives" debate', *Br J Educ Tech*, 39, 2008.

[27] Selwyn N., 'The digital native: myth and reality', *Aslib Proc*, 61, 2009.

[28] Calvani A. et al., 'Are young generations in secondary school digitally competent?', *Comput Educ*, 58, 2012.

[29] Tricot A., in Miller M., 'Etre un "digital native" ne rend pas meilleur pour prendre des notes', lemonde.fr, 2018.

[30] Kennedy G. et al., 'Beyond natives and immigrants', *J Comput Assist Lear*, 26, 2010.

[31] Bekebrede G. et al., 'Reviewing the need for gaming in education to accommodate the net generation', *Comput Educ*, 57, 2011.

[32] Jones C. et al., 'Net generation or digital natives', *Comput Educ*, 54, 2010.

[33] Zhang M., 'Internet use that reproduces educational inequalities', *Comput Educ*, 86, 2015.

[34] Lai K. et al., 'Technology use and learning characteristics of students in higher education: do generational differences exist?', *Brit J Educ Tech*, 46, 2015.

[35] Rideout V., 'The common sense census: media use by tweens and teens', Common Sense Media, 2015.

[36] Fraillon J. et al., 'Preparing for life in a digital age: international computer and information literacy study', Springer Open, 2014.

[37] Demirbilek M., 'The "digital natives" debate', *Eurasia J Math Sci Tech*, 10, 2014.

[38] Romero M. et al., 'Do UOC students fit in the net generation profile?', *Int Rev Res Open Distrib Lear*, 14, 2013.

[39] Hargittai E., 'Digital na(t)ives? Variation in Internet skills and uses among members of the "net generation"', *Sociol Inq*, 80, 2010.

40 Nasah A. et al., 'The digital literacy debate', *Educ Tech Res Dev*, 58, 2010.

41 Rideout V. et al., 'The common sense census: media use by tweens and teens', Common Sense Media, 2019.

42 Stoerger S., 'The digital melting pot', *First Monday*, 14, 2009.

43 'Evaluating information: the cornerstone of civic online reasoning', report from the Stanford History Education Group, Stanford History Education Group, 2016.

44 'Computerkenntnisse der ÖsterreicherInnen (Austrian Computer Society)', Austrian Computer Society, 2014.

45 'Security of the digital natives', Tech and Law Center Project, 2014.

46 'Information behaviour of the researcher of the future', University College London, 2008.

47 Johnson L. et al., 'Horizon Report Europe: 2014 schools edition', Publications Office of the European Union & The New Media Consortium, 2014.

48 Rowlands I. et al., 'The Google generation', *Aslib Proc*, 60, 2008.

49 Thirion P. et al., 'Enquête sur les compétences documentaires et informationnelles des étudiants qui accèdent à l'enseignement supérieur en Communauté française de Belgique', enssib.fr, 2008.

50 Julien H. et al., 'How high-school students find and evaluate scientific information', *Libr Inform Sci Res*, 31, 2009.

51 Gross M. et al., 'What's skill got to do with it?', *J Am Soc Inf Sci Technol*, 63, 2012.

52 Perret C., 'Pratiques de recherche documentaire et réussite universitaire des étudiants de première année', *Carrefours de l'Éducation*, 35, 2013.

53 Dumouchel G. et al., 'Mon ami Google', *Can J Learn Tech*, 43, 2017.

54 TNS Sofres, 'Les millennials passent un jour par semaine sur leur smartphone', tns-sofres.com, 2015.

55 Lhenart A., 'Teens, social media & technology overview 2015', Pew Research Center, 2015.

56 Rideout V. et al., 'Generation M2: media in the lives of 8–18 year-olds', Kaiser Family Foundation, 2010.

57 Dumais S., 'Cohort and gender differences in extracurricular participation', *Sociol Spectr*, 29, 2009.

58 Lauricella A. et al., 'The common sense census: plugged in parents of tweens and teens', Common Sense Media, 2016.

59 Ofcom, 'Adults' media use and attitudes (report 2016)', ofcom.org, 2016.

60 Greenwood S. et al., 'Social media update 2016', Pew Research Center, 2016.

61 Anderson M. et al., 'Tech adoption climbs among older adults', Pew Research Center, 2017.

62 Richtel M., 'A Silicon Valley school that doesn't compute', nytimes.com, 2011.

63 AAP, 'Media and young minds: American Academy of Pediatrics. Council on Communications and Media', *Pediatrics*, 138, 2016.

[64] Christodoulou D., *Seven Myths About Education*, Routledge, 2014.

[65] *Paroles de Poilus*, J'ai Lu, 2013.

[66] Fourgous J., 'Réussir l'école numérique: rapport de la mission parlementaire sur la modernisation de l'école par le numérique', La Documentation Française, 2010.

[67] Fourgous J., '"Apprendre autrement" à l'ère numérique: rapport de la mission parlementaire de Jean-Michel Fourgous', 2012.

[68] Small G. et al., *iBrain*, HarperCollins, 2009.

[69] Fourgous J., *Réussir à l'École avec le Numérique*, Odile Jacob, 2011.

[70] Des Deserts S., 'Nos enfants, ces mut@nts', nouvelobs.com, 2012.

[71] Serres M., *Thumbelina: The Culture and Technology of Millennials*, translated by Daniel W. Smith, Rowman & Littlefield International, 2015.

[72] Small G. et al., in *Digital Divide* (ed. Bauerlein M.), 'Your brain is evolving right now', Penguin, 2011.

[73] Bisson J., 'Le cerveau de nos enfants n'aura plus la même architecture', lefigaro.fr, 2012.

[74] Prensky M., *Brain Gain*, St Martin's Press, 2012.

[75] Kuhn S. et al., 'Amount of lifetime video gaming is positively associated with entorhinal, hippocampal and occipital volume', *Mol Psychiatry*, 19, 2014.

[76] Kuhn S. et al., 'Playing Super Mario induces structural brain plasticity', *Mol Psychiatry*, 19, 2014.

[77] Kuhn S. et al., 'Positive association of video game playing with left frontal cortical thickness in adolescents', *PLoS One*, 9, 2014.

[78] Gong D. et al., 'Enhanced functional connectivity and increased gray matter volume of insula related to action video game playing', *Sci Rep*, 5, 2015.

[79] Tanaka S. et al., 'Larger right posterior parietal volume in action video game experts', *PLoS One*, 8, 2013.

[80] 'Jouer à Super Mario augmente le volume de matière grise', lexpress.fr, 2013.

[81] Gracci F., 'Les adeptes des jeux vidéos ont plus de matière grise et une meilleure connectivité cérébrale', science-et-vie.com, 2015.

[82] DiSalvo D., 'The surprising connection between playing video games and a thicker brain', forbes.com, 2014.

[83] Bergland C., 'Video gaming can increase brain size and connectivity', psychologytoday.com, 2013.

[84] Costandi M., *Neuroplasticity*, MIT Press, 2016.

[85] Draganski B. et al., 'Neuroplasticity', *Nature*, 427, 2004.

[86] Munte T. F. et al., 'The musician's brain as a model of neuroplasticity', *Nat Rev Neurosci*, 3, 2002.

[87] Becker M. P. et al., 'Longitudinal changes in white matter microstructure after heavy cannabis use', *Dev Cogn Neurosci*, 16, 2015.

[88] Preissler S. et al., 'Gray matter changes following limb amputation with high and low intensities of phantom limb pain', *Cereb Cortex*, 23, 2013.

[89] Maguire E. A. et al., 'Recalling routes around London', *J Neurosci*, 17, 1997.

[90] Takeuchi H. et al., 'The impact of television viewing on brain structures', *Cereb Cortex*, 25, 2015.

[91] Takeuchi H. et al., 'Impact of reading habit on white matter structure', *Neuroimage*, 133, 2016.

[92] Killgore W. D. et al., 'Physical exercise habits correlate with gray matter volume of the hippocampus in healthy adult humans', *Sci Rep*, 3, 2013.

[93] Fritel J., 'Jeux vidéo: les nouveaux maîtres du monde', documentaire Arte, 15 November 2016.

[94] Kanai R. et al., 'The structural basis of inter-individual differences in human behaviour and cognition', *Nat Rev Neurosci*, 12, 2011.

[95] Shaw P. et al., 'Intellectual ability and cortical development in children and adolescents', *Nature*, 440, 2006.

[96] Schnack H. G. et al., 'Changes in thickness and surface area of the human cortex and their relationship with intelligence', *Cereb Cortex*, 25, 2015.

[97] Luders E. et al., 'The link between callosal thickness and intelligence in healthy children and adolescents', *Neuroimage*, 54, 2011.

[98] Takeuchi H. et al., 'Impact of videogame play on the brain's microstructural properties', *Mol Psychiatry*, 21, 2016.

[99] Li W. et al., 'Brain structures and functional connectivity associated with individual differences in Internet tendency in healthy young adults', *Neuropsychologia*, 70, 2015.

[100] 'Brain regions can be specifically trained with video games', sciencedaily.com, 2013.

[101] Boehly A., 'Super Mario joue sur notre cerveau', sciencesetavenir.fr, 2013.

[102] Richardson A. et al., 'Video game experience predicts virtual, but not real navigation performance', *Comput Hum Behav*, 27, 2011.

[103] West G. L. et al., 'Impact of video games on plasticity of the hippocampus', *Mol Psychiatry*, 2017.

[104] Tanji J. et al., 'Role of the lateral prefrontal cortex in executive behavioral control', *Physiol Rev*, 88, 2008.

[105] Matsumoto K. et al., 'The role of the medial prefrontal cortex in achieving goals', *Curr Opin Neurobiol*, 14, 2004.

[106] Funahashi S., 'Space representation in the prefrontal cortex', *Prog Neurobiol*, 103, 2013.

[107] Ballard I. C. et al., 'Dorsolateral prefrontal cortex drives mesolimbic dopaminergic regions to initiate motivated behavior', *J Neurosci*, 31, 2011.

[108] Weinstein A. et al., 'Internet addiction or excessive Internet use', *Am J Drug Alcohol Abuse*, 36, 2010.

[109] Weinstein A. et al., 'New developments in brain research of Internet and gaming disorder', *Neurosci Biobehav Rev*, 75, 2017.

[110] Meng Y. et al., 'The prefrontal dysfunction in individuals with Internet gaming disorder', *Addict Biol*, 20, 2015.

[111] Kuss D. J. et al., 'Neurobiological correlates in Internet gaming disorder: a systematic literature review', *Front Psychiatry*, 9, 2018.

[112] Yuan K. et al., 'Cortical thickness abnormalities in late adolescence with online gaming addiction', *PLoS One*, 8, 2013.

[113] Juraska J. M. et al., 'Pubertal onset as a critical transition for neural development and cognition', *Brain Res*, 1654, 2017.

[114] Konrad K. et al., 'Brain development during adolescence', *Dtsch Arztebl Int*, 110, 2013.

[115] Selemon L. D., 'A role for synaptic plasticity in the adolescent development of executive function', *Transl Psychiatry*, 3, 2013.

[116] Sisk C. L., 'Development: pubertal hormones meet the adolescent brain', *Curr Biol*, 27, 2017.

[117] Caballero A. et al., 'Mechanisms contributing to prefrontal cortex maturation during adolescence', *Neurosci Biobehav Rev*, 70, 2016.

[118] Caballero A. et al., 'GABAergic function as a limiting factor for prefrontal maturation during adolescence', *Trends Neurosci*, 39, 2016.

[119] Paus T. et al., 'Why do many psychiatric disorders emerge during adolescence?', *Nat Rev Neurosci*, 9, 2008.

[120] Sawyer S. M. et al., 'Adolescence: a foundation for future health', *Lancet*, 379, 2012.

[121] Oei A. C. et al., 'Are videogame training gains specific or general?', *Front Syst Neurosci*, 8, 2014.

[122] Przybylski A. K. et al., 'A large scale test of the gaming-enhancement hypothesis', *PeerJ*, 4, 2016.

[123] van Ravenzwaaij D. et al., 'Action video games do not improve the speed of information processing in simple perceptual tasks', *J Exp Psychol Gen*, 143, 2014.

[124] Jäncke L. et al., 'Expertise in video gaming and driving skills', *Z Neuropsychol*, 22, 2011.

[125] Gaspar J. G. et al., 'Are gamers better crossers? An examination of action video game experience and dual task effects in a simulated street crossing task', *Hum Factors*, 56, 2014.

[126] Owen A. M. et al., 'Putting brain training to the test', *Nature*, 465, 2010.

[127] Simons D. J. et al., 'Do "brain-training" programs work?', *Psychol Sci Public Interest*, 17, 2016.

[128] Azizi E. et al., 'The influence of action video game playing on eye movement behaviour during visual search in abstract, in-game and natural scenes', *Atten Percept Psychophys*, 79, 2017.

[129] Sala G. et al., 'Video game training does not enhance cognitive ability', *Psychol Bull*, 144, 2018.

[130] Bavelier D. et al., 'Brain plasticity through the life span', *Annu Rev Neurosci*, 35, 2012.

[131] Koziol L. F. et al., 'Consensus paper: the cerebellum's role in movement and cognition', *Cerebellum*, 13, 2014.

[132] Manto M. et al., 'Consensus paper: roles of the cerebellum in motor control', *Cerebellum*, 11, 2012.

[133] Kennedy A. M. et al., 'Video gaming enhances psychomotor skills but not visuospatial and perceptual abilities in surgical trainees', *J Surg Educ*, 68, 2011.

[134] Desmurget M., *Imitation et Apprentissages Moteurs*, Solal, 2007.

Part Two

[1] *Pensées de Monsieur le Comte d'Oxenstirn sur Divers Sujets (volume 2)*, 'Aux dépens de la société', 1787.

[2] Bach J. et al., *L'Enfant et les Écrans: Un Avis de l'Académie des Sciences*, Le Pommier, 2013.

[3] Vandewater E. A. et al., 'Measuring children's media use in the digital age', *Am Behav Sci*, 52, 2009.

[4] Anderson D. R. et al., 'Estimates of young children's time with television', *Child Dev*, 56, 1985.

[5] Desmurget M., *TV Lobotomie*, J'ai Lu, 2013.

[6] Donaldson-Pressman S. et al., *The Learning Habit*, Penguin, 2014.

[7] American Optometric Association, 'Survey reveals parents drastically underestimate the time kids spend on electronic devices', aoa.org, 2014.

[8] Lee H. et al., 'Comparing the self-report and measured smartphone usage of college students', *Psychiatry Investig*, 14, 2017.

[9] Otten J. J. et al., 'Relationship between self-report and an objective measure of television-viewing time in adults', *Obesity (Silver Spring)*, 18, 2010.

[10] Rideout V., 'The common sense census: media use by tweens and teens', Common Sense Media, 2015.

[11] Rideout V., 'The common sense census: media use by kids age zero to eight', Common Sense Media, 2017.

[12] Roberts D. F. et al., 'Generation M: media in the lives of 8–18 year-olds', Kaiser Family Foundation, 2005.

[13] 'Esteban: étude de santé sur l'environnement, la biosurveillance, l'activité physique et la nutrition, 2014–2016', santepubliquefrance.fr, 2017.

[14] 'Santé des collégiens en France /2014' (données françaises de l'enquête internationale HBSC), santepubliquefrance.fr, 2016.

[15] Barr R. et al., 'Amount, content and context of infant media exposure', *Int J Early Years Educ*, 18, 2010.

[16] Garrison M. M. et al., 'The impact of a healthy media use intervention on sleep in preschool children', *Pediatrics*, 130, 2012.

[17] Sisson S. B. et al., 'Television, reading, and computer time', *J Phys Act Health*, 8, 2011.

[18] Felisoni D. et al., 'Cell phone usage and academic performance', *Comput Educ*, 117, 2018.

[19] Rideout V. et al., 'Generation M2: media in the lives of 8–18 year-olds', Kaiser Family Foundation, 2010.

[20] Rideout V., 'Zero to eight: children's media use in America 2013', Common Sense Media, 2013.

[21] Rideout V. et al., 'The media family: electronic media in the lives of infants, toddlers, preschoolers and their parents', Kaiser Family Foundation, 2006.

[22] Médiamat Annuel 2017, Médiamétrie.

[23] Ofcom, 'Children and parents: media use and attitudes report', ofcom.org, 2017.

[24] Hysing M. et al., 'Sleep and use of electronic devices in adolescence', *BMJ Open*, 5, 2015.

[25] Australian Institute of Family Studies, 'The Longitudinal Study of Australian Children annual statistical report 2015', GrowingUpInAustralia.gov.au, 2016.

[26] Winn M., *The Plug-In-Drug* (revised edition), Penguin, 2002.

[27] Lee S. J. et al., 'Predicting children's media use in the USA', *Br J Dev Psychol*, 27, 2009.

[28] Chiu Y. C. et al., 'The amount of television that infants and their parents watched influenced children's viewing habits when they got older', *Acta Paediatr*, 106, 2017.

[29] Biddle S. J. et al., 'Tracking of sedentary behaviours of young people', *Prev Med*, 51, 2010.

[30] Cadoret G. et al., 'Relationship between screen-time and motor proficiency in children', *Early Child Dev Care*, 188, 2018.

[31] Trinh M. H. et al., 'Association of trajectory and covariates of children's screen media time', *JAMA Pediatr*, 2019.

[32] Olsen A. et al., 'Early origins of overeating', *Curr Obes Rep*, 2, 2013.

[33] Rossano M. J., 'The essential role of ritual in the transmission and reinforcement of social norms', *Psychol Bull*, 138, 2012.

[34] Dehaene-Lambertz G. et al., in *L'Acquisition du Langage: Le Langage en Émergence* (eds. Kail M. et al.), 'Bases cérébrales de l'acquisition du langage', PUF, 2000.

[35] Uylings H., 'Development of the human cortex and the concept of "critical" or "sensitive" periods', *Lang Learn*, 56, 2006.

[36] Nelson C. A., 3rd et al., 'Cognitive recovery in socially deprived young children', *Science*, 318, 2007.

[37] Zeanah C. H. et al., 'Sensitive periods', *Monogr Soc Res Child Dev*, 76, 2011.

[38] Knudsen E. I., 'Sensitive periods in the development of the brain and behavior', *J Cogn Neurosci*, 16, 2004.

[39] Hensch T. K., 'Critical period regulation', *Annu Rev Neurosci*, 27, 2004.

[40] Friedmann N. et al., 'Critical period for first language', *Curr Opin Neurobiol*, 35, 2015.

[41] McLaughlin K. A. et al., 'Neglect as a violation of species-expectant experience: neurodevelopmental consequences', *Biol Psychiatry*, 82, 2017.

[42] Anderson V. et al., 'Do children really recover better? Neurobehavioural plasticity after early brain insult', *Brain*, 134, 2011.

[43] Beuriat P. A. et al., 'Cerebellar lesions at a young age predict poorer long-term functional recovery', *Brain Commun*, 2, 2020.

[44] Chaput J. P. et al., 'Sleeping hours: what is the ideal number and how does age impact this?', *Nat Sci Sleep*, 10, 2018.

[45] Skinner J. D. et al., 'Meal and snack patterns of infants and toddlers', *J Am Diet Assoc*, 104, 2004.

[46] Ziegler P. et al., 'Feeding infants and toddlers study', *J Am Diet Assoc*, 106, 2006.

[47] Jia R. et al., 'New parents' psychological adjustment and trajectories of early parental involvement', *J Marriage Fam*, 78, 2016.

[48] Kotila L. E. et al., 'Time in parenting activities in dual-earner families at the transition to parenthood', *Fam Relat*, 62, 2013.

[49] 'American Time Use Survey 2016', bls.gov, 2017.

[50] 'Horaires d'enseignement des écoles maternelles et élémentaires – France', education.gouv.fr, 2015.

[51] 'Number of instructional days and hours in the school year, by state: 2018', nces.ed.gov, 2018.

[52] Hart B. et al., *Meaningful Differences*, Paul H. Brookes, 1995.

[53] Wartella E. et al., 'Parenting in the age of digital technology', Center on Media and Human Development, School of Communication, Northwestern University, 2014.

[54] Mendelsohn A. L. et al., 'Do verbal interactions with infants during electronic media exposure mitigate adverse impacts on their language development as toddlers?', *Infant Child Dev*, 19, 2010.

[55] Chonchaiya W. et al., 'Elevated background TV exposure over time increases behavioural scores of 18-month-old toddlers', *Acta Paediatr*, 104, 2015.

[56] Duch H. et al., 'Association of screen time use and language development in Hispanic toddlers', *Clin Pediatr (Phila)*, 52, 2013.

[57] Kabali H. K. et al., 'Exposure and use of mobile media devices by young children', *Pediatrics*, 136, 2015.

[58] Ericsson A. et al., 'The role of deliberate practice in the acquisition of expert performance', *Psychol Rev*, 100, 1993.

[59] Fetler M., 'Television viewing and school achievement', *J Commun*, 34, 1984.

[60] Beentjes J. et al., 'Television's impact on children's reading skills', *Read Res Q*, 23, 1988.

[61] Comstock G., in *Thinking and Literacy: The Mind at Work* (eds. Hedley C. N. et al.), 'Television and the American child', LEA, 1995.

[62] Jackson L. et al., 'A longitudinal study of the effects of Internet use and videogame playing on academic performance and the roles of gender, race and income in these relationships', *Comput Hum Behav*, 27, 2011.

[63] Rideout V. et al., 'The common sense census: media use by tweens and teens', Common Sense Media, 2019.

[64] 'L'emploi du temps de votre enfant au collège', education.gouv.fr, 2017.

[65] 'Average annual hours actually worked (2019 or latest available)', data. oecd.org, 2020.

[66] Orben A. et al., 'The association between adolescent well-being and digital technology use', *Nat Hum Behav*, 3, 2019.

[67] Orben A. et al., 'Screens, teens, and psychological well-being: evidence from three time-use-diary studies', *Psychol Sci*, 30, 2019.

[68] Kasser T., *The High Price of Materialism*, MIT Press, 2002.

[69] Public Health England, 'How healthy behaviour supports children's wellbeing', gov.uk, 2013.

[70] Kross E. et al., 'Facebook use predicts declines in subjective well-being in young adults', *PLoS One*, 8, 2013.

[71] Yang F. et al., 'Electronic screen use and mental well-being of 10–12-year-old children', *Eur J Public Health*, 23, 2013.

[72] Verduyn P. et al., 'Passive Facebook usage undermines affective well-being: experimental and longitudinal evidence', *J Exp Psychol Gen*, 144, 2015.

[73] Tromholt M., 'The Facebook experiment', *Cyberpsychol Behav Soc Netw*, 19, 2016.

[74] Lin L. Y. et al., 'Association between social media use and depression among U.S. young adults', *Depress Anxiety*, 33, 2016.

[75] Primack B. A. et al., 'Social media use and perceived social isolation among young adults in the U.S.', *Am J Prev Med*, 53, 2017.

[76] Primack B. A. et al., 'Association between media use in adolescence and depression in young adulthood', *Arch Gen Psychiatry*, 66, 2009.

[77] Costigan S. A. et al., 'The health indicators associated with screen-based sedentary behavior among adolescent girls', *J Adolesc Health*, 52, 2013.

[78] Shakya H. B. et al., 'Association of Facebook use with compromised well-being', *Am J Epidemiol*, 185, 2017.

[79] Babic M. et al., 'Longitudinal associations between changes in screen-time and mental health outcomes in adolescents', *Ment Health Phys Act*, 12, 2017.

[80] Twenge J. et al., 'Increases in depressive symptoms, suicide-related outcomes, and suicide rates among U.S. adolescents after 2010 and links to increased new media screen time', *Clin Psychol Sci*, 6, 2018.

[81] Twenge J. M. et al., 'Decreases in psychological well-being among American adolescents after 2012 and links to screen time during the rise of smartphone technology', *Emotion*, 2018.

[82] Kelly Y. et al., 'Social media use and adolescent mental health', *EClinicalMedicine*, 2019.

[83] Demirci K. et al., 'Relationship of smartphone use severity with sleep quality, depression, and anxiety in university students', *J Behav Addict*, 4, 2015.

[84] Hinkley T. et al., 'Early childhood electronic media use as a predictor of poorer well-being', *JAMA Pediatr*, 168, 2014.

[85] Hunt M. et al., 'No more FOMO', *J Soc Clin Psychol*, 37, 2018.

[86] Seo J. H. et al., 'Late use of electronic media and its association with sleep, depression, and suicidality among Korean adolescents', *Sleep Med*, 29, 2017.

[87] Tournier P., in Weynants E., '"Les collégiens ont trop d'heures de cours"', lexpress.fr, 2010.

[88] Dupiot C., '"L'école? On va finir par y dormir"', liberation.fr, 2012.

[89] Gladwell M., *Outliers*, Black Bay Books, 2008.

[90] Tough P., *How Children Succeed*, Random House, 2013.

[91] Angrist J. D. et al., 'Who benefits from KIPP?', *J Policy Anal Manag*, 31, 2012.

[92] Dennison B. A. et al., 'Television viewing and television in bedroom associated with overweight risk among low-income preschool children', *Pediatrics*, 109, 2002.

[93] Borzekowski D. L. et al., 'The remote, the mouse, and the no. 2 pencil', *Arch Pediatr Adolesc Med*, 159, 2005.

[94] Barr-Anderson D. J. et al., 'Characteristics associated with older adolescents who have a television in their bedrooms', *Pediatrics*, 121, 2008.

[95] Granich J. et al., 'Individual, social, and physical environment factors associated with electronic media use among children', *J Phys Act Health*, 8, 2011.

[96] Sisson S. B. et al., 'TVs in the bedrooms of children', *Prev Med*, 52, 2011.

[97] Ramirez E. R. et al., 'Adolescent screen time and rules to limit screen time in the home', *J Adolesc Health*, 48, 2011.

[98] Garrison M. M. et al., 'Media use and child sleep', *Pediatrics*, 128, 2011.

[99] Tandon P. S. et al., 'Home environment relationships with children's physical activity, sedentary time, and screen time by socioeconomic status', *Int J Behav Nutr Phys Act*, 9, 2012.

[100] Wethington H. et al., 'The association of screen time, television in the bedroom, and obesity among school-aged youth', *J Sch Health*, 83, 2013.

[101] Dumuid D. et al., 'Does home equipment contribute to socioeconomic gradients in Australian children's physical activity, sedentary time and screen time?', *BMC Public Health*, 16, 2016.

[102] Li S. et al., 'The impact of media use on sleep patterns and sleep disorders among school-aged children in China', *Sleep*, 30, 2007.

[103] Brockmann P. E. et al., 'Impact of television on the quality of sleep in preschool children', *Sleep Med*, 20, 2016.

[104] Van den Bulck J., 'Television viewing, computer game playing, and Internet use and self-reported time to bed and time out of bed in secondary-school children', *Sleep*, 27, 2004.

[105] Gentile D. A. et al., 'Bedroom media', *Dev Psychol*, 53, 2017.

[106] Shochat T. et al., 'Sleep patterns, electronic media exposure and daytime sleep-related behaviours among Israeli adolescents', *Acta Paediatr*, 99, 2010.

[107] Owens J. et al., 'Television-viewing habits and sleep disturbance in school children', *Pediatrics*, 104, 1999.

[108] Veldhuis L. et al., 'Parenting style, the home environment, and screen time of 5-year-old children; the "be active, eat right" study', *PLoS One*, 9, 2014.

[109] Pempek T. et al., 'Young children's tablet use and associations with maternal well-being', *J Child Fam Stud*, 25, 2016.

[110]Lauricella A. R. et al., 'Young children's screen time', *J Appl Dev Psychol*, 36, 2015.

[111]Jago R. et al., 'Cross-sectional associations between the screen-time of parents and young children', *Int J Behav Nutr Phys Act*, 11, 2014.

[112]Jago R. et al., 'Parent and child screen-viewing time and home media environment', *Am J Prev Med*, 43, 2012.

[113]De Decker E. et al., 'Influencing factors of screen time in preschool children', *Obes Rev*, 13 Suppl. 1, 2012.

[114]Bleakley A. et al., 'The relationship between parents' and children's television viewing', *Pediatrics*, 132, 2013.

[115]Collier K. M. et al., 'Does parental mediation of media influence child outcomes? A meta-analysis on media time, aggression, substance use, and sexual behavior', *Dev Psychol*, 52, 2016.

[116]Bandura A., *Social Learning Theory*, Prentice Hall, 1977.

[117]Durlak A. et al., *Handbook of Social and Emotional Learning*, Guilford Press, 2015.

[118]Jago R. et al., 'Parental sedentary restriction, maternal parenting style, and television viewing among 10- to 11-year-olds', *Pediatrics*, 128, 2011.

[119]Buchanan L. et al., 'Reducing recreational sedentary screen time: a community guide systematic review', *Am J Prev Med*, 50, 2016.

[120]Community Preventive Services Task Force, 'Reducing children's recreational sedentary screen time', *Am J Prev Med*, 50, 2016.

[121]Desmurget M., *L'Antirégime au Quotidien*, Belin, 2017.

[122]Wansink B., *Mindless Eating*, Bantam Books, 2007.

[123]Feeley J., 'Children's content interest: a factor analytic study', paper presented at the Annual Meeting of the National Council of Teachers of English, Minneapolis, Minnesota, 23–5 November 1972.

[124]Killingsworth M. A. et al., 'A wandering mind is an unhappy mind', *Science*, 330, 2010.

[125]Koerth-Baker M., 'Why boredom is anything but boring', *Nature*, 529, 2016.

[126]Milyavskaya M. et al., 'Reward sensitivity following boredom and cognitive effort: a high-powered neurophysiological investigation', *Neuropsychologia*, 2018.

[127]Wilson T. D. et al., 'Just think', *Science*, 345, 2014.

[128]Havermans R. C. et al., 'Eating and inflicting pain out of boredom', *Appetite*, 85, 2015.

[129]Maushart S., *The Winter of Our Disconnect*, Tarcher/Penguin, 2011.

[130]Dunkley V., 'Gray matters: too much screen time damages the brain', psychologytoday.com, 2014.

[131]Walton A., 'Investors pressure Apple over psychological risks of screen time for kids', forbes.com, 2018.

[132]Huerre P., in Picut G., 'Comment aider son enfant à ne pas devenir accro aux écrans?', lexpress.fr, 2014.

[133]Brand M. et al., 'Prefrontal control and Internet addiction: a theoretical

model and review of neuropsychological and neuroimaging findings', *Front Hum Neurosci*, 8, 2014.

[134]De-Sola Gutierrez J. et al., 'Cell-phone addiction', *Front Psychiatry*, 7, 2016.

[135]Cerniglia L. et al., 'Internet addiction in adolescence', *Neurosci Biobehav Rev*, 76, 2017.

[136]Kuss D. J. et al., 'Neurobiological correlates in Internet gaming disorder: a systematic literature review', *Front Psychiatry*, 9, 2018.

[137]Meng Y. et al., 'The prefrontal dysfunction in individuals with Internet gaming disorder', *Addict Biol*, 20, 2015.

[138]Park B. et al., 'Neurobiological findings related to Internet use disorders', *Psychiatry Clin Neurosci*, 71, 2017.

[139]Weinstein A. et al., 'New developments in brain research of Internet and gaming disorder', *Neurosci Biobehav Rev*, 75, 2017.

[140]Gentile D. A. et al., 'Internet gaming disorder in children and adolescents', *Pediatrics*, 140, 2017.

[141]Griffiths M. et al., 'A brief overview of Internet gaming disorder and its treatment', *Austr Clin Psychol*, 2, 2016.

[142]He Q. et al., 'Brain anatomy alterations associated with social networking site (SNS) addiction', *Sci Rep*, 7, 2017.

[143]OMS, 'Trouble du jeu vidéo', who.int, 2018.

[144]Anderson E. L. et al., 'Internet use and problematic Internet use', *Int J Adolesc Youth*, 2016.

[145]Kuss D. J. et al., 'Internet addiction', *Curr Pharm Des*, 20, 2014.

[146]Petry N. M. et al., 'Griffiths et al.'s comments on the international consensus statement of Internet gaming disorder', *Addiction*, 111, 2016.

[147]Griffiths M. D. et al., 'Working towards an international consensus on criteria for assessing Internet gaming disorder: a critical commentary on Petry et al. 2014', *Addiction*, 111, 2016.

[148]Weinstein A. et al., 'Internet addiction or excessive Internet use', *Am J Drug Alcohol Abuse*, 36, 2010.

[149]Durkee T. et al., 'Prevalence of pathological Internet use among adolescents in Europe: demographic and social factors', *Addiction*, 107, 2012.

[150]Feng W. et al., 'Internet gaming disorder: trends in prevalence 1998–2016', *Addict Behav*, 75, 2017.

[151]Mihara S. et al., 'Cross-sectional and longitudinal epidemiological studies of Internet gaming disorder: a systematic review of the literature', *Psychiatry Clin Neurosci*, 71, 2017.

[152]INSEE, 'Population par sexe et groupe d'âges en 2018', insee.fr, 2018.

[153]United States Census, '2017 national population projections tables', census.gov, 2017.

[154]Ballet V., 'Jeux vidéo: "ma pratique était excessive, mais le mot 'addiction' me semblait exagéré"', liberation.fr, 2018.

[155]Young K. S., 'Internet addiction', *CyberPsychol Behav*, 1, 1998.

[156]Douglas A. et al., 'Internet addiction', *Comput Hum Behav*, 24, 2008.

[157] Kuss D. et al., 'Excessive Internet use and psychopathology', *Clin Neuropsychiatry*, 14, 2017.

[158] Hubel D. H. et al., 'The period of susceptibility to the physiological effects of unilateral eye closure in kittens', *J Physiol*, 206, 1970.

[159] de Villers-Sidani E. et al., 'Critical period window for spectral tuning defined in the primary auditory cortex (A1) in the rat', *J Neurosci*, 27, 2007.

[160] Kral A., 'Auditory critical periods', *Neuroscience*, 247, 2013.

[161] Kral A. et al., 'Developmental neuroplasticity after cochlear implantation', *Trends Neurosci*, 35, 2012.

[162] Bailey J. A. et al., 'Early musical training is linked to gray matter structure in the ventral premotor cortex and auditory-motor rhythm synchronization performance', *J Cogn Neurosci*, 26, 2014.

[163] Steele C. J. et al., 'Early musical training and white-matter plasticity in the corpus callosum', *J Neurosci*, 33, 2013.

[164] Johnson J. S. et al., 'Critical period effects in second language learning', *Cogn Psychol*, 21, 1989.

[165] Kuhl P. K., 'Brain mechanisms in early language acquisition', *Neuron*, 67, 2010.

[166] Kuhl P. et al., 'Neural substrates of language acquisition', *Annu Rev Neurosci*, 31, 2008.

[167] Gervain J. et al., 'Speech perception and language acquisition in the first year of life', *Annu Rev Psychol*, 61, 2010.

[168] Werker J. F. et al., 'Critical periods in speech perception: new directions', *Annu Rev Psychol*, 66, 2015.

[169] Flege J. et al., 'Amount of native-language (L1) use affects the pronunciation of an L2', *J Phon*, 25, 1997.

[170] Weber-Fox C. M. et al., 'Maturational constraints on functional specializations for language processing', *J Cogn Neurosci*, 8, 1996.

[171] Piaget J., *The Origins of Intelligence in Children*, International Universities Press, 1952.

[172] *The New Jerusalem Bible: Standard Edition*, Doubleday, 1999.

[173] Duff D. et al., 'The influence of reading on vocabulary growth', *J Speech Lang Hear Res*, 58, 2015.

[174] Perc M., 'The Matthew effect in empirical data', *J R Soc Interface*, 11, 2014.

[175] Cunningham A. et al., *Book Smart*, Oxford University Press, 2014.

[176] Hirsch E., *The Knowledge Deficit*, Houghton Mifflin Harcourt, 2006.

[177] Mol S. E. et al., 'To read or not to read', *Psychol Bull*, 137, 2011.

[178] Petersen A. M. et al., 'Quantitative and empirical demonstration of the Matthew effect in a study of career longevity', *Proc Natl Acad Sci USA*, 108, 2011.

[179] Rigney D., *The Matthew Effect*, Columbia University Press, 2010.

[180] Heckman J. J., 'Skill formation and the economics of investing in disadvantaged children', *Science*, 312, 2006.

[181] van den Heuvel M. et al., 'Mobile media device use is associated with expressive language delay in 18-month-old children', *J Dev Behav Pediatr*, 40, 2019.

[182] Wen L. M. et al., 'Correlates of body mass index and overweight and obesity of children aged 2 years', *Obesity (Silver Spring)*, 22, 2014.

[183] Tomopoulos S. et al., 'Infant media exposure and toddler development', *Arch Pediatr Adolesc Med*, 164, 2010.

[184] Pagani L. S. et al., 'Prospective associations between early childhood television exposure and academic, psychosocial, and physical well-being by middle childhood', *Arch Pediatr Adolesc Med*, 164, 2010.

[185] Christakis D. A. et al., 'How early media exposure may affect cognitive function', *Proc Natl Acad Sci USA*, 115, 2018.

[186] Nikkelen S. W. et al., 'Media use and ADHD-related behaviors in children and adolescents', *Dev Psychol*, 50, 2014.

[187] Rueb E., 'W.H.O. says limited or no screen time for children under 5', nytimes.com, 2019.

[188] WHO, 'To grow up healthy, children need to sit less and play more', who.int, 2019.

[189] AAP, 'Media education: American Academy of Pediatrics. Committee on Public Education', *Pediatrics*, 104, 1999.

[190] Australian Department of Health, 'Is your family missing out on the benefits of being active every day?', health.gov.au, 2014.

[191] AAP, 'Media and young minds: American Academy of Pediatrics. Council on Communications and Media', *Pediatrics*, 138, 2016.

[192] Canadian Paediatric Society, Digital Health Task Force, Ottawa, Ontario, 'Screen time and young children: promoting health and development in a digital world', *Paediatr Child Health*, 22, 2017.

[193] Conseil Supérieur de l'Audiovisuel, 'Utiliser les écrans, ça s'apprend', csa.fr, September 2018.

[194] Kostyrka-Allchorne K. et al., 'The relationship between television exposure and children's cognition and behaviour', *Dev Rev*, 44, 2017.

[195] Madigan S. et al., 'Associations between screen use and child language skills: a systematic review and meta-analysis', *JAMA Pediatr*, 2020.

[196] Murray L. et al., 'Randomized controlled trial of a book-sharing intervention in a deprived South African community', *J Child Psychol Psychiatry*, 57, 2016.

[197] Vally Z. et al., 'The impact of dialogic book-sharing training on infant language and attention', *J Child Psychol Psychiatry*, 56, 2015.

[198] Hayes D., 'Speaking and writing', *J Mem Lang*, 27, 1988.

[199] Cunningham A. et al., 'What reading does for the mind', *Am Educ*, 22, 1998.

[200] AAP, 'Children and adolescents and digital media: American Academy of Pediatrics. Council on Communications and Media', *Pediatrics*, 138, 2016.

[201] Rymer R., *Genie: A Scientific Tragedy*, HarperPerennial, 1994.

[202] Whitebread D. et al., in *Creativity and the Wandering Mind* (eds. Preiss

D. et al.), 'Pretend play in young children and the emergence of creativity', Academic Press, 2020.

[203] Nicolopoulou A. et al., 'What do we know about pretend play and narrative development?', *Am J Play*, 6, 2013.

[204] Rao Z. et al., in *The SAGE Handbook of Developmental Psychology and Early Childhood Education* (eds. Whitebread D. et al.), 'The role of pretend play in supporting young children's emotional development', SAGE, 2019.

[205] Vandewater E. A. et al., 'Time well spent? Relating television use to children's free-time activities', *Pediatrics*, 117, 2006.

[206] Hancox R. J. et al., 'Association of television viewing during childhood with poor educational achievement', *Arch Pediatr Adolesc Med*, 159, 2005.

[207] Zheng F. et al., 'Association between mobile phone use and inattention in 7102 Chinese adolescents', *BMC Public Health*, 14, 2014.

[208] Stettler N. et al., 'Electronic games and environmental factors associated with childhood obesity in Switzerland', *Obes Res*, 12, 2004.

[209] Exelmans L. et al., 'Sleep quality is negatively related to video gaming volume in adults', *J Sleep Res*, 24, 2015.

[210] Gopinath B. et al., 'Influence of physical activity and screen time on the retinal microvasculature in young children', *Arterioscler Thromb Vasc Biol*, 31, 2011.

[211] Dunstan D. W. et al., 'Television viewing time and mortality', *Circulation*, 121, 2010.

[212] Strasburger V. C. et al., 'Children, adolescents, and the media', *Pediatr Clin North Am*, 59, 2012.

[213] AAP, 'Policy statement: media violence', *Pediatrics*, 124, 2009.

[214] MacDonald K., 'How much screen time is too much for kids? It's complicated', theguardian.com, 2018.

[215] Ibid.

[216] Desmurget M., *L'Antirégime*, Belin, 2015.

[217] USDA et al., 'Dietary Guidelines for Americans, 2010: 7th Edition', U.S. Department of Agriculture and U.S. Department of Health and Human Services, 2010.

[218] Morgenstern M. et al., 'Smoking in movies and adolescent smoking', *Thorax*, 66, 2011.

[219] Morgenstern M. et al., 'Smoking in movies and adolescent smoking initiation', *Am J Prev Med*, 44, 2013.

[220] Dalton M. A. et al., 'Early exposure to movie smoking predicts established smoking by older teens and young adults', *Pediatrics*, 123, 2009.

[221] Dalton M. A. et al., 'Effect of viewing smoking in movies on adolescent smoking initiation: a cohort study', *Lancet*, 362, 2003.

[222] Sargent J. D. et al., 'Exposure to movie smoking', *Pediatrics*, 116, 2005.

[223] Wingood G. M. et al., 'A prospective study of exposure to rap music videos and African American female adolescents' health', *Am J Public Health*, 93, 2003.

[224] Chandra A. et al., 'Does watching sex on television predict teen pregnancy?

Findings from a national longitudinal survey of youth', *Pediatrics*, 122, 2008.

[225] Collins R. L. et al., 'Relationships between adolescent sexual outcomes and exposure to sex in media', *Dev Psychol*, 47, 2011.

[226] O'Hara R. E. et al., 'Greater exposure to sexual content in popular movies predicts earlier sexual debut and increased sexual risk taking', *Psychol Sci*, 23, 2012.

[227] Postman N., *Amusing Ourselves to Death*, Penguin, 2005/1985.

Part Three

[1] Bauerlein M., *The Dumbest Generation*, Tarcher/Penguin, 2009.

Preamble

[1] Vriend J. et al., 'Emotional and cognitive impact of sleep restriction in children', *Sleep Med Clin*, 10, 2015.

[2] Kirszenblat L. et al., 'The yin and yang of sleep and attention', *Trends Neurosci*, 38, 2015.

[3] Lowe C. J. et al., 'The neurocognitive consequences of sleep restriction', *Neurosci Biobehav Rev*, 80, 2017.

[4] Tarokh L. et al., 'Sleep in adolescence', *Neurosci Biobehav Rev*, 70, 2016.

[5] Curcio G. et al., 'Sleep loss, learning capacity and academic performance', *Sleep Med Rev*, 10, 2006.

[6] Carskadon M. A., 'Sleep's effects on cognition and learning in adolescence', *Prog Brain Res*, 190, 2011.

[7] Shochat T. et al., 'Functional consequences of inadequate sleep in adolescents', *Sleep Med Rev*, 18, 2014.

[8] Schmidt R. E. et al., 'The relations between sleep, personality, behavioral problems, and school performance in adolescents', *Sleep Med Clin*, 10, 2015.

[9] Bryant P. A. et al., 'Sick and tired', *Nat Rev Immunol*, 4, 2004.

[10] Kurien P. A. et al., 'Sick and tired', *Curr Opin Neurobiol*, 23, 2013.

[11] Irwin M. R. et al., 'Sleep health', *Neuropsychopharmacology*, 42, 2017.

[12] Baxter S. D. et al., 'The relationship of school absenteeism with body mass index, academic achievement, and socioeconomic status among fourth-grade children', *J Sch Health*, 81, 2011.

[13] Sigfusdottir I. D. et al., 'Health behaviour and academic achievement in Icelandic school children', *Health Educ Res*, 22, 2007.

[14] Blaya C., 'L'absentéisme des collégiens', *Les Sciences de l'Éducation – Pour l'Ère Nouvelle*, 42, 2009.

[15] Frank M. G., 'Sleep and developmental plasticity not just for kids', *Prog Brain Res*, 193, 2011.

[16] Telzer E. H. et al., 'Sleep variability in adolescence is associated with altered brain development', *Dev Cogn Neurosci*, 14, 2015.

[17] Dutil C. et al., 'Influence of sleep on developing brain functions and structures in children and adolescents', *Sleep Med Rev*, 2018.

[18] Patel S. R. et al., 'Short sleep duration and weight gain', *Obesity (Silver Spring)*, 16, 2008.

[19] Chen X. et al., 'Is sleep duration associated with childhood obesity? A systematic review and meta-analysis', *Obesity (Silver Spring)*, 16, 2008.

[20] Fatima Y. et al., 'Longitudinal impact of sleep on overweight and obesity in children and adolescents', *Obes Rev*, 16, 2015.

[21] Miller M. A. et al., 'Sleep duration and incidence of obesity in infants, children, and adolescents', *Sleep*, 41, 2018.

[22] Taras H. et al., 'Obesity and student performance at school', *J Sch Health*, 75, 2005.

[23] Karnehed N. et al., 'Obesity and attained education', *Obesity (Silver Spring)*, 14, 2006.

[24] Pont S. J. et al., 'Stigma experienced by children and adolescents with obesity', *Pediatrics*, 140, 2017.

[25] Puhl R.M. et al., 'The stigma of obesity', *Obesity (Silver Spring)*, 17, 2009.

[26] Puhl R. M. et al., 'Stigma, obesity, and the health of the nation's children', *Psychol Bull*, 133, 2007.

[27] Shore S. M. et al., 'Decreased scholastic achievement in overweight middle school students', *Obesity (Silver Spring)*, 16, 2008.

[28] Geier A. B. et al., 'The relationship between relative weight and school attendance among elementary schoolchildren', *Obesity (Silver Spring)*, 15, 2007.

[29] Desmurget M., *L'Antirégime*, Belin, 2015.

[30] Karsay K. et al., '"Weak, sad, and lazy fatties": adolescents' explicit and implicit weight bias following exposure to weight loss reality TV shows', *Media Psychol*, 22, 2019.

[31] Institute of Medicine of the National Academies, *Sleep Disorders and Sleep Deprivation: An Unmet Public Health Problem*, National Academies Press, 2006.

[32] Goldstein A. N. et al., 'The role of sleep in emotional brain function', *Annu Rev Clin Psychol*, 10, 2014.

[33] Uehli K. et al., 'Sleep problems and work injuries', *Sleep Med Rev*, 18, 2014.

[34] St-Onge M. P. et al., 'Sleep duration and quality', *Circulation*, 134, 2016.

[35] Bioulac S. et al., 'Risk of motor vehicle accidents related to sleepiness at the wheel', *Sleep*, 41, 2018.

[36] Spira A. P. et al., 'Impact of sleep on the risk of cognitive decline and dementia', *Curr Opin Psychiatry*, 27, 2014.

[37] Lindstrom H. A. et al., 'The relationships between television viewing in midlife and the development of Alzheimer's disease in a case-control study', *Brain Cogn*, 58, 2005.

[38]Lo J. C. et al., 'Sleep duration and age-related changes in brain structure and cognitive performance', *Sleep*, 37, 2014.

[39]Ju Y. E. et al., 'Sleep and Alzheimer disease pathology: a bidirectional relationship', *Nat Rev Neurol*, 10, 2014.

[40]Zhang F. et al., 'The missing link between sleep disorders and age-related dementia', *J Neural Transm (Vienna)*, 124, 2017.

[41]Macedo A. C. et al., 'Is sleep disruption a risk factor for Alzheimer's disease?', *J Alzheimer's Dis*, 58, 2017.

[42]Wu L. et al., 'A systematic review and dose-response meta-analysis of sleep duration and the occurrence of cognitive disorders', *Sleep Breath*, 22, 2018.

[43]Barnes D. E. et al., 'The projected effect of risk factor reduction on Alzheimer's disease prevalence', *Lancet Neurol*, 10, 2011.

[44]Ostria V., 'Par le petit bout de la lucarne', *Les Inrockuptibles*, 792, 2011.

Academic success

[1]Garcia S., *Le Goût de l'Effort*, PUF, 2018.

[2]Lahire B., *Enfances de Classe*, Seuil, 2019.

[3]Bourdieu P. et al., *The Inheritors*, University of California Press, 1979/1964.

[4]Sirin S., 'Socioeconomic status and academic achievement', *Rev Educ Res*, 75, 2005.

[5]Bumgarner E. et al., in *International Guide to Student Achievement* (eds. Hattie J. et al.), 'Socioeconomic status and student achievement', Routledge, 2013.

[6]Corder K. et al., 'Revising on the run or studying on the sofa', *Int J Behav Nutr Phys Act*, 12, 2015.

[7]Dimitriou D. et al., 'The role of environmental factors on sleep patterns and school performance in adolescents', *Front Psychol*, 6, 2015.

[8]Garcia-Continente X. et al., 'Factors associated with media use among adolescents', *Eur J Public Health*, 24, 2014.

[9]Garcia-Hermoso A. et al., 'Relationship of weight status, physical activity and screen time with academic achievement in adolescents', *Obes Res Clin Pract*, 11, 2017.

[10]Pressman R. et al., 'Examining the interface of family and personal traits, media, and academic imperatives using the Learning Habit Study', *Am J Fam Ther*, 42, 2014.

[11]Jacobsen W. C. et al., 'The wired generation', *Cyberpsychol Behav Soc Netw*, 14, 2011.

[12]Lizandra J. et al., 'Does sedentary behavior predict academic performance in adolescents or the other way round? A longitudinal path analysis', *PLoS One*, 11, 2016.

[13]Mossle T. et al., 'Media use and school achievement: boys at risk?', *Br J Dev Psychol*, 28, 2010.

[14] Peiro-Velert C. et al., 'Screen media usage, sleep time and academic performance in adolescents', *PLoS One*, 9, 2014.

[15] Poulain T. et al., 'Cross-sectional and longitudinal associations of screen time and physical activity with school performance at different types of secondary school', *BMC Public Health*, 18, 2018.

[16] Syvaoja H. J. et al., 'Physical activity, sedentary behavior, and academic performance in Finnish children', *Med Sci Sports Exerc*, 45, 2013.

[17] Syvaoja H. J. et al., 'The relation of physical activity, sedentary behaviors, and academic achievement is mediated by fitness and bedtime', *J Phys Act Health*, 15, 2018.

[18] Ishii K. et al., 'Joint associations of leisure screen time and physical activity with academic performance in a sample of Japanese children', *Int J Environ Res Public Health*, 17, 2020.

[19] Desmurget M., *TV Lobotomie*, J'ai Lu, 2013.

[20] Keith T. et al., 'Parental involvement, homework, and TV time', *J Educ Psychol*, 78, 1986.

[21] Comstock G., in *Thinking and Literacy: The Mind at Work* (eds. Hedley C. N. et al.), 'Television and the American child', LEA, 1995.

[22] Ozmert E. et al., 'Behavioral correlates of television viewing in primary school children evaluated by the Child Behavior Checklist', *Arch Pediatr Adolesc Med*, 156, 2002.

[23] Shin N., 'Exploring pathways from television viewing to academic achievement in school age children', *J Genet Psychol*, 165, 2004.

[24] Hunley S. A. et al., 'Adolescent computer use and academic achievement', *Adolescence*, 40, 2005.

[25] Borzekowski D. L. et al., 'The remote, the mouse, and the no. 2 pencil', *Arch Pediatr Adolesc Med*, 159, 2005.

[26] Hancox R. J. et al., 'Association of television viewing during childhood with poor educational achievement', *Arch Pediatr Adolesc Med*, 159, 2005.

[27] Johnson J. G. et al., 'Extensive television viewing and the development of attention and learning difficulties during adolescence', *Arch Pediatr Adolesc Med*, 161, 2007.

[28] Espinoza F., 'Using project-based data in physics to examine television viewing in relation to student performance in science', *J Sci Educ Technol*, 18, 2009.

[29] Sharif I. et al., 'Association between television, movie, and video game exposure and school performance', *Pediatrics*, 118, 2006.

[30] Sharif I. et al., 'Effect of visual media use on school performance', *J Adolesc Health*, 46, 2010.

[31] Pagani L. S. et al., 'Prospective associations between early childhood television exposure and academic, psychosocial, and physical well-being by middle childhood', *Arch Pediatr Adolesc Med*, 164, 2010.

[32] Walsh J. L. et al., 'Female college students' media use and academic outcomes', *Emerg Adulthood*, 1, 2013.

[33] Gentile D. A. et al., 'Bedroom media', *Dev Psychol*, 53, 2017.

[34] Ribner A. et al., 'Family socioeconomic status moderates associations between television viewing and school readiness skills', *J Dev Behav Pediatr*, 38, 2017.

[35] Shejwal B. R. et al., 'Television viewing of higher secondary students: does it affect their academic achievement and mathematical reasoning?', *Psychol Dev Soc*, 18, 2006.

[36] Vassiloudis I. et al., 'Academic performance in relation to adherence to the Mediterranean diet and energy balance behaviors in Greek primary schoolchildren', *J Nutr Educ Behav*, 46, 2014.

[37] Adelantado-Renau M. et al., 'Association between screen media use and academic performance among children and adolescents: a systematic review and meta-analysis', *JAMA Pediatr*, 2019.

[38] Landhuis C. E. et al., 'Association between childhood and adolescent television viewing and unemployment in adulthood', *Prev Med*, 54, 2012.

[39] Anderson C. A. et al., 'Video games and aggressive thoughts, feelings, and behavior in the laboratory and in life', *J Pers Soc Psychol*, 78, 2000.

[40] Jaruratanasirikul S. et al., 'Electronic game play and school performance of adolescents in southern Thailand', *Cyberpsychol Behav*, 12, 2009.

[41] Chan P. A. et al., 'A cross-sectional analysis of video games and attention deficit hyperactivity disorder symptoms in adolescents', *Ann Gen Psychiatry*, 5, 2006.

[42] Hastings E. C. et al., 'Young children's video/computer game use', *Issues Ment Health Nurs*, 30, 2009.

[43] Li D. et al., 'Effects of digital game play among young Singaporean gamers', *J Virtual Worlds Res*, 5, 2012.

[44] Gentile D., 'Pathological video-game use among youth ages 8 to 18', *Psychol Sci*, 20, 2009.

[45] Gentile D. A. et al., 'The effects of violent video game habits on adolescent hostility, aggressive behaviors, and school performance', *J Adolesc*, 27, 2004.

[46] Jackson L. et al., 'A longitudinal study of the effects of Internet use and videogame playing on academic performance and the roles of gender, race and income in these relationships', *Comput Hum Behav*, 27, 2011.

[47] Jackson L. et al., 'Internet use, videogame playing and cell phone use as predictors of children's body mass index (BMI), body weight, academic performance, and social and overall self-esteem', *Comput Hum Behav*, 27, 2011.

[48] Stinebrickner R. et al., 'The causal effect of studying on academic performance', *BE J Econom Anal Policy*, 8, 2008.

[49] Weis R. et al., 'Effects of video-game ownership on young boys' academic and behavioral functioning', *Psychol Sci*, 21, 2010.

[50] Spitzer M., 'Outsourcing the mental? From knowledge-on-demand to Morbus Google', *Trends Neurosci Educ*, 5, 2016.

[51] Sanchez-Martinez M. et al., 'Factors associated with cell phone use in

adolescents in the community of Madrid (Spain)', *Cyberpsychol Behav*, 12, 2009.

[52] Junco R. et al., 'No A 4 U', *Comput Educ*, 59, 2012.

[53] Lepp A. et al., 'The relationship between cell phone use, academic performance, anxiety, and satisfaction with life in college students', *Comput Hum Behav*, 31, 2014.

[54] Lepp A. et al., 'The relationship between cell phone use and academic performance in a sample of U.S. college students', *SAGE Open*, 5, 2015.

[55] Li J. et al., 'Locus of control and cell phone use', *Comput Hum Behav*, 52, 2015.

[56] Baert S. et al., 'Smartphone use and academic performance: IZA Discussion Paper No. 11455', iza.org, 2018.

[57] Harman B. et al., 'Cell phone use and grade point average among undergraduate university students', *Coll Stud J*, 45, 2011.

[58] Seo D. et al., 'Mobile phone dependency and its impacts on adolescents' social and academic behaviors', *Comput Hum Behav*, 63, 2016.

[59] Hawi N. et al., 'To excel or not to excel', *Comput Educ*, 98, 2016.

[60] Samaha M. et al., 'Relationships among smartphone addiction, stress, academic performance, and satisfaction with life', *Comput Hum Behav*, 57, 2016.

[61] Dempsey S. et al., 'Later is better', *Econ Innovat New Tech*, 2018.

[62] Felisoni D. et al., 'Cell phone usage and academic performance', *Comput Educ*, 117, 2018.

[63] Abdoul-Maninroudine A., 'Classement des PACES: où réussit-on le mieux le concours de médecine?', letudiant.fr, 2017.

[64] Kirschner P. et al., 'Facebook® and academic performance', *Comput Hum Behav*, 26, 2010.

[65] Junco R., 'Too much face and not enough books', *Comput Hum Behav*, 28, 2012.

[66] Paul J. et al., 'Effect of online social networking on student academic performance', *Comput Hum Behav*, 28, 2012.

[67] Rosen L. et al., 'Facebook and texting made me do it', *Comput Hum Behav*, 29, 2013.

[68] Karpinski A. et al., 'An exploration of social networking site use, multitasking, and academic performance among United States and European university students', *Comput Hum Behav*, 29, 2013.

[69] Tsitsika A. K. et al., 'Online social networking in adolescence', *J Adolesc Health*, 55, 2014.

[70] Giunchiglia F. et al., 'Mobile social media usage and academic performance', *Comput Hum Behav*, 82, 2018.

[71] Lau W., 'Effects of social media usage and social media multitasking on the academic performance of university students', *Comput Hum Behav*, 68, 2017.

[72] Liu D. et al., 'A meta-analysis of the relationship of academic performance and social network site use among adolescents and young adults', *Comput Hum Behav*, 77, 2017.

[73] Gregory P. et al., 'The instructional network', *J Comput Math Sci Teach*, 33, 2014.

[74] Hansen J. D. et al., 'Democratizing education? Examining access and usage patterns in massive open online courses', *Science*, 350, 2015.

[75] Perna L. et al., 'The life cycle of a million MOOC users: paper presented at the MOOC Research Initiative Conference, 5–6 December 2013', upenn. edu, 2013.

[76] Kolowich S., 'San Jose State U. puts MOOC project with Udacity on hold', chronicle.com, 2013.

[77] Fairlie R., 'Do boys and girls use computers differently, and does it contribute to why boys do worse in school than girls? IZA Discussion Paper No. 9302', iza.org, 2015.

[78] Fairlie R. et al., 'Experimental evidence on the effects of home computers on academic achievement among schoolchildren: NBER Working Paper No. 19060', nber.org, 2013.

[79] Fuchs T. et al., 'Computers and student learning', Ifo Working Paper No. 8, 2005.

[80] Malamud O. et al., 'Home computer use and the development of human capital', *Q J Econ*, 126, 2011.

[81] Vigdor J. et al., 'Scaling the digital divide', *Econ Inq*, 52, 2014.

[82] Spitzer M., 'Information technology in education', *Trends Neurosci Educ*, 3, 2014.

[83] Even if this quotation is often associated with Aldous Huxley's *Brave New World*, it does not actually appear in the book (or in *Brave New World Revisited*). It seems to come from a report by Annie Degré Lassalle, ici. radio-canada.ca.

[84] Postman N., *Amusing Ourselves to Death*, Penguin, 2005/1985.

[85] Keith T., 'Time spent on homework and high school grades', *J Educ Psychol*, 74, 1982.

[86] Keith T. et al., 'Longitudinal effects of in-school and out-of-school homework on high school grades', *School Psychol Q*, 19, 2004.

[87] Cooper H. et al., 'Does homework improve academic achievement? A synthesis of research, 1987–2003', *Rev Educ Res*, 76, 2006.

[88] Fan H. et al., 'Homework and students' achievement in math and science', *Educ Res Rev*, 20, 2017.

[89] Rawson K. et al., 'Homework and achievement', *J Educ Psychol*, 109, 2017.

[90] Bempechat J., 'The motivational benefits of homework', *Theory Pract*, 43, 2004.

[91] Ramdass D. et al., 'Developing self-regulation skills', *J Adv Acad*, 22, 2011.

[92] Hampshire P. et al., 'Homework plans', *Teach Except Child*, 46, 2014.

[93] Göllner R. et al., 'Is doing your homework associated with becoming more conscientious?', *J Res Pers*, 71, 2017.

[94] Duckworth A. L. et al., 'Self-discipline outdoes IQ in predicting academic performance of adolescents', *Psychol Sci*, 16, 2005.

[95] Duckworth A. L., *Grit*, Scribner, 2016.

[96] Ericsson A. et al., *Peak*, Houghton Mifflin Harcourt, 2016.

[97] Dweck C., *Mindset*, Ballantine Books, 2008.

[98] Colvin G., *Talent Is Overrated*, Portfolio, 2010.

[99] Baumeister R. et al., *Willpower*, Penguin, 2011.

[100] Duckworth A. et al., 'Self-regulation strategies improve self-discipline in adolescents: benefits of mental contrasting and implementation intentions', *Educ Psychol*, 31, 2011.

[101] Donaldson-Pressman S. et al., *The Learning Habit*, Penguin, 2014.

[102] Wiecha J. L. et al., 'Household television access', *Ambul Pediatr*, 1, 2001.

[103] Vandewater E. A. et al., 'Time well spent? Relating television use to children's free-time activities', *Pediatrics*, 117, 2006.

[104] Cummings H. M. et al., 'Relation of adolescent video game play to time spent in other activities', *Arch Pediatr Adolesc Med*, 161, 2007.

[105] Barr-Anderson D. J. et al., 'Characteristics associated with older adolescents who have a television in their bedrooms', *Pediatrics*, 121, 2008.

[106] Ruest S. et al., 'The inverse relationship between digital media exposure and childhood flourishing', *J Pediatr*, 197, 2018.

[107] Armstrong G. et al., 'Background television as an inhibitor of cognitive processing', *Human Comm Res*, 16, 1990.

[108] Pool M. et al., 'Background television as an inhibitor of performance on easy and difficult homework assignments', *Comm Res*, 27, 2000.

[109] Pool M. et al., 'The impact of background radio and television on high school students' homework performance', *J Commun*, 53, 2003.

[110] Calderwood C. et al., 'What else do college students "do" while studying? An investigation of multitasking', *Comput Educ*, 75, 2014.

[111] Jeong S.-H. et al., 'Does multitasking increase or decrease persuasion? Effects of multitasking on comprehension and counterarguing', *J Commun*, 62, 2012.

[112] Srivastava J., 'Media multitasking performance', *Comput Hum Behav*, 29, 2013.

[113] Foerde K. et al., 'Modulation of competing memory systems by distraction', *Proc Natl Acad Sci USA*, 103, 2006.

[114] Kirschner P. et al., 'The myths of the digital native and the multitasker', *Teach Teach Educ*, 67, 2017.

[115] Guglielminetti B., 'One Laptop Per Child réussit son défi', LeDevoir.com, 2007.

[116] '£50 laptop to teach Third World children', dailymail.co.uk, 2007.

[117] 'Ethiopian kids teach themselves with tablets', WashingtonPost.com, 2013.

[118] Ehlers F., 'The miracle of Wenchi: Ethiopian kids using tablets to teach themselves', Spiegel.de, 2012.

[119] Guégan Y., 'Apprendre à lire sans prof? Les enfants éthiopiens s'y emploient', nouvelobs.com, 2012.

[120] Beaumont P., 'Rwanda's laptop revolution', theguardian.com, 2010.

[121]'Ces enfants éthiopiens ont hacké leurs tablettes OLPC en 5 mois!', 20minutes.fr, 2012.

[122]Thomson L., 'African kids learn to read, hack Android on OLPC fondleslab', theregister.co.uk, 2012.

[123]Ozler B., 'One Laptop Per Child is not improving reading or math: but, are we learning enough from these evaluations?', WorldBank.org, 2012.

[124]deMelo G. et al., 'The impact of a One Laptop per Child Program on learning: evidence from Uruguay', IZA Discussion Paper No. 8489, 2014.

[125]Beuermann D. W. et al., 'One Laptop per Child at home', *AEJ: Applied Economics*, 7, 2015.

[126]Meza-Cordero J. A., 'Learn to play and play to learn', *J Int Dev*, 29, 2017.

[127]Sharma U., 'Can computers increase human capital in developing countries? An evaluation of Nepal's One Laptop per Child program', paper presented at the AAEA Annual Meeting, Minneapolis, 2014.

[128]Cristia J. et al., 'Technology and child development', *Am Econ J Appl Econ*, 9, 2017.

[129]Mora T. et al., 'Computers and students' achievement: an analysis of the One Laptop per Child program in Catalonia', *Int J Educ Res*, 92, 2018.

[130]Warschauer M. et al., 'Can One Laptop per Child save the world's poor?', *J Int Aff*, 64, 2010.

[131]Champeau G., 'Des enfants illettrés s'éduquent seuls avec une tablette', Numerama.com, 2012.

[132]Murray L. et al., 'Randomized controlled trial of a book-sharing intervention in a deprived South African community', *J Child Psychol Psychiatry*, 57, 2016.

[133]Vally Z. et al., 'The impact of dialogic book-sharing training on infant language and attention', *J Child Psychol Psychiatry*, 56, 2015.

[134]Bohannon J., 'I fooled millions into thinking chocolate helps weight loss: here's how', io9.gizmodo.com, 2015.

[135]Lieury A. et al., 'Loisirs numériques et performances cognitives et scolaires', *Bulletin de Psychologie*, 530, 2014.

[136]'Liste des revues AERES pour le domaine: psychologie–éthologie–ergonomie', Agence d'Évaluation de la Recherche et de l'Enseignement, 2009.

[137]Lieury A. et al., 'L'impact des loisirs des adolescents sur les performances scolaires', Cahiers Pédagogiques, 2014.

[138]'Les ados accros à la téléréalité sont moins bons à l'école', 20minutes.fr, 2014.

[139]'Téléréalité et réussite scolaire ne font pas bon ménage', atlantico.fr, 2014.

[140]Mondoloni M., 'Plus on regarde de la téléréalité, moins on est bon à l'école', francetvinfo.fr, 2014.

[141]Mouloud L., 'Alain Lieury "La télé-réalité, un loisir nocif pour les résultats scolaires"', humanite.fr, 2014.

[142]'Si tu regardes la télé-réalité, tu auras des mauvaises notes à l'école', lexpress.fr, 2014.

[143] Radier V., '"La télé-réalité fait chuter les notes des ados"', nouvelobs.com, 2014.

[144] Simon P., 'Éducation: trop de téléréalité fait baisser les notes en classe', ouest-france.fr, 2014.

[145] 'La téléréalité nuit aux résultats scolaires', leparisien.fr, 2014.

[146] Médias, Le Magazine, France 5, invité Lieury A., 9 February 2014.

[147] CSA, 'Etude sur les stéréotypes féminins pouvant être véhiculés dans les émissions de divertissement', csa.fr, 2014.

[148] Gibson B. et al., 'Narcissism on the Jersey shore', *Psychol Pop Media Cult*, 7, 2018.

[149] Gibson B. et al., 'Just "harmless entertainment"? Effects of surveillance reality TV on physical aggression', *Psychol Pop Media Cult*, 5, 2016.

[150] Martins N. et al., 'The relationship between "teen mom" reality programming and teenagers' beliefs about teen parenthood', *Mass Commun Soc*, 17, 2014.

[151] Martins N. et al., 'The role of media exposure on relational aggression: a meta-analysis', *Aggress Violent Behav*, 47, 2019.

[152] van Oosten J. et al., 'Adolescents' sexual media use and willingness to engage in casual sex: differential relations and underlying processes', *Hum Commun Res*, 43, 2017.

[153] Riddle K. et al., 'A Snooki effect? An exploration of the surveillance subgenre of reality TV and viewers' beliefs about the "real" real world', *Psychol Pop Media Cult*, 2, 2013.

[154] Posso A., 'Internet usage and educational outcomes among 15-year-old Australian students', *Int J Commun*, 10, 2016.

[155] Gevaudan C., 'Les ados qui jouent en ligne ont de meilleures notes', liberation.fr, 2016.

[156] Griffiths S., 'Playing video games could boost children's intelligence (but Facebook will ruin their school grades)', dailymail.co.uk, 2016.

[157] Scutti S., 'Teen gamers do better at math than social media stars, study says', cnn.com, 2016.

[158] Fisné A., 'Selon une étude, les jeux vidéo permettraient d'avoir de meilleures notes', lefigaro.fr, 2016.

[159] Gibbs S., 'Positive link between video games and academic performance, study suggests', theguardian.com, 2016.

[160] Dotinga R., 'What video games, social media may mean for kids' grades', cbsnews.com, 2016.

[161] Bodkin H., 'Teenagers regularly using social media do less well at school, new survey finds', telegraph.co.uk, 2016.

[162] Devauchelle B., in Fisné A., 'Selon une étude, les jeux vidéo permettraient d'avoir de meilleures notes', lefigaro.fr, 2016.

[163] 'L'usage des jeux vidéo corrélé à de meilleures notes au lycée, selon une étude australienne', lemonde.fr, 2016.

[164] Oei A. C. et al., 'Are videogame training gains specific or general?', *Front Syst Neurosci*, 8, 2014.

[165] Przybylski A. K. et al., 'A large scale test of the gaming-enhancement hypothesis', *PeerJ*, 4, 2016.

[166] van Ravenzwaaij D. et al., 'Action video games do not improve the speed of information processing in simple perceptual tasks', *J Exp Psychol Gen*, 143, 2014.

[167] Jäncke L. et al., 'Expertise in video gaming and driving skills', *Z Neuropsychol*, 22, 2011.

[168] Gaspar J. G. et al., 'Are gamers better crossers? An examination of action video game experience and dual task effects in a simulated street crossing task', *Hum Factors*, 56, 2014.

[169] Owen A. M. et al., 'Putting brain training to the test', *Nature*, 465, 2010.

[170] Simons D. J. et al., 'Do "brain-training" programs work?', *Psychol Sci Public Interest*, 17, 2016.

[171] Azizi E. et al., 'The influence of action video game playing on eye movement behaviour during visual search in abstract, in-game and natural scenes', *Atten Percept Psychophys*, 79, 2017.

[172] Sala G. et al., 'Video game training does not enhance cognitive ability', *Psychol Bull*, 144, 2018.

[173] Drummond A. et al., 'Video-games do not negatively impact adolescent academic performance in science, mathematics or reading', *PLoS One*, 9, 2014.

[174] Borgonovi F., 'Video gaming and gender differences in digital and printed reading performance among 15-year-old students in 26 countries', *J Adolesc*, 48, 2016.

[175] OECD, 'The ABC of gender equality in education', OECD, 2015.

[176] Humphreys J., 'Playing video games can boost exam performance, OECD claims', IrishTimes.com, 2015.

[177] Eleftheriou-Smith L., 'Teenagers who play video games do better at school – but not if they're gaming every day', Independent.co.uk, 2015.

[178] Nunès E., 'Jouer (avec modération) aux jeux vidéo ne nuit pas à la scolarité', lemonde.fr, 2015.

[179] Bingham J., 'Video games are good for children (sort of)', telegraph.co.uk, 2015.

[180] Hu X. et al., 'The relationship between ICT and student literacy in mathematics, reading, and science across 44 countries', *Comput Educ*, 125, 2018.

[181] OECD, 'PISA 2015 Assessment and Analytical Framework', 2017.

[182] Vandewater E. A. et al., 'Measuring children's media use in the digital age', *Am Behav Sci*, 52, 2009.

[183] Edison T., in Saettler P., *The Evolution of American Educational Technology*, IAP, 1990.

[184] Edison T., in Cuban L., *Teachers and the Machines*, Teachers College Press, 1986.

[185] Darrow B., in Cuban L., *Teachers and the Machines*, Teachers College Press, 1986.

[186] Wischner G. et al., 'Some thoughts on television as an educational tool', *Am Psychol*, 10, 1955.

[187]Johnson L., in Cuban L., *Teachers and the Machines*, Teachers College Press, 1986.

[188]Boileau N., *Oeuvres Poétiques*, vol. 1, Imprimerie Générale, 1872.

[189]Fourgous J., 'Oser la pédagogie numérique!', lemonde.fr, 2011.

[190]Spitzer M., 'M-learning? When it comes to learning, smartphones are a liability, not an asset', *Trends Neurosci Educ*, 4, 2015.

[191]Longcamp M. et al., 'Learning through hand- or typewriting influences visual recognition of new graphic shapes', *J Cogn Neurosci*, 20, 2008.

[192]Longcamp M. et al., 'Remembering the orientation of newly learned characters depends on the associated writing knowledge', *Hum Mov Sci*, 25, 2006.

[193]Longcamp M. et al., 'The influence of writing practice on letter recognition in preschool children', *Acta Psychol (Amst)*, 119, 2005.

[194]Tan L. H. et al., 'China's language input system in the digital age affects children's reading development', *Proc Natl Acad Sci USA*, 110, 2013.

[195]Fitzgerald J. et al., 'Reading and writing relations and their development', *Educ Psychol*, 35, 2000.

[196]Tan L. H. et al., 'Reading depends on writing, in Chinese', *Proc Natl Acad Sci USA*, 102, 2005.

[197]Longcamp M. et al., 'Contribution de la motricité graphique à la reconnaissance visuelle des lettres', *Psychol Fr*, 55, 2010.

[198]Ahmed Y. et al., 'Developmental relations between reading and writing at the word, sentence and text levels', *J Educ Psychol*, 106, 2014.

[199]Li J. X. et al., 'Handwriting generates variable visual output to facilitate symbol learning', *J Exp Psychol Gen*, 145, 2016.

[200]James K. H. et al., 'The effects of handwriting experience on functional brain development in pre-literate children', *Trends Neurosci Educ*, 1, 2012.

[201]Mueller P. A. et al., 'The pen is mightier than the keyboard', *Psychol Sci*, 25, 2014.

[202]Abadie A., 'Twitter en maternelle, le cahier de vie scolaire 2.0', lemonde.fr, 2012.

[203]Davidenkoff E., 'La pédagogie doit s'adapter à l'outil', *Femme Actuelle*, 1544, April 2014.

[204]Kirkpatrick H. et al., 'Computers make kids smarter – right?', *Technos Quarterly*, 7, 1998.

[205]Smith H. et al., 'Interactive whiteboards: boon or bandwagon? A critical review of the literature', *J Comput Assist Lear*, 21, 2005.

[206]Goolsbee A. et al., 'World wide wonder?', *Educ Next*, 6, 2006.

[207]Clark R. et al., in *The Cambridge Handbook of Multimedia Learning* (ed. Mayer R. E.), 'Ten common but questionable principles of multimedia learning', Cambridge University Press, 2014.

[208]Bihouix P. et al., *Le Désastre de l'École Numérique*, Seuil, 2016.

[209]Angrist J. et al., 'New evidence on classroom computers and pupil learning', *Econ J*, 112, 2002.

[210]Spiel C. et al. 'Evaluierung des österreichischen Modellversuchs "e-Learning

und e-Teaching mit SchülerInnen-Notebooks"', Bundesministeriums für Bildung, Wissenschaft und Kultur, 2003.

[211] Rouse C. et al., 'Putting computerized instruction to the test', *Econ Educ Rev*, 23, 2004.

[212] Goolsbee A. et al., 'The impact of Internet subsidies in public schools', *Rev Econ Stat*, 88, 2006.

[213] Schaumburg H. et al., 'Lernen in Notebook-Klassen: Endbericht zur Evaluation des Projekts "1000mal1000: Notebooks im Schulranzen"', Schulen ans Netz e. V., 2007.

[214] Wurst C. et al., 'Ubiquitous laptop usage in higher education', *Comput Educ*, 51, 2008.

[215] Barrera-Osorio F. et al., 'The use and misuse of computers in education: evidence from a randomized experiment in Colombia', World Bank Policy Research Working Paper No. 4836, World Bank, 2009.

[216] Gottwald A. et al., 'Hamburger Notebook-Projekt', Behördefür Schule und Berufsbildung, 2010.

[217] Leuven E. et al., 'The effect of extra funding for disadvantaged pupils on achievement', *Rev Econ Stat*, 89, 2007.

[218] OECD, 'Students, computers and learning: making the connection (PISA)', oecd.org, 2015.

[219] OECD, 'Connectés pour apprendre? Les élèves et les nouvelles technologies (principaux résultats)', oecd.org, 2015.

[220] USDE, 'Effectiveness of reading and mathematics software products: findings from the first student cohort (report to Congress)', ies.ed.gov, 2007.

[221] USDE, 'Reviewing the evidence on how teacher professional development affects student achievement (REL 2007, no 033)', ies.ed.gov, 2007.

[222] Rockoff J., 'The impact of individual teachers on student achievement', *Am Econ Rev*, 94, 2004.

[223] Ripley A., *The Smartest Kids in the World*, Simon & Schuster, 2013.

[224] Darling-Hammond L., 'Teacher quality and student achievement', *Educ Policy Analysis Arch*, 8, 2000.

[225] Darling-Hammond L., *Empowered Educators*, Jossey-Bass, 2017.

[226] Chetty R. et al., 'Measuring the impacts of teachers II', *Am Econ Rev*, 104, 2014.

[227] OECD, 'Effective teacher policies: insights from PISA', oecd.org, 2018.

[228] Joy B., in Bauerlein M., *The Dumbest Generation*, Tarcher/Penguin, 2009.

[229] Johnson L. et al., 'Horizon Report Europe: 2014 schools edition', Publications Office of the European Union & The New Media Consortium, 2014.

[230] 'A l'université Lyon 3, les connexions sur Facebook et Netflix ralentissent le Wifi', lefigaro.fr, 2018.

[231] Nunès E., 'Quand les réseaux sociaux accaparent la bande passante de l'université Lyon-III', lemonde.fr, 2018.

[232] Gazzaley A. et al., *The Distracted Mind*, MIT Press, 2016.

[233] Junco R., 'In-class multitasking and academic performance', *Comput Hum Behav*, 28, 2012.

[234] Burak L., 'Multitasking in the university classroom', *Int J Scholar Teach Learn*, 8, 2012.

[235] Bellur S. et al., 'Make it our time', *Comput Hum Behav*, 53, 2015.

[236] Bjornsen C. et al., 'Relations between college students' cell phone use during class and grades', *Scholarsh Teach Learn Psychol*, 1, 2015.

[237] Carter S. et al., 'The impact of computer usage on academic performance', *Econ Educ Rev*, 56, 2017.

[238] Patterson R. et al., 'Computers and productivity', *Econ Educ Rev*, 57, 2017.

[239] Lawson D. et al., 'The costs of texting in the classroom', *Coll Teach*, 63, 2015.

[240] Zhang W., 'Learning variables, in-class laptop multitasking and academic performance', *Comput Educ*, 81, 2015.

[241] Gaudreau P. et al., 'Canadian university students in wireless classrooms', *Comput Educ*, 70, 2014.

[242] Ravizza S. et al., 'Non-academic Internet use in the classroom is negatively related to classroom learning regardless of intellectual ability', *Comput Educ*, 78, 2014.

[243] Clayson D. et al., 'An introduction to multitasking and texting: prevalence and impact on grades and GPA in marketing classes', *J Mark Educ*, 35, 2013.

[244] Wood E. et al., 'Examining the impact of off-task multi-tasking with technology on real-time classroom learning', *Comput Educ*, 58, 2012.

[245] Fried C., 'In-class laptop use and its effects on student learning', *Comput Educ*, 50, 2008.

[246] Beland L. et al., 'Ill communication', *Labour Econ*, 41, 2016.

[247] Jamet E. et al., 'Does multitasking in the classroom affect learning outcomes? A naturalistic study', *Comput Hum Behav*, 106, 2020.

[248] Tindell D. et al., 'The use and abuse of cell phones and text messaging in the classroom', *Coll Teach*, 60, 2012.

[249] Aagaard J., 'Drawn to distraction: a qualitative study of off-task use of educational technology', *Comput Educ*, 87, 2015.

[250] Judd T., 'Making sense of multitasking', *Comput Educ*, 70, 2014.

[251] Rosenfeld B. et al., 'East vs. West', *Coll Stud J*, 48, 2014.

[252] Ugur N. et al., 'Time for digital detox', *Procedia Soc Behav Sci*, 195, 2015.

[253] Ragan E. et al., 'Unregulated use of laptops over time in large lecture classes', *Comput Educ*, 78, 2014.

[254] Kraushaar J. et al., 'Examining the affects of student multitasking with laptops during the lecture', *J Inf Syst Educ*, 21, 2010.

[255] Hembrooke H. et al., 'The laptop and the lecture', *J Comput High Educ*, 15, 2003.

[256] Bowman L. et al., 'Can students really multitask? An experimental study of instant messaging while reading', *Comput Educ*, 54, 2010.

[257] Ellis Y. et al., 'The effect of multitasking on the grade performance of business students', *Res High Educ J*, 8, 2010.

[258] End C. et al., 'Costly cell phones', *Teach Psychol*, 37, 2010.

[259] Barks A. et al., 'Effects of text messaging on academic performance', *Signum Temporis*, 4, 2011.

[260] Froese A. et al., 'Effects of classroom cell phone use on expected and actual learning', *Coll Stud J*, 46, 2012.

[261] Kuznekoff J. et al., 'The impact of mobile phone usage on student learning', *Commun Educ*, 62, 2013.

[262] Sana F. et al., 'Laptop multitasking hinders classroom learning for both users and nearby peers', *Comput Educ*, 62, 2013.

[263] Gingerich A. et al., 'OMG! Texting in class = U fail', *Teach Psychol*, 41, 2014.

[264] Thornton B. et al., 'The mere presence of a cell phone may be distracting', *Soc Psychol*, 45, 2014.

[265] Rideout V. et al., 'The common sense census: media use by tweens and teens', Common Sense Media, 2019.

[266] Rideout V., 'The common sense census: media use by tweens and teens', Common Sense Media, 2015.

[267] Morrisson C., 'La faisabilité politique de l'ajustement', *Cahier de Politique Économique*, 13, 1996.

[268] Bourhan S., 'Alerte, on manque de profs!', franceinter.fr, 2018.

[269] Mediavilla L., 'L'éducation nationale peine toujours à recruter ses enseignants', lesechos.fr, 2018.

[270] Adams R., 'Secondary teacher recruitment in England falls short of targets', theguardian.com, 2019.

[271] Yan H. et al., 'Desperate to fill teacher shortages, US schools are hiring teachers from overseas', cnn.com, 2019.

[272] Richtel M., 'Teachers resist high-tech push in Idaho schools', nytimes.com, 2012.

[273] Herrera L., 'In Florida, virtual classrooms with no teachers', nytimes.com, 2011.

[274] Frohlich T., 'Teacher pay: states where educators are paid the most and least', usatoday.com, 2018.

[275] Davidenkoff E., *Le Tsunami Numérique*, Stock, 2014.

[276] Davidenkoff E., 'La révolution MOOC', huffingtonpost.fr, 2013.

[277] Khan Academy, 'Pythagorean theorem proof using similarity', khanacademy.org, 2020.

[278] Allione G. et al., 'Mass attrition', *J Econ Educ*, 47, 2016.

[279] Onah D. et al., 'Dropout rates of massive open online courses: behavioral patterns', Proceedings of EDULEARN14, Barcelona, Spain, 2014.

[280] Breslow L., in *From Books to MOOCs?* (eds. De Corte E. et al.), 'MOOC research', Portland Press, 2016.

[281] Evans B. et al., 'Persistence patterns in massive open online courses (MOOCs)', *J High Educ*, 87, 2016.

[282] Selingo J., 'Demystifying the MOOC', nytimes.com, 2014.

[283] Dubson M. et al., 'Apples vs. oranges: comparison of student performance in a MOOC vs. a brick-and-mortar course', PERC Proceedings 2014.

[284] Miller M. A., 'Les MOOCs font pshitt', lemonde.fr, 2017.

[285] Barth I., 'Faut-il avoir peur des grands méchants MOOCs?', educpros.fr, 2013.

[286] Azer S. A., 'Is Wikipedia a reliable learning resource for medical students? Evaluating respiratory topics', *Adv Physiol Educ*, 39, 2015.

[287] Azer S. A. et al., 'Accuracy and readability of cardiovascular entries on Wikipedia', *BMJ Open*, 5, 2015.

[288] Vilensky J. A. et al., 'Anatomy and Wikipedia', *Clin Anat*, 28, 2015.

[289] Hasty R. T. et al., 'Wikipedia vs peer-reviewed medical literature for information about the 10 most costly medical conditions', *J Am Osteopath Assoc*, 114, 2014.

[290] Lee S. et al., 'Evaluating the quality of Internet information for femoroacetabular impingement', *Arthroscopy*, 30, 2014.

[291] Lavsa S. et al., 'Reliability of Wikipedia as a medication information source for pharmacy students', *Curr Pharm Teach Learn*, 3, 2011.

[292] Berlatsky N., 'Google search algorithms are not impartial', nbcnews.com, 2018.

[293] Murray D., *The Madness of Crowds*, Bloomsbury Continuum, 2019.

[294] Solon A. et al., 'How Google's search algorithm spreads false information with a rightwing bias', theguardian.com, 2016.

[295] Grind K. et al., 'How Google interferes with its search algorithms and changes your results', wsj.com, 2019.

[296] Lynch P. M., *The Internet of Us*, Liveright, 2016.

[297] http://pensees.bibliques.over-blog.org/article-2590229.html.

[298] https://christiananswers.net/french/q-aig/aig-c030f.html.

[299] https://datanews.levif.be/ict/actualite/qu-est-il-arrive-aux-dinosaures/article-normal-299437.html.

[300] http://fr.pursuegod.org/whats-the-biblical-view-on-dinosaurs.

[301] Hirsch E., *The Knowledge Deficit*, Houghton Mifflin Harcourt, 2006.

[302] Willingham D., *Why Don't Students Like School?*, Jossey-Bass, 2009.

[303] Christodoulou D., *Seven Myths About Education*, Routledge, 2014.

[304] Tricot A. et al., 'Domain-specific knowledge and why teaching generic skills does not work', *Educ Psychol Rev*, 26, 2014.

[305] Metzger M. et al., 'Believing the unbelievable', *J Child Med*, 9, 2015.

[306] Saunders L. et al., 'Don't they teach that in high school? Examining the high school to college information literacy gap', *Libr Inform Sci Res*, 39, 2017.

[307] Recht D. et al., 'Effect of prior knowledge on good and poor readers' memory of text', *J Educ Psychol*, 80, 1988.

[308] Rowlands I. et al., 'The Google generation', *Aslib Proc*, 60, 2008.

[309] Thirion P. et al., 'Enquête sur les compétences documentaires et informationnelles des étudiants qui accèdent à l'enseignement supérieur en Communauté française de Belgique', enssib.fr, 2008.

[310] Julien H. et al., 'How high-school students find and evaluate scientific information', *Libr Inform Sci Res*, 31, 2009.

[311] Gross M. et al., 'What's skill got to do with it?', *J Am Soc Inf Sci Technol*, 63, 2012.

[312] Perret C., 'Pratiques de recherche documentaire et réussite universitaire des étudiants de première année', *Carrefours de l'Éducation*, 35, 2013.

[313] Dumouchel G. et al., 'Mon ami Google', *Can J Learn Tech*, 43, 2017.

[314] 'Evaluating information: the cornerstone of civic online reasoning', report from the Stanford History Education Group, Stanford History Education Group, 2016.

[315] McNamara D. et al., 'Are good texts always better? Interactions of text coherence, background knowledge, and levels of understanding in learning from text', *Cognition Instruct*, 14, 1996.

[316] Amadieu F. et al., 'Exploratory study of relations between prior knowledge, comprehension, disorientation and on-line processes in hypertext', *Ergon Open J*, 2, 2009.

[317] Amadieu F. et al., 'Prior knowledge in learning from a non-linear electronic document: disorientation and coherence of the reading sequences', *Comput Hum Behav*, 25, 2009.

[318] Amadieu F. et al., 'Effects of prior knowledge and concept-map structure on disorientation, cognitive load, and learning', *Learn Instr*, 19, 2009.

[319] Khosrowjerdi M. et al., 'Prior knowledge and information-seeking behavior of PhD and MA students', *Libr Inform Sci Res*, 33, 2011.

[320] Kalyuga S., 'Effects of learner prior knowledge and working memory limitations on multimedia learning', *Procedia Soc Behav Sci*, 83, 2013.

[321] Guillou M., 'Profs débutants: 10 bonnes raisons d'échapper au numérique', educavox.fr, 2013.

[322] Guéno J., *Mémoires de Maîtres, Paroles d'Élèves*, J'ai Lu, 2012.

[323] Camus A., in Bersihand N., 'Lettre de Camus à Louis Germain, son premier instituteur', huffingtonpost.fr, 2014.

Development

[1] Dehaene-Lambertz G. et al., 'The infancy of the human brain', *Neuron*, 88, 2015.

[2] Otsuka Y., 'Face recognition in infants', *Jpn Psychol Res*, 56, 2014.

[3] Bonini L. et al., 'Evolution of mirror systems', *Ann N Y Acad Sci*, 1225, 2011.

[4] Grossmann T., 'The development of social brain functions in infancy', *Psychol Bull*, 141, 2015.

[5] Piaget J., *The Origins of Intelligence in Children*, International Universities Press, 1952.

[6] Cassidy J. et al., *Handbook of Attachment: Theory, Research, and Clinical Applications* (3rd edition), Guilford Press, 2016.

[7] Tottenham N., 'The importance of early experiences for neuro-affective development', *Curr Top Behav Neurosci*, 16, 2014.

[8] Grusec J. E., 'Socialization processes in the family', *Annu Rev Psychol*, 62, 2011.

[9] Kuhl P. K., 'Brain mechanisms in early language acquisition', *Neuron*, 67, 2010.

[10] Eshel N. et al., 'Responsive parenting', *Bull World Health Organ*, 84, 2006.

[11] Champagne F. A. et al., 'How social experiences influence the brain', *Curr Opin Neurobiol*, 15, 2005.

[12] Hart B. et al., *Meaningful Differences*, Paul H. Brookes, 1995.

[13] Farley J. P. et al., 'The development of adolescent self-regulation', *J Adolesc*, 37, 2014.

[14] Hair E. et al., 'The continued importance of quality parent–adolescent relationships during late adolescence', *J Res Adolesc*, 18, 2008.

[15] Morris A. S. et al., 'The role of the family context in the development of emotion regulation', *Soc Dev*, 16, 2007.

[16] Smetana J. G. et al., 'Adolescent development in interpersonal and societal contexts', *Annu Rev Psychol*, 57, 2006.

[17] Forehand R. et al., 'Home predictors of young adolescents' school behavior and academic performance', *Child Dev*, 57, 1986.

[18] Dettmer A. M. et al., 'Neonatal face-to-face interactions promote later social behaviour in infant rhesus monkeys', *Nat Commun*, 7, 2016.

[19] Cunningham A. et al., *Book Smart*, Oxford University Press, 2014.

[20] Neuman S. et al., *Handbook of Early Literacy Research* (vols. 1 to 3), Guilford Press, 2001–11.

[21] Black S. et al., 'Older and wiser? Birth order and IQ of young men', NBER Working Paper No. 13237, 2007.

[22] Black S. et al., 'The more the merrier? The effect of family size and birth order on children's education', *Q J Econ*, 120, 2005.

[23] Kantarevic J. et al., 'Birth order, educational attainment, and earnings', *J Hum Resour*, XLI, 2006.

[24] Lehmann J. et al., 'The early origins of birth order differences in children's outcomes and parental behavior', *J Hum Resour*, 53, 2018.

[25] Coude G. et al., 'Grasping neurons in the ventral premotor cortex of macaques are modulated by social goals', *J Cogn Neurosci*, 2018.

[26] Ferrari P. F., 'The neuroscience of social relations: a comparative-based approach to empathy and to the capacity of evaluating others' action value', *Behaviour*, 151, 2014.

[27] Salo V. C. et al., 'The role of the motor system in action understanding and communication', *Dev Psychobiol*, 2018.

[28] Ferrari P. F. et al., 'Mirror neurons responding to the observation of ingestive and communicative mouth actions in the monkey ventral premotor cortex', *Eur J Neurosci*, 17, 2003.

[29] Jarvelainen J. et al., 'Stronger reactivity of the human primary motor cortex during observation of live rather than video motor acts', *Neuroreport*, 12, 2001.

[30]Perani D. et al., 'Different brain correlates for watching real and virtual hand actions', *Neuroimage*, 14, 2001.

[31]Shimada S. et al., 'Infant's brain responses to live and televised action', *Neuroimage*, 32, 2006.

[32]Jola C. et al., 'In the here and now', *Cogn Neurosci*, 4, 2013.

[33]Ruysschaert L. et al., 'Neural mirroring during the observation of live and video actions in infants', *Clin Neurophysiol*, 124, 2013.

[34]Troseth G. L. et al., 'The medium can obscure the message', *Child Dev*, 69, 1998.

[35]Troseth G. L. et al., 'Young children's use of video as a source of socially relevant information', *Child Dev*, 77, 2006.

[36]Kuhl P. K. et al., 'Foreign-language experience in infancy', *Proc Natl Acad Sci USA*, 100, 2003.

[37]Schmidt K. L. et al., 'Television and reality', *Media Psychol*, 4, 2002.

[38]Schmidt K. L. et al., 'Two-year-olds' object retrieval based on television: testing a perceptual account', *Media Psychol*, 9, 2007.

[39]Kirkorian H. et al., 'Video deficit in toddlers' object retrieval', *Infancy*, 21, 2016.

[40]Kim D. H. et al., 'Effects of live and video form action observation training on upper limb function in children with hemiparetic cerebral palsy', *Technol Health Care*, 26, 2018.

[41]Reiß M. et al., 'Theory of mind and the video deficit effect', *Media Psychol*, 22, 2019.

[42]Barr R. et al., 'Developmental changes in imitation from television during infancy', *Child Dev*, 70, 1999.

[43]Hayne H. et al., 'Imitation from television by 24- and 30-month-olds', *Dev Sci*, 6, 2003.

[44]Thierry K. et al., 'A real-life event enhances the accuracy of preschoolers' recall', *Appl Cogn Psychol*, 18, 2004.

[45]Yadav S. et al., 'Children aged 6–24 months like to watch YouTube videos but could not learn anything from them', *Acta Paediatr*, 107, 2018.

[46]Madigan S. et al., 'Association between screen time and children's performance on a developmental screening test', *JAMA Pediatr*, 2019.

[47]Kildare C. et al., 'Impact of parents mobile device use on parent–child interaction', *Comput Hum Behav*, 75, 2017.

[48]Napier C., 'How use of screen media affects the emotional development of infants', *Prim Health Care*, 24, 2014.

[49]Radesky J. et al., 'Maternal mobile device use during a structured parent–child interaction task', *Acad Pediatr*, 15, 2015.

[50]Radesky J. S. et al., 'Patterns of mobile device use by caregivers and children during meals in fast food restaurants', *Pediatrics*, 133, 2014.

[51]Stockdale L. et al., 'Parent and child technoference and socioemotional behavioral outcomes', *Comput Hum Behav*, 88, 2018.

[52]Kushlev K. et al., 'Smartphones distract parents from cultivating feelings

of connection when spending time with their children', *J Soc Pers Relat*, 36, 2018.

[53]Rotondi V. et al., 'Connecting alone', *J Econ Psychol*, 63, 2017.

[54]Dwyer R. et al., 'Smartphone use undermines enjoyment of face-to-face social interactions', *J Exp Soc Psychol*, 78, 2018.

[55]Christakis D. A. et al., 'Audible television and decreased adult words, infant vocalizations, and conversational turns', *Arch Pediatr Adolesc Med*, 163, 2009.

[56]Kirkorian H. L. et al., 'The impact of background television on parent–child interaction', *Child Dev*, 80, 2009.

[57]Tomopoulos S. et al., 'Is exposure to media intended for preschool children associated with less parent–child shared reading aloud and teaching activities?', *Ambul Pediatr*, 7, 2007.

[58]Tanimura M. et al., 'Television viewing, reduced parental utterance, and delayed speech development in infants and young children', *Arch Pediatr Adolesc Med*, 161, 2007.

[59]Vandewater E. A. et al., 'Time well spent? Relating television use to children's free-time activities', *Pediatrics*, 117, 2006.

[60]Chaput J. P. et al., 'Sleeping hours: what is the ideal number and how does age impact this?', *Nat Sci Sleep*, 10, 2018.

[61]Rideout V., 'The common sense census: media use by tweens and teens', Common Sense Media, 2015.

[62]Rideout V., 'The common sense census: media use by kids age zero to eight', Common Sense Media, 2017.

[63]Wartella E. et al., 'Parenting in the age of digital technology', Center on Media and Human Development, School of Communication, Northwestern University, 2014.

[64]Donnat O., *Les Pratiques Culturelles des Français à l'Ère Numérique: Enquête 2008*, La Découverte, 2009.

[65]Desmurget M., *TV Lobotomie*, J'ai Lu, 2013.

[66]Schmidt M. E. et al., 'The effects of background television on the toy play behavior of very young children', *Child Dev*, 79, 2008.

[67]Kubey R. et al., 'Television addiction is no mere metaphor', *Sci Am*, 286, 2002.

[68]Huston A. C. et al., 'Communicating more than content', *J Commun*, 31, 1981.

[69]Bermejo Berros J., *Génération Télévision*, De Boeck, 2007.

[70]Lachaux J., *Le Cerveau Attentif*, Odile Jacob, 2011.

[71]Przybylski A. et al., 'Can you connect with me now? How the presence of mobile communication technology influences face-to-face conversation quality', *J Soc Pers Relatsh*, 30, 2013.

[72]McDaniel B. et al., '"Technoference"', *Psychol Pop Media Cult*, 5, 2016.

[73]McDaniel B. et al., '"Technoference" and implications for mothers' and fathers' couple and coparenting relationship quality', *Comput Hum Behav*, 80, 2018.

[74]Roberts J. et al., 'My life has become a major distraction from my cell phone', *Comput Hum Behav*, 54, 2016.

[75]Halpern D. et al., 'Texting's consequences for romantic relationships', *Comput Hum Behav*, 71, 2017.

[76]Winn M., *The Plug-In-Drug* (revised edition), Penguin, 2002.

[77]Coyne S. et al., 'Gaming in the game of love', *Fam Relat*, 61, 2012.

[78]Ahlstrom M. et al., 'Me, my spouse, and my avatar', *J Leis Res*, 44, 2012.

[79]Parke R. D., 'Development in the family', *Annu Rev Psychol*, 55, 2004.

[80]El-Sheikh M. et al., 'Family conflict, autonomic nervous system functioning, and child adaptation', *Dev Psychopathol*, 23, 2011.

[81]Lucas-Thompson R. G. et al., 'Family relationships and children's stress responses', *Adv Child Dev Behav*, 40, 2011.

[82]Sternberg R., in *The Nature of Vocabulary Acquisition* (eds. McKeown M. et al.), 'Most vocabulary is learned from context', Lawrence Erlbaum Associates, 1987.

[83]Duch H. et al., 'Association of screen time use and language development in Hispanic toddlers', *Clin Pediatr (Phila)*, 52, 2013.

[84]Lin L. Y. et al., 'Effects of television exposure on developmental skills among young children', *Infant Behav Dev*, 38, 2015.

[85]Pagani L. S. et al., 'Early childhood television viewing and kindergarten entry readiness', *Pediatr Res*, 74, 2013.

[86]Tomopoulos S. et al., 'Infant media exposure and toddler development', *Arch Pediatr Adolesc Med*, 164, 2010.

[87]Zimmerman F. J. et al., 'Associations between media viewing and language development in children under age 2 years', *J Pediatr*, 151, 2007.

[88]Byeon H. et al., 'Relationship between television viewing and language delay in toddlers', *PLoS One*, 10, 2015.

[89]Chonchaiya W. et al., 'Television viewing associates with delayed language development', *Acta Paediatr*, 97, 2008.

[90]van den Heuvel M. et al., 'Mobile media device use is associated with expressive language delay in 18-month-old children', *J Dev Behav Pediatr*, 40, 2019.

[91]Collet M. et al., 'Case-control study found that primary language disorders were associated with screen exposure', *Acta Paediatr*, 2018.

[92]Madigan S. et al., 'Associations between screen use and child language skills: a systematic review and meta-analysis', *JAMA Pediatr*, 2020.

[93]Tremblay M. S. et al., 'Canadian 24-Hour Movement guidelines for children and youth: an integration of physical activity, sedentary behaviour, and sleep', *Appl Physiol Nutr Metab*, 41, 2016.

[94]Walsh J. J. et al., 'Associations between 24-hour movement behaviours and global cognition in US children', *Lancet Child Adolesc Health*, 2, 2018.

[95]Takeuchi H. et al., 'The impact of television viewing on brain structures', *Cereb Cortex*, 25, 2015.

[96]Takeuchi H. et al., 'Impact of videogame play on the brain's microstructural properties', *Mol Psychiatry*, 21, 2016.

[97] Mitra P. et al., 'Clinical and molecular aspects of lead toxicity', *Crit Rev Clin Lab Sci*, 54, 2017.

[98] Chiodo L. M. et al., 'Blood lead levels and specific attention effects in young children', *Neurotoxicol Teratol*, 29, 2007.

[99] Horowitz-Kraus T. et al., 'Brain connectivity in children is increased by the time they spend reading books and decreased by the length of exposure to screen-based media', *Acta Paediatr*, 107, 2018.

[100] Takeuchi H. et al., 'Impact of frequency of Internet use on development of brain structures and verbal intelligence: longitudinal analyses', *Hum Brain Mapp*, 39, 2018.

[101] Hutton J. S. et al., 'Potential association of screen use with brain development in preschool-aged children: reply', *JAMA Pediatr*, 2020.

[102] Farah M. J., 'The neuroscience of socioeconomic status: correlates, causes, and consequences', *Neuron*, 96, 2017.

[103] Mohammed A. H. et al., 'Environmental enrichment and the brain', *Prog Brain Res*, 138, 2002.

[104] van Praag H. et al., 'Neural consequences of environmental enrichment', *Nat Rev Neurosci*, 1, 2000.

[105] Huttenlocher J. et al., 'Early vocabulary growth', *Dev Psychol*, 27, 1991.

[106] Walker D. et al., 'Prediction of school outcomes based on early language production and socioeconomic factors', *Child Dev*, 65, 1994.

[107] Hoff E., 'The specificity of environmental influence', *Child Dev*, 74, 2003.

[108] Zimmerman F. J. et al., 'Teaching by listening', *Pediatrics*, 124, 2009.

[109] Cartmill E. A. et al., 'Quality of early parent input predicts child vocabulary 3 years later', *Proc Natl Acad Sci USA*, 110, 2013.

[110] Bloom P., *How Children Learn the Meaning of Words*, MIT Press, 2000.

[111] Takeuchi H. et al., 'Impact of reading habit on white matter structure', *Neuroimage*, 133, 2016.

[112] Gilkerson J. et al., 'Language experience in the second year of life and language outcomes in late childhood', *Pediatrics*, 142, 2018.

[113] Hart B. et al., 'American parenting of language-learning children', *Dev Psychol*, 28, 1992.

[114] Romeo R. R. et al., 'Language exposure relates to structural neural connectivity in childhood', *J Neurosci*, 38, 2018.

[115] Damgé M., 'Écrans et capacités cognitives, une relation complexe', lemonde.fr, 2019.

[116] Davis N., 'Study links high levels of screen time to slower child development', theguardian.com, 2019.

[117] Kostyrka-Allchorne K. et al., 'The relationship between television exposure and children's cognition and behaviour', *Dev Rev*, 44, 2017.

[118] Krcmar M., 'Word learning in very young children from infant-directed DVDs', *J Commun*, 61, 2011.

[119] Richert R. A. et al., 'Word learning from baby videos', *Arch Pediatr Adolesc Med*, 164, 2010.

[120] Robb M. B. et al., 'Just a talking book? Word learning from watching baby videos', *Br J Dev Psychol*, 27, 2009.

[121] DeLoache J. S. et al., 'Do babies learn from baby media?', *Psychol Sci*, 21, 2010.

[122] Kaminski J. et al., 'Word learning in a domestic dog', *Science*, 304, 2004.

[123] Carey S., in *Linguistic Theory and Psychological Reality* (eds. Halle M. et al.), 'The child as word learner', MIT Press, 1978.

[124] Krcmar M., 'Can infants and toddlers learn words from repeat exposure to an infant directed DVD?', *J Broadcast Electron Media*, 58, 2014.

[125] Gola A. A. H. et al., in *Handbook of Children and the Media* (2nd edition) (eds. Singer D. G. et al.), 'Television as incidental language teacher', SAGE, 2012.

[126] Van Lommel S. et al., 'Foreign-grammar acquisition while watching subtitled television programmes', *Br J Educ Psychol*, 76, 2006.

[127] Roseberry S. et al., 'Live action: can young children learn verbs from video?', *Child Dev*, 80, 2009.

[128] Baudelaire C., *Oeuvres Complètes (IV): Petits Poèmes en Prose*, Michel Lévy Frères, 1869.

[129] Brown P. et al., *Make it Stick*, Harvard University Press, 2014.

[130] Veneziano E., in *L'Acquisition du Langage: Le Langage en Émergence. De la Naissance à Trois Ans* (eds. Kail M. et al.), 'Interaction, conversation et acquisition du langage dans les trois premières années de la vie', PUF, 2000.

[131] Hickok G. et al., 'The cortical organization of speech processing', *Nat Rev Neurosci*, 8, 2007.

[132] Lopez-Barroso D. et al., 'Word learning is mediated by the left arcuate fasciculus', *Proc Natl Acad Sci USA*, 110, 2013.

[133] Collectif, 'Children and adolescents and digital media', *Pediatrics*, 138, 2016.

[134] Stanovich K., in *Advances of Child Development and Behavior* (vol. 24) (ed. Reese H.), 'Does reading make you smarter? Literacy and the development of verbal intelligence', Academic Press, 1993.

[135] Hayes D., 'Speaking and writing', *J Mem Lang*, 27, 1988.

[136] Cunningham A. et al., 'What reading does for the mind', *Am Educ*, 22, 1998.

[137] Collectif, 'Rentrée 2008: évaluation du niveau d'orthographe et de grammaire des élèves qui entrent en classe de seconde', sauv.net, 2009.

[138] Mathieu-Colas M., 'Maîtrise du français', lefigaro.fr, 2010.

[139] Anderson R. et al., 'Growth in reading and how children spend their time outside of school', *Read Res Q*, 23, 1988.

[140] Esteban-Cornejo I. et al., 'Objectively measured and self-reported leisure-time sedentary behavior and academic performance in youth', *Prev Med*, 77, 2015.

[141] Sullivan A. et al., 'Social inequalities in cognitive scores at age 16: the role of reading', CLS Working Paper 2013/10, Centre for Longitudinal Studies, Institute of Education, University of London, 2013.

[142] Mol S. E. et al., 'To read or not to read', *Psychol Bull*, 137, 2011.

[143] NEA, 'To read or not to read', Research Report No. 47, National Endowment for the Arts, 2007.

[144] Shin N., 'Exploring pathways from television viewing to academic achievement in school age children', *J Genet Psychol*, 165, 2004.

[145] Head Zauche L. et al., 'The power of language nutrition for children's brain development, health, and future academic achievement', *J Pediatr Health Care*, 31, 2017.

[146] Barr-Anderson D. J. et al., 'Characteristics associated with older adolescents who have a television in their bedrooms', *Pediatrics*, 121, 2008.

[147] Merga M. et al., 'The influence of access to eReaders, computers and mobile phones on children's book reading frequency', *Comput Educ*, 109, 2017.

[148] Gentile D. A. et al., 'Bedroom media', *Dev Psychol*, 53, 2017.

[149] Rideout V. et al., 'Generation M2: media in the lives of 8–18 year-olds', Kaiser Family Foundation, 2010.

[150] Garcia-Continente X. et al., 'Factors associated with media use among adolescents', *Eur J Public Health*, 24, 2014.

[151] Wiecha J. L. et al., 'Household television access', *Ambul Pediatr*, 1, 2001.

[152] Gadberry S., 'Effects of restricting first graders' TV-viewing on leisure time use, IQ change, and cognitive style', *J Appl Dev Psychol*, 1, 1980.

[153] Cummings H. M. et al., 'Relation of adolescent video game play to time spent in other activities', *Arch Pediatr Adolesc Med*, 161, 2007.

[154] Corteen R. S. et al., in *The Impact of Television: A Natural Experiment in Three Communities* (ed. MacBeth Williams T.), 'Television and reading skills', Academic Press, 1986.

[155] Vandewater E. A. et al., 'When the television is always on', *Am Behav Sci*, 48, 2005.

[156] Koolstra C. M. et al., 'Television's impact on children's reading comprehension and decoding skills', *Read Res Q*, 32, 1997.

[157] 'Children's reading for pleasure: trends and challenges (Egmont Books Report)', egmont.co.uk, 2020.

[158] Clark C. et al., 'Children and young people's reading in 2019 (National Literacy Trust research report)', literacytrust.org.uk, 2020.

[159] Lombardo P. et al., 'Cinquante ans de pratiques culturelles en France', culture.gouv.fr, 2020.

[160] Rideout V. et al., 'The common sense census: media use by tweens and teens', Common Sense Media, 2019.

[161] Mauléon F., in Rollot O., 'Nouvelles pédagogies: "l'étudiant doit être la personne la plus importante dans une école"', lemonde.fr, 2013.

[162] Manilève V., 'Dire que les "jeunes lisent moins qu'avant" n'a plus aucun sens à l'heure d'Internet', slate.fr, 2015.

[163] Octobre S., *Deux Pouces et des Neurones*, Ministère de la Culture et de la Communication, 2014.

[164] Octobre S., in Buratti L., 'Les jeunes lisent toujours, mais pas des livres', lemonde.fr, 2014.

[165] Duncan L. G. et al., 'Adolescent reading skill and engagement with digital and traditional literacies as predictors of reading comprehension', *Br J Psychol*, 107, 2016.

[166] Pfost M. et al., 'Students' extracurricular reading behavior and the development of vocabulary and reading comprehension', *Learn Individ Differ*, 26, 2013.

[167] Mangen A. et al., 'Reading linear texts on paper versus computer screen', *Int J Educ Res*, 58, 2013.

[168] Kong Y. et al., 'Comparison of reading performance on screen and on paper', *Comput Educ*, 123, 2018.

[169] Delgado P. et al., 'Don't throw away your printed books', *Educ Res Rev*, 25, 2018.

[170] Singer L. et al., 'Reading across mediums', *J Exp Educ*, 85, 2017.

[171] Toulon A., 'Des jeux-vidéo pour lutter contre la dyslexie', Europe1.fr, 2014.

[172] 'Video games "help reading in children with dyslexia"', bbc.com, 2013.

[173] Serna J., 'Study: a day of video games tops a year of therapy for dyslexic readers', LaTimes.com, 2013.

[174] Solis M., 'Video games may treat dyslexia', scientificamerican.com, 2013.

[175] Harrar V. et al., 'Multisensory integration and attention in developmental dyslexia', *Curr Biol*, 24, 2014.

[176] 'Les jeux vidéo d'action recommandés aux dyslexiques', CNewsMatin.fr, 2014.

[177] de la Bigne Y., 'Les juex viédos conrte la dislexye', Europe1.fr, 2014.

[178] Kipling R., *Histoires Comme Ça*, Livre de Poche, 2007.

[179] Franceschini S. et al., 'Action video games make dyslexic children read better', *Curr Biol*, 23, 2013.

[180] Tressoldi P. E. et al., 'The development of reading speed in Italians with dyslexia', *J Learn Disabil*, 34, 2001.

[181] Tressoldi P. E. et al., 'Efficacy of an intervention to improve fluency in children with developmental dyslexia in a regular orthography', *J Learn Disabil*, 40, 2007.

[182] Collins N., 'Video games "teach dyslexic children to read"', Telegraph.co.uk, 2013.

[183] Guarini D., '9 ways video games can actually be good for you', huffingtonpost.com, 2013.

[184] Green C. S. et al., 'Action video game modifies visual selective attention', *Nature*, 423, 2003.

[185] Blakeslee S., 'Video-game killing builds visual skills, researchers report', nytimes.com, 2003.

[186] Debroise A., 'Les effets positifs des jeux vidéo', LePoint.fr, 2012.

[187] 'Les jeux de tirs sont bons pour le cerveau', lefigaro.fr, 2012.

[188] Fleming N., 'Why video games may be good for you', bbc.com, 2013.

[189] Bach J. et al., *L'Enfant et les Écrans: Un Avis de l'Académie des Sciences*, Le Pommier, 2013.

[190] Bavelier D. et al., 'Brain plasticity through the life span', *Annu Rev Neurosci*, 35, 2012.

[191] Weisburg R. W., in *Handbook of Creativity* (ed. Sternberg R.), 'Creativity and knowledge', Cambridge University Press, 1999.

[192] Colvin G., *Talent is Overrated*, Portfolio, 2010.

[193] Gladwell M., *Outliers*, Black Bay Books, 2008.

[194] Ericsson A. et al., *Peak*, Houghton Mifflin Harcourt, 2016.

[195] Cain S., *Quiet*, Broadway Paperbacks, 2013.

[196] Dunnette M. et al., 'The effect of group participation on brainstorming effectiveness for 2 industrial samples', *J Appl Psychol*, 47, 1963.

[197] Mongeau P. et al., 'Reconsidering brainstorming', *Group Facilitation*, 1, 1999.

[198] Furnham A., 'The brainstorming myth', *Bus Strategy Rev*, 11, 2000.

[199] Dye M. W. et al., 'Increasing speed of processing with action video games', *Curr Dir Psychol Sci*, 18, 2009.

[200] Castel A. D. et al., 'The effects of action video game experience on the time course of inhibition of return and the efficiency of visual search', *Acta Psychol (Amst)*, 119, 2005.

[201] Green C. S. et al., 'Improved probabilistic inference as a general learning mechanism with action video games', *Curr Biol*, 20, 2010.

[202] Murphy K. et al., 'Playing video games does not make for better visual attention skills', *JASNH*, 6, 2009.

[203] Boot W. R. et al., 'The effects of video game playing on attention, memory, and executive control', *Acta Psychol (Amst)*, 129, 2008.

[204] Boot W. R. et al., 'Do action video games improve perception and cognition?', *Front Psychol*, 2, 2011.

[205] Irons J. et al., 'Not so fast', *Aust J Psychol*, 63, 2011.

[206] Donohue S. E. et al., 'Cognitive pitfall! Videogame players are not immune to dual-task costs', *Atten Percept Psychophys*, 74, 2012.

[207] Boot W. R. et al., 'The pervasive problem with placebos in psychology: why active control groups are not sufficient to rule out placebo effects', *Perspect Psychol Sci*, 8, 2013.

[208] Collins E. et al., 'Video game use and cognitive performance', *Cyberpsychol Behav Soc Netw*, 17, 2014.

[209] Gobet F. et al., '"No level up!"', *Front Psychol*, 5, 2014.

[210] Unsworth N. et al., 'Is playing video games related to cognitive abilities?', *Psychol Sci*, 26, 2015.

[211] Redick T. S. et al., 'Don't shoot the messenger: a reply to Green et al. (2017)', *Psychol Sci*, 28, 2017.

[212] Memmert D. et al., 'The relationship between visual attention and expertise in sports', *Psychol Sport Exerc*, 10, 2009.

[213] Kida N. et al., 'Intensive baseball practice improves the Go/Nogo reaction time, but not the simple reaction time', *Brain Res Cogn Brain Res*, 22, 2005.

[214] Azemar G. et al., *Neurobiologie des Comportements Moteurs*, INSEP, 1982.

[215] Ripoll H. et al., *Neurosciences du Sport*, INSEP, 1987.

[216] Underwood G. et al., 'Visual search while driving', *Transp Res Part F*, 5, 2002.

[217] Savelsbergh G. J. et al., 'Visual search, anticipation and expertise in soccer goalkeepers', *J Sports Sci*, 20, 2002.

[218] Muller S. et al., 'Expert anticipatory skill in striking sports', *Res Q Exerc Sport*, 83, 2012.

[219] Helsen W. et al., 'The relationship between expertise and visual information processing in sport', *Adv Psychol*, 102, 1993.

[220] Steffens M., 'Video games are good for you', abc.net.au, 2009.

[221] Jäncke L. et al., 'Expertise in video gaming and driving skills', *Z Neuropsychol*, 22, 2011.

[222] Ciceri M. et al., 'Does driving experience in video games count? Hazard anticipation and visual exploration of male gamers as function of driving experience', *Transp Res Part F*, 22, 2014.

[223] Fischer P. et al., 'The effects of risk-glorifying media exposure on risk-positive cognitions, emotions, and behaviors', *Psychol Bull*, 137, 2011.

[224] Fischer P. et al., 'The racing-game effect', *Pers Soc Psychol Bull*, 35, 2009.

[225] Beullens K. et al., 'Excellent gamer, excellent driver? The impact of adolescents' video game playing on driving behavior', *Accid Anal Prev*, 43, 2011.

[226] Beullens K. et al., 'Predicting young drivers' car crashes', *Media Psychol*, 16, 2013.

[227] Beullens K. et al., 'Driving game playing as a predictor of adolescents' unlicensed driving in Flanders', *J Child Med*, 7, 2013.

[228] Hull J. G. et al., 'A longitudinal study of risk-glorifying video games and behavioral deviance', *J Pers Soc Psychol*, 107, 2014.

[229] Rozières G., 'Jouer à Mario Kart fait de vous un meilleur conducteur, c'est scientifiquement prouvé', huffingtonpost.fr, 2016.

[230] 'Jouer à Mario Kart fait de vous un meilleur conducteur, c'est scientifiquement prouvé!', Elle.fr, 2017.

[231] Priam E., 'Jouer à Mario Kart fait de vous un meilleur conducteur', femmeactuelle.fr, 2017.

[232] Aratani L., 'Study confirms "Mario Kart" really does make you a better driver: see, mom!', huffingtonpost.com, 2016.

[233] 'Playing Mario Kart CAN make you a better driver', dailymail.co.uk, 2016.

[234] Li L. et al., 'Playing action video games improves visuomotor control', *Psychol Sci*, 27, 2016.

[235] 'Les fans de Mario Kart seraient de meilleurs conducteurs, selon la science', public.fr, 2017.

[236] Bediou B. et al., 'Meta-analysis of action video game impact on perceptual, attentional, and cognitive skills', *Psychol Bull*, 144, 2018.

[237] Powers K. L. et al., 'Effects of video-game play on information processing', *Psychon Bull Rev*, 20, 2013.

[238] Schlickum M. K. et al., 'Systematic video game training in surgical novices improves performance in virtual reality endoscopic surgical simulators', *World J Surg*, 33, 2009.

[239] Rosser J. C., Jr. et al., 'The impact of video games on training surgeons in the 21st century', *Arch Surg*, 142, 2007.

[240] McKinley R. A. et al., 'Operator selection for unmanned aerial systems', *Aviat Space Environ Med*, 82, 2011.

[241] Oei A. C. et al., 'Are videogame training gains specific or general?', *Front Syst Neurosci*, 8, 2014.

[242] Przybylski A. K. et al., 'A large scale test of the gaming-enhancement hypothesis', *PeerJ*, 4, 2016.

[243] van Ravenzwaaij D. et al., 'Action video games do not improve the speed of information processing in simple perceptual tasks', *J Exp Psychol Gen*, 143, 2014.

[244] Gaspar J. G. et al., 'Are gamers better crossers? An examination of action video game experience and dual task effects in a simulated street crossing task', *Hum Factors*, 56, 2014.

[245] Owen A. M. et al., 'Putting brain training to the test', *Nature*, 465, 2010.

[246] Simons D. J. et al., 'Do "brain-training" programs work?', *Psychol Sci Public Interest*, 17, 2016.

[247] Azizi E. et al., 'The influence of action video game playing on eye movement behaviour during visual search in abstract, in-game and natural scenes', *Atten Percept Psychophys*, 79, 2017.

[248] Sala G. et al., 'Video game training does not enhance cognitive ability', *Psychol Bull*, 144, 2018.

[249] Conti J., 'Ces jeux vidéo qui vous font du bien', LeTemps.ch, 2013.

[250] Fritel J., 'Jeux vidéo: les nouveaux maîtres du monde', documentaire Arte, 15 November 2016.

[251] Dehaene S., 'Matinale de France Inter, le grand entretien', franceinter.fr, 2018.

[252] Gazzaley A. et al., *The Distracted Mind*, MIT Press, 2016.

[253] Katsuki F. et al., 'Bottom-up and top-down attention', *Neuroscientist*, 20, 2014.

[254] Chun M. M. et al., 'A taxonomy of external and internal attention', *Annu Rev Psychol*, 62, 2011.

[255] Johansen-Berg H. et al., 'Attention to touch modulates activity in both primary and secondary somatosensory areas', *Neuroreport*, 11, 2000.

[256] Duncan G. J. et al., 'School readiness and later achievement', *Dev Psychol*, 43, 2007.

[257] Pagani L. S. et al., 'School readiness and later achievement', *Dev Psychol*, 46, 2010.

[258] Horn W. et al., 'Early identification of learning problems', *J Educ Psychol*, 77, 1985.

[259] Polderman T. J. et al., 'A systematic review of prospective studies on attention problems and academic achievement', *Acta Psychiatr Scand*, 122, 2010.

[260] Rhoades B. et al., 'Examining the link between preschool social-emotional competence and first grade academic achievement', *Early Child Res Q*, 26, 2011.

[261] Johnson J. G. et al., 'Extensive television viewing and the development of attention and learning difficulties during adolescence', *Arch Pediatr Adolesc Med*, 161, 2007.

[262] Frazier T. W. et al., 'ADHD and achievement', *J Learn Disabil*, 40, 2007.

[263] Loe I. M. et al., 'Academic and educational outcomes of children with ADHD', *J Pediatr Psychol*, 32, 2007.

[264] Hinshaw S. P., 'Externalizing behavior problems and academic under-achievement in childhood and adolescence', *Psychol Bull*, 111, 1992.

[265] Inoue S. et al., 'Working memory of numerals in chimpanzees', *Curr Biol*, 17, 2007.

[266] Wilson D. E. et al., 'Practice in visual search produces decreased capacity demands but increased distraction', *Percept Psychophys*, 70, 2008.

[267] Bailey K. et al., 'A negative association between video game experience and proactive cognitive control', *Psychophysiology*, 47, 2010.

[268] Chan P. A. et al., 'A cross-sectional analysis of video games and attention deficit hyperactivity disorder symptoms in adolescents', *Ann Gen Psychiatry*, 5, 2006.

[269] Gentile D., 'Pathological video-game use among youth ages 8 to 18', *Psychol Sci*, 20, 2009.

[270] Gentile D. et al., 'Video game playing, attention problems, and impulsiveness', *Psychol Pop Media Cult*, 1, 2012.

[271] Swing E. L. et al., 'Television and video game exposure and the development of attention problems', *Pediatrics*, 126, 2010.

[272] Swing E. L., 'Plugged in: the effects of electronic media use on attention problems, cognitive control, visual attention, and aggression', PhD dissertation, Iowa State University, 2012.

[273] Hastings E. C. et al., 'Young children's video/computer game use', *Issues Ment Health Nurs*, 30, 2009.

[274] Rosen L. D. et al., 'Media and technology use predicts ill-being among children, preteens and teenagers independent of the negative health impacts of exercise and eating habits', *Comput Hum Behav*, 35, 2014.

[275] Trisolini D. C. et al., 'Is action video gaming related to sustained attention of adolescents?', *Q J Exp Psychol (Hove)*, 71, 2017.

[276] Bavelier D. et al., 'Brains on video games', *Nat Rev Neurosci*, 12, 2011.

[277] Thivent V., 'Quand l'Académie des sciences penche en faveur des jeux vidéo', lemonde.fr, 2014.

[278] Suchert V. et al., 'Sedentary behavior and indicators of mental health in school-aged children and adolescents', *Prev Med*, 76, 2015.

[279] Nikkelen S. W. et al., 'Media use and ADHD-related behaviors in children and adolescents', *Dev Psychol*, 50, 2014.

[280] Mundy L. K. et al., 'The association between electronic media and emotional and behavioral problems in late childhood', *Acad Pediatr*, 17, 2017.

[281] Christakis D. A. et al., 'Early television exposure and subsequent attentional problems in children', *Pediatrics*, 113, 2004.

[282] Landhuis C. E. et al., 'Does childhood television viewing lead to attention problems in adolescence? Results from a prospective longitudinal study', *Pediatrics*, 120, 2007.

[283] Miller C. J. et al., 'Television viewing and risk for attention problems in preschool children', *J Pediatr Psychol*, 32, 2007.

[284] Ozmert E. et al., 'Behavioral correlates of television viewing in primary school children evaluated by the child behavior checklist', *Arch Pediatr Adolesc Med*, 156, 2002.

[285] Zimmerman F. J. et al., 'Associations between content types of early media exposure and subsequent attentional problems', *Pediatrics*, 120, 2007.

[286] Kushlev K. et al., '"Silence your phones": smartphone notifications increase inattention and hyperactivity symptoms', Proceedings of the 2016 CHI Conference on Human Factors in Computing Systems, 2016.

[287] Levine L. et al., 'Mobile media use, multitasking and distractibility', *Int J Cyber Behav Psychol*, 2, 2012.

[288] Seo D. et al., 'Mobile phone dependency and its impacts on adolescents' social and academic behaviors', *Comput Hum Behav*, 63, 2016.

[289] Zheng F. et al., 'Association between mobile phone use and inattention in 7102 Chinese adolescents', *BMC Public Health*, 14, 2014.

[290] Borghans L. et al., 'What grades and achievement tests measure', *Proc Natl Acad Sci USA*, 113, 2016.

[291] Duckworth A. L. et al., 'Self-discipline outdoes IQ in predicting academic performance of adolescents', *Psychol Sci*, 16, 2005.

[292] Bushman B. J. et al., 'Media violence and the American public: scientific facts versus media misinformation', *Am Psychol*, 56, 2001.

[293] Tamana S. K. et al., 'Screen-time is associated with inattention problems in preschoolers', *PLoS One*, 14, 2019.

[294] Microsoft Canada, 'Attention spans', Consumer Insights, 2015.

[295] Dahl R. E., 'The impact of inadequate sleep on children's daytime cognitive function', *Semin Pediatr Neurol*, 3, 1996.

[296] Lim J. et al., 'Sleep deprivation and vigilant attention', *Ann N Y Acad Sci*, 1129, 2008.

[297] Lim J. et al., 'A meta-analysis of the impact of short-term sleep deprivation on cognitive variables', *Psychol Bull*, 136, 2010.

[298] Beebe D. W., 'Cognitive, behavioral, and functional consequences of inadequate sleep in children and adolescents', *Pediatr Clin North Am*, 58, 2011.

[299] Maass A. et al., 'Does media use have a short-term impact on cognitive performance?', *J Media Psychol*, 23, 2011.

[300] Kuschpel M. S. et al., 'Differential effects of wakeful rest, music and video game playing on working memory performance in the n-back task', *Front Psychol*, 6, 2015.

[301] Lillard A. S. et al., 'Further examination of the immediate impact of television on children's executive function', *Dev Psychol*, 51, 2015.

[302] Lillard A. S. et al., 'Television and children's executive function', *Adv Child Dev Behav*, 48, 2015.

[303] Lillard A. S. et al., 'The immediate impact of different types of television on young children's executive function', *Pediatrics*, 128, 2011.

[304] Markowetz A., *Digitaler Burnout*, Droemer, 2015.

[305] 'Usages mobiles', deloitte.com, 2017.

[306] Pielot M. et al., 'An in-situ study of mobile phone notifications', Proceedings of the 16th International Conference on Human–Computer Interaction with Mobile Devices, Toronto, Canada, 2014.

[307] Shirazi A. et al., 'Large-scale assessment of mobile notifications', Proceedings of the 32nd Annual ACM Conference on Human Factors in Computing Systems, Toronto, Canada, 2014.

[308] Greenfield S., *Mind Change*, Rider, 2014.

[309] Gottlieb J. et al., 'Information-seeking, curiosity, and attention', *Trends Cogn Sci*, 17, 2013.

[310] Kidd C. et al., 'The psychology and neuroscience of curiosity', *Neuron*, 88, 2015.

[311] Wolniewicz C. A. et al., 'Problematic smartphone use and relations with negative affect, fear of missing out, and fear of negative and positive evaluation', *Psychiatry Res*, 262, 2018.

[312] Beyens I. et al., '"I don't want to miss a thing"', *Comput Hum Behav*, 64, 2016.

[313] Elhai J. et al., 'Fear of missing out, need for touch, anxiety and depression are related to problematic smartphone use', *Comput Hum Behav*, 63, 2016.

[314] Rosen L. et al., 'Facebook and texting made me do it', *Comput Hum Behav*, 29, 2013.

[315] Thornton B. et al., 'The mere presence of a cell phone may be distracting', *Soc Psychol*, 45, 2014.

[316] Stothart C. et al., 'The attentional cost of receiving a cell phone notification', *J Exp Psychol Hum Percept Perform*, 41, 2015.

[317] Altmann E. M. et al., 'Momentary interruptions can derail the train of thought', *J Exp Psychol Gen*, 143, 2014.

[318] Lee B. et al., 'The effects of task interruption on human performance', *Hum Factors Man*, 25, 2015.

[319] Borst J. et al., 'What makes interruptions disruptive?', Proceedings of the 33rd Annual ACM Conference on Human Factors in Computing Systems, Seoul, Korea, 2015.

[320] Mark G. et al., 'No task left behind?', Proceedings of the SIGCHI

Conference on Human Factors in Computing Systems, Portland, Oregon, 2005.

[321] APA, 'Multitasking: switching costs', American Psychological Association, 2006.

[322] Klauer S. G. et al., 'Distracted driving and risk of road crashes among novice and experienced drivers', *N Engl J Med*, 370, 2014.

[323] Caird J. K. et al., 'A meta-analysis of the effects of texting on driving', *Accid Anal Prev*, 71, 2014.

[324] Olson R. et al., 'Driver distraction in commercial vehicle operations: Report No. FMCSA-RRR-09-042', fmcsa.dot.gov, 2009.

[325] Roney L. et al., 'Distracted driving behaviors of adults while children are in the car', *J Trauma Acute Care Surg*, 75, 2013.

[326] Kirschner P. et al., 'The myths of the digital native and the multitasker', *Teach Teach Educ*, 67, 2017.

[327] Greenfield P. M., 'Technology and informal education', *Science*, 323, 2009.

[328] Pashler H., 'Dual-task interference in simple tasks', *Psychol Bull*, 116, 1994.

[329] Koechlin E. et al., 'The role of the anterior prefrontal cortex in human cognition', *Nature*, 399, 1999.

[330] Braver T. S. et al., 'The role of frontopolar cortex in subgoal processing during working memory', *Neuroimage*, 15, 2002.

[331] Dux P. E. et al., 'Isolation of a central bottleneck of information processing with time-resolved FMRI', *Neuron*, 52, 2006.

[332] Roca M. et al., 'The role of Area 10 (BA10) in human multitasking and in social cognition: a lesion study', *Neuropsychologia*, 49, 2011.

[333] Foerde K. et al., 'Modulation of competing memory systems by distraction', *Proc Natl Acad Sci USA*, 103, 2006.

[334] Dindar M. et al., 'Effects of multitasking on retention and topic interest', *Learn Instr*, 41, 2016.

[335] Uncapher M. R. et al., 'Media multitasking and memory', *Psychon Bull Rev*, 23, 2016.

[336] Mueller P. et al., 'Technology and note-taking in the classroom, boardroom, hospital room, and courtroom', *Trends Neurosci Educ*, 5, 2016.

[337] Mueller P. A. et al., 'The pen is mightier than the keyboard', *Psychol Sci*, 25, 2014.

[338] Diemand-Yauman C. et al., 'Fortune favors the bold (and the italicized)', *Cognition*, 118, 2011.

[339] Hirshman E. et al., 'The generation effect', *J Exp Psychol Learn Mem Cogn*, 14, 1988.

[340] 'The social dilemma', Documentary, Netflix, 2020.

[341] Lanier J., *Ten Arguments for Deleting Your Social Media Accounts Right Now*, Vintage, 2019.

[342] Solon O., 'Ex-Facebook president Sean Parker: site made to exploit human "vulnerability"', theguardian.com, 2017.

[343] Guyonnet P., 'Facebook a été conçu pour exploiter les faiblesses des gens, prévient son ancien président Sean Parker', huffingtonpost.fr, 2017.

[344] Wong J., 'Former Facebook executive: social media is ripping society apart', guardian.com, 2017.

[345] 'D'anciens cadres de Facebook expriment leurs remords d'avoir contribué à son succès', lemonde.fr, 2017.

[346] Bowles N., 'A dark consensus about screens and kids begins to emerge in Silicon Valley', nytimes.com, 2018.

[347] Ophir E. et al., 'Cognitive control in media multitaskers', *Proc Natl Acad Sci USA*, 106, 2009.

[348] Cain M. S. et al., 'Media multitasking in adolescence', *Psychon Bull Rev*, 23, 2016.

[349] Cain M. S. et al., 'Distractor filtering in media multitaskers', *Perception*, 40, 2011.

[350] Sanbonmatsu D. M. et al., 'Who multitasks and why? Multitasking ability, perceived multitasking ability, impulsivity, and sensation seeking', *PLoS One*, 8, 2013.

[351] Gorman T. E. et al., 'Short-term mindfulness intervention reduces the negative attentional effects associated with heavy media multitasking', *Sci Rep*, 6, 2016.

[352] Lopez R. B. et al., 'Media multitasking is associated with altered processing of incidental, irrelevant cues during person perception', *BMC Psychol*, 6, 2018.

[353] Yang X. et al., 'Predictors of media multitasking in Chinese adolescents', *Int J Psychol*, 51, 2016.

[354] Moisala M. et al., 'Media multitasking is associated with distractibility and increased prefrontal activity in adolescents and young adults', *Neuroimage*, 134, 2016.

[355] Uncapher M. R. et al., 'Minds and brains of media multitaskers', *Proc Natl Acad Sci USA*, 115, 2018.

[356] Hadar A. et al., 'Answering the missed call: initial exploration of cognitive and electrophysiological changes associated with smartphone use and abuse', *PLoS One*, 12, 2017.

[357] *Le Trésor de la Langue Française Informatisé*, http://atilf.atilf.fr.

[358] Greenough W. T. et al., 'Experience and brain development', *Child Dev*, 58, 1987.

[359] Christakis D. A. et al., 'How early media exposure may affect cognitive function', *Proc Natl Acad Sci USA*, 115, 2018.

[360] Christakis D. A. et al., 'Overstimulation of newborn mice leads to behavioral differences and deficits in cognitive performance', *Sci Rep*, 2, 2012.

[361] Ravinder S. et al., 'Excessive sensory stimulation during development alters neural plasticity and vulnerability to cocaine in mice', *eNeuro*, 3, 2016.

[362] Capusan A. J. et al., 'Comorbidity of adult ADHD and its subtypes with

substance use disorder in a large population-based epidemiological study', *J Atten Disord*, 2016.

[363] Karaca S. et al., 'Comorbidity between behavioral addictions and attention deficit/hyperactivity disorder', *Int J Ment Health Addiction*, 15, 2017.

[364] Wilens T. et al., in *Oxford Textbook of Attention Deficit Hyperactivity Disorder* (eds. Banaschewski T. et al.), 'ADHD and substance misuse', Oxford University Press, 2018.

[365] Hadas I. et al., 'Exposure to salient, dynamic sensory stimuli during development increases distractibility in adulthood', *Sci Rep*, 6, 2016.

[366] Wachs T., 'Noise in the nursery', *Child Environ Q*, 3, 1986.

[367] Wachs T. et al., 'Cognitive development in infants of different age levels and from different environmental backgrounds', *Merrill Palmer Q*, 17, 1971.

[368] Klaus R. A. et al., 'The early training project for disadvantaged children', *Monogr Soc Res Child Dev*, 33, 1968.

[369] Heft H., 'Background and focal environmental conditions of the home and attention in young children', *J Appl Soc Psychol*, 9, 1979.

[370] Raman S. R. et al., 'Trends in attention-deficit hyperactivity disorder medication use', *Lancet Psychiatry*, 5, 2018.

[371] Visser S. N. et al., 'Trends in the parent-report of health care provider-diagnosed and medicated attention-deficit/hyperactivity disorder: United States, 2003–2011', *J Am Acad Child Adolesc Psychiatry*, 53, 2014.

[372] Xu G. et al., 'Twenty-year trends in diagnosed attention-deficit/hyperactivity disorder among US children and adolescents, 1997–2016', *JAMA Netw Open*, 1, 2018.

[373] Ra C. K. et al., 'Association of digital media use with subsequent symptoms of attention-deficit/hyperactivity disorder among adolescents', *JAMA*, 320, 2018.

[374] Weiss M. D. et al., 'The screens culture', *Atten Defic Hyperact Disord*, 3, 2011.

[375] Rymer R., *Genie: A Scientific Tragedy*, HarperPerennial, 1994.

Health

[1] Christakis D. A. et al., 'Media as a public health issue', *Arch Pediatr Adolesc Med*, 160, 2006.

[2] Strasburger V. C. et al., 'Health effects of media on children and adolescents', *Pediatrics*, 125, 2010.

[3] Strasburger V. C. et al., 'Children, adolescents, and the media', *Pediatr Clin North Am*, 59, 2012.

[4] Desmurget M., *TV Lobotomie*, J'ai Lu, 2013.

[5] Bach J. et al., *L'Enfant et les Écrans: Un Avis de l'Académie des Sciences*, Le Pommier, 2013.

[6] Duflo S., *Quand les Écrans Deviennent Neurotoxiques*, Marabout, 2018.

[7] Freed R., *Wired Child*, CreateSpace, 2015.

[8] Winn M., *The Plug-In-Drug* (revised edition), Penguin, 2002.

[9] Siniscalco M. et al., *Parents, Enfants, Écrans*, Nouvelle Cité, 2014.

[10] Institute of Medicine of the National Academies, *Sleep Disorders and Sleep Deprivation: An Unmet Public Health Problem*, National Academies Press, 2006.

[11] Owens J. et al., 'Insufficient sleep in adolescents and young adults', *Pediatrics*, 134, 2014.

[12] Buysse D. J., 'Sleep health', *Sleep*, 37, 2014.

[13] Gangwisch J. E. et al., 'Earlier parental set bedtimes as a protective factor against depression and suicidal ideation', *Sleep*, 33, 2010.

[14] Goldstein A. N. et al., 'The role of sleep in emotional brain function', *Annu Rev Clin Psychol*, 10, 2014.

[15] Gujar N. et al., 'Sleep deprivation amplifies reactivity of brain reward networks, biasing the appraisal of positive emotional experiences', *J Neurosci*, 31, 2011.

[16] Yoo S. S. et al., 'The human emotional brain without sleep: a prefrontal amygdala disconnect', *Curr Biol*, 17, 2007.

[17] Desmurget M., *L'Antirégime au Quotidien*, Belin, 2017.

[18] Desmurget M., *L'Antirégime*, Belin, 2015.

[19] Chaput J. P. et al., 'Risk factors for adult overweight and obesity', *Obes Facts*, 3, 2010.

[20] Brondel L. et al., 'Acute partial sleep deprivation increases food intake in healthy men', *Am J Clin Nutr*, 91, 2010.

[21] Greer S. M. et al., 'The impact of sleep deprivation on food desire in the human brain', *Nat Commun*, 4, 2013.

[22] Benedict C. et al., 'Acute sleep deprivation reduces energy expenditure in healthy men', *Am J Clin Nutr*, 93, 2011.

[23] Seegers V. et al., 'Short persistent sleep duration is associated with poor receptive vocabulary performance in middle childhood', *J Sleep Res*, 25, 2016.

[24] Jones J. J. et al., 'Association between late-night tweeting and next-day game performance among professional basketball players', *Sleep Health*, 5, 2019.

[25] Harrison Y. et al., 'The impact of sleep deprivation on decision making', *J Exp Psychol Appl*, 6, 2000.

[26] Venkatraman V. et al., 'Sleep deprivation elevates expectation of gains and attenuates response to losses following risky decisions', *Sleep*, 30, 2007.

[27] Venkatraman V. et al., 'Sleep deprivation biases the neural mechanisms underlying economic preferences', *J Neurosci*, 31, 2011.

[28] Kirszenblat L. et al., 'The yin and yang of sleep and attention', *Trends Neurosci*, 38, 2015.

[29] Lim J. et al., 'Sleep deprivation and vigilant attention', *Ann N Y Acad Sci*, 1129, 2008.

[30] Lim J. et al., 'A meta-analysis of the impact of short-term sleep deprivation on cognitive variables', *Psychol Bull*, 136, 2010.

[31] Lowe C. J. et al., 'The neurocognitive consequences of sleep restriction', *Neurosci Biobehav Rev*, 80, 2017.

[32] Sadeh A. et al., 'Infant sleep predicts attention regulation and behavior problems at 3–4 years of age', *Dev Neuropsychol*, 40, 2015.

[33] Beebe D. W., 'Cognitive, behavioral, and functional consequences of inadequate sleep in children and adolescents', *Pediatr Clin North Am*, 58, 2011.

[34] Dahl R. E., 'The impact of inadequate sleep on children's daytime cognitive function', *Semin Pediatr Neurol*, 3, 1996.

[35] Chen Z. et al., 'Deciphering neural codes of memory during sleep', *Trends Neurosci*, 40, 2017.

[36] Diekelmann S., 'Sleep for cognitive enhancement', *Front Syst Neurosci*, 8, 2014.

[37] Diekelmann S. et al., 'The memory function of sleep', *Nat Rev Neurosci*, 11, 2010.

[38] Frank M. G., 'Sleep and developmental plasticity not just for kids', *Prog Brain Res*, 193, 2011.

[39] Dutil C. et al., 'Influence of sleep on developing brain functions and structures in children and adolescents', *Sleep Med Rev*, 2018.

[40] Tarokh L. et al., 'Sleep in adolescence', *Neurosci Biobehav Rev*, 70, 2016.

[41] Telzer E. H. et al., 'Sleep variability in adolescence is associated with altered brain development', *Dev Cogn Neurosci*, 14, 2015.

[42] Gruber R. et al., 'Short sleep duration is associated with poor performance on IQ measures in healthy school-age children', *Sleep Med*, 11, 2010.

[43] Touchette E. et al., 'Associations between sleep duration patterns and behavioral/cognitive functioning at school entry', *Sleep*, 30, 2007.

[44] Lewis P. A. et al., 'How memory replay in sleep boosts creative problem-solving', *Trends Cogn Sci*, 22, 2018.

[45] Curcio G. et al., 'Sleep loss, learning capacity and academic performance', *Sleep Med Rev*, 10, 2006.

[46] Dewald J. F. et al., 'The influence of sleep quality, sleep duration and sleepiness on school performance in children and adolescents', *Sleep Med Rev*, 14, 2010.

[47] Hysing M. et al., 'Sleep and academic performance in later adolescence', *J Sleep Res*, 25, 2016.

[48] Schmidt R. E. et al., 'The relations between sleep, personality, behavioral problems, and school performance in adolescents', *Sleep Med Clin*, 10, 2015.

[49] Shochat T. et al., 'Functional consequences of inadequate sleep in adolescents', *Sleep Med Rev*, 18, 2014.

[50] Astill R. G. et al., 'Sleep, cognition, and behavioral problems in school-age children', *Psychol Bull*, 138, 2012.

[51] Litwiller B. et al., 'The relationship between sleep and work', *J Appl Psychol*, 102, 2017.

[52] Rosekind M. R. et al., 'The cost of poor sleep', *J Occup Environ Med*, 52, 2010.

[53] Roberts R. E. et al., 'The prospective association between sleep deprivation and depression among adolescents', *Sleep*, 37, 2014.

[54] Short M. A. et al., 'Sleep deprivation leads to mood deficits in healthy adolescents', *Sleep Med*, 16, 2015.

[55] Baum K. T. et al., 'Sleep restriction worsens mood and emotion regulation in adolescents', *J Child Psychol Psychiatry*, 55, 2014.

[56] Pilcher J. J. et al., 'Effects of sleep deprivation on performance', *Sleep*, 19, 1996.

[57] Liu X., 'Sleep and adolescent suicidal behavior', *Sleep*, 27, 2004.

[58] Gregory A. M. et al., 'The direction of longitudinal associations between sleep problems and depression symptoms', *Sleep*, 32, 2009.

[59] Pires G. N. et al., 'Effects of experimental sleep deprivation on anxiety-like behavior in animal research', *Neurosci Biobehav Rev*, 68, 2016.

[60] Touchette E. et al., 'Short nighttime sleep-duration and hyperactivity trajectories in early childhood', *Pediatrics*, 124, 2009.

[61] Paavonen E. J. et al., 'Short sleep duration and behavioral symptoms of attention-deficit/hyperactivity disorder in healthy 7- to 8-year-old children', *Pediatrics*, 123, 2009.

[62] Kelly Y. et al., 'Changes in bedtime schedules and behavioral difficulties in 7 year old children', *Pediatrics*, 132, 2013.

[63] Telzer E. H. et al., 'The effects of poor quality sleep on brain function and risk taking in adolescence', *Neuroimage*, 71, 2013.

[64] Kamphuis J. et al., 'Poor sleep as a potential causal factor in aggression and violence', *Sleep Med*, 13, 2012.

[65] Cappuccio F. P. et al., 'Meta-analysis of short sleep duration and obesity in children and adults', *Sleep*, 31, 2008.

[66] Chaput J. P. et al., 'Lack of sleep as a contributor to obesity in adolescents', *Int J Behav Nutr Phys Act*, 13, 2016.

[67] Chen X. et al., 'Is sleep duration associated with childhood obesity? A systematic review and meta-analysis', *Obesity (Silver Spring)*, 16, 2008.

[68] Fatima Y. et al., 'Longitudinal impact of sleep on overweight and obesity in children and adolescents', *Obes Rev*, 16, 2015.

[69] Miller M. A. et al., 'Sleep duration and incidence of obesity in infants, children, and adolescents', *Sleep*, 41, 2018.

[70] Wu Y. et al., 'Short sleep duration and obesity among children', *Obes Res Clin Pract*, 11, 2017.

[71] Shan Z. et al., 'Sleep duration and risk of type 2 diabetes', *Diabetes Care*, 38, 2015.

[72] Dutil C. et al., 'Inadequate sleep as a contributor to type 2 diabetes in children and adolescents', *Nutr Diabetes*, 7, 2017.

[73] Cappuccio F. P. et al., 'Sleep and cardio-metabolic disease', *Curr Cardiol Rep*, 19, 2017.

[74] Cappuccio F. P. et al., 'Sleep duration predicts cardiovascular outcomes', *Eur Heart J*, 32, 2011.

[75] Gangwisch J. E., 'A review of evidence for the link between sleep duration and hypertension', *Am J Hypertens*, 27, 2014.

[76] Miller M. A. et al., 'Biomarkers of cardiovascular risk in sleep-deprived people', *J Hum Hypertens*, 27, 2013.

[77] St-Onge M. P. et al., 'Sleep duration and quality', *Circulation*, 134, 2016.

[78] Irwin M. R., 'Why sleep is important for health', *Annu Rev Psychol*, 66, 2015.

[79] Irwin M. R. et al., 'Sleep health', *Neuropsychopharmacology*, 42, 2017.

[80] Bryant P. A. et al., 'Sick and tired', *Nat Rev Immunol*, 4, 2004.

[81] Zada D. et al., 'Sleep increases chromosome dynamics to enable reduction of accumulating DNA damage in single neurons', *Nat Commun*, 10, 2019.

[82] Grandner M. A. et al., 'Mortality associated with short sleep duration', *Sleep Med Rev*, 14, 2010.

[83] Cappuccio F. P. et al., 'Sleep duration and all-cause mortality', *Sleep*, 33, 2010.

[84] Bioulac S. et al., 'Risk of motor vehicle accidents related to sleepiness at the wheel', *Sleep*, 40, 2017.

[85] Horne J. et al., 'Vehicle accidents related to sleep', *Occup Environ Med*, 56, 1999.

[86] Uehli K. et al., 'Sleep problems and work injuries', *Sleep Med Rev*, 18, 2014.

[87] Spira A. P. et al., 'Impact of sleep on the risk of cognitive decline and dementia', *Curr Opin Psychiatry*, 27, 2014.

[88] Ju Y. E. et al., 'Sleep and Alzheimer disease pathology: a bidirectional relationship', *Nat Rev Neurol*, 10, 2014.

[89] Zhang F. et al., 'The missing link between sleep disorders and age-related dementia', *J Neural Transm (Vienna)*, 124, 2017.

[90] Macedo A. C. et al., 'Is sleep disruption a risk factor for Alzheimer's disease?', *J Alzheimer's Dis*, 58, 2017.

[91] Wu L. et al., 'A systematic review and dose-response meta-analysis of sleep duration and the occurrence of cognitive disorders', *Sleep Breath*, 22, 2018.

[92] Lo J. C. et al., 'Sleep duration and age-related changes in brain structure and cognitive performance', *Sleep*, 37, 2014.

[93] Vriend J. et al., 'Emotional and cognitive impact of sleep restriction in children', *Sleep Med Clin*, 10, 2015.

[94] Vriend J. L. et al., 'Manipulating sleep duration alters emotional functioning and cognitive performance in children', *J Pediatr Psychol*, 38, 2013.

[95] Dewald-Kaufmann J. F. et al., 'The effects of sleep extension on sleep and cognitive performance in adolescents with chronic sleep reduction', *Sleep Med*, 14, 2013.

[96] Dewald-Kaufmann J. F. et al., 'The effects of sleep extension and sleep hygiene advice on sleep and depressive symptoms in adolescents', *J Child Psychol Psychiatry*, 55, 2014.

[97] Sadeh A. et al., 'The effects of sleep restriction and extension on school-age children', *Child Dev*, 74, 2003.

[98] Gruber R. et al., 'Impact of sleep extension and restriction on children's emotional lability and impulsivity', *Pediatrics*, 130, 2012.

[99] Chaput J. P. et al., 'Sleep duration estimates of Canadian children and adolescents', *J Sleep Res*, 25, 2016.

[100] Hawkins S. S. et al., 'Social determinants of inadequate sleep in US children and adolescents', *Public Health*, 138, 2016.

[101] Patte K. A. et al., 'Sleep duration trends and trajectories among youth in the COMPASS study', *Sleep Health*, 3, 2017.

[102] Rognvaldsdottir V. et al., 'Sleep deficiency on school days in Icelandic youth, as assessed by wrist accelerometry', *Sleep Med*, 33, 2017.

[103] Twenge J. M. et al., 'Decreases in self-reported sleep duration among U.S. adolescents 2009–2015 and association with new media screen time', *Sleep Med*, 39, 2017.

[104] LeBourgeois M. K. et al., 'Digital media and sleep in childhood and adolescence', *Pediatrics*, 140, 2017.

[105] Keyes K. M. et al., 'The great sleep recession', *Pediatrics*, 135, 2015.

[106] Cain N. et al., 'Electronic media use and sleep in school-aged children and adolescents', *Sleep Med*, 11, 2010.

[107] Carter B. et al., 'Association between portable screen-based media device access or use and sleep outcomes', *JAMA Pediatr*, 170, 2016.

[108] AAP, 'Children and adolescents and digital media: American Academy of Pediatrics. Council on Communications and Media', *Pediatrics*, 138, 2016.

[109] Arora T. et al., 'Associations between specific technologies and adolescent sleep quantity, sleep quality, and parasomnias', *Sleep Med*, 15, 2014.

[110] Chahal H. et al., 'Availability and night-time use of electronic entertainment and communication devices are associated with short sleep duration and obesity among Canadian children', *Pediatr Obes*, 8, 2013.

[111] Cheung C. H. et al., 'Daily touchscreen use in infants and toddlers is associated with reduced sleep and delayed sleep onset', *Sci Rep*, 7, 2017.

[112] Falbe J. et al., 'Sleep duration, restfulness, and screens in the sleep environment', *Pediatrics*, 135, 2015.

[113] Hysing M. et al., 'Sleep and use of electronic devices in adolescence', *BMJ Open*, 5, 2015.

[114] Scott H. et al., 'Fear of missing out and sleep', *J Adolesc*, 68, 2018.

[115] Twenge J. M. et al., 'Associations between screen time and sleep duration are primarily driven by portable electronic devices', *Sleep Med*, 2018.

[116] Owens J. et al., 'Television-viewing habits and sleep disturbance in school children', *Pediatrics*, 104, 1999.

[117] Brockmann P. E. et al., 'Impact of television on the quality of sleep in preschool children', *Sleep Med*, 20, 2016.

[118] Gentile D. A. et al., 'Bedroom media', *Dev Psychol*, 53, 2017.

[119] Li S. et al., 'The impact of media use on sleep patterns and sleep disorders among school-aged children in China', *Sleep*, 30, 2007.

[120] Shochat T. et al., 'Sleep patterns, electronic media exposure and daytime sleep-related behaviours among Israeli adolescents', *Acta Paediatr*, 99, 2010.

[121] Sisson S. B. et al., 'TVs in the bedrooms of children', *Prev Med*, 52, 2011.

[122] Van den Bulck J., 'Television viewing, computer game playing, and

Internet use and self-reported time to bed and time out of bed in secondary-school children', *Sleep*, 27, 2004.

[123] Garrison M. M. et al., 'Media use and child sleep', *Pediatrics*, 128, 2011.

[124] AAP, 'School start times for adolescents', *Pediatrics*, 134, 2014.

[125] Minges K. E. et al., 'Delayed school start times and adolescent sleep', *Sleep Med Rev*, 28, 2016.

[126] Chang A. M. et al., 'Evening use of light-emitting eReaders negatively affects sleep, circadian timing, and next-morning alertness', *Proc Natl Acad Sci USA*, 112, 2015.

[127] Tosini G. et al., 'Effects of blue light on the circadian system and eye physiology', *Mol Vis*, 22, 2016.

[128] Touitou Y. et al., 'Disruption of adolescents' circadian clock', *J Physiol Paris*, 110, 2016.

[129] Rosen L. et al., 'Sleeping with technology', *Sleep Health*, 2, 2016.

[130] Gradisar M. et al., 'The sleep and technology use of Americans: findings from the National Sleep Foundation's 2011 Sleep in America poll', *J Clin Sleep Med*, 9, 2013.

[131] Van den Bulck J., 'Adolescent use of mobile phones for calling and for sending text messages after lights out', *Sleep*, 30, 2007.

[132] Munezawa T. et al., 'The association between use of mobile phones after lights out and sleep disturbances among Japanese adolescents', *Sleep*, 34, 2011.

[133] Thomee S. et al., 'Mobile phone use and stress, sleep disturbances, and symptoms of depression among young adults: a prospective cohort study', *BMC Public Health*, 11, 2011.

[134] Schoeni A. et al., 'Symptoms and cognitive functions in adolescents in relation to mobile phone use during night', *PLoS One*, 10, 2015.

[135] Adams S. et al., 'Sleep quality as a mediator between technology-related sleep quality, depression, and anxiety', *Cyberpsychol Behav Soc Netw*, 16, 2013.

[136] Paavonen E. J. et al., 'TV exposure associated with sleep disturbances in 5- to 6-year-old children', *J Sleep Res*, 15, 2006.

[137] Dworak M. et al., 'Impact of singular excessive computer game and television exposure on sleep patterns and memory performance of school-aged children', *Pediatrics*, 120, 2007.

[138] Walker M. P., 'The role of slow wave sleep in memory processing', *J Clin Sleep Med*, 5, 2009.

[139] Wilckens K. A. et al., 'Slow-wave activity enhancement to improve cognition', *Trends Neurosci*, 41, 2018.

[140] King D. L. et al., 'The impact of prolonged violent video-gaming on adolescent sleep: an experimental study', *J Sleep Res*, 22, 2013.

[141] OECD, 'L'égalité des sexes dans l'éducation', OECD, 2015.

[142] Tisseron S., in Buthigieg R. et al., 'La télévision est-elle un danger pour les enfants?', TeleStar No. 1830, 29 October–4 November 2011.

[143] Vandewater E. A. et al., 'Digital childhood: electronic media and technology use among infants, toddlers, and preschoolers', *Pediatrics*, 119, 2007.

[144] Eggermont S. et al., 'Nodding off or switching off? The use of popular media as a sleep aid in secondary-school children', *J Paediatr Child Health*, 42, 2006.

[145] Wise R. A., 'Brain reward circuitry', *Neuron*, 36, 2002.

[146] Hinkley T. et al., 'Early childhood electronic media use as a predictor of poorer well-being', *JAMA Pediatr*, 168, 2014.

[147] Kasser T., *The High Price of Materialism*, MIT Press, 2002.

[148] Public Health England, 'How healthy behaviour supports children's wellbeing', gov.uk, 2013.

[149] Kross E. et al., 'Facebook use predicts declines in subjective well-being in young adults', *PLoS One*, 8, 2013.

[150] Verduyn P. et al., 'Passive Facebook usage undermines affective well-being: experimental and longitudinal evidence', *J Exp Psychol Gen*, 144, 2015.

[151] Tromholt M., 'The Facebook experiment', *Cyberpsychol Behav Soc Netw*, 19, 2016.

[152] Lin L. Y. et al., 'Association between social media use and depression among U.S. young adults', *Depress Anxiety*, 33, 2016.

[153] Primack B. A. et al., 'Social media use and perceived social isolation among young adults in the U.S.', *Am J Prev Med*, 53, 2017.

[154] Primack B. A. et al., 'Association between media use in adolescence and depression in young adulthood', *Arch Gen Psychiatry*, 66, 2009.

[155] Costigan S. A. et al., 'The health indicators associated with screen-based sedentary behavior among adolescent girls', *J Adolesc Health*, 52, 2013.

[156] Shakya H. B. et al., 'Association of Facebook use with compromised well-being', *Am J Epidemiol*, 185, 2017.

[157] Babic M. et al., 'Longitudinal associations between changes in screen-time and mental health outcomes in adolescents', *Ment Health Phys Act*, 12, 2017.

[158] Twenge J. et al., 'Increases in depressive symptoms, suicide-related outcomes, and suicide rates among U.S. adolescents after 2010 and links to increased new media screen time', *Clin Psychol Sci*, 6, 2018.

[159] Twenge J. M. et al., 'Decreases in psychological well-being among American adolescents after 2012 and links to screen time during the rise of smartphone technology', *Emotion*, 2018.

[160] Kelly Y. et al., 'Social media use and adolescent mental health', *EClinicalMedicine*, 2019.

[161] Demirci K. et al., 'Relationship of smartphone use severity with sleep quality, depression, and anxiety in university students', *J Behav Addict*, 4, 2015.

[162] Hunt M. et al., 'No more FOMO', *J Soc Clin Psychol*, 37, 2018.

[163] Seo J. H. et al., 'Late use of electronic media and its association with sleep, depression, and suicidality among Korean adolescents', *Sleep Med*, 29, 2017.

[164] Hoare E. et al., 'The associations between sedentary behaviour and mental health among adolescents', *Int J Behav Nutr Phys Act*, 13, 2016.

[165] Hoge E. et al., 'Digital media, anxiety, and depression in children', *Pediatrics*, 140, 2017.

[166] Tisseron S., in Buthigieg R., 'La télévision nuit-elle au sommeil?', TeleStar No. 1800, 2–8 April 2011.

[167] 'Enquête de santé: abus d'écrans: notre cerveau en danger?', France 5, 23 June 2020.

[168] Royant-Parola S. et al., 'The use of social media modifies teenagers' sleep-related behavior [in French]', *Encephale*, 44, 2018.

[169] '18ème journée du sommeil: le sommeil des jeunes (15–24 ans)', Enquête INSV/MGEN, institut-sommeil-vigilance.org, March 2018.

[170] Galland B. C. et al., 'Establishing normal values for pediatric nighttime sleep measured by actigraphy: a systematic review and meta-analysis', *Sleep*, 41, 2018.

[171] Chaput J. P. et al., 'Sleeping hours: what is the ideal number and how does age impact this?', *Nat Sci Sleep*, 10, 2018.

[172] Przybylski A. K., 'Digital screen time and pediatric sleep: evidence from a preregistered cohort study', *J Pediatr*, 205, 2019.

[173] Maccoby E. E., 'Television: its impact on school children', *Public Opin Q*, 15, 1951.

[174] Asaoka S. et al., 'Does television viewing cause delayed and/or irregular sleep–wake patterns?', *Sleep Biol Rhythms*, 5, 2007.

[175] Owen N. et al., 'Too much sitting', *Exerc Sport Sci Rev*, 38, 2010.

[176] Booth F. W. et al., 'Role of inactivity in chronic diseases: evolutionary insight and pathophysiological mechanisms', *Physiol Rev*, 97, 2017.

[177] Dunstan D. W. et al., 'Television viewing time and mortality', *Circulation*, 121, 2010.

[178] Basterra-Gortari F. J. et al., 'Television viewing, computer use, time driving and all-cause mortality', *J Am Heart Assoc*, 3, 2014.

[179] Stamatakis E. et al., 'Screen-based entertainment time, all-cause mortality, and cardiovascular events: population-based study with ongoing mortality and hospital events follow-up', *J Am Coll Cardiol*, 57, 2011.

[180] Katzmarzyk P. T. et al., 'Sedentary behaviour and life expectancy in the USA', *BMJ Open*, 2, 2012.

[181] Veerman J. L. et al., 'Television viewing time and reduced life expectancy', *Br J Sports Med*, 46, 2012.

[182] Grontved A. et al., 'Television viewing and risk of type 2 diabetes, cardiovascular disease, and all-cause mortality', *JAMA*, 305, 2011.

[183] Keadle S. K. et al., 'Causes of death associated with prolonged TV viewing', *Am J Prev Med*, 49, 2015.

[184] Allen M. S. et al., 'Sedentary behaviour and risk of anxiety', *J Affect Disord*, 242, 2019.

[185] van Uffelen J. G. et al., 'Sitting-time, physical activity, and depressive symptoms in mid-aged women', *Am J Prev Med*, 45, 2013.

[186] Ellingson L. D. et al., 'Changes in sedentary time are associated with changes in mental wellbeing over 1 year in young adults', *Prev Med Rep*, 11, 2018.

[187] Falck R. S. et al., 'What is the association between sedentary behaviour and cognitive function? A systematic review', *Br J Sports Med*, 51, 2017.

[188] Hamilton M. T. et al., 'Role of low energy expenditure and sitting in obesity, metabolic syndrome, type 2 diabetes, and cardiovascular disease', *Diabetes*, 56, 2007.

[189] Zderic T. W. et al., 'Identification of hemostatic genes expressed in human and rat leg muscles and a novel gene (LPP1/PAP2A) suppressed during prolonged physical inactivity (sitting)', *Lipids Health Dis*, 11, 2012.

[190] Hamburg N. M. et al., 'Physical inactivity rapidly induces insulin resistance and microvascular dysfunction in healthy volunteers', *Arterioscler Thromb Vasc Biol*, 27, 2007.

[191] Pagani L. S. et al., 'Prospective associations between early childhood television exposure and academic, psychosocial, and physical well-being by middle childhood', *Arch Pediatr Adolesc Med*, 164, 2010.

[192] Babey S. H. et al., 'Adolescent sedentary behaviors', *J Adolesc Health*, 52, 2013.

[193] Barr-Anderson D. J. et al., 'Characteristics associated with older adolescents who have a television in their bedrooms', *Pediatrics*, 121, 2008.

[194] Bennett G. G. et al., 'Television viewing and pedometer-determined physical activity among multiethnic residents of low-income housing', *Am J Public Health*, 96, 2006.

[195] Carlson S. A. et al., 'Influence of limit-setting and participation in physical activity on youth screen time', *Pediatrics*, 126, 2010.

[196] Jago R. et al., 'BMI from 3–6 y of age is predicted by TV viewing and physical activity, not diet', *Int J Obes (Lond)*, 29, 2005.

[197] Salmon J. et al., 'Television viewing habits associated with obesity risk factors', *Med J Aust*, 184, 2006.

[198] LeBlanc A. G. et al., 'Correlates of total sedentary time and screen time in 9–11 year-old children around the world', *PLoS One*, 10, 2015.

[199] MacBeth Williams T. et al., in *The Impact of Television: A Natural Experiment in Three Communities* (ed. MacBeth Williams T.), 'Television and other leisure activities', Academic Press, 1986.

[200] Tomkinson G. et al., in *Pediatric Fitness: Secular Trends and Geographic Variability* (eds. Tomkinson G. et al.), 'Secular changes in pediatric aerobic fitness test performance', Karger, 2007.

[201] Tomkinson G. R. et al., 'Temporal trends in the cardiorespiratory fitness of children and adolescents representing 19 high-income and upper middle-income countries between 1981 and 2014', *Br J Sports Med*, 53, 2019.

[202] Morales-Demori R. et al., 'Trend of endurance level among healthy inner-city children and adolescents over three decades', *Pediatr Cardiol*, 38, 2017.

[203] Fédération Française de Cardiologie, 'Depuis 40 ans, les enfants ont perdu près de 25% de leur capacité cardio-vasculaire!', Communiqué de presse, fedecardio.org, February 2016.

[204] Ferreira I. et al., 'Environmental correlates of physical activity in youth: a review and update', *Obes Rev*, 8, 2007.

[205] Ding D. et al., 'Neighborhood environment and physical activity among youth: a review', *Am J Prev Med*, 41, 2011.

[206] Tremblay M. S. et al., 'Systematic review of sedentary behaviour and health indicators in school-aged children and youth', *Int J Behav Nutr Phys Act*, 8, 2011.

[207] de Rezende L. F. et al., 'Sedentary behavior and health outcomes', *PLoS One*, 9, 2014.

[208] Chinapaw M. J. et al., 'Relationship between young peoples' sedentary behaviour and biomedical health indicators', *Obes Rev*, 12, 2011.

[209] Landhuis E. et al., 'Programming obesity and poor fitness', *Obesity (Silver Spring)*, 16, 2008.

[210] Lepp A. et al., 'The relationship between cell phone use, physical and sedentary activity, and cardiorespiratory fitness in a sample of U.S. college students', *Int J Behav Nutr Phys Act*, 10, 2013.

[211] Gopinath B. et al., 'Influence of physical activity and screen time on the retinal microvasculature in young children', *Arterioscler Thromb Vasc Biol*, 31, 2011.

[212] Newman A. R. et al., 'Review of paediatric retinal microvascular changes as a predictor of cardiovascular disease', *Clin Exp Ophthalmol*, 45, 2017.

[213] Li L. J. et al., 'Can the retinal microvasculature offer clues to cardiovascular risk factors in early life?', *Acta Paediatr*, 102, 2013.

[214] Li L. J. et al., 'Retinal vascular imaging in early life', *J Physiol*, 594, 2016.

[215] Sasongko M. B. et al., 'Retinal arteriolar changes', *Microcirculation*, 17, 2010.

[216] George M. G. et al., 'Prevalence of cardiovascular risk factors and strokes in younger adults', *JAMA Neurol*, 74, 2017.

[217] Bejot Y. et al., 'Trends in the incidence of ischaemic stroke in young adults between 1985 and 2011', *J Neurol Neurosurg Psychiatry*, 85, 2014.

[218] Santana C. C. A. et al., 'Physical fitness and academic performance in youth', *Scand J Med Sci Sports*, 27, 2017.

[219] de Greeff J. W. et al., 'Effects of physical activity on executive functions, attention and academic performance in preadolescent children', *J Sci Med Sport*, 21, 2018.

[220] Donnelly J. E. et al., 'Physical activity, fitness, cognitive function, and academic achievement in children', *Med Sci Sports Exerc*, 48, 2016.

[221] Poitras V. J. et al., 'Systematic review of the relationships between objectively measured physical activity and health indicators in school-aged children and youth', *Appl Physiol Nutr Metab*, 41, 2016.

[222] Janssen I. et al., 'Systematic review of the health benefits of physical activity and fitness in school-aged children and youth', *Int J Behav Nutr Phys Act*, 7, 2010.

[223] '2018 Physical Activity Guidelines Advisory Committee Scientific Report', U.S. Department of Health and Human Services, health.gov, February 2018.

[224] OMS, 'Global recommendations on physical activity for health', who.int, 2010.

[225] Piercy K. L. et al., 'The Physical Activity Guidelines for Americans', *JAMA*, 320, 2018.

[226] Kahlmeier S. et al., 'National physical activity recommendations', *BMC Public Health*, 15, 2015.

[227] Kalman M. et al., 'Secular trends in moderate-to-vigorous physical activity in 32 countries from 2002 to 2010', *Eur J Public Health*, 25 Suppl 2, 2015.

[228] ONAP, 'Etat des lieux de l'activité physique et de la sédentarité en France', onaps.fr, 2018.

[229] Katzmarzyk P. T. et al., 'Results from the United States 2018 Report Card on Physical Activity for Children and Youth', *J Phys Act Health*, 15, 2018.

[230] Varma V. R. et al., 'Re-evaluating the effect of age on physical activity over the lifespan', *Prev Med*, 101, 2017.

[231] AAP, 'Active healthy living', *Pediatrics*, 117, 2006.

[232] de Saint-Exupéry A., *Le Petit Prince*, Gallimard, 1945/1999.

[233] Wikenheiser A. M. et al., 'Over the river, through the woods', *Nat Rev Neurosci*, 17, 2016.

[234] Morton N. W. et al., 'Memory integration constructs maps of space, time, and concepts', *Curr Opin Behav Sci*, 17, 2017.

[235] Eichenbaum H., 'Memory', *Annu Rev Psychol*, 68, 2017.

[236] Meyer D. E. et al., 'Facilitation in recognizing pairs of words', *J Exp Psychol*, 90, 1971.

[237] Anderson J., 'A spreading activation theory of memory', *J Verbal Learning Verbal Behav*, 22, 1983.

[238] Roediger H. et al., 'Creating false memories', *J Exp Psychol Learn Mem Cogn*, 21, 1995.

[239] Seamon J. et al., 'Creating false memories of words with or without recognition of list items', *Psychol Sci*, 9, 1998.

[240] Eichenbaum H., 'On the integration of space, time, and memory', *Neuron*, 95, 2017.

[241] Uitvlugt M. G. et al., 'Temporal proximity links unrelated news events in memory', *Psychol Sci*, 30, 2019.

[242] Plassmann H. et al., 'Marketing actions can modulate neural representations of experienced pleasantness', *Proc Natl Acad Sci USA*, 105, 2008.

[243] Koenigs M. et al., 'Prefrontal cortex damage abolishes brand-cued changes in cola preference', *Soc Cogn Affect Neurosci*, 3, 2008.

[244] Kuhn S. et al., 'Does taste matter? How anticipation of cola brands influences gustatory processing in the brain', *PLoS One*, 8, 2013.

[245] McClure S. M. et al., 'Neural correlates of behavioral preference for culturally familiar drinks', *Neuron*, 44, 2004.

[246] Robinson T. N. et al., 'Effects of fast food branding on young children's taste preferences', *Arch Pediatr Adolesc Med*, 161, 2007.

[247] Hinton P., 'Implicit stereotypes and the predictive brain', *Palgrave Commun*, 3, 2017.

[248] Mlodinow L., *Subliminal*, Vintage, 2012.

[249] Greenwald A. et al., 'Implicit bias', *Cal L Rev*, 94, 2006.

[250] Greenwald A. G. et al., 'Statistically small effects of the Implicit Association Test can have societally large effects', *J Pers Soc Psychol*, 108, 2015.

[251] Custers R. et al., 'The unconscious will', *Science*, 329, 2010.

[252] Dijksterhuis A. et al., 'The perception–behavior expressway', *Adv Exp Soc Psychol*, 33, 2001.

[253] Dijksterhuis A. et al., 'Goals, attention, and (un)consciousness', *Annu Rev Psychol*, 61, 2010.

[254] Reuben E. et al., 'How stereotypes impair women's careers in science', *Proc Natl Acad Sci USA*, 111, 2014.

[255] Shih M. et al., 'Stereotype susceptibility', *Psychol Sci*, 10, 1999.

[256] Bargh J. A. et al., 'Automaticity of social behavior', *J Pers Soc Psychol*, 71, 1996.

[257] Brunner T. A. et al., 'Reduced food intake after exposure to subtle weight-related cues', *Appetite*, 58, 2012.

[258] Aarts H. et al., 'Preparing and motivating behavior outside of awareness', *Science*, 319, 2008.

[259] Ostria V., 'Par le petit bout de la lucarne', *Les Inrockuptibles*, 792, 2011.

[260] Anizon E. et al., '"On me transforme en marchand de cerveaux": quand Patrick Le Lay tentait de se défendre', telerama.fr, 2020.

[261] OMS, 'Tabagisme', who.int, 2018.

[262] CDC, 'Tobacco-related mortality', cdc.gov, 2018.

[263] Ribassin-Majed L. et al., 'Trends in tobacco-attributable mortality in France', *Eur J Public Health*, 25, 2015.

[264] Banque mondiale, 'Données de population 2017', banquemondiale.org.

[265] US Census Bureau, '2019 Population estimates', data.census.gov.

[266] Goodchild M. et al., 'Global economic cost of smoking-attributable diseases', *Tob Control*, 27, 2018.

[267] OFDT, 'Le coût social des drogues en France', Note de Synthèse 2015–04, ofdt.fr, 2015.

[268] WHO, 'WHO report on the global tobacco epidemic', who.int, 2008.

[269] WHO, 'Tobacco industry interference', who.int, 2012.

[270] OMS, 'WHO report on the global tobacco epidemic 2017: monitoring tobacco use and prevention policies', who.int, 2017.

[271] WHO, 'Tobacco', who.int, 2020.

[272] CDC, 'Youth and tobacco use', cdc.gov, 2019.

[273] Gaillard B., 'Un cow-boy Marlboro meurt du cancer du poumon', europe1.fr, 2014.

[274] Pearce M., 'At least four Marlboro Men have died of smoking-related diseases', latimes.com, 2014.

[275] OMS, 'Smoke-free movies: from evidence to action', who.int, 2015.

[276] Millett C. et al., 'European governments should stop subsidizing films with tobacco imagery', *Eur J Public Health*, 22, 2012.

[277] Glantz S. A. et al., *The Cigarette Papers*, University of California Press, 1998.

[278] Oreskes N. et al., *Merchants of Doubt*, Bloomsbury, 2010.

[279] Desmurget M., 'La cigarette dans les films, un débat plus narquois qu'étayé', lemonde.fr, 2017.

[280] Commentaires en réactions à l'article de Desmurget M., 'La cigarette dans les films, un débat plus narquois qu'étayé', lemonde.fr, 2017.

[281] Felder A., 'How comments shape perception of sites' quality and affect traffic', theatlantic.com, 2014.

[282] Polansky J. et al., 'Smoking in top-grossing US movies 2018', escholarship.org, 2019.

[283] Gabrielli J. et al., 'Industry television ratings for violence, sex, and substance use', *Pediatrics*, 138, 2016.

[284] FCC, 'The V-chip: options to restrict what your children watch on TV', fcc.gov, 2019.

[285] Barrientos-Gutierrez I. et al., 'Comparison of tobacco and alcohol use in films produced in Europe, Latin America, and the United States', *BMC Public Health*, 15, 2015.

[286] 'Tabac et cinéma: étude conjoints IPSOS, Ligue contre le cancer', ligue-cancer.net, 2012.

[287] 'While you were streaming', truthinitiative.org, 2018.

[288] 'Preventing tobacco use among youth and young adults. A report of the Surgeon General', U.S. Department of Health and Human Services, 2012.

[289] OMS, 'WHO report on the global tobacco epidemic 2013: enforcing bans on tobacco advertising, promotion and sponsorship', who.int, 2013.

[290] Freeman B., 'New media and tobacco control', *Tob Control*, 21, 2012.

[291] Ribisl K. M. et al., 'Tobacco control is losing ground in the Web 2.0 era', *Tob Control*, 21, 2012.

[292] Elkin L. et al., 'Connecting world youth with tobacco brands', *Tob Control*, 19, 2010.

[293] Richardson A. et al., 'The cigar ambassador', *Tob Control*, 23, 2014.

[294] Liang Y. et al., 'Exploring how the tobacco industry presents and promotes itself in social media', *J Med Internet Res*, 17, 2015.

[295] Liang Y. et al., 'Characterizing social interaction in tobacco-oriented social networks', *Sci Rep*, 5, 2015.

[296] Kostygina G. et al., '"Sweeter than a swisher"', *Tob Control*, 25, 2016.

[297] Cortese D. et al., 'Smoking selfies', *SM+S*, 4, 2018.

[298] Barrientos-Gutierrez T. et al., 'Video games and the next tobacco frontier: smoking in the Starcraft universe', *Tob Control*, 21, 2012.

[299] Forsyth S. R. et al., 'Tobacco content in video games', *Nicotine Tob Res*, 21, 2019.

[300] Forsyth S. R. et al., '"Playing the movie directly"', *Annu Rev Nurs Res*, 36, 2018.

[301] 'Played: smoking and video game', truthinitiative.org, 2016.

[302] 'Some video games glamorize smoking so much that cigarettes can help players win', truthinitiative.org, 2018.

[303] 'Are video games glamorizing tobacco use?', truthinitiative.org, 2017.

[304] Ferguson S. et al., 'An analysis of tobacco placement in YouTube cartoon series The Big Lez Show', *Nicotine Tob Res*, 2019.

[305] Richardson A. et al., 'YouTube: a promotional vehicle for little cigars and cigarillos?', *Tob Control*, 23, 2014.

[306] Tsai F. J. et al., 'Portrayal of tobacco in Mongolian language YouTube videos: policy gaps', *Tob Control*, 25, 2016.

[307] Forsyth S. R. et al., '"I'll be your cigarette: light me up and get on with it"', *Nicotine Tob Res*, 12, 2010.

[308] Cranwell J. et al., 'Adolescents' exposure to tobacco and alcohol content in YouTube music videos', *Addiction*, 110, 2015.

[309] Cranwell J. et al., 'Adult and adolescent exposure to tobacco and alcohol content in contemporary YouTube music videos in Great Britain', *J Epidemiol Community Health*, 70, 2016.

[310] Knutzen K. E. et al., 'Combustible and electronic tobacco and marijuana products in hip-hop music videos, 2013–2017', *JAMA Intern Med*, 178, 2018.

[311] Forsyth S. R. et al., 'Tobacco imagery in video games', *Tob Control*, 25, 2016.

[312] Gentile D., 'Pathological video-game use among youth ages 8 to 18', *Psychol Sci*, 20, 2009.

[313] Feldman C., 'Grand Theft Auto IV steals sales records', cnn.com, 2008.

[314] 'Grand Theft Auto V "has made more money than any film in history"', telegraph.co.uk, 2018.

[315] Rideout V. et al., 'Generation M2: media in the lives of 8–18 year-olds', Kaiser Family Foundation, 2010.

[316] Worth K. et al., 'Character smoking in top box office movies', truthinitiative.org, 2007.

[317] Charlesworth A. et al., 'Smoking in the movies increases adolescent smoking', *Pediatrics*, 116, 2005.

[318] Polansky J. et al., 'First-run smoking presentations in U.S. movies 1999–2006', Center for Tobacco Control Research and Education (UCSF), 2007.

[319] National Cancer Institute, 'Davis R.M., "The role of the media in promoting and reducing tobacco use", Tobacco Control Monograph No. 19, National Cancer Institute, 2008', cancer.gov, 2008.

[320] 'The health consequences of smoking: 50 years of progress: a report of the Surgeon General', U.S. Department of Health and Human Services, 2014.

[321] CDC, 'Smoking in the movies', cdc.gov, 2017.

[322] Cancer Council Australia, 'Position statement: smoking in movies', cancer.org.au, 2007.

[323] NCI, 'Tobacco Control Monograph No. 19: the role of the media in promoting and reducing tobacco use', National Cancer Institute, 2008.

[324] Arora M. et al., 'Tobacco use in Bollywood movies, tobacco promotional activities and their association with tobacco use among Indian adolescents', *Tob Control*, 21, 2012.

[325] Hanewinkel R. et al., 'Exposure to smoking in popular contemporary movies and youth smoking in Germany', *Am J Prev Med*, 32, 2007.

[326] Hull J. G. et al., 'A longitudinal study of risk-glorifying video games and behavioral deviance', *J Pers Soc Psychol*, 107, 2014.

[327] Morgenstern M. et al., 'Smoking in movies and adolescent smoking', *Thorax*, 66, 2011.

[328] Sargent J. D. et al., 'Exposure to movie smoking', *Pediatrics*, 116, 2005.

[329] Sargent J. D. et al., 'Effect of seeing tobacco use in films on trying smoking among adolescents', *BMJ*, 323, 2001.

[330] Thrasher J. F. et al., 'Exposure to smoking imagery in popular films and adolescent smoking in Mexico', *Am J Prev Med*, 35, 2008.

[331] Depue J. B. et al., 'Encoded exposure to tobacco use in social media predicts subsequent smoking behavior', *Am J Health Promot*, 29, 2015.

[332] Cranwell J. et al., 'Alcohol and tobacco content in UK video games and their association with alcohol and tobacco use among young people', *Cyberpsychol Behav Soc Netw*, 19, 2016.

[333] Dalton M. A. et al., 'Early exposure to movie smoking predicts established smoking by older teens and young adults', *Pediatrics*, 123, 2009.

[334] Sargent J. D. et al., 'Influence of motion picture rating on adolescent response to movie smoking', *Pediatrics*, 130, 2012.

[335] Hancox R. J. et al., 'Association between child and adolescent television viewing and adult health', *Lancet*, 364, 2004.

[336] Watkins S. S. et al., 'Neural mechanisms underlying nicotine addiction', *Nicotine Tob Res*, 2, 2000.

[337] Gutschoven K. et al., 'Television viewing and smoking volume in adolescent smokers', *Prev Med*, 39, 2004.

[338] Lochbuehler K. et al., 'Attentional bias in smokers', *J Psychopharmacol*, 25, 2011.

[339] Baumann S. B. et al., 'Smoking cues in a virtual world provoke craving in cigarette smokers', *Psychol Addict Behav*, 20, 2006.

[340] Sargent J. D. et al., 'Movie smoking and urge to smoke among adult smokers', *Nicotine Tob Res*, 11, 2009.

[341] Tong C. et al., 'Smoking-related videos for use in cue-induced craving paradigms', *Addict Behav*, 32, 2007.

[342] Shmueli D. et al., 'Effect of smoking scenes in films on immediate smoking', *Am J Prev Med*, 38, 2010.

[343] Wagner D. D. et al., 'Spontaneous action representation in smokers when watching movie characters smoke', *J Neurosci*, 31, 2011.

[344] OMS, 'Global status report on alcohol and health 2018', who.int, 2018.

[345] 'Australian guidelines to reduce health risks from drinking alcohol', nhmrc.gov.au, 2009.

[346] 'The Surgeon General's call to action to prevent and reduce underage drinking', nih.gov, 2007.

[347] IARD, 'Minimum legal age limits', 2019.

[348] Squeglia L. M. et al., 'Alcohol and drug use and the developing brain', *Curr Psychiatry Rep*, 18, 2016.

[349] Squeglia L. M. et al., 'The effect of alcohol use on human adolescent brain structures and systems', *Handb Clin Neurol*, 125, 2014.

[350] Grant B. F. et al., 'Age at onset of alcohol use and its association with DSM-IV alcohol abuse and dependence', *J Subst Abuse*, 9, 1997.

[351] INVS, 'L'alcool, toujours un facteur de risque majeur pour la santé en France', *BEH*, 16–18, 2013.

[352] Bonnie R. J. et al., 'Reducing underage drinking: a collective responsibility', report from the National Research Council, National Academies Press, 2004.

[353] 'The impact of alcohol advertising', report of the National Foundation for Alcohol Prevention, europa.eu, 2007.

[354] CDC, 'Youth exposure to alcohol advertising on television', *Morb Mortal Wkly Rep*, 62, 2013.

[355] Dal Cin S. et al., 'Youth exposure to alcohol use and brand appearances in popular contemporary movies', *Addiction*, 103, 2008.

[356] Jernigan D. H. et al., 'Self-reported youth and adult exposure to alcohol marketing in traditional and digital media', *Alcohol Clin Exp Res*, 41, 2017.

[357] Barry A. E. et al., 'Alcohol marketing on Twitter and Instagram', *Alcohol Alcohol*, 51, 2016.

[358] Simons A. et al., 'Alcohol marketing on social media', eucam.info, 2017.

[359] Eisenberg M. E. et al., 'What are we drinking? Beverages shown in adolescents' favorite television shows', *J Acad Nutr Diet*, 117, 2017.

[360] Hendriks H. et al., 'Social drinking on social media', *J Med Internet Res*, 20, 2018.

[361] Keller-Hamilton B. et al., 'Tobacco and alcohol on television', *Prev Chronic Dis*, 15, 2018.

[362] Lobstein T. et al., 'The commercial use of digital media to market alcohol products', *Addiction*, 112 Suppl. 1, 2017.

[363] Primack B. A. et al., 'Portrayal of alcohol intoxication on YouTube', *Alcohol Clin Exp Res*, 39, 2015.

[364] Primack B. A. et al., 'Portrayal of alcohol brands popular among underage youth on YouTube', *J Stud Alcohol Drugs*, 78, 2017.

[365] Anderson P. et al., 'Impact of alcohol advertising and media exposure on adolescent alcohol use', *Alcohol Alcohol*, 44, 2009.

[366] Hanewinkel R. et al., 'Portrayal of alcohol consumption in movies and drinking initiation in low-risk adolescents', *Pediatrics*, 133, 2014.

[367] Hanewinkel R. et al., 'Exposure to alcohol use in motion pictures and teen drinking in Germany', *Int J Epidemiol*, 36, 2007.

[368] Jernigan D. et al., 'Alcohol marketing and youth alcohol consumption', *Addiction*, 112 Suppl. 1, 2017.

[369] Mejia R. et al., 'Exposure to alcohol use in movies and problematic use of alcohol', *J Stud Alcohol Drugs*, 80, 2019.

370 Waylen A. et al., 'Alcohol use in films and adolescent alcohol use', *Pediatrics*, 135, 2015.

371 Hanewinkel R. et al., 'Longitudinal study of parental movie restriction on teen smoking and drinking in Germany', *Addiction*, 103, 2008.

372 Hanewinkel R. et al., 'Longitudinal study of exposure to entertainment media and alcohol use among German adolescents', *Pediatrics*, 123, 2009.

373 Tanski S. E. et al., 'Parental R-rated movie restriction and early-onset alcohol use', *J Stud Alcohol Drugs*, 71, 2010.

374 Engels R. C. et al., 'Alcohol portrayal on television affects actual drinking behaviour', *Alcohol Alcohol*, 44, 2009.

375 Koordeman R. et al., 'Effects of alcohol portrayals in movies on actual alcohol consumption', *Addiction*, 106, 2011.

376 Koordeman R. et al., 'Do we act upon what we see? Direct effects of alcohol cues in movies on young adults' alcohol drinking', *Alcohol Alcohol*, 46, 2011.

377 Koordeman R. et al., 'Exposure to soda commercials affects sugar-sweetened soda consumption in young women: an observational experimental study', *Appetite*, 54, 2010.

378 OMS, 'Obésité et surpoids', who.int, 2018.

379 GBD et al., 'Health effects of overweight and obesity in 195 countries over 25 years', *N Engl J Med*, 377, 2017.

380 AAP, 'Children, adolescents, obesity, and the media', *Pediatrics*, 128, 2011.

381 Robinson T. N. et al., 'Screen media exposure and obesity in children and adolescents', *Pediatrics*, 140, 2017.

382 World Cancer Research Fund, 'Diet, nutrition and physical activity', wcrf.org, 2018.

383 Wu L. et al., 'The effect of interventions targeting screen time reduction', *Medicine (Baltimore)*, 95, 2016.

384 Kelly C., 'Lutte contre l'obésité infantile: les paradoxes de la télévision, partenaire d'une régulation à la française', lemonde.fr, 2010.

385 'Association of Canadian Advertisers comment for the consultation regarding Health Canada's June 10, 2017 "Marketing to Children" proposal', acaweb.ca, 2017.

386 Wilcock D. et al., 'Boris's junk food ad ban would be a "slap in the face" for food industry after it "worked so hard during coronavirus", insiders say – as advertisers blast "significant impact at a time when the economy is already under strain"', dailymail.co.uk, 2020.

387 Zimmerman F. J., 'Using marketing muscle to sell fat', *Annu Rev Public Health*, 32, 2011.

388 Cairns G. et al., 'Systematic reviews of the evidence on the nature, extent and effects of food marketing to children: a retrospective summary', *Appetite*, 62, 2013.

389 Boyland E. J. et al., 'Television advertising and branding: effects on eating behaviour and food preferences in children', *Appetite*, 62, 2013.

[390] Boyland E. J. et al., 'Advertising as a cue to consume: a systematic review and meta-analysis of the effects of acute exposure to unhealthy food and nonalcoholic beverage advertising on intake in children and adults', *Am J Clin Nutr*, 103, 2016.

[391] Boyland E. et al., 'Digital food marketing to young people: a substantial public health challenge', *Ann Nutr Metab*, 76, 2020.

[392] Castello-Martinez A. et al., 'Obesity and food-related content aimed at children on YouTube', *Clin Obes*, 10, 2020.

[393] Qutteina Y. et al., 'Media food marketing and eating outcomes among pre-adolescents and adolescents: a systematic review and meta-analysis', *Obes Rev*, 20, 2019.

[394] Qutteina Y. et al., 'What do adolescents see on social media? A diary study of food marketing images on social media', *Front Psychol*, 10, 2019.

[395] Smith R. et al., 'Food marketing influences children's attitudes, preferences and consumption: a systematic critical review', *Nutrients*, 11, 2019.

[396] Russell S. J. et al., 'The effect of screen advertising on children's dietary intake: a systematic review and meta-analysis', *Obes Rev*, 20, 2019.

[397] Harris J. L. et al., 'A crisis in the marketplace', *Annu Rev Public Health*, 30, 2009.

[398] Zimmerman F. J. et al., 'Associations of television content type and obesity in children', *Am J Public Health*, 100, 2010.

[399] Veerman J. L. et al., 'By how much would limiting TV food advertising reduce childhood obesity?', *Eur J Public Health*, 19, 2009.

[400] Chou S. et al., 'Food restaurant advertising on television and its influence on childhood obesity', *J Law Econ*, 51, 2008.

[401] Lobstein T. et al., 'Evidence of a possible link between obesogenic food advertising and child overweight', *Obes Rev*, 6, 2005.

[402] UFC-QueChoisir, 'Marketing télévisé pour les produits alimentaires à destination des enfants', quechoisir.org, 2010.

[403] Dalton M. A. et al., 'Child-targeted fast-food television advertising exposure is linked with fast-food intake among pre-school children', *Public Health Nutr*, 20, 2017.

[404] Utter J. et al., 'Associations between television viewing and consumption of commonly advertised foods among New Zealand children and young adolescents', *Public Health Nutr*, 9, 2006.

[405] Miller S. A. et al., 'Association between television viewing and poor diet quality in young children', *Int J Pediatr Obes*, 3, 2008.

[406] Dixon H. G. et al., 'The effects of television advertisements for junk food versus nutritious food on children's food attitudes and preferences', *Soc Sci Med*, 65, 2007.

[407] Wiecha J. L. et al., 'When children eat what they watch', *Arch Pediatr Adolesc Med*, 160, 2006.

[408] Hill J. O., 'Can a small-changes approach help address the obesity epidemic? A report of the Joint Task Force of the American Society

for Nutrition, Institute of Food Technologists, and International Food Information Council', *Am J Clin Nutr*, 89, 2009.

[409] Hall K. D. et al., 'Quantification of the effect of energy imbalance on bodyweight', *Lancet*, 378, 2011.

[410] Birch L. L., 'Development of food preferences', *Annu Rev Nutr*, 19, 1999.

[411] Gugusheff J. R. et al., 'The early origins of food preferences', *FASEB J*, 29, 2015.

[412] Breen F. M. et al., 'Heritability of food preferences in young children', *Physiol Behav*, 88, 2006.

[413] Haller R. et al., 'The influence of early experience with vanillin on food preference later in life', *Chem Senses*, 24, 1999.

[414] Whitaker R. C. et al., 'Predicting obesity in young adulthood from childhood and parental obesity', *N Engl J Med*, 337, 1997.

[415] Bouchard C., 'Childhood obesity', *Am J Clin Nutr*, 89, 2009.

[416] Boswell R. G. et al., 'Food cue reactivity and craving predict eating and weight gain', *Obes Rev*, 17, 2016.

[417] Schor J., *The Overspent American*, HarperPerennial, 1998.

[418] Schor J., *The Overworked American*, Basic Books, 1991.

[419] 'Étude Nutrinet-Santé: état d'avancement et résultats préliminaires 3 ans après le lancement', etude-nutrinet-sante.fr, 2012.

[420] Rubinstein S. et al., 'Is Miss America an undernourished role model?', *JAMA*, 283, 2000.

[421] Volonte P., 'The thin ideal and the practice of fashion', *J Consum Cult*, 19, 2019.

[422] Record K. L. et al., '"Paris thin": a call to regulate life-threatening starvation of runway models in the US fashion industry', *Am J Public Health*, 106, 2016.

[423] Swami V. et al., 'Body image concerns in professional fashion models: are they really an at-risk group?', *Psychiatry Res*, 207, 2013.

[424] Tovee M. J. et al., 'Supermodels: stick insects or hourglasses?', *Lancet*, 350, 1997.

[425] Fryar C. et al., 'Prevalence of underweight among adults aged 20 and over: United States, 1960–1962 through 2015–2016', cdc.gov, 2018.

[426] Mears A., *Pricing Beauty: The Making of a Fashion Model*, University of California Press, 2011.

[427] Effron L. et al., 'Fashion models: by the numbers', abcnews.go.com, 14 September 2011.

[428] CDC, 'Anthropometric reference data for children and adults: United States, 2011–2014', cdc.gov, 2016.

[429] Greenberg B. S. et al., 'Portrayals of overweight and obese individuals on commercial television', *Am J Public Health*, 93, 2003.

[430] Flegal K. M. et al., 'Prevalence and trends in obesity among US adults, 1999–2008', *JAMA*, 303, 2010.

[431] Pont S. J. et al., 'Stigma experienced by children and adolescents with obesity', *Pediatrics*, 140, 2017.

[432] Puhl R. M. et al., 'The stigma of obesity', *Obesity (Silver Spring)*, 17, 2009.

[433] Puhl R. M. et al., 'Stigma, obesity, and the health of the nation's children', *Psychol Bull*, 133, 2007.

[434] Karsay K. et al., '"Weak, sad, and lazy fatties": adolescents' explicit and implicit weight bias following exposure to weight loss reality TV shows', *Media Psychol*, 22, 2019.

[435] Grabe S. et al., 'The role of the media in body image concerns among women', *Psychol Bull*, 134, 2008.

[436] Becker A. E. et al., 'Eating behaviours and attitudes following prolonged exposure to television among ethnic Fijian adolescent girls', *Br J Psychiatry*, 180, 2002.

[437] AAP, 'Policy statement: sexuality, contraception, and the media', *Pediatrics*, 126, 2010.

[438] Kunkel D. et al., 'Sex on TV -4', kff.org, 2005.

[439] Bleakley A. et al., 'Trends of sexual and violent content by gender in top-grossing U.S. films, 1950–2006', *J Adolesc Health*, 51, 2012.

[440] Bleakley A. et al., 'It works both ways', *Media Psychol*, 11, 2008.

[441] Ashby S. L. et al., 'Television viewing and risk of sexual initiation by young adolescents', *Arch Pediatr Adolesc Med*, 160, 2006.

[442] Collins R. L. et al., 'Relationships between adolescent sexual outcomes and exposure to sex in media', *Dev Psychol*, 47, 2011.

[443] Brown J. D. et al., 'Sexy media matter', *Pediatrics*, 117, 2006.

[444] O'Hara R. E. et al., 'Greater exposure to sexual content in popular movies predicts earlier sexual debut and increased sexual risk taking', *Psychol Sci*, 23, 2012.

[445] Wright P., 'Mass media effects on youth sexual behavior: assessing the claim for causality', *Ann Int Comm Ass*, 35, 2011.

[446] Collins R. L. et al., 'Watching sex on television predicts adolescent initiation of sexual behavior', *Pediatrics*, 114, 2004.

[447] Chandra A. et al., 'Does watching sex on television predict teen pregnancy? Findings from a national longitudinal survey of youth', *Pediatrics*, 122, 2008.

[448] Wingood G. M. et al., 'A prospective study of exposure to rap music videos and African American female adolescents' health', *Am J Public Health*, 93, 2003.

[449] Quadrara A. et al., 'The effects of pornography on children and young people: research report, Australian Institute of Family Studies', aifs.gov.au, 2017.

[450] Australian Psychological Society, 'Submission to the Senate Environment and Communications References Committee Inquiry into the harm being done to Australian children through access to pornography on the Internet', psychology.org.au, 2016.

[451] Flood M., 'The harms of pornography exposure among children and young people', *Child Abuse Review*, 18, 2009.

[452] Ybarra M. L. et al., 'X-rated material and perpetration of sexually aggressive behavior among children and adolescents: is there a link?', *Aggress Behav*, 37, 2011.

[453] Peter J. et al., 'Adolescents and pornography: a review of 20 years of research', *J Sex Res*, 53, 2016.

[454] Collins R. L. et al., 'Sexual media and childhood well-being and health', *Pediatrics*, 140, 2017.

[455] Principi N. et al., 'Consumption of sexually explicit Internet material and its effects on minors' health: latest evidence from the literature', *Minerva Pediatr*, 2019.

[456] Gestos M. et al., 'Representation of women in video games: a systematic review of literature in consideration of adult female wellbeing', *Cyberpsychol Behav Soc Netw*, 21, 2018.

[457] Dill K. et al., 'Effects of exposure to sex-stereotyped video game characters on tolerance of sexual harassment', *J Exp Soc Psychol*, 44, 2008.

[458] Stermer S. et al., 'SeX-Box: exposure to sexist video games predicts benevolent sexism', *Psychol Pop Media Cult*, 4, 2015.

[459] Stermer S. et al., 'Xbox or SeXbox? An examination of sexualized content in video games', *Soc Pers Psychol Comp*, 6, 2012.

[460] Ward L., 'Media and sexualization: state of empirical research, 1995–2015', *J Sex Res*, 53, 2016.

[461] Gabbiadini A. et al., 'Grand Theft Auto is a "sandbox" game, but there are weapons, criminals, and prostitutes in the sandbox: response to Ferguson and Donnellan (2017)', *J Youth Adolesc*, 46, 2017.

[462] Gabbiadini A. et al., 'Acting like a tough guy: violent-sexist video games, identification with game characters, masculine beliefs, & empathy for female violence victims', *PLoS One*, 11, 2016.

[463] Fox J. et al., 'Lifetime video game consumption, interpersonal aggression, hostile sexism, and rape myth acceptance: a cultivation perspective', *J Interpers Violence*, 31, 2016.

[464] Begue L. et al., 'Video games exposure and sexism in a representative sample of adolescents', *Front Psychol*, 8, 2017.

[465] Kahneman D., *Thinking, Fast and Slow*, Farrar, Straus and Giroux, 2011.

[466] Danziger S. et al., 'Extraneous factors in judicial decisions', *Proc Natl Acad Sci USA*, 108, 2011.

[467] Wansink B., *Mindless Eating*, Bantam Books, 2007.

[468] Zuboff S., *The Age of Surveillance Capitalism*, Profile Books, 2019.

[469] Cadwalladr C., 'Fresh Cambridge Analytica leak "shows global manipulation is out of control"', theguardian.com, 2020.

[470] Confessore N., 'Cambridge Analytica and Facebook: the scandal and the fallout so far', nytimes.com, 2018.

[471] Wylie C., *Mindf*ck*, Random House, 2019.

[472] 'The great hack', documentary, Netflix, 2019.

[473] Dixon T., in *Race and Gender in Electronic Media* (ed. Lind R.), 'Understanding how the Internet and social media accelerate racial

stereotyping and social division: the socially mediated stereotyping model', Taylor & Francis, 2017.

[474] Dixon T. et al., in *Oxford Research Encyclopedia of Communication*, 'Media constructions of culture, race, and ethnicity', Oxford University Press, 2019.

[475] Appel M. et al., 'Do mass mediated stereotypes harm members of negatively stereotyped groups? A meta-analytical review on media-generated stereotype threat and stereotype lift', *Comm Res*, 2017.

[476] Collectif, 'Virtual violence (AAP Council on Communications and Media)', *Pediatrics*, 138, 2016.

[477] Anderson C. A. et al., 'Violent video game effects on aggression, empathy, and prosocial behavior in Eastern and Western countries', *Psychol Bull*, 136, 2010.

[478] Greitemeyer T. et al., 'Video games do affect social outcomes: a meta-analytic review of the effects of violent and prosocial video game play', *Pers Soc Psychol Bull*, 40, 2014.

[479] Bushman B. J. et al., 'Understanding causality in the effects of media violence', *Am Behav Sci*, 59, 2015.

[480] Bushman B. J., 'Violent media and hostile appraisals: a meta-analytic review', *Aggress Behav*, 42, 2016.

[481] Anderson C. et al., 'SPSSI research summary on media violence', *Anal Soc Issues Public Policy*, 15, 2015.

[482] Calvert S. L. et al., 'The American Psychological Association Task Force assessment of violent video games', *Am Psychol*, 72, 2017.

[483] Bender P. K. et al., 'The effects of violent media content on aggression', *Curr Opin Psychol*, 19, 2018.

[484] Prescott A. T. et al., 'Metaanalysis of the relationship between violent video game play and physical aggression over time', *Proc Natl Acad Sci USA*, 115, 2018.

[485] Plante C. et al., in *The Wiley Handbook of Violence and Aggression*, vol. 1 (ed. Sturmey P.), 'Media, violence, aggression, and antisocial behavior: is the link causal?', Wiley-Blackwell, 2017.

[486] Carey B., 'Shooting in the dark', nytimes.com, 2013.

[487] Soullier L., 'Jeux vidéo: le coupable idéal', lexpress.fr, 2012.

[488] Bushman B. J. et al., 'There is broad consensus', *Psychol Pop Media Cult*, 4, 2015.

[489] Bushman B. et al., 'Agreement across stakeholders is consensus', *Psychol Pop Media Cult*, 4, 2015.

[490] Anderson C. et al., 'Consensus on media violence effects', *Psychol Pop Media Cult*, 4, 2015.

[491] 'Surgeon General's Scientific Advisory Committee on Television and Social Behavior: television and growing up: the impact of televised violence', US Government Printing Office, 1972.

[492] NSF, 'Youth violence: what we need to know', National Science Foundation, 2013.

[493] 'Joint statement on the impact of entertainment violence on children', Congressional Public Health Summit, 26 July 2000, signed by The American Academy of Pediatrics, The American Academy of Child & Adolescent Psychiatry, The American Psychological Association, The American Medical Association, The American Academy of Family Physicians and The American Psychiatric Association, aap.org.

[494] AAP, 'Policy statement: media violence', *Pediatrics*, 124, 2009.

[495] Appelbaum M. et al., 'Technical report on the violent video game literature', APA Task Force on Violent Media, 2015.

[496] ISRA, 'Report of the Media Violence Commission', *Aggress Behav*, 38, 2012.

[497] Bushman B. J. et al., 'Short-term and long-term effects of violent media on aggression in children and adults', *Arch Pediatr Adolesc Med*, 160, 2006.

[498] Huesmann L. R. et al., 'The role of media violence in violent behavior', *Annu Rev Public Health*, 27, 2006.

[499] Paik H. et al., 'The effects of television violence on antisocial behavior', *Comm Res*, 21, 1994.

[500] Anderson C. A. et al., 'Effects of violent video games on aggressive behavior, aggressive cognition, aggressive affect, physiological arousal, and prosocial behavior', *Psychol Sci*, 12, 2001.

[501] Bushman B. et al., 'Twenty-five years of research on violence in digital games and aggression revisited', *Eur Psychol*, 19, 2014.

[502] Mifflin L., 'Many researchers say link is already clear on media and youth violence', nytimes.com, 1999.

[503] Bushman B. J. et al., 'Media violence and the American public: scientific facts versus media misinformation', *Am Psychol*, 56, 2001.

[504] Martins N. et al., 'A content analysis of print news coverage of media violence and aggression research', *J Commun*, 63, 2013.

[505] Rideout V., 'The common sense census: media use by tweens and teens', Common Sense Media, 2015.

[506] Strasburger V. C. et al., 'Why is it so hard to believe that media influence children and adolescents?', *Pediatrics*, 133, 2014.

[507] Ferguson C. J., 'No consensus among scholars on media violence', huffingtonpost.com, 2013.

[508] Ferguson C. J., 'Video games don't make kids violent', time.com, 2011.

[509] Ferguson C. J., 'Stop blaming violent video games', usnews.com, 2016.

[510] DeCamp W. et al., 'The impact of degree of exposure to violent video games, family background, and other factors on youth violence', *J Youth Adolesc*, 46, 2017.

[511] Ferguson C. J., 'Do Angry Birds make for angry children? A meta-analysis of video game influences on children's and adolescents' aggression, mental health, prosocial behavior, and academic performance', *Perspect Psychol Sci*, 10, 2015.

[512] Ferguson C. J., 'A further plea for caution against medical professionals overstating video game violence effects', *Mayo Clin Proc*, 86, 2011.

[513] Ferguson C. J. et al., 'The public health risks of media violence', *J Pediatr*, 154, 2009.

[514] Ferguson C. J., 'The good, the bad and the ugly', *Psychiatr Q*, 78, 2007.

[515] Ferguson C., 'Evidence for publication bias in video game violence effects literature', *Aggress Violent Behav*, 12, 2007.

[516] Bushman B. et al., 'Much ado about something: reply to Ferguson and Kilburn (2010)', *Psychol Bull*, 136, 2010.

[517] Gentile D. A., 'What is a good skeptic to do? The case for skepticism in the media violence discussion', *Perspect Psychol Sci*, 10, 2015.

[518] Boxer P. et al., 'Video games do indeed influence children and adolescents' aggression, prosocial behavior, and academic performance', *Perspect Psychol Sci*, 10, 2015.

[519] Rothstein H. R. et al., 'Methodological and reporting errors in meta-analytic reviews make other meta-analysts angry: a commentary on Ferguson (2015)', *Perspect Psychol Sci*, 10, 2015.

[520] See the website meta-analysis.com.

[521] Borenstein M. et al., *Introduction to Meta-Analysis*, Wiley, 2009.

[522] Borenstein M. et al., *Computing Effect Sizes for Meta-Analysis*, Wiley, 2018.

[523] Rothstein H. R. et al., *Publication Bias in Meta-Analysis*, Wiley, 2005.

[524] Borenstein M. et al., 'A basic introduction to fixed-effect and random-effects models for meta-analysis', *Res Synth Methods*, 1, 2010.

[525] Borenstein M. et al., 'Basics of meta-analysis', *Res Synth Methods*, 8, 2017.

[526] Valentine J. C. et al., 'How many studies do you need?', *J Educ Behav Stat*, 35, 2010.

[527] Anderson C. A. et al., 'Psychology: the effects of media violence on society', *Science*, 295, 2002.

[528] Federman J., *National Television Violence Study*, vol. 3, SAGE, 1998.

[529] Carver C. S. et al., 'Modeling: an analysis in terms of category accessibility', *J Exp Soc Psychol*, 19, 1983.

[530] Bushman B., 'Priming effects of media violence on the accessibility of aggressive constructs in memory', *Pers Soc Psychol Bull*, 24, 1998.

[531] Zillmann D. et al., 'Effects of prolonged exposure to gratuitous media violence on provoked and unprovoked hostile behavior', *J Appl Soc Psychol*, 29, 1999.

[532] Leyens J. P. et al., 'Effects of movie violence on aggression in a field setting as a function of group dominance and cohesion', *J Pers Soc Psychol*, 32, 1975.

[533] Lovaas O. I., 'Effect of exposure to symbolic aggression on aggressive behavior', *Child Dev*, 32, 1961.

[534] Liebert R. M. et al., in *Television and Social Behavior. Reports and Papers, Vol. II. Television and Social Learning* (eds. Murray J. P. et al.), 'Short term effects of television aggression on children's aggressive behavior', U.S. Government Printing Office, 1972.

[535]Hasan Y. et al., 'The more you play, the more aggressive you become: a long-term experimental study of cumulative violent video game effects on hostile expectations and aggressive behavior', *J Exp Soc Psychol*, 49, 2013.

[536]Robinson T. N. et al., 'Effects of reducing children's television and video game use on aggressive behavior: a randomized controlled trial', *Arch Pediatr Adolesc Med*, 155, 2001.

[537]Joy L. A. et al., in *The Impact of Television: A Natural Experiment in Three Communities* (ed. MacBeth Williams T.), 'Television and children's aggressive behavior', Academic Press, 1986.

[538]Zimmerman F. J. et al., 'Early cognitive stimulation, emotional support, and television watching as predictors of subsequent bullying among grade-school children', *Arch Pediatr Adolesc Med*, 159, 2005.

[539]Christakis D. A. et al., 'Violent television viewing during preschool is associated with antisocial behavior during school age', *Pediatrics*, 120, 2007.

[540]Huesmann L. R. et al., 'Longitudinal relations between children's exposure to TV violence and their aggressive and violent behavior in young adulthood', *Dev Psychol*, 39, 2003.

[541]Anderson C. A. et al., 'Longitudinal effects of violent video games on aggression in Japan and the United States', *Pediatrics*, 122, 2008.

[542]Graber J. et al., 'A longitudinal examination of family, friend, and media influences on competent versus problem behaviors among urban minority youth', *Appl Dev Sci*, 10, 2006.

[543]Johnson J. G. et al., 'Television viewing and aggressive behavior during adolescence and adulthood', *Science*, 295, 2002.

[544]Krahe B. et al., 'Longitudinal effects of media violence on aggression and empathy among German adolescents', *J Appl Dev Psychol*, 31, 2010.

[545]Moller I. et al., 'Exposure to violent video games and aggression in German adolescents: a longitudinal analysis', *Aggress Behav*, 35, 2009.

[546]Bandura A., *Social Learning Theory*, Prentice Hall, 1977.

[547]Dominick J. et al., in *Television and Social Behavior. Reports and Papers, Vol. III. Television and Adolescent Aggressiveness* (eds. Comstock G. et al.), 'Attitudes towards violence', US Government Printing Office, 1972.

[548]Huesmann L. R. et al., 'Children's normative beliefs about aggression and aggressive behavior', *J Pers Soc Psychol*, 72, 1997.

[549]Funk J. B. et al., 'Violence exposure in real-life, video games, television, movies, and the Internet: is there desensitization?', *J Adolesc*, 27, 2004.

[550]Krahe B. et al., 'Playing violent electronic games, hostile attributional style, and aggression-related norms in German adolescents', *J Adolesc*, 27, 2004.

[551]Uhlmann E. et al., 'Exposure to violent video games increases automatic aggressiveness', *J Adolesc*, 27, 2004.

[552]Tighe T. et al., *Habituation*, Routledge, 1976.

[553]Dalton P., 'Psychophysical and behavioral characteristics of olfactory adaptation', *Chem Senses*, 25, 2000.

[554] Anderson C. A. et al., 'The influence of media violence on youth', *Psychol Sci Public Interest*, 4, 2003.

[555] Nias D. K., 'Desensitisation and media violence', *J Psychosom Res*, 23, 1979.

[556] Brockmyer J. F., 'Playing violent video games and desensitization to violence', *Child Adolesc Psychiatr Clin N Am*, 24, 2015.

[557] Prot S. et al., 'Long-term relations among prosocial-media use, empathy, and prosocial behavior', *Psychol Sci*, 25, 2014.

[558] Hummer T., 'Media violence effects on brain development', *Am Behav Sci*, 59, 2015.

[559] Kelly C. R. et al., 'Repeated exposure to media violence is associated with diminished response in an inhibitory frontolimbic network', *PLoS One*, 2, 2007.

[560] Strenziok M. et al., 'Fronto-parietal regulation of media violence exposure in adolescents', *Soc Cogn Affect Neurosci*, 6, 2011.

[561] Strenziok M. et al., 'Lower lateral orbitofrontal cortex density associated with more frequent exposure to television and movie violence in male adolescents', *J Adolesc Health*, 46, 2010.

[562] Cline V. B. et al., 'Desensitization of children to television violence', *J Pers Soc Psychol*, 27, 1973.

[563] Thomas M. H. et al., 'Desensitization to portrayals of real-life aggression as a function of exposure to television violence', *J Pers Soc Psychol*, 35, 1977.

[564] Bartholow B. et al., 'Chronic violent video game exposure and desensitization to violence: behavioral and event-related brain potential data', *J Exp Soc Psychol*, 42, 2006.

[565] Montag C. et al., 'Does excessive play of violent first-person-shooter-video-games dampen brain activity in response to emotional stimuli?', *Biol Psychol*, 89, 2012.

[566] Gentile D. et al., 'Differential neural recruitment during violent video game play in violent- and nonviolent-game players', *Psychol Pop Media Cult*, 5, 2016.

[567] Engelhardt C. et al., 'This is your brain on violent video games', *J Exp Soc Psychol*, 47, 2011.

[568] Fanti K. A. et al., 'Desensitization to media violence over a short period of time', *Aggress Behav*, 35, 2009.

[569] Cantor J., in *Handbook of Children and the Media* (eds. Singer D. G. et al.), 'The media and children's fears, anxieties, and perception of danger', SAGE, 2001.

[570] Houston J., 'Media coverage of terrorism: a meta-analytic assessment of media use and posttraumatic stress', *Journal Mass Commun Q*, 86, 2009.

[571] Wilson B. J., 'Media and children's aggression, fear, and altruism', *Future Child*, 18, 2008.

[572] Hopwood T. et al., 'Psychological outcomes in reaction to media exposure to disasters and large-scale violence: a meta-analysis', *Psychol Violence*, 7, 2017.

[573] Pearce L. et al., 'The impact of "scary" TV and film on children's internalizing emotions: a meta-analysis', *Hum Commun Res*, 42, 2016.

[574] Pettit H., 'Countries that play more violent video games such as Grand Theft Auto and Call of Duty have FEWER murders', dailymail.co.uk, 2017.

[575] Fisher M., 'Ten-country comparison suggests there's little or no link between video games and gun murders', thewashingtonpost.com, 2012.

[576] Abad-Santos A., 'Don't blame violent video games for Monday's mass shooting', theatlantic.com, 2013.

[577] Murphy M., 'Nations where video games like Call of Duty, Halo, and Grand Theft Auto are hugely popular have FEWER murders and violent assaults', thesun.co.uk, 2017.

[578] Roeder O. et al., 'What caused the crime decline?', Brennan Center for Justice, 2015.

[579] Carpenter D. O. et al., 'Environmental causes of violence', *Physiol Behav*, 99, 2010.

[580] National Research Council, *Understanding Crime Trends: Workshop Report*, National Academies Press, 2008.

[581] Shader M., 'Risk factors for delinquency', US Department of Justice, 2004.

[582] Levitt S., 'Understanding why crime fell in the 1990s: four factors that explain the decline and six that do not', *J Econ Perspect*, 18, 2004.

[583] Greenfeld L., 'Alcohol and crime', US Department of Justice, 1998.

[584] Kain E., 'As video game sales climb year over year, violent crime continues to fall', forbes.com, 2012.

[585] Markey P. et al., 'Violent video games and real-world violence', *Psychol Pop Media Cult*, 4, 2015.

[586] Garcia V., 'Les jeux vidéo violents réduisent-ils la criminalité?', lexpress. fr, 2014.

[587] 'Les jeux vidéo violents réduiraient la criminalité', 7sur7.be, 2014.

[588] ESA, 'Essential facts about games and violence', theesa.com, 2016.

[589] Supreme Court of the United States, *Brown vs EMA* (No. 08-1448), supremecourt.gov, June 2011.

[590] Bushman B. J. et al., 'Supreme Court decision on violent video games was based on the First Amendment, not scientific evidence', *Am Psychol*, 69, 2014.

[591] Liptak A., 'Justices reject ban on violent video games for children', nytimes.com, 2011.

Epilogue

[1] Reich W., *Listen, Little Man!*, Penguin, 1975.

[2] Postman N., *The Disappearance of Childhood*, Vintage, 1994/1982.

[3] Santi P., 'Écrans: appel des académies à une "vigilance raisonnée"', lemonde.fr, 2019.

[4] Sophocles, *Antigone*, Hachette, 1868.
[5] Bowles N., 'A dark consensus about screens and kids begins to emerge in Silicon Valley', nytimes.com, 2018.
[6] Desmurget M., *L'Antirégime au Quotidien*, Belin, 2017.
[7] Castellion S., in Zweig S., *The Right to Heresy: Castellio Against Calvin*, Viking Press, 1936.

INDEX

Page numbers in *italics* refer to figures.